D1555618

On Earth or in Poems

On Earth or in Poems

THE MANY LIVES OF AL-ANDALUS

Eric Calderwood

HARVARD UNIVERSITY PRESS

Cambridge, Massachusetts, and London, England · 2023

Copyright © 2023 by the President and Fellows of Harvard College
All rights reserved
Printed in the United States of America

FIRST PRINTING

Publication of this book has been supported through the generous provisions of the
Maurice and Lula Bradley Smith Memorial Fund

Library of Congress Cataloging-in-Publication Data

Names: Calderwood, Eric, 1979– author.
Title: On earth or in poems : the many lives of al-Andalus / Eric Calderwood.
Description: Cambridge, Massachusetts : Harvard University Press, 2023. |
    Includes bibliographical references and index.
Identifiers: LCCN 2022032506 | ISBN 9780674980365 (hardcover)
Subjects: LCSH: Islamic civilization. | Collective memory. | Andalusia (Spain)—
    Civilization. | Spain—Civilization—711-1516.
Classification: LCC DP103 .C35 2023 | DDC 946/.02—dc23/eng/20220929
LC record available at https://lccn.loc.gov/2022032506

For Jamie

Contents

Note on Transliteration

For Arabic words, I have followed, in general, the transliteration system of the *International Journal of Middle East Studies*. There are, however, some exceptions to this rule. Many of the authors I discuss in this book write in multiple languages, including Arabic and one or more European languages. If I am referring exclusively or primarily to an author's Arabic-language body of work, then I transliterate the author's name according to the *IJMES* system. When discussing authors whose work is primarily in English, Spanish, or French, I use the spelling preferred by the author in question.

On Earth or in Poems

And in the end we will ask ourselves: Was al-Andalus
Here or there? On earth . . . or in poems?

MAHMUD DARWISH

Introduction

In the summer of 2010 a controversy erupted over plans to build an Islamic community center in lower Manhattan, a few blocks from the site of the 9/11 attacks.[1] Opponents to the project—primarily right-wing pundits and provocateurs—dubbed it the "Ground Zero Mosque." The project's leaders called it "Cordoba House." One of them, a prominent Egyptian American imam named Feisal Abdul Rauf, explained the inspiration behind the name in an op-ed piece that he published in the *New York Times* in the heat of the controversy. "Our name, Cordoba," he wrote, "was inspired by the city in Spain where Muslims, Christians and Jews co-existed in the Middle Ages during a period of great cultural enrichment created by Muslims."[2] As this quote shows, Abdul Rauf viewed medieval Muslim Cordoba as a historical model for Muslim-Christian-Jewish coexistence, a model that could, perhaps, inspire a similar spirit of coexistence in twenty-first-century New York. The controversy that broke out in 2010 prevented Abdul Rauf from building Cordoba House in lower Manhattan. But the idea persisted, and the organization eventually launched operations in a different space in October 2015. Since then, Cordoba House has offered a range of educational and religious programs from a rented space inside East End Temple, a reform synagogue near Union Square. In other words, Cordoba House exists today as a Muslim organization housed inside a synagogue. This arrangement is a fitting tribute to Abdul Rauf's original vision for interfaith coexistence (Figure I.1).[3]

The story of Cordoba House illustrates some of the issues that will be central to this book. First, it shows that the history of Muslim rule in the Iberian Peninsula (today's Spain and Portugal) has had a long cultural afterlife that continues to resonate in the present. From 711 to 1492, large parts of today's Spain and Portugal were ruled by Muslims, and this territory was

Figure I.1. Image from Cordoba House website. cordobahouse.com.

known as al-Andalus.[4] Al-Andalus ceased to exist as a place in 1492, but its memories and legacies have survived in many forms and have animated a diverse range of cultural and political projects throughout today's world. Indeed, something that the case of New York's Cordoba House demonstrates is that stories and ideas about al-Andalus circulate today far from the historical site of al-Andalus in the Iberian Peninsula. Another thing it illustrates is that modern-day claims about al-Andalus are often as much (or more) about addressing the needs of the present as they are about understanding the past. It is no coincidence, for instance, that Abdul Rauf turned to the memory of al-Andalus in the years that followed the 9/11 attacks, a time when many American Muslims faced suspicion about their place in US society. Against this backdrop, Abdul Rauf evoked Muslim Cordoba as a model of interfaith tolerance—a time and a place where Muslims, Jews, and Christians coexisted peacefully. He would articulate this vision in several of his writings and projects from the first decade of the twenty-first century. For example, in a 2004 book calling for "a new vision for Muslims and the West," Abdul Rauf wrote, "We strive for a 'New Cordoba,' a time when Jews, Christians, Muslims, and all other faith traditions will live together in peace."[5] The Cordoba House project emerged from this call to build a "New Cordoba" in the United States in the twenty-first century. Abdul Rauf envisioned the project as one that could, in his words, "help heal the wounds of 9/11."[6] Cordoba House was, then, a tribute to the memory of al-Andalus and, at the same time, a response to the political and cultural demands that American Muslims faced in the post-9/11 years.

For Abdul Rauf, the primary lesson of al-Andalus was one of religious tolerance. Time and time again, he wrote of al-Andalus as a place "where Muslims, Christians and Jews co-existed." This particular vision of al-Andalus as a place of exceptional tolerance has a deep and complicated history that has received much attention from scholars in recent years.[7] It also has a name: *convivencia,* a Spanish word that means "living together" and that refers, in particular, to the idea that Muslims, Jews, and Christians lived together in relative peace and harmony in al-Andalus. *Convivencia* is one of the most hotly debated concepts in the scholarship on al-Andalus. Many specialists have distanced themselves from the concept, arguing that it is a simplistic or anachronistic framework for understanding the complexity of interfaith relations in medieval Iberia.[8] Yet, although *convivencia* has been the target of a mounting wave of scholarly critique, it cannot be easily cast aside, for the simple reason that the term *convivencia* and the associated idea of interfaith tolerance have played a large role in contemporary conversations about al-Andalus, exerting influence on a wide range of scholars, writers, and public figures.[9] My approach to this problem is to treat *convivencia* as a term that is both insufficient and necessary—insufficient because it does not provide a satisfactory explanation of interfaith relations in the past, and necessary because it has shaped long-standing debates about al-Andalus and its legacy.[10]

But *convivencia* is just one of many ideas associated today with al-Andalus. In contemporary culture, the memory of al-Andalus is like a Swiss Army knife, a varied kit of tools ready to address all sorts of problems and needs. Al-Andalus is the name of a world music ensemble from the United States, a park in Cairo, a shopping mall in Saudi Arabia, a historic movie house in the West Bank, and an Israeli publisher that specializes in the translation of Arabic literature into Hebrew. Al-Andalus is a symbol of intercultural coexistence while also being a rhetorical weapon deployed by extremists of all stripes, from ISIS operatives in Syria to right-wing Islamophobes in Europe and the United States. Al-Andalus is a major driver of tourism to Spain as well as a cornerstone of Moroccan national identity. In al-Andalus, generations of Palestinian poets have found a metaphor for their homeland, while generations of feminist thinkers have found in al-Andalus a model for women's empowerment and creativity. In short, al-Andalus has proven incredibly

useful and malleable for writers, scholars, artists, politicians, and businesspeople around the world.[11]

In *On Earth or in Poems,* I explore the uses and meanings of al-Andalus
in contemporary culture. In particular, I examine representations of al-
Andalus in literature, cinema, television, music, tourism, and political discourse from a broad array of contexts, spanning Europe, North Africa, the
Middle East, and the United States. This book challenges a tradition of scholarship that has treated al-Andalus as a symbol of tolerance and cross-cultural
understanding while too often disregarding what Arabs and Muslims have had
to say about the modern legacy of al-Andalus.[12] For much of the nineteenth and
twentieth centuries, *convivencia* was not the only, or even the predominant,
understanding of al-Andalus among Arab and Muslim authors, artists, and
thinkers. In this book I center Arab and Muslim voices and, in so doing,
offer a wide-ranging and multilingual account of the various understandings
of al-Andalus in contemporary culture. Along the way, I examine a diverse
body of cultural works in Arabic, Spanish, French, and English. Guiding my
readings of these diverse works is the conviction that the story of al-Andalus
is not about learning to tolerate difference, but instead about learning to
tolerate contradiction. Al-Andalus means many different things to many
different people, and the ethical challenge is to keep all of these disparate
meanings in mind without having one dominate the others. Thus, I do not
approach the problem of al-Andalus as if it were a struggle over scarce resources.
Instead, I take al-Andalus as an invitation to a mode of cultural memory that
is capacious enough to accommodate, and even welcome, competing claims
on the past.[13]

This book is not a history of al-Andalus; instead it is a study of how that
history has been imagined and deployed in modern times, from the nineteenth century to the present. However, to understand the story I want to tell
here, readers must have a basic grasp of the history of al-Andalus, since it is
the raw material from which later stories about al-Andalus are forged. For
that reason, I will offer here a brief overview of some major events in the
history of al-Andalus.[14] Over the course of its history, from 711 to 1492, al-
Andalus was ruled by a succession of Muslim dynasties originating in Syria
or North Africa. In 711, roughly a century after the advent of Islam, an army
led by North African general Tariq b. Ziyad crossed the Strait of Gibraltar,
the narrow sliver of water that separates Europe from Africa, and conquered

much of the Iberian Peninsula, which was, at the time, under Visigoth rule. For the next four decades, al-Andalus was ruled by governors answerable to the Umayyad caliphs, based in Damascus. In the middle of the eighth century, a momentous event rocked the Muslim world and, with it, the history of al-Andalus. A new dynasty, the Abbasids, violently overthrew the Umayyads and moved the capital of the caliphate from Damascus to Baghdad. One member of the Umayyad clan, 'Abd al-Rahman b. Mu'awiya (also known as 'Abd al-Rahman I), escaped the carnage and fled from Syria across North Africa to al-Andalus, where in 756 he resettled and claimed rule in the name of the Umayyads. For the next two centuries, al-Andalus was a semiautonomous Umayyad state with a capital in Cordoba and a nominal allegiance to the Abbasid caliphate in Baghdad. That arrangement held until 929, when 'Abd al-Rahman III, a descendant of 'Abd al-Rahman I, proclaimed himself caliph, marking al-Andalus's formal independence from the Abbasids in Baghdad and a new player, the Fatimid dynasty in Egypt. The Umayyad caliphs' rule lasted until the early eleventh century, when al-Andalus descended into a period of civil strife commonly known as the *fitna* (Arabic for "discord" or "strife").

The Umayyad caliphate was officially dissolved in 1031, and al-Andalus splintered into a number of rival kingdoms known as the *taifa* kingdoms (from the Arabic *ṭā'ifa,* "faction"). This period of political division provided an opportunity for the Christian kings, based in the north of the Iberian Peninsula, to gather strength and mount the first sustained attempts at conquering the territories that Muslims had ruled since the early eighth century. Facing this threat from the north, some of the *taifa* kings of al-Andalus turned to the south for military assistance, asking the Almoravids, a North African dynasty, to intervene in al-Andalus. In 1086, a joint army of Almoravid and Andalusi troops defeated the forces of Alfonso VI of Castile at Zallaqa (Sagrajas, in Spanish). Soon after, the Almoravids took control of al-Andalus.

From the late eleventh century until the middle of the thirteenth century, al-Andalus was ruled by two different North African dynasties—first the Almoravids and then their successors, the Almohads. During this period, large parts of today's Spain, Portugal, and Morocco were united in a single political territory, with major urban centers on both sides of the Strait of Gibraltar. This state of affairs came to an end in the thirteenth century, when the Almohads suffered a string of military defeats, culminating in the

Castilian conquests of Cordoba and Seville in 1236 and 1248, respectively. From this point until the end of the fifteenth century, the territory of al-Andalus was reduced to a small kingdom, the kingdom of Granada, whose rulers, known as the Nasrids, built the Alhambra, one of the most famous monuments from al-Andalus. In 1492, Nasrid Granada, the last remnant of Muslim rule in al-Andalus, fell to the forces of the so-called Catholic Monarchs, Isabella of Castile and Ferdinand of Aragon.

Soon after the conquest of Granada, Isabella and Ferdinand ordered the expulsion of Jews from their territories, forcing the members of Iberia's long-standing Jewish communities to disperse throughout the Mediterranean. Muslims, on the other hand, were initially allowed to remain in Spain after the conquest of Granada. The peace treaty that the Catholic Monarchs signed with the last Muslim ruler of Granada guaranteed that the remaining Muslims would be free to practice their religion and to keep their private property. However, in 1500, less than a decade after the conquest of Granada, the Spanish authorities began a series of brutal campaigns to forcibly convert all Spanish Muslims to Christianity. The conversion campaigns drove many Spanish Muslims into exile in North Africa, but some chose to remain behind and submit to conversion. Many of those who converted to Christianity continued to observe their Islamic faith in secrecy. The crypto-Muslims and descendants of Muslims who remained in Spain after 1492 are commonly known today as "Moriscos," though some North African historians prefer to call them the "late Andalusis" (*al-andalusiyyūn al-muta'akhkhirūn*).[15] Between 1609 and 1614, King Philip III of Spain issued a series of expulsion decrees that forced the Moriscos into exile, marking a tragic conclusion to the history of al-Andalus.

What this brief historical summary reveals is that al-Andalus is, and always was, a moving target. Over the course of nearly 800 years, from 711 to 1492, the name *al-Andalus* referred to a territory whose borders and affiliations were in constant flux. Over its long life, al-Andalus witnessed many different dynasties, centers of power, and sociocultural arrangements. At times al-Andalus spilled beyond the borders of the Iberian Peninsula; at other times it was reduced to a small kingdom centered on Granada. For the first three centuries of its existence, most of the rulers of al-Andalus were Arabs who claimed a direct genealogical link to the Umayyad caliphs of Syria. Over the next few centuries, most of the rulers came from North Africa, and some even spoke a variant of Amazigh, or Berber, umbrella terms for the family of languages spoken by the inhabitants of northwest Africa before the arrival of Muslim Arab conquerors in the seventh century.[16] Many of the rulers of al-Andalus worked closely with Jewish and Christian advisors, some persecuted Jews and Christians, and some did both. The last kingdom of al-Andalus fell in 1492, and yet even after that date, a sizable community of Muslims and crypto-Muslims remained in Spain and maintained a close sense of affiliation with the culture that their ancestors had developed over several centuries.

Given the vast and complicated histories nested within the term *al-Andalus,* one might rightfully wonder whether it is helpful to retain it at all. My short answer is yes. The reason is that, while al-Andalus obfuscates certain kinds of diversity, it also enables others. It is precisely the capaciousness of al-Andalus—the wide range of places, periods, and peoples encompassed in the term—that makes it so appealing as a site of memory-making and collective belonging. Under the loose heading of al-Andalus, diverse circuits of affiliation become possible: Syrians can imagine a connection to the Umayyad rulers of Cordoba; North Africans can claim a link to the Almohad rulers of al-Andalus; and Palestinians can imagine themselves as "Moriscos," the spiritual descendants of a people who faced occupation and cultural erasure. (I discuss examples of all three cases in the following chapters.) These routes of affiliation crisscross the Mediterranean, but they also move beyond it. Under the loose heading of al-Andalus, a Palestinian American musician can play flamenco in Chicago and visual artists based in Australia and New York can advocate for women's rights in Saudi Arabia. Relinquishing the term *al-Andalus* would mean losing the vast world of imagination that the term makes possible. Al-Andalus is the thread tying together this far-flung network of diverse peoples who imagine themselves in a relationship with al-Andalus, even as they sometimes fail to imagine themselves in a relationship with each other.

As I have worked to get a handle on an unruly object of study, I have found two conceptual tools to be of particular relevance: metonymy and position. The first of these tools, metonymy, refers to the widespread practice of taking a part of Andalusi history—the Umayyads, the Almohads, Moriscos, Cordoba, female poets, and so on—as representative of the broader whole. AbdoolKarim Vakil draws attention to this issue when he observes that al-Andalus "is a constellation of symbolic dates, iconic buildings, exemplary figures, historical personalities or literary characters, names, words, sounds and sites: each can stand for the whole, certainly, but the choice renders the whole in the image of the part."[17] Like Vakil, I am interested in how different writers, artists, readers, and communities establish metonymic relationships with al-Andalus, laying claim to a particular slice of the Andalusi heritage, while treating that slice as a stand-in for the whole. In this vein, many of my cases studies boil down to figuring out which Andalus is the Andalus that is at work in a particular text and why. Such metonymic relationships are, in turn, largely dependent on the place and time in which a particular vision of al-Andalus is articulated.

This point leads me to my second conceptual tool: position—or, to borrow a phrase from Stuart Hall, the "politics of position."[18] Drawing inspiration from Hall's work, I ask: How do writers, artists, and their audiences position themselves with respect to al-Andalus, and how are they positioned by al-Andalus?[19] The point I'm trying to elucidate here is that representations of al-Andalus always implicate the positions from which different subjects speak, write, read, perform, or live. To put this point in more concrete terms, I would say that the Andalus that emerges in a cultural text from Palestine in the 1920s is often quite distinct from the Andalus that emerges in a text from Spain in the 2000s, even if both texts may be understood as contributions to the wide-ranging and unfinished business of grappling with al-Andalus. One's cultural position does not necessarily predetermine one's vision of al-Andalus, but it certainly does structure the angle of approach, the points of reference, the sense of proximity (or distance), and the perceived relationship between past and present.

By bringing together the tools of position and metonymy, I have sought, in this book, to think about how different subject positions have enabled different angles of approach to al-Andalus (and its legacy), leading to different understandings of what al-Andalus was and how its legacies have shaped the conditions of the present and the contours of the future. As I have studied a diverse range of stories and discourses about al-Andalus, I have tried to remain mindful of how they match up with the material and documentary evidence we have from medieval Iberia, but I have ultimately placed far greater emphasis on a different set of concerns. In particular, I have been guided by the following questions: How do contemporary authors, artists, and public figures imagine their relationship to al-Andalus? On what sources do they draw to form and legitimate their visions of al-Andalus? How do visions of al-Andalus vary across geographic and cultural contexts? How do these visions translate into political actions or aspirations? In short, rather than asking what al-Andalus *is,* I ask what it *does.*[20] The point I want to underline here is that contemporary representations of al-Andalus perform meaningful cultural and political work, even when they have only a tenuous relationship to events in medieval Muslim Iberia.

This book builds on a growing body of scholarship about the long cultural afterlife of al-Andalus. The existing scholarship on this topic has helped me to identify some of the sources that I discuss in the following chapters, and it has also, more importantly, helped me to identify some useful conceptual frameworks for thinking about al-Andalus and its legacies. For example, Christina Civantos has taken translation as the central conceit of her book about the cultural afterlife of al-Andalus. Civantos calls for a shift from a "Cordoba paradigm," based on interfaith harmony, to a "Toledo paradigm," named after the city that was a famous center for translation between Arabic, Latin, and Romance languages in the twelfth and thirteenth centuries.[21] For Civantos, translation serves as a metaphor for the afterlife of al-Andalus, not only because the legacy of al-Andalus moves between languages, but also because it illuminates, and thrives on, the movement of ideas, stories, and texts across space and time. In a similar vein, Rachel Scott and AbdoolKarim Vakil treat al-Andalus not as an object of historical study but instead as a "traveling concept" that acquires meaning and ideological freight as it moves across different times and spaces.[22] Jonathan Shannon, for his part, has taken performance as the central conceit of his book about modern musical traditions that originated, or claim to have originated, in al-Andalus. For Shannon, performance is not just an object of study but also an analytical tool, one that reveals how al-Andalus is a protean form that is constantly made and remade through concerts, festivals, recordings, and other musical practices.[23] Shannon joins another scholar, José Antonio González Alcantud, in viewing al-Andalus as myth—not in the colloquial sense of the word, meaning a made-up story, but in the anthropological sense, meaning a story that has social utility. Both Shannon and González Alcantud borrow a famous phrase from French anthropologist Claude Lévi-Strauss to argue that al-Andalus is "good to think with."[24] In other words, they argue that al-Andalus is useful for making sense of the world and for thinking about the relationship between past and present. Their approach, like mine, is indebted to the scholarship on Andalusi history but is ultimately more interested in how that history makes meaning and does work in public culture and debate today.

A book about the uses of the past might, at first blush, appear to be a book about nostalgia. And undoubtedly the texts that I will consider here do, at times, express a sense of longing for al-Andalus. This nostalgic mode is summed up in one of the most common nicknames for al-Andalus in modern Arabic literature: *al-firdaws al-mafqūd,* "the lost paradise."[25] However, just as there is, at times, a nostalgia for al-Andalus, there is also something that I would call "al-Andalus futurism," an imaginative mode whose horizon is not the past but instead the future.[26] In this mode, the question "What was al-Andalus?" morphs into a number of alternatives, including: What might al-Andalus have been, and what could it be now or later? This is an al-Andalus that exists in the subjunctive mood and in multiple tenses—past, present, and future.

My engagement with the complex temporality of al-Andalus draws inspiration from other scholars who have wrestled with this problem. For instance, William Granara has observed that writing about al-Andalus in modern Arabic literature "lies less in the act of remembering, less in fashioning a poetics of nostalgia for a paradise lost, but rather in the desire and need to articulate the anxieties and concerns of the present, and by extension the hopes and aspirations for the future."[27] Building on Granara's observation, I hope to show that representations of al-Andalus in contemporary culture not only intervene in debates about the meaning of the past but also propel conversations about the needs and hopes of the present and the future. In other words, many authors, artists, and thinkers look back at al-Andalus in order, paradoxically, to look forward to the future. Through their engagements with al-Andalus, they produce a layered sense of time that we might call "Andalus time," where multiple pasts, presents, and futures commingle in different configurations and trajectories.[28]

While acknowledging my debt to the existing scholarship on the legacy of al-Andalus, I also hope to push the conversation in new directions. The existing studies on this topic have been organized by either chronology, national context, place represented (for instance, Cordoba or Granada), or historical figure represented (such as Tariq b. Ziyad or 'Abd al-Rahman I).[29] All of these organizational schemes come with certain advantages, but they can also make it difficult to establish connections across national, cultural, and temporal lines. Furthermore, they often lead to a focus on what a given text (or body of texts) is *about*, instead of a focus on what it is *doing*. The questions that drive my study are not so much "What?" and "Where?" but "How?" and "Why?" That is, how and why does al-Andalus perform specific cultural and political work in different contexts across the globe?[30] With these questions in mind, I have organized the book thematically. Each chapter identifies one of the specific uses or meanings that al-Andalus has acquired in contemporary culture. For each case, I ask: How and why did this particular understanding of al-Andalus come into being, how has it found expression in a wide range of cultural texts, what are the political and cultural needs that it has served, and what are the identities and communities that have formed around it? The result of these inquiries is not so much a history of al-Andalus as it is "a history of the present" through the prism of al-Andalus.[31]

In Chapters 1 and 2, I explore how the legacy of al-Andalus intersects with debates about ethnic identities in the Middle East and North Africa. Since the medieval period and until the present day, many Arab writers and intellectuals have cast al-Andalus as an Arab and Arabic phenomenon, rather than a Muslim one. That is, they have identified al-Andalus in ethnic and linguistic terms, rather than religious ones. Chapter 1, "The Arab al-Andalus," charts the history and political implications of this idea, from the nineteenth century to the present. I show, in particular, how it has centered Arab identity and associated al-Andalus with Syria and the Arab heartlands in the Middle East, while sidelining other ethnic groups, especially North African Berbers, and downplaying Islam's role in the formation of al-Andalus. Put more bluntly, I argue that the "Arab al-Andalus" has served to make al-Andalus whiter, less religious, and more compatible with dominant notions of Western identity. In Chapter 2, "The Berber al-Andalus," I examine efforts by North African writers, scholars, and filmmakers to reclaim the contributions that Berbers, the indigenous peoples of North Africa, made to al-Andalus. These projects have sought to remap the cultural legacy of al-Andalus along a north–south axis, asserting al-Andalus's debts to North African cultures. So, Chapter 1 presents an al-Andalus from the east, whereas Chapter 2 presents an Andalus "from below" in two senses: from the south and from the perspective of peoples who have historically been marginalized in Middle Eastern and European accounts of al-Andalus.

In Chapter 3, "The Feminist al-Andalus," I turn from ethnic identities to gender identities. Since the late nineteenth century, al-Andalus has figured prominently in the imaginary of Arab and Muslim feminists and, in particular, in their efforts to articulate an indigenous feminism, independent from the history of feminist movements in Europe and the United States. In Chapter 3, I trace the modern emergence of a "feminist al-Andalus," highlighting the work of writers and artists who have imagined al-Andalus as a place of exceptional freedom and creativity for Arab and Muslim women. One of the authors whose work I analyze in this chapter, the Egyptian writer Radwa 'Ashur, was a long-standing champion of the Palestinian cause. 'Ashur was, in fact, just one of many authors who have connected al-Andalus to the question of Palestine. Chapter 4, "The Palestinian al-Andalus," picks up this thread, analyzing the varied uses and meanings of al-Andalus in Palestine / Israel. Since the early twentieth century, al-Andalus has been an important point of reference for Palestinian writers, who have turned to it to reflect on the political plight of their homeland, to decry occupation and cultural erasure, to call for resistance, and to imagine a future for Palestine—a future that one Palestinian poet, Mahmud Darwish, calls "the Andalus of the possible."[32] While Chapter 4 focuses on Palestinian perspectives, it also addresses, in the conclusion, some aspects of the cultural and political work that al-Andalus has performed in contemporary Israeli culture. In recent decades, several Israeli intellectuals, authors, and musicians have promoted al-Andalus as a model of Jewish-Arab coexistence and as an identity symbol for the *Mizrahim,* Jews from the Middle East and North Africa.

In Chapter 5, "The Harmonious al-Andalus," I pick up the question of *convivencia* and engage it through a different cultural medium: music. I explore how artists from a diverse range of cultural backgrounds have used music to perform, imagine, or engage with the legacy of al-Andalus. Many of the projects I discuss in this chapter are collaborations between performers of different ethnic, religious, or cultural backgrounds. These collaborative projects frequently claim to recover both the sounds and the spirit of al-Andalus. By studying these projects, I hope to trace the diverse imprints that al-Andalus has left on contemporary music and, at the same time, to think about what it means to treat music as "a historical medium" (a formulation that I have borrowed from Charles Hirschkind).[33] Put differently, I ask, in Chapter 5: What does al-Andalus sound like, and what does it mean to sound the depths of al-Andalus with music?

In the Epilogue, I return to the memory of Muslim Cordoba, approaching it through the story of two mosques, one in Cordoba and the other in the town where I live in central Illinois. The aim of the epilogue is to show that debates about the meaning of Cordoba are both widespread and unresolved. At the center of the epilogue is a controversy that, in recent years, has engulfed Europe's oldest Islamic monument: the Mosque-Cathedral of Cordoba, built by the Umayyads in the eighth century and transformed into a cathedral in 1236. For some this famous building embodies the multicultural heritage of the Andalusi legacy, while for others it elicits anxieties about the role that Muslims and Islam have played in Spain, past and present. Like its namesake Cordoba House, the Mosque-Cathedral of Cordoba is both a vibrant reminder of the cultural splendor of al-Andalus and a Rorschach test for lingering debates about the conceptual and historical relationship between Islam and the West.

The primary advantage of my book's thematic structure is that it allows me to track how different ways of talking about al-Andalus have emerged and coalesced to serve the needs and aspirations of specific communities spread across the globe. A potential drawback of my approach is that it might give the erroneous impression that these different ways of talking about al-Andalus, and the communities that engage in them, are siloed off from each other—as if, for example, conversations about ethnicity in al-Andalus had nothing to do with conversations about gender in al-Andalus. In response to this concern, I have tried, throughout the book, to identify the predominant meanings that al-Andalus has accrued in contemporary culture, while, at the same time, signaling moments of exchange, cross-pollination, and debate between the different discourses about al-Andalus. The result is that each chapter in the book tells a story that can stand on its own but also is deeply intertwined with the stories told in the other chapters.

As will become clear over the course of this book, the politics of imagining al-Andalus and laying claim to its legacy are messy. Often, representations of al-Andalus will subvert some power structures (say, anti-Muslim bias in Europe) while consolidating others (say, notions of Arab superiority over Berbers). The legacy of al-Andalus encompasses many cultural groups, and yet these groups do not always recognize each other's claims on the past (or the present). Al-Andalus can create connections between different groups, but it can also serve to draw boundaries or to shore up hierarchies. An additional complication is that the cultural afterlife of al-Andalus is deeply enmeshed with the history of colonialism. The colonial encounter between Europe, North Africa, and the Middle East refracted previously existing ideas about al-Andalus while spawning new ones, and the legacy of colonialism continues to inflect contemporary debates over the meanings of al-Andalus. As I track different imaginings of al-Andalus in contemporary culture, my aim will be to draw attention to the possibilities they afford, while also being mindful of the fraught histories they carry and the people they sometimes exclude. In short, I have sought to lean into the messiness of al-Andalus, treating it as an opportunity instead of an obstacle.

In mapping the afterlives of al-Andalus, I have attempted to cast a wide net, incorporating voices from Europe, North Africa, the Middle East, and the United States, with occasional forays into other contexts. Despite the broad reach of my study, I've still had to leave many stones unturned. For example, I give no account here of the tremendous importance that al-Andalus had for the identity of the Arab diaspora communities in Latin America in the early twentieth century.[34] I also have not been able to tell the story of al-Andalus's influence on writers from Turkey and South Asia.[35] These omissions are, in part, the result of my training and of the time constraints that come with writing any book. But those factors are only part of the story. I also believe that al-Andalus is inexhaustible. Getting your hands around it is not simply a matter of adding another example, another chapter. The power of al-Andalus resides, in great part, in its extreme plasticity, its ability to mold and adapt to different places and times, transcending seemingly insurmountable boundaries of culture, language, religion, and politics. The study of al-Andalus and its legacies demands a dose of methodological humility, a recognition that limitations—of language, perspective, and knowledge—are woven into the task of studying al-Andalus. They are a feature, not a bug. If I take away one lesson from the story of al-Andalus, it is that there are many stories about al-Andalus, and that no one gets the last word, not even someone (such as myself) who has spent decades studying al-Andalus. Even though al-Andalus no longer exists as a place on the map, it continues to enjoy a vibrant life as a place in discourse. It is in this arena where the work of al-Andalus is ongoing and unfinished. Its meanings are still under debate, and each turn of the debate gives rise to new possibilities for imagining the interconnections between past, present, and future, as well as between Europe, North Africa, the Middle East, and beyond.

1

The Arab al-Andalus

In February 1966 the Lebanese superstar Fayruz (b. 1935), one of the most popular Arab singers of the twentieth century, performed before an adoring audience at Cinema al-Andalus, Kuwait's premier movie palace and concert venue.[1] At the beginning of the show, with the stage curtain still down, the strings in Fayruz's orchestra played a tremolo. Over it, an off-stage male narrator recited the first two lines of a famous poem by Ibn al-Khatib (1313–1375), a poet from Muslim Granada:

> Jādaka al-ghaythu idhā al-ghaythu hamā / yā zamān al-waṣli
>   bi-l-Andalusi
> lam yakun waṣluka illā hulumā / fī al-karā aw khilsat al-mukhtalisi.
> [May the rain cloud shower you when the rain cloud pours / O time
>   of union in al-Andalus
> Union with you was but a dream / in slumber, or the deception of a
>   deceiver.][2]

After a brief musical overture, the curtain rose to reveal a medieval market scene, with two-tone arches whose design evoked the arches in the Mosque of Cordoba. Fayruz and her orchestra then broke into "Arji'i ya alfa layla," the first track from the album *Andalusiyyat* (1966), whose title roughly translates as "Songs from al-Andalus."[3] Arguably the most famous song from that album is Fayruz's rendition of Ibn al-Khatib's poem "Jadaka al-ghayth," the very same poem that was recited at the beginning of Fayruz's concert at Cinema al-Andalus. Later in the concert, at the end of the first act, Fayruz brought down the house when she performed her rendition of Ibn al-Khatib's poem. In the song's climactic final bars, as the tempo and volume increased, the male members of Fayruz's chorus sang, "O time of union in al-Andalus!"; then the female members of the chorus echoed, "O time of union in al-Andalus!"; then, Fayruz chimed in, "O time of union in al-Andalus!"; finally, everyone on stage shouted in unison, "In al-Andalus!" The crowd erupted in cheers as the curtain drew to a close.

Let us pause here to consider the intricate web of cultural references that underpin this scene: Fayruz, a Lebanese Christian performer, sings a poem by Ibn al-Khatib, a Muslim poet from fourteenth-century Granada, in Cinema al-Andalus, a Kuwaiti concert venue named after a place that is 3,000 miles away and after a historical period that predated the creation of the modern state of Kuwait by several centuries. What system of meaning and memory makes it possible for these disparate threads to cohere into an intelligible web? It is not a system based on geographic or temporal proximity to al-Andalus, nor is it one based on nation-state identification or religious affiliation. After all, Fayruz, the Andalusi poet Ibn al-Khatib, and the audience in Kuwait do not share a country of origin, historical context, or religion. Rather, what connects them is the notion of *Arabness,* an identity rooted in a common language (Arabic) and in the perception of a common ethnic and cultural heritage, one that encompasses Arabs of different faiths, as well as Arabs in different historical contexts, from medieval al-Andalus to the modern Gulf states.

Fayruz's performance in 1966 is part of a long-standing cultural tradition that traces its roots back to the time of al-Andalus itself. Since the medieval period and until the present day, many Arab writers and artists have cast al-Andalus as a primarily Arab and Arabic phenomenon, rather than a Muslim one. That is, they have identified al-Andalus in ethnic and linguistic terms, rather than religious ones. This view of Andalusi history champions the period in which the Umayyads, an Arab dynasty that originated in Damascus, ruled al-Andalus, with Cordoba as their capital. The Arab-centric view of Andalusi culture emerged in conjunction with the foundation of the Umayyad state in al-Andalus in the eighth century and has survived intermittently until the present. Historically, this view has associated al-Andalus with the Levant and with the Greco-Roman heritage, while distancing al-Andalus from North Africa. My aim, in this chapter, is to trace the modern career of this idea, illuminating its origins, its stakeholders, its modes of circulation, and its limitations. Along the way, I ask: When, why, and for whom has it been useful to claim the *Arabness* of al-Andalus, and who is excluded from such claims?

The argument I want to pursue here is that the "Arab al-Andalus" is a discourse that has empowered Arabs of different faiths and animated celebrations of pan-Arab identity, while also ignoring, or even openly rejecting, the contributions that North Africans and Andalusis of North African descent made to al-Andalus.[4]

In the long career of this discourse, one of the most enduring themes is the connection between Cordoba (the Umayyad capital in al-Andalus) and Damascus (the birthplace of the Umayyad dynasty). The first Umayyad ruler in al-Andalus, 'Abd al-Rahman I (d. 788), fled his native Damascus in 750, escaping the massacre of his family perpetuated by the Abbasids as part of their struggle to claim the caliphate. 'Abd al-Rahman made his way from Syria to al-Andalus, where he claimed the title of *amīr* (prince, or ruler). Once in al-Andalus, he proceeded to lay the groundwork for an Arab Andalusi culture that, as Alexander Elinson has argued, constantly looked eastward to the Arab heartlands to define itself.[5] In an early and illustrative example of this trend, 'Abd al-Rahman I named his estate in Cordoba "al-Rusafa," after the Umayyad estate of the same name in Syria. Through such gestures, 'Abd al-Rahman I and the Umayyad rulers and elites who came in his wake asserted their affiliation with Syria and, more broadly, with the people and culture of the Mashriq (the Arab heartlands to the east).

While stressing the links between Cordoba and Damascus, proponents of the Arab al-Andalus would find a foil in the Maghrib (North Africa) and its peoples—and especially in the people known collectively as Berbers (a problematic term that I discuss in Chapter 2) or Imazighen (sing. Amazigh), the inhabitants of North Africa before the arrival of Islam in the seventh century.[6] It is worth noting here that Berber / Amazigh groups were key players in the story of al-Andalus from the very beginning. In fact, the Muslim invasion of the Iberian Peninsula in 711 was led by a North African commander of Berber descent, Tariq b. Ziyad. Tariq led an army that was primarily composed of North African Berber soldiers, who were the pioneers in a network of mobility and exchange that would link al-Andalus and North Africa for many centuries. Despite the important contributions that Berbers made to al-Andalus, ethnic tensions between Arabs and Berbers were a common problem in Andalusi society, especially during the period of Umayyad rule (711–1031), when Arab elites often asserted their cultural superiority over Berbers.[7] The long-standing tensions between Arabs and Berbers came to a

head during the civil war (1008–1031) that led to the dissolution of the
Umayyad caliphate in the eleventh century. One of the most infamous episodes of this civil war came in 1010, when Berber soldiers sacked and pillaged
Madinat al-Zahra', a magnificent city and palace complex built near Cordoba
by 'Abd al-Rahman III (r. 912–961). This event has often been seen—by
eleventh-century observers as well as by modern historians—as the end of a
period in which al-Andalus was united under Arab rulers whose legitimacy
and prestige were closely associated with their claims of descent from the
Mashriq.[8]

In the centuries following the collapse of the Umayyad caliphate, assertions of the superiority of al-Andalus over the Maghrib—and of Arabs over
Berbers—persisted and coalesced into a literary genre known as the *risāla fī
faḍl al-Andalus* (epistle on the superiority of al-Andalus).[9] The most famous
example of this genre is a treatise written by the Andalusi scholar al-Shaqundi
(d. 1231–1232) during the period when the Almohad dynasty was in control
of al-Andalus.[10] The overriding theme of al-Shaqundi's work is that al-Andalus
is a place of beauty and cultural splendor, whereas the Maghrib is a land of
bumpkins and desert wastelands. It would have been politically unwise for
al-Shaqundi to criticize the ruling Almohad dynasty (at whose pleasure he
served), so he directed his most savage attacks at the Almoravids, the North
African dynasty that preceded the Almohads.

In what is perhaps the most famous passage from al-Shaqundi's treatise,
the author ridicules Yusuf b. Tashfin (d. 1106), the Berber commander who
led the Almoravid conquest of al-Andalus at the end of the eleventh century.
Ignoring Ibn Tashfin's military exploits, al-Shaqundi focuses instead on the
commander's alleged lack of education and refinement. He depicts Ibn Tashfin
as an ignoramus who was incapable of understanding the poetry that a group
of eminent Andalusi writers composed in his honor after he took control
of al-Andalus.[11] According to al-Shaqundi, Ibn Tashfin's grasp of Arabic was
so weak that he had to ask the ruler of Seville, al-Mu'tamid ibn 'Abbad (himself an accomplished poet), to intervene and explain the poetry to him. The
force of this anecdote—and of al-Shaqundi's mockery of Ibn Tashfin—
hinges on the author's implicit assumption that cultural refinement is closely
associated with a strong command of Arabic and with an appreciation of Arabic poetry. Arabic language and poetry were, for al-Shaqundi and his contemporaries in al-Andalus, strong markers of Arabness—and, in particular,

markers that affiliated them with the elite literary culture of the Arab heart-lands in the east.[12]

My intention here is not to offer a detailed account of how Andalusi elites constructed their ethnic and cultural identities by affiliating themselves with the Mashriq and distancing themselves from the Maghrib. Rather, my goal is to show that modern celebrations of the Arabness of al-Andalus (such as Fayruz's performance in Kuwait) tap into a long history, one that stretches from the eighth century to the present. Giving an exhaustive account of this phenomenon would be nearly impossible, since the "Arab al-Andalus" is likely the most enduring and resilient of the competing visions of al-Andalus that I will analyze in this book. What will concern me, in the following pages, is the revival of this notion in the second half of the nineteenth century and its persistence from then until the present.

In what follows, I will focus on two snapshots in the long history of "Ara-bizing" al-Andalus. The first comes from the late nineteenth and early twen-tieth centuries, when Arab writers and intellectuals turned to al-Andalus with renewed interest and made it the subject of popular travel narratives and historical novels aimed at a broad, pan-Arab audience. I will focus, in partic-ular, on the work of Jurji Zaydan (1861–1914), a Lebanese novelist, journalist, publisher, and scholar who wrote three historical novels about al-Andalus in the first decade of the twentieth century. Zaydan's historical novels are, in my view, the predecessors of a much more recent phenomenon: the rise, in the early part of the twenty-first century, of Arabic-language television dramas set in al-Andalus and broadcast to audiences throughout the Arab world. Both Zaydan's novels about al-Andalus and the popular television dramas on the same theme contribute to creating a particular form of pan-Arab consciousness whose contours I will outline here.

The Return to al-Andalus in an Age of Revival

From the early nineteenth century to the early twentieth century, a diverse group of Arab writers and thinkers, mostly based in Egypt and the Levant, pursued a project of cultural revival known as the Nahda (lit. "the awak-ening").[13] At the same time, al-Andalus enjoyed a resurgence of interest among writers and readers in the Middle East and Europe. These overlapping phe-nomena were loosely related, in the sense that both were implicated in the colonial encounter between Europe and the Arab world.[14] European and Arab writers turned to the memory of al-Andalus to make sense of the colonial encounter and to situate European imperialism in a longer history of contact, conflict, and exchange between Europe, North Africa, and the Middle East.[15] For Arab writers associated with the Nahda, al-Andalus was not only a symbol of the Arab world's long-standing relations with (and contributions to) Europe; it was also a model of achievement that could serve to inspire the projects of cultural revival that were unfolding in the face of Europe's rising imperial power.

The long nineteenth century was also a time that witnessed an increased traffic in ideas between the Middle East and Europe, and this traffic extended to ideas about al-Andalus. For example, the growing body of European Orientalist scholarship on al-Andalus made its way—through diverse circuits of translation, citation, and commentary—to Arab writers and readers like Jurji Zaydan, who drew on European scholarship, among other sources, for his influential historical novels about al-Andalus. Turning to such complex moments of exchange, I aim to explore, in this section, how the memories and legacies of al-Andalus intersected with debates about Arab identity in an age of cultural revival framed by colonial encounter. Writings about al-Andalus from the Nahda not only echoed and amplified long-standing assertions about the centrality of Arabs and Arabness to al-Andalus, but also refracted those ideas through new lenses—especially the lens of race. As such, al-Andalus helped writers of the Nahda to articulate a pan-Arab identity, while also helping them to assert Arab contributions to European civilization and, in some cases, to lay claim to whiteness.

Of course, it was not only ideas that were on the move in this period, but also people. Starting in the late nineteenth century, Spain became a popular travel destination for Arab writers from the Mashriq. These writers—including such luminaries as Ahmad Zaki and Shakib Arslan—would travel to Spain to find inspiration in the monuments of al-Andalus and to memorialize those monuments in popular travel narratives written for Arabic readers.[16] By the middle of the twentieth century, this practice had become so common that the Iraqi writer Safa' Khulusi was able to write the following on the cover of his *Bint al-Sarraj* (1952): "I bear witness before God that I have fulfilled the duty of the nationalist pilgrimage [*al-ḥajj al-qawmī*] by visiting Arab Muslim Spain."[17] What is striking about this statement is that Khulusi describes his visit to Spain as a *ḥajj,* a term normally reserved for the pilgrimage to Mecca and Medina. Khulusi thus suggests that, by the time of his journey, Spain had become something like a second Mecca for Arab writers, who performed the "nationalist pilgrimage" to Spain as a duty to Arab nationalism.

The nineteenth century saw not only a boom in Arab travelers to Spain but also a notable rise in European scholarship on al-Andalus. At the forefront of this burgeoning field of research was Dutch Orientalist Reinhart Dozy (1820–1883). Dozy's four-volume history of al-Andalus, *Histoire des Musulmans d'Espagne* (History of the Muslims of Spain, 1861), marked a watershed moment in European Orientalist scholarship and remained the standard history of al-Andalus in Europe for nearly a century.[18] Dozy also codified a certain way of narrating Andalusi history—one that begins and ends with Arab rule. Although the title of his major work promises a history "of the Muslims of Spain," what the work actually offers is a historical narrative that begins in pre-Islamic Arabia and ends with the Almoravid (that is, North African) conquest of al-Andalus in the late eleventh century. This narrative of Andalusi history—one that effectively ends in the eleventh century—would cast a long shadow over future generations of scholars and has continued to exercise influence in the twenty-first century.[19]

Dozy's account of Andalusi history not only centered the period of Arab Umayyad rule but also consolidated a clear binary distinction between Arabs and Berbers, associating the former with civilization and the latter with barbarity. For example, Dozy calls the Arab rulers of al-Andalus "modern" and "enlightened" (*éclairé*), whereas he reserves adjectives like "crude" and "barbarian" for the Berbers.[20] Indeed, it is revealing that Dozy describes the civil war that broke out in al-Andalus in the early eleventh century as a conflict between "the Cordobans" and "the Berbers," as if the former category could not include the latter.[21] Here, for example, is how Dozy describes the entrance of Berber troops into Cordoba in April 1013: "The Berbers began to roam the streets, shouting ferocious cries. Here, they pillaged; there, they raped; everywhere, they massacred. The most inoffensive men fell victim to their blind fury."[22] In this description, Dozy dehumanizes the Berber troops by depicting them as a violent mob that emitted "ferocious cries" while killing innocent people in a state of "blind fury." He continues in this vein when he later describes the Berber troops as the "ferocious hordes [*hordes féroces*] that had ravaged the whole empire."[23] In all these examples, the contrast between Arabs and Berbers appears to stand in for the opposition between civilization and barbarity and between human and nonhuman. Read against the broader backdrop of European imperialism, Dozy's descriptions of the Berbers in al-Andalus associate them with the savagery and irrationality often attributed to non-European peoples in nineteenth-century European writings, especially within the field of Orientalism.

The racial politics of Dozy's approach to al-Andalus are particularly apparent in a passage about the Almoravid take-over of al-Andalus, led by Yusuf b. Tashfin in 1086. According to Dozy, Yusuf and the Almoravids,

> when they arrived in Spain, were illiterate, it is true, but pious, brave, honest, and accustomed to the simple and frugal life of the desert . . . The civilization of al-Andalus was for them quite a new spectacle. Feeling shame for their barbarity [*barbarie*], they wanted to become initiated in it, and they took as models the princes that they had dethroned. Unfortunately, their epidermis was too tough to be able to appropriate the delicateness, the tact, the finesse of the Andalusians. Everything about them carried the stamp of servile and weak imitation. They began to protect the men of letters and to order poems to be recited for them and books to be dedicated to them, but they did all of that awkwardly, without grace or taste. Whatever they tried, they remained half savages [*demi sauvages*].[24]

This passage revolves around a series of oppositions between al-Andalus and the Almoravid rulers who came to power in the late eleventh century. On the side of al-Andalus stand "civilization," "delicateness," "tact," "finesse," and poetry; on the side of Yusuf b. Tashfin and his men stand illiteracy, "barbarity," half-savagery, and servile and awkward imitation. Dozy's description evokes the famous passage from al-Shaqundi, who, in the thirteenth century, mocked Yusuf b. Tashfin for his inability to understand the refined Arabic poetry of al-Andalus. In al-Shaqundi's passage, the ethno-racial subtext is implicit, buried underneath a network of values that associated Arab identity with elite Arabic literary culture. In Dozy's text, in contrast, the racial overtones are impossible to miss. The Dutch scholar asserts that the Almoravids' "epidermis was too tough to be able to appropriate the delicateness, the tact, the finesse of the Andalusians." In other words, he claims that the Almoravids carried their "barbarity" on their skin ("epidermis"). His description of the Almoravids takes inspiration from a long-standing tendency to celebrate the Arab contributions to al-Andalus, but it puts this tendency to the service of a nineteenth-century worldview that associated racialized others, especially Africans, with "savagery" and "barbarity." It is not a coincidence that Dozy frequently refers to Berbers as "Africans."[25] His history of al-Andalus reflects the race thinking of nineteenth-century Europe.[26]

Dozy's scholarship on al-Andalus warrants such scrutiny not only because of the tremendous influence it exercised in Europe, but also because of the impact it would have on Arabic-language accounts of al-Andalus. One of Dozy's most avid readers in the Arab world was none other than Jurji Zaydan, who, as I have already indicated, played an important role in reviving popular interest in al-Andalus and in connecting the memory of al-Andalus to a nascent pan-Arab nationalism. Zaydan frequently cited Dozy's work in the footnotes to the three historical novels that he wrote about al-Andalus in the first decade of the twentieth century. Like Dozy, Zaydan espoused a vision of al-Andalus that celebrated Arabness, tying al-Andalus to the Arab heartlands in the east and distancing it from North Africans. Zaydan's Andalus also carried the imprint of the scientific racism that was circulating between European and Arab intellectuals in the late nineteenth and early twentieth centuries.

Jurji Zaydan was born to a poor Greek Orthodox family in Beirut in 1861.[27] Although largely an autodidact, he spent a short but formative stint as a young man at the Syrian Protestant College, where he refined his literary Arabic (*al-fuṣḥā*) and came into contact with new intellectual trends, such as Darwin's theory of evolution. In 1883 Zaydan moved to Cairo and landed a job at a newspaper owned by another Syrian immigrant in Egypt. Over the next several years, he would contribute to several prominent Arabic periodicals in Cairo. He combined this work with various teaching positions and with stints of self-guided study, including an extended stay in London, where he spent several weeks in the reading rooms of the British Museum, acquainting himself with European Orientalist scholarship.[28] (It is likely that the British Museum is where Zaydan encountered the work of Reinhart Dozy.) After returning to Cairo in the late 1880s, Zaydan worked as the editor of the well-known journal *al-Muqtataf* and as a teacher at Cairo's Greek Orthodox School.

In the early 1890s Zaydan embarked on the projects that would launch him to fame and that would occupy him for the rest of his life. In 1891 Zaydan published his first historical novel, *al-Mamluk al-sharid* (The fugitive Mamluk).[29] The following year, he founded the monthly cultural journal *al-Hilal* and a publishing house of the same name. The success of these ventures allowed Zaydan to resign from his other jobs and to devote himself entirely to writing.[30] Over the course of the next two decades, Zaydan would go on to write twenty more historical novels, all of which were published in serialized form in the journal *al-Hilal*.[31] In the pages of *al-Hilal*, Zaydan also published his extensive writings on the Arabic language, the history of the Arabs (including pre-Islamic Arab history), and the history of Arabic literature. These writings served as the foundation for Zaydan's major nonfiction works, including his *Tarikh adab al-lugha al-'arabiyya* (History of the literatures of the Arabic language, 1911), often hailed as the first modern literary history written in Arabic.[32]

Although Zaydan made important contributions to several fields, he is best known for his historical novels, which were wildly popular during his lifetime and are still reprinted today. Since the time of their first publication, Zaydan's historical novels have introduced generations of readers to major figures and events from Arab history, thereby helping to create a popular historical consciousness among readers of the Arabic language.[33] There are many testimonies to the immense popularity that Zaydan's novels enjoyed during his lifetime and throughout the twentieth century. One of the most eloquent comes from none other than Taha Husayn (1889–1973), arguably the most significant Egyptian cultural figure of the twentieth century.[34] In an essay published in 1942, Husayn vividly recollects how Zaydan's historical novels captivated his imagination when he was young.[35] For Husayn and other readers of his generation, Zaydan's work not only introduced a new literary genre—the historical novel—but also ignited a passion for, and awareness of, Arab history, conceived as such. For that reason, Husayn credits Zaydan with "a revival in Arab history" (*ihyā' li-l-tārikh al-'arabi*).[36]

Zaydan saw his novels as a crucial element in the broader project of generating consciousness of, and interest in, a shared Arab history, explicitly framed in nationalist terms. Zaydan referred to himself as a *kātib 'āmm*, a phrase that has been translated as "non-specialist writer," though I think that an even better translation would be "public writer."[37] Zaydan defined the *kātib ʿāmm* as "the servant of the nation [*al-umma*] and the guardian of its instruction."[38] The "nation" to which Zaydan refers here is not Egypt or Syria, but instead the "Arab nation," a construct that Zaydan himself helped to build. Anne-Laure Dupont has compared the role of the *kātib ʿāmm* to that of the French *instituteur,* "both the nation's teacher and the one who institutes it, who creates it through his teaching."[39] Zaydan positioned himself as the Arab nation's teacher—or, rather, as the teacher who would help build the Arab nation through a didactic program of public writing.

Writing in 1902, Zaydan explained why the historical novel was the ideal vehicle for such a program. "Because reading pure history," Zaydan wrote, "is burdensome for the reading public, especially in our country where science is still in the stage of infancy. We had no choice but to use trickery in order to spread science among us, with the aim of exciting people's interest in reading. And novels are the best means for this aim."[40] Zaydan describes his novels as a kind of "trickery" (*iḥtiyāl*)—the spoonful of sugar that lets the medicine of history go down. The phrase he uses to describe the intended audience for his novels is *jumhūr al-qurrāʾ*: "the reading public," or, more literally, "the public of readers." Zaydan, through his historical novels, set out not only to communicate with such a reading public but also, in some sense, to create it. He indicated as much when he stated, in an article published in *al-Hilal* in 1899: "Readers are simply the creation of writers."[41] In his role as "public writer," Zaydan set out to spread the knowledge of history among the public and also, more importantly, to create a national community of readers who share a common set of historical narratives.

I am reminded here of Benedict Anderson's classic work on the origins of nationalism and, in particular, of Anderson's assertion that the newspaper, the novel, and other forms of print capitalism played an important role in the creation of the "imagined community" of the nation.[42] In this regard it seems noteworthy that Zaydan's historical novels, like most of his published work, first appeared in the pages of his magazine *al-Hilal,* one of the most successful Arabic-language print ventures of the nineteenth and twentieth centuries.[43] Anderson's study of nationalism offers a helpful framework for thinking about Zaydan's work as a novelist, journalist, and public writer, but there are also some important differences between Anderson's approach and

Zaydan's projects.[44] The first difference is that Zaydan was trying to imagine a national community that was not bound by a specific nation-state. Zaydan's imagined community was not Egypt or Syria, but instead the Arab nation, defined by language and a common cultural heritage.

This point leads to a second key difference between Anderson and Zaydan. Anderson's account emphasizes the rise of national vernaculars, their displacement of transnational sacred languages (such as Latin), and their consolidation and dissemination through print culture. Anderson's emphasis on the mutually reinforcing relationship between vernacular languages and print capitalism is helpful for understanding the rise of nationalism in Europe but is less helpful for understanding Zaydan and his historical milieu. Zaydan was aiming, not to consolidate a national vernacular (be it Egyptian or Syrian), but instead to create a simplified and accessible transnational print language that would be appealing to a broad pan-Arab readership. Zaydan was, as other scholars have noted, both a witness to, and an agent of, the reform and renovation of the Arabic language in the modern era.[45] The result of this process of reform was the language that we now call "Modern Standard Arabic." Zaydan was an ardent defender of this language, without which his imagined audience of readers would cease to exist. In fact, he argued against British attempts to turn the Egyptian dialect into a written language because he saw those attempts as a threat to pan-Arab identity. On this point, Zaydan declared, in an article published in 1893: "Arab collective identity depends on preserving the literary language."[46]

Building on this vision of an intimate relationship between language and identity, Zaydan would speak of his pan-Arab audience as "the nation of language" (*ummat al-lugha*) or "the Arabic linguistic society" (*al-mujtama' al-lughawī al-'arabī*).[47] For Zaydan, the Arabic language was a force (perhaps the only force) that could forge a common identity among Arabs of different faiths and from different places and times. This view was likely informed by Zaydan's own experience as a Syrian Christian immigrant writing in Muslim-majority Egypt at a time when Egyptian nationalism was on the rise.[48] Zaydan and other Christian Arab intellectuals of his generation asserted a place for themselves in Egyptian and Levantine society by advocating for a pan-Arab identity based on a common language instead of a common religion.

This vision of pan-Arab identity comes to the fore in Zaydan's historical novels—in particular, in his three novels set in al-Andalus. The first one, *Fath*

al-Andalus (1903, translated into English as *The Conquest of Andalusia*), tells
the story of the events leading up to the Muslim invasion of the Iberian Peninsula in 711, focusing on the political discord and palace intrigue that led
to the demise of Visigoth rule in Iberia.[49] Zaydan's second Andalus-themed
novel, *Sharl wa-ʿAbd al-Rahman* (1904, translated into English as *The Battle
of Poitiers*), follows the campaign of the Arab commander ʿAbd al-Rahman
al-Ghafiqi into today's France, culminating with the defeat of ʿAbd al-
Rahman's army in the Battle of Poitiers in 732, the first major setback of Islam's rapid expansion into medieval Europe.[50] Zaydan's third and final novel
set in al-Andalus, *ʿAbd al-Rahman al-Nasir* (1910), focuses on the reign of ʿAbd
al-Rahman al-Nasir (r. 912–961), highlighting the cultural splendor of
Umayyad Cordoba but also hinting at the political and ethnic tensions that
would eventually lead to the demise of Umayyad rule in the eleventh century.[51]
The three novels illustrate Zaydan's efforts to claim al-Andalus as a chapter
in Arab cultural history—that is, to emphasize al-Andalus's Arab identity
while deemphasizing its connection to North African Muslims.[52]

It bears noting that Zaydan's Andalus trilogy, much like Dozy's history of
al-Andalus, covers only the period in which al-Andalus was under the control of Arab rulers who claimed descent from Syria. Zaydan's Andalus effectively ends in the tenth century, before the decline of the Umayyad caliphate
in the early eleventh century. It is no accident that Zaydan and Dozy converge on a similar vision of the history of al-Andalus. Dozy's work was, in
fact, one of the main sources Zaydan consulted while doing the research for
the historical background for his Andalus novels. These novels, like many of
Zaydan's works, include footnotes citing authoritative sources, often European Orientalist scholarship.[53] The footnotes serve to validate and legitimate
the historical information that Zaydan presents, giving his novels a certain
degree of scholarly gravitas. Dozy is one of the authors most frequently cited
in the footnotes of Zaydan's novels set in al-Andalus.[54] Another frequently
cited author is Charles Romey, whose multivolume *Histoire d'Espagne* (1839)
not only provided Zaydan with information about the Visigoths but also bolstered the writer's pro-Arab bias. To mention just one illustrative example,
Romey blames the defeat of ʿAbd al-Rahman al-Ghafiqi's army at the Battle
of Poitiers on the greed and insincerity of the Arab commander's Berber
troops, a view that becomes a central theme in the second part of Zaydan's
Andalus trilogy, *Sharl wa-ʿAbd al-Rahman*.[55] In sum, Jurji Zaydan, in his

attempt to offer an "Arab view" of al-Andalus, relied heavily on European sources that emphasized the Arab contributions to al-Andalus and that attributed the eventual demise of al-Andalus to the rivalry between Arabs and Berbers.

In the first installment of Zaydan's Andalus trilogy, *The Conquest of al-Andalus* (*Fath al-Andalus*), one of Zaydan's main rhetorical strategies is to depict the rapid expansion of Islam in the seventh and eighth centuries as the peaceful expansion of Arab rule, from the Mashriq to Europe. Zaydan frequently refers to the "Arab," rather than the "Muslim," conquests of North Africa and al-Andalus. In other words, Zaydan tends to conflate the adjectives "Arab" and "Muslim" and to shift subtly between a religious mode of identification and an ethnic one. This slippage is particularly surprising in the case of the conquest of al-Andalus, in which the Berber commander Tariq b. Ziyad led an army primary composed of Berber soldiers.[56]

Zaydan's emphasis on the Arabness of the Muslim conquests is paired with a related theme: Arab tolerance toward Jews and Christians. In *The Conquest of al-Andalus,* many of the Jewish and Christian characters oppose King Roderic and support the Muslim (or, in the novel's terms, "Arab") invasion because they believe that they will enjoy greater freedom under the new rulers. This theme underpins a pivotal scene in which one of the main Jewish characters, Sulayman, tries to convince one of the main Christian characters, Alfonso, that he should not fear the coming Muslim invasion. Sulayman assures Alfonso that he and his fellow Christians will enjoy autonomy and religious freedom under the new rulers:

> I don't blame you for being so surprised, since this is totally unprecedented according to what you know of these lands, where rulers meddle in all aspects of people's lives and even regard their subjects as their slaves. But these Arabs are different. Once they have conquered a country and imposed the poll tax [*al-jizya*] and the land tax, they take up residence in its outskirts and build cities for themselves . . . Jewish and Christian subjects have been much better off under Arab rule than that of others.[57]

Here, Sulayman describes the poll tax paid by Jews, Christians, and other protected non-Muslim communities (known as *ahl al-dhimma*) living under

Muslim rule. Yet Sulayman attributes this system of protection to "Arab rule" rather than Muslim jurisprudence. Indeed, this passage illustrates Zaydan's tendency to slip between religious categories ("Jews and Christians") and ethnic ones ("Arab").

In this passage, and throughout the novel, Zaydan makes some interrelated claims: he suggests that Arab rule is tolerant by nature, that Islam is most tolerant when its leaders are Arab, and that there is a natural alliance between Arabs, Jews, and Christians. Sulayman returns to the last point in another key scene, where he lays out the Jewish case for supporting the new rulers over the Visigoths: "The Jews are closely related to the Arabs because, as you know, both groups come from a single ancestor, Abraham."[58] Although the figure of Abraham often serves as a symbol of cooperation between the three major monotheistic faiths (Judaism, Christianity, and Islam), its function here is different: here, it serves as the origin of a network of kinship linking Jews and Arabs.

The Battle of Poitiers (*Sharl wa-'Abd al-Rahman*), the second part of Zaydan's Andalus trilogy, picks up on these themes, casting the Muslim conquest of al-Andalus as an Arab enterprise and celebrating the tolerance of Arabs toward other peoples, especially Christians. According to the summary that appeared on the cover of the first edition (1904), the novel "covers *the Arabs'* conquests in the lands of France . . . and the reasons that led to *the Arabs'* failure and to Europe's salvation from them."[59] The novel posits that the defeat at the Battle of Poitiers was due, not to the military or political superiority of the Franks, but to the treachery and greed of the Berber soldiers in 'Abd al-Rahman al-Ghafiqi's army. In other words, the novel blames Berbers for the failure of the Muslim forces to establish a permanent foothold in today's France.

The Battle of Poitiers casts the Berbers as a threat to the Arab spirit of al-Andalus—and, in particular, to the tolerance that Arab rulers allegedly show to their Christian subjects. This theme emerges early in the novel, when a faction of Berber troops led by the Berber commander Bustam pillages and loots the cathedral of Bordeaux. News of this incident reaches the Arab general 'Abd al-Rahman al-Ghafiqi from an Arabic-speaking Christian woman named Salma, who is taken captive with her daughter during the assault on Bordeaux. When 'Abd al-Rahman learns about the Berbers soldiers' looting of the cathedral, he is outraged, and he summons Bustam to reprimand him and remind him of the obligation that Muslims have to treat Christians with respect.[60] In the exchange between 'Abd al-Rahman and Bustam, the Arab general represents a vision of Islamic governance that welcomes and respects Christians.

This vision finds a powerful ally and spokesperson in Salma, the Arabic-speaking Christian captive from Bordeaux. Later in the novel, it is revealed that Salma was once the wife of Roderic, the last Visigoth king in Iberia. After Roderic's defeat in 711, Salma (then known by another name) remained in Toledo, where she met and fell in love with 'Abd al-'Aziz b. Musa b. Nusayr (d. 716), one of the first Muslim rulers of al-Andalus.[61] She married 'Abd al-'Aziz on the condition that she could remain a Christian. From their marriage was born a daughter, Maryam—conveniently named after a figure, Mary, who is revered in both the Christian and Muslim traditions. Indeed, the character Maryam, the daughter of an Iberian Christian mother and an Arab Muslim father, symbolizes, in the novel, the promise of interethnic and interfaith coexistence that could be actualized under the banner of Arab rule. Likewise, her mother, Salma, serves as an advocate for Arab-Christian solidarity throughout the novel.

Soon after being captured in Bordeaux, Salma volunteers to serve as a mediator between 'Abd al-Rahman and the Christian Gauls, many of whom, she claims, "prefer the victory of the Arab Muslims to the victory of the Frankish Christians."[62] In her new role as mediator, Salma leaves 'Abd al-Rahman's camp and makes her way back to Bordeaux, where she gets an audience with the archbishop and tries to convince him to throw his support behind the Arab cause. As the narrator explains:

> She assured him that the Arabs are the greatest of nations in terms of their gentle treatment of their subjects and prisoners, and that wherever their sovereignty extends, to the east and west, the people of those lands, regardless of their faiths, enjoy freedom of religion and civil treatment not customary in the Frankish nations in that period. [Finally, she assured him] that the pillaging of the cathedral of Bordeaux happened on account of the negligence of some greedy non-Arab [ghayr al-'arab] followers of the Muslim army.[63]

Salma tries to assure the archbishop that the real threat comes not from Muslims but instead from non-Arabs. To bolster this claim, she points to the "freedom of religion" that people of all faiths enjoy under Arab sovereignty, and she blames the looting of Bordeaux's cathedral on greedy "non-Arab followers of the Muslim army"—that is, on Berbers.

Not surprisingly, the novel's villain is a Berber: the Berber commander Bustam. He embodies the negative qualities that Zaydan attributes to Berbers: greed, disloyalty, lust, and an insincere commitment to Islam. These qualities are emphasized early in the novel, in the narrator's first description of Bustam:

> Among them was a Berber commander named Bustam. He and his tribe had only converted to Islam out of greed for profit, plunder, booty, and the like. He was strong-bodied and ill-tempered. Anyone who laid eyes on him would shudder at the sight of him on account of his huge head, his wide face, his enormous nose, and his inflated nostrils ... To say nothing of his oily color, the harsh crudeness on display in his entire appearance, and his thick lips of the darkest night, suggesting lewd pleasures.[64]

The narrator suggests here that Bustam and other North African Berbers converted to Islam only out of greed and a desire for plunder. This idea frequently surfaces in the novel, including in the novel's final sequence, when 'Abd al-Rahman's Berber troops abandon him in the Battle of Poitiers in order to protect their war booty.

Yet perhaps what is most striking about the narrator's description of Bustam is not the claim about his insincere faith but instead the attention to Bustam's physical features. Put bluntly, Zaydan's narrator *Africanizes* Bustam, attributing to him features that are commonly associated with people of African descent, such as a dark complexion, a wide face, and thick lips. Furthermore, these physical features are explicitly associated with moral flaws, such as lewdness, crudeness, and an ill temper. The passage illustrates Zaydan's adherence to the principles of nineteenth-century physiognomy— and, in particular, to the belief that the study of someone's physical features reveals truths about the person's underlying moral character.

It bears noting here that Zaydan, before publishing his Andalus trilogy, had shown a sustained interest in physiognomy and other related European race sciences. These sciences played a pivotal role in sustaining European claims of racial supremacy in the nineteenth and twentieth centuries and often served as justifications for Europe's colonization of Africa (and elsewhere).[65] Zaydan's interest in European race science culminated in the publication of his *Kitab 'ilm al-firasa al-hadith* (Book on the modern science of physiognomy, 1901), whose cover promised readers a guide to "judging people's character, ability, talents, and varieties of actions from the shape of their limbs."[66] In fact, Zaydan cites this very work in the footnotes to his novel *The Conquest of al-Andalus,* in a passage where the narrator praises a Christian character's physical attributes and associates them with positive moral traits, such as "a strong sense of what is right."[67] In other words, the implied association between Bustam's physical appearance and his moral character is not haphazard; rather, it is part of a systematic attempt to represent Berbers as racialized others with moral and cultural deficiencies.

These efforts not only rely on ideas taken from European race science but also build on long-standing ideas about the cultural superiority of Arabs over Berbers. It is not a coincidence that the novel draws attention to Bustam's linguistic difference, in addition to his racial difference. In a passage in which Bustam tries to force himself on Salma's daughter Maryam, the narrator notes that he speaks "in an Arabic language made un-Arabic [*musta'jama*] by the intonation of the Berbers."[68] The phrase hinges on an Arabic participle made from a root that refers to non-Arabs (*al-'ajam* is a collective noun meaning "non-Arabs"). In other words, the narrator suggests that the Arabic language becomes "non-Arab" in Bustam's mouth. This emphasis on linguistic difference is particularly striking when one considers that the novel repeatedly draws attention to how well Salma and her daughter Maryam speak the Arabic language, even though it is not their native tongue. Arabness, it would seem, is a cultural ideal that, in Zaydan's novel, is fluid enough to be open to some Christians, but not to North African Berbers.

The system of racial and cultural difference that underpins Zaydan's *The Battle of Poitiers* comes into greater focus when we compare the novel's descriptions of Bustam to its descriptions of Hani, an Arab commander who is 'Abd al-Rahman's right-hand man and Bustam's rival for Maryam's love. Here is the narrator's first description of Hani:

Hani was tall and broad chested, and people recognized him immediately. Wherever he appeared, his outstanding qualities were easy to detect. He was in the prime of his youth, with clearly defined features, prominent eyebrows, high cheek bones, piercing eyes, a small nose and mouth, a prominent chin, a sparse beard, and jet black hair, with a face ever smiling but nonetheless dignified.[69]

Hani, like Bustam, is clearly racialized. The narrator attributes to Hani physical traits that are commonly associated with whiteness, such as high cheek bones and a small nose and mouth. Hani's whiteness is associated not only with physical beauty but also with dignity and other "outstanding qualities." Hani and his foil, Bustam, thus exist within a system that valorizes whiteness and demonizes blackness. Crucially, they also exist within a system that associates Berbers with blackness, Arabs with whiteness, and al-Andalus with Arabs (and therefore with whiteness).

These racial hierarchies correspond with a spatial imaginary that links al-Andalus and the Levant to Europe, while distancing them from Africa. Zaydan's Andalus trilogy particularly emphasizes the links between al-Andalus and the Mashriq, but it also points to the links between al-Andalus and the Greco-Roman heritage. For example, in *The Conquest of al-Andalus,* Zaydan depicts the Muslim (or, to use his adjective, "Arab") conquest of Iberia as a restoration of the Roman heritage. Along these lines, the narrator explains:

> The Goths conquered [Spain], but they were unable to substitute their language [for Latin], as the Arabs were able to substitute Arabic for the languages in the areas that they conquered in the eastern Roman kingdoms. In their conquests of former Roman kingdoms, the Goths and Arabs shared a lot in common . . . But it was the Arabs who managed to achieve something that the Goths did not: building on the vestiges of Roman civilization, they managed to erect a new one that was uniquely their own. With the passing of generations, they managed to mold the various nations with whom they came into contact into a single nation that spoke a single language.[70]

The narrator's comment establishes a contrast between the Visigoths, who were unable to forge a unified cultural identity in their territories, and the Arabs, who were able to create a "single nation" (*umma wāḥida*) built on the shared use of the Arabic language. In this account of Mediterranean history, the *Pax Romana* passes the torch to the *Pax Arabica,* and Latin gives way to Arabic as the language of cultural prestige in the Mediterranean. Zaydan suggests that the Arabs are the heirs to the Romans in the sense that both peoples were able to forge an ecumenical national identity based on the shared use of a language. He also suggests that the Arabic language is not only the basis for Arab national identity but also the bridge that brought ancient Roman civilization ("the vestiges of Roman civilization") to Europe.

The third installment of Zaydan's Andalus trilogy, *'Abd al-Rahman al-Nasir* (1910), reinforces the idea that al-Andalus is a hub in a cultural map linking Iberia to the eastern Mediterranean, the Mashriq, and the Greco-Roman heritage. The novel focuses on the reign of 'Abd al-Rahman III (also known as 'Abd al-Rahman *al-Nāṣir,* "the Victor"), the first Umayyad caliph in al-Andalus. One of the novel's main themes is that 'Abd al-Rahman derives his authority from his affiliation with the memory of Umayyad Damascus, and, as a corollary, that the primary threats to his rule come from North Africa and from non-Arab elements. The novel follows a plot to overthrow the Umayyad state led by a spy from the Fatimid court, a rival dynasty that rose to power in North Africa in the early tenth century and challenged the Umayyads' claim to the caliphate. In other words, the novel dramatizes yet another threat to Umayyad rule emanating from North Africa. It also highlights internal tensions in tenth-century Umayyad Cordoba: in particular, the popular discontent with the rising power and influence of foreign elements in 'Abd al-Rahman's court—especially the northern European eunuchs known as "Slavs" (*al-ṣaqāliba*). In short, *'Abd al-Rahman al-Nasir* pays tribute to the splendor of Umayyad Cordoba but also foreshadows the end of a period in which al-Andalus was dominated by Arab rulers with genealogical and cultural connections to the eastern Mediterranean.

The novel's action begins with the news of the arrival of emissaries from the court of Constantine VII, the emperor of the Byzantine empire. This plotline is based on a historical event: an embassy from the Byzantine emperor to the court of 'Abd al-Rahman III in 948 or 949.[71] In Zaydan's novel, the emissaries arrive at 'Abd al-Rahman's palace in Madinat al-Zahra' and present the caliph with a letter from the Byzantine emperor. The letter is addressed, in Greek, to "'Abd al-Rahman, the caliph, ruler of the Arabs in al-Andalus."[72] The emissaries also bear two gifts: a book in Greek and a book in Latin. The first of these books is an illustrated copy of Dioscorides's treatise on medicinal plants, commonly known by its Latin title *De materia medica* and described by Zaydan's narrator as "the Book of Herbs, the work by the famous botanist Dioscorides."[73] The second book is "the book of Orosius [*Kitāb Hurūshiyūs*]"—that is, Orosius's *Historiae adversus paganos* (ca. 416).[74] The books come with a note encouraging the caliph to have the books translated into Arabic. Here again, Zaydan bases the plot on historical events. In the tenth century, 'Abd Rahman III sponsored an Arabic translation of Dioscorides's botanical treatise, and in the ninth or tenth century, Orosius's work was translated from Latin into Arabic by scholars working in Umayyad Cordoba.[75]

The scene described above captures three key elements of Zaydan's view of al-Andalus. First of all, it depicts al-Andalus as the bridge between the Greco-Roman world and medieval Europe, highlighting the important role that Andalusi scholars and patrons played in the translation and transmission of ancient Greek and Latin texts into Europe.[76] Second, the scene depicts al-Andalus as a site of prestige and political power—that is, as a place where the most powerful rulers in the world, such as Byzantine emperor, send their emissaries. This theme reemerges later in the novel, when 'Abd al-Rahman III receives diplomatic delegations from "the kings of France and Italy."[77] Finally, the scene depicts an Andalus that is Arab in terms of culture, language, and ethnic hierarchy. The letter from the Byzantine emperor calls 'Abd al-Rahman the "ruler of the Arabs in al-Andalus," even though 'Abd al-Rahman was, in fact, the ruler of a diverse society with multiple ethnic, religious, and linguistic communities.

In *'Abd al-Rahman al-Nasir,* the title character is represented as the rightful heir to the Umayyads of Damascus, and his court is depicted as a restoration of Umayyad culture on Iberian soil. Comparisons between Cordoba and Damascus abound in the novel. For example, when two members of 'Abd al-Rahman's court observe the caliph as he prepares to meet the emissaries from Constantinople, one of them comments to the other:

Look at the staff that is in his hand: it is the staff of the caliphate . . . And look at him now wearing the turban studded with jewels and wearing an outer cloak like the ones the caliphs used to wear. But he made it white so that it would resemble the clothes of his forefathers, the Umayyads in Syria. And you see below the outer cloak an embroidered

garment. It is also the dress that the Umayyads would use during the
time of their dynasty in Syria.[78]

Zaydan's 'Abd al-Rahman dresses himself, quite literally, in the cloak of his
Umayyad forefathers in Damascus. His claim to the caliphate is explicitly
grounded in his genealogical connection to the Umayyad caliphate in the
east. Likewise, the splendor of his Cordoba is predicated on his ability to
restore the protocols and trappings of Umayyad Damascus. The passage,
then, depicts an Andalus with a foot in Europe and an eye on the Mashriq, an
Andalus whose dominant culture patterns itself after a lost homeland in the
east, turning its back on North Africans and other cultural groups that contributed to the building of al-Andalus.

The Arab al-Andalus on Screen

Jurji Zaydan's Andalus trilogy disseminated an Arab-centric view of al-
Andalus that would persist in Arabic literature through much of the twentieth century. This view was particularly popular among the numerous
Levantine and Egyptian writers who visited Spain in the twentieth century to
write about the monuments of al-Andalus.[79] Two prominent examples of this
trend are the Syrian writers Nizar Qabbani (1923–1998) and Salma al-Haffar
al-Kuzbari (1923–2006), both of whom lived in Spain in the 1960s and wrote
works that celebrated the deep historical ties between Spain and the Arab
world—and, in particular, between Cordoba and Damascus.[80] Al-Haffar al-
Kuzbari would hammer home this theme in a lecture she delivered in 1965
at the Damascus Social Club, where she told her audience, "Talking about
Spain, ladies and gentlemen, is a pleasant topic, but it is also one that carries
with it sorrows that shake all Arabs—and that shake us Syrians especially.
For, Spain is the beautiful name of a great and beautiful country in whose
Andalus was born an original civilization of Arab characteristics through the
labor of our ancestors, the Umayyads."[81] I will discuss al-Haffar al-Kuzbari's
writings about al-Andalus at greater length in Chapter 3. For now, I want
to highlight two things about her remarks to the audience in Damascus in
1965. First, al-Haffar al-Kuzbari emphasizes the Arabness of al-Andalus
by describing al-Andalus as "an original civilization of Arab characteristics."
Second, she uses the phrase "our ancestors, the Umayyads" to invite her

Syrian Arab audience to imagine themselves as the descendants of the Umayyad rulers who helped give rise to al-Andalus. In al-Haffar al-Kuzbari's lecture, as in Jurji Zaydan's novels, the cultural legacy of al-Andalus runs a relay on an east–west axis, moving from Damascus to Cordoba in the eighth century and then back to Damascus in the twentieth century.[82]

Although the Arab al-Andalus has persisted as a historical imaginary in Arabic literature, it has also made the leap from literature to visual culture, including cinema and television. In the 1990s, al-Andalus was brought to the big screen in such films as Nacer Khemir's *The Dove's Lost Necklace* (*Le collier perdu de la colombe,* 1991) and Youssef Chahine's *Destiny* (*al-Masir,* 1997), both of which premiered to great acclaim at European film festivals.[83] For the purposes of my argument, though, I am less interested in art-house cinema than I am in a more popular form of entertainment: Arabic television drama—in particular, a form of Arabic television drama known as the *musalsal* (pl. *musalsalāt*). *Musalsalāt* are thirty-episode dramatic miniseries that generally premiere on the first night of Ramadan, air on consecutive nights during the month of Ramadan, and are rebroadcast throughout the year and online.[84] The thirty-episode format of the *musalsal* thus molds itself to the lunar month of Ramadan, offering a popular cultural ritual that unfolds alongside the sacred rituals of Ramadan. In recent decades al-Andalus has figured prominently in this mass cultural phenomenon, for reasons that I will briefly outline here.

Ramadan television is big business—something akin to the sweeps season in the United States.[85] During Ramadan, the Arabic-language television industry releases its best and most anticipated programs, and viewership and advertising rates soar. Egyptian dramas dominated the television industry in the 1970s and 1980s, but the advent of pan-Arab satellite television channels in the 1990s radically altered the geography of Arabic television production and of consumption patterns.[86] With the rise of satellite television, producers and writers needed to create content that would appeal to a transnational pan-Arab audience. In this new media landscape, Syrian television producers emerged as leaders in the industry, specializing in the production of historical epics and costume dramas, often written and performed in Modern Standard Arabic (as opposed to the Egyptian dialect used in many Egyptian dramas). Starting in the 1990s, Syrian drama creators increasingly worked in close collaboration with the pan-Arab satellite networks based in the

wealthy Gulf countries. In this arrangement, the Syrian creators would produce much of the dramatic content for the Gulf-based networks, and these
networks would, in turn, broadcast the Syrian dramas to a wide audience in the
Arab world (and throughout the worldwide Arab diaspora).[87] The fruitful and
mutually beneficial collaboration between Syrian drama creators and Gulf-
based satellite networks ushered in a boom in Syrian television production—
a boom that critics and the press called "the outpouring of drama" (*al-fawra
al-dramiyya*).[88]

In the first decade of the twenty-first century, during the heyday of the
"outpouring of drama," al-Andalus emerged as a popular theme in Ramadan
television. Between 2002 and 2005, at least six big-budget historical epics
set in al-Andalus aired during Ramadan.[89] Among them, the most famous
was a trilogy of dramas directed by Hatim ʿAli (1962–2020), a star of the
Syrian television industry, and written by a Palestinian-Jordanian screen-
writer, Walid Sayf (b. 1948). The trilogy comprises *Saqr Quraysh* (The
hawk of Quraysh, 2002), *Rabiʿ Qurtuba* (The spring of Cordoba, 2003), and
Muluk al-tawaʾif (The *taifa* kings, 2005). The trilogy enjoyed both commercial
and critical success, garnering top awards at festivals in Egypt, Syria, and
Tunisia.[90]

In addition to offering a fascinating window into contemporary views of
al-Andalus, the trilogy also illustrates the increasingly transnational nature
of contemporary Arabic television production. Directed by a Syrian and
written by a Jordanian-Palestinian, the trilogy was produced by Syrian Art
Production International, a Syrian company with close ties to the Asad regime, and was broadcast by the premier pan-Arab satellite entertainment network, MBC, which is based in Saudi Arabia.[91] It featured a star-studded cast
of Syrian and Moroccan actors, including some of the biggest names in Arabic television, such as Syrian actors Jamal Sulayman, Khalid Taja, and Taym
Hasan. As this sketch of the trilogy's production illuminates, Syrian artists,
such as director Hatim ʿAli, are leaders in the production of dramatic miniseries and, at the same time, players in an expansive, transnational network
that involves actors, producers, writers, viewers, and financial entities in the
Gulf and throughout the Arab world.

As I hope to illustrate over the following pages, the Andalus trilogy created by Hatim ʿAli and Walid Sayf revived the spirit of the cultural project
that Jurji Zaydan pursued at the turn of the twentieth century. Like Zaydan's

historical novels about al-Andalus, 'Ali and Sayf's Andalus trilogy targeted a broad, Arabic-speaking audience with the goal of promoting a pan-Arab historical consciousness that includes, but is not centered on, Islam. Zaydan's historical novels and 'Ali and Sayf's trilogy also follow a similar historical arc, telling a story of al-Andalus that is centered on Arab Umayyad rule. The first part of 'Ali and Sayf's trilogy, *Saqr Quraysh* (The hawk of Quraysh, 2002), traces the fall of the Umayyad caliphate in Syria and the restoration of Umayyad power in al-Andalus through the story of 'Abd al-Rahman I (also known as 'Abd al-Rahman *al-Dākhil,* "the Immigrant"). The second part of the trilogy, *Rabi' Qurtuba* (The spring of Cordoba, 2003), focuses on the heyday of the Umayyad caliphate in tenth-century al-Andalus, especially during the reign of the first two Umayyad caliphs, 'Abd al-Rahman III and al-Hakam II (r. 961–976). While the series pays tribute to the cultural splendor and political power of Umayyad Cordoba, it also dramatizes some of the political and ethnic rivalries that would lead to the eventual demise of the Umayyad state in al-Andalus. These tensions come to a head in the third and final installment of the trilogy, *Muluk al-tawa'if* (The *taifa* kings, 2005), which tells the story of the small kingdoms (known as *taifa* kingdoms) that emerged in al-Andalus in the eleventh century after the collapse of the Cordoba caliphate. In the series, the *taifa* kings fight among themselves for control of al-Andalus, while facing threats from the Christian territories to the north and from a new political rival in North Africa, the Almoravids. By the end of the series, the Almoravids have conquered al-Andalus.

In sum, 'Ali and Sayf's Andalus trilogy presents a story about al-Andalus that begins in Syria (with 'Abd al-Rahman I) and ends with the rise of the North African Almoravid dynasty, which conquers al-Andalus from the south. This particular narration of al-Andalus sets aside the last four centuries of Andalusi history and presents the demise of Arab Umayyad rule as the beginning of a long decline that inexorably leads to the loss of al-Andalus in 1492. In other words, the trilogy is a distillation of the vision I've been calling "the Arab al-Andalus." Like Zaydan's novels, the trilogy associates al-Andalus with the ideal of Arabness, locates the origins of Arabness in the Levant, and identifies the main threats to al-Andalus as intra-Arab conflict and the political ascendancy of non-Arab groups, such as North African Berbers. Moreover, the trilogy transmits this historical imaginary through a cultural form that is aimed at a broad, transnational, Arabic-speaking audience: the *musalsal.* At the turn of the twentieth century, Zaydan engaged in a project of public history through the form of the serialized novel; at the turn of the twenty-first century, 'Ali and Sayf picked up the torch and pursued a similar project through the form of the *musalsal.*

The first part of the trilogy, *Saqr Quraysh,* celebrates the restoration of Umayyad Syria in al-Andalus. As such, the plot does not begin with the founding moment of Andalusi history, the Muslim conquest of the Iberian Peninsula in 711; rather, it begins a few decades later, and thousands of miles away, in Syria. The first episode of the series opens in Rusafa, the summer residence that the Umayyad caliph Hisham (r. 724–743) built in the Syrian desert. The main plotline centers on Hisham's grandson, 'Abd al-Rahman, who flees Syria after the Abbasid massacre of his family and makes his way to al-Andalus. In the final episodes of the series, after 'Abd al-Rahman has become the ruler of al-Andalus, he decides to build an estate outside of Cordoba and to call it Rusafa, after his grandfather's estate in Syria. The two Rusafas—one in Syria and the other in Cordoba—serve as bookends for the plot. *Saqr Quraysh,* thus, tells a story that moves from the Rusafa of the east (in Syria) to the Rusafa of the west (in Cordoba), and from the fall of the Umayyads in Syria to the rise of the Umayyads in al-Andalus.

This cultural itinerary is foreshadowed early in the series. In episode 3, 'Abd al-Rahman and his brothers go to the caliph's palace in Rusafa to see their grandfather, Hisham. One of the caliph's advisors meets the brothers in the palace's courtyard, and when he sees 'Abd al-Rahman, he is blinded by a sudden flash of light (a moment that is accentuated in the score by the crash of a cymbal). The caliph's advisor approaches the young 'Abd al-Rahman, examines his face, and then greets him as "the prince [*amīr*] of al-Andalus." The caliph Hisham (played by Syrian actor Khalid Taja) observes the exchange from a window that faces the courtyard. At the end of the scene, the caliph asks his advisor why he gave more attention to 'Abd al-Rahman than to his brothers, and the advisor responds: "I saw the signs on him . . . This is the Umayyad who will revive the Umayyad state in the West [*al-Maghrib*], after its removal in the East [*al-Mashriq*]."[92] This prophecy is reiterated in the following episode (episode 4), when caliph Hisham is on his deathbed. In the last moments of his life, Hisham grabs his grandson 'Abd al-Rahman by the shirt, draws him near, and urges him to fulfill his destiny: "Renew our rule in al-Andalus. At that point, remember your grandfather Hisham . . .

And make al-Andalus an image of Syria."[93] Hisham's dying words to 'Abd al-Rahman mark the narrative path that the series will follow. They frame 'Abd al-Rahman's mission as one of restoration and replication—one of "making al-Andalus an image of Syria."

'Abd al-Rahman's destiny as the figure who will revive Umayyad rule in a new land is a theme that runs throughout the series, reemerging at key points in the narrative. Perhaps nowhere is this theme more pronounced than in one of the main storylines of the last third of the series: 'Abd al-Rahman's construction of Rusafa, a palace complex on the outskirts of Cordoba. This storyline unfolds over several episodes, from episode 22 to episode 30, and provides a vantage point from which 'Abd al-Rahman can look back on the events of the series—and back on the home that he left behind in Syria.

The pivotal scene comes in episode 23, when 'Abd al-Rahman brings his family and his entourage to the new Rusafa for the first time. 'Abd al-Rahman leads the group to an open field, where he has planted a lone date palm tree. The prince points to the tree and hails it as "the first date palm [*nakhla*] in al-Andalus!" The actor playing 'Abd al-Rahman (Jamal Sulayman) then approaches the palm tree and recites a poem that is attributed to the historical 'Abd al-Rahman:

> A palm tree stands in the middle of Rusafa, born in the West, far
> from the land of palms.
> I said to it: "How like me you are, far away and in exile, in long
> separation from family and friends.
> You have sprung from soil in which you are a stranger; and I, like
> you, am far from home."[94]

The poem suggests a parallel between the prince and the palm tree. Both are, in the poem's words, "strangers" that have sprung up "far from the land of palms." The implied meaning is that 'Abd al-Rahman and his palm tree are both transplants, springing up far from their "natural" home in the east. The camerawork in this scene emphasizes the intimate link between the Umayyad prince and the palm tree: the camera shows 'Abd al-Rahman standing in profile in front of the tree, a framing that is repeated in several subsequent scenes (Figure 1.1).

Figure 1.1. 'Abd al-Rahman I and the palm tree in *Saqr Quraysh*. *Saqr Quraysh*, episode 23, Syrian Art Production International, 2002.

Alexander Elinson has interpreted 'Abd al-Rahman's poem for the palm tree in Rusafa as an illustration of how the Umayyad leader and his successors built the cultural prestige of Umayyad al-Andalus through a nostalgic practice of looking back to Syria and the Arab East.[95] In the case of the series *Saqr Quraysh*, there is at least one more layer of nostalgia in play. Here, a Syrian director (Hatim 'Ali), a Syrian actor (Jamal Sulayman), and a Syrian producer (Syrian Art Production International), working from a present in which Arab Umayyad rule has long since disappeared, look back at a moment in which Syrian Arabs established a great state in al-Andalus, a state whose grandeur and prestige were intimately linked to its Syrian roots. Thus, a twenty-first-century Syrian claim on the legacy of al-Andalus is layered on top of an eighth-century poem that links al-Andalus back to a lost Umayyad home in Syria. While 'Abd al-Rahman's poem moves from al-Andalus to Syria, 'Ali and Sayf's *Saqr Quraysh* adds another leg to this cultural relay: it moves from present-day Syria to eighth-century al-Andalus, and from there back to Syria.

In *Saqr Quraysh*, the main threats to al-Andalus come from two sources: the threat of non-Arab rule and the danger of intra-Arab rivalries. 'Abd al-Rahman must confront both threats in order to lay the groundwork for an

Arab Umayyad state in al-Andalus. It is, therefore, not a coincidence that one of 'Abd al-Rahman's main rivals in the series is a Berber: Shaqya b. 'Abd al-Wahid, a historical figure who led an uprising against 'Abd al-Rahman from roughly 768 to 777.[96] In *Saqr Quraysh,* Shaqya's revolt poses a threat that has both religious and ethnic dimensions. On the religious front, Shaqya claims a genealogical lineage that closely links him to Shi'i Islam. In episodes 26 and 27, Shaqya uses a forged document to convince his followers that he descends from the Prophet's daughter Fatima and her son, al-Husayn, a revered figure in Shi'i Islam. This plotline portrays Shaqya as a religious outsider who represents a dangerous challenge to the Sunni Islam practiced by the Umayyad rulers. But Shaqya is a threat to not only the religious order but also the ethnic order in Umayyad al-Andalus. His followers, in *Saqr Quraysh,* are clearly marked as North African Berbers. Most of them are dark-skinned and wear the blue robes that distinguish Berber characters in *Saqr Quraysh.* Shaqya also makes frequent allusions to his family roots in the Miknasa, a prominent Berber group originating in North Africa. Finally, Shaqya often refers to his followers as "the sons of Tariq b. Ziyad," an allusion to one of the most famous Berber figures from the history of al-Andalus. For example, in a speech to his followers in episode 27, Shaqya says, "O ye Muslims, o sons of Tariq b. Ziyad, my call has reached you. So, who will follow me to fight this apostate Umayyad and to unite him to the fate of his ancestors in the Mashriq?"[97] Shaqya's call to arms reveals a confrontation between two ethnic and genealogical imaginaries: on the one hand, the Berbers of al-Andalus, the "sons of Tariq b. Ziyad," and on the other hand, 'Abd al-Rahman, the "apostate Umayyad," who traces his legitimacy back to his ancestors in the Mashriq.

The character Shaqya in *Saqr Quraysh* conforms to a type of Berber villain that appears in other Arab representations of al-Andalus. For instance, Shaqya bears some striking resemblances to Jurji Zaydan's character Bustam, the Berber villain in Zaydan's novel *The Battle of Poitiers* (1904). Like Bustam, Shaqya is ill-tempered, lascivious, violent, and hypocritical. The two characters appear in texts that are separated by nearly a century, and yet they attest to a remarkably consistent discursive tradition of negative portrayals of Berbers in Mashriqi texts about al-Andalus. Both characters claim to act in the name of Islam, and yet both are impious in similar ways. Zaydan's character Bustam is frequently drunk, despite his supposed conversion to

Islam. In one scene in Zaydan's novel, the Arab commander Hani confronts Bustam and finds him stumbling around drunk; in another, Bustam threatens to assault the heroine Maryam while reeking of alcohol.[98] Likewise, Shaqya, the Berber villain in *Saqr Quraysh,* is brought down by his lust and his penchant for drink. After rising to power, Shaqya spends his time at home consorting with concubines and drinking wine. Shaqya's ten-year revolt comes to an ignominious end when his wife and his followers turn against him. His wife, fed up with her husband's infidelities, reveals to two of his followers that Shaqya's prophetic lineage is a fiction. She also informs them that Shaqya secretly drinks wine. The two followers confront Shaqya and find him in a drunken stupor, with an empty bottle of wine next to him. They murder Shaqya on the spot. It is hard to assess whether this ending bears any resemblance to the actual demise of the eighth-century rebel Shaqya (the medieval sources are vague on this point).[99] What the portrayal of Shaqya in *Saqr Quraysh* does undoubtedly reveal is an abiding hostility to Berbers in modern texts produced by Mashriqi Arabs as well as a tendency to view the Berbers as the enemies to the Arab Umayyad project in al-Andalus.

Saqr Quraysh sets the agenda for the two series that come after it. The next installment in the trilogy, *Rabiʿ Qurtuba* (The spring of Cordoba), opens with a reprise of a scene from the last episode of *Saqr Quraysh.* ʿAbd al-Rahman, now an old man, goes to visit his palm tree in Rusafa at dusk. The crepuscular setting highlights the fact that the Umayyad prince is reaching the end of his days. While ʿAbd al-Rahman looks at the palm tree, there are flashbacks to key moments from *Saqr Quraysh,* including images of ʿAbd al-Rahman's escape from Syria and of the scene in which he picks the spot to build Rusafa, his estate near Cordoba. ʿAbd al-Rahman and Rusafa thus serve as bridges between part one and part two of the trilogy, marking the continuity between ʿAbd al-Rahman's story (the main plot of *Saqr Quraysh*) and the story of the Umayyad caliphate in tenth-century al-Andalus, the setting for *Rabiʿ Qurtuba.*

This continuity becomes quite explicit in the following scene, where ʿAbd al-Rahman lies on his deathbed. As ʿAbd al-Rahman draws his last breaths, an off-screen narrator says:

> The life of the Hawk of Quraysh, ʿAbd al-Rahman al-Dakhil, did not come to an end until he had fulfilled his destiny and realized a dream that first seemed impossible: he set in place the pillars of the Andalusi state that would become one of the greatest kingdoms on earth, the link

between the East and the West, and a mighty example of the blending [*imtizāj*] of civilizations and cultures, until it reached its pinnacle in the era of the caliph 'Abd al-Rahman al-Nasir.[100]

After the voice-over, the action jumps from 788, the year of 'Abd al-Rahman I's death, to 958, toward the end of the reign of 'Abd al-Rahman III. Thus, in a few short minutes the first episode of *Rabi' Qurtuba* moves from 'Abd al-Rahman I in the eighth century to 'Abd al-Rahman III in the tenth century, and it traces the path from Umayyad Syria (seen in 'Abd al-Rahman's flash-back) to the foundation of the Umayyad state in al-Andalus (represented by Rusafa) to the apex of the Umayyad caliphate in al-Andalus (embodied by 'Abd al-Rahman III).

The voice-over also marks a new theme in 'Ali and Sayf's trilogy: the idea that Umayyad al-Andalus was a site of cross-cultural exchange—"a mighty example of the blending of civilizations." This idea is a variant of the long-standing motif of *convivencia,* and it responds to the post–9/11 context in which the trilogy was made. Hatim 'Ali spoke directly to this issue in an interview with anthropologist Christa Salamandra in 2007. In the interview, the Syrian director described the circumstances that led him to make a trilogy about al-Andalus:

> I think we are on the brink of a true war of civilizations, one that is not limited to a battle of ideas, but is about to develop into a confrontation using traditional and probably not traditional weapons, in the future. In light of this, I began a project about the rise of the Andalusian state, which is probably a unique, exceptional experiment in the history of human kind, where you found, in one place on earth, Muslims of all ideologies, ideas, and aspirations, along with Christians—the original inhabitants of the land, and Jews. The presence of all of these in one place, in a democratic atmosphere, in a dialogue of civilizations, allowed for the establishment of one of the most important human civilizations, the Andalusian civilization, which was, I think, the gate through which Greek civilization entered what is today called Europe.[101]

In these revealing comments about the genesis of his Andalus trilogy, 'Ali draws on a few key terms that dominated geopolitical debates at the turn of the millennium. First, 'Ali positions his trilogy as a response to a mounting "war of civilizations"—a phrase that seems to be an allusion to Samuel Huntington's much-debated notion of the "clash of civilizations." Huntington's thesis, formulated in the early 1990s, was that the primary source of conflict in the post–Cold War world would be competing cultural and religious identities.[102] Huntington warned, in particular, of an inevitable clash between "Western civilization" (his phrase) and the Muslim world. Huntington's thesis sparked a broad range of responses in the fields of international diplomacy and political science. Among them was the UN's decision, in 1998, to designate the year 2001 as the "United Nations Year of Dialogue among Civilizations."[103] The UN initiative, which stretched beyond 2001, was presented as an alternative (and even a rebuke) to Huntington's ideas. For instance, a UN press release about the initiative quoted a member of the UN General Assembly saying: "Instead of accepting that international dynamics would lead *civilizations to clash,* the international community should strive to create a bounteous crossroad of civilization."[104] This comment illustrates the binary opposition between the UN's "dialogue of civilizations" and Huntington's "clash of civilizations"—an opposition that would become even more pronounced in the wake of the 9/11 attacks and the emergence of the Bush administration's "war on terror."

These debates form the background for understanding Hatim 'Ali's remarks about the genesis of his Andalus trilogy. 'Ali aligns al-Andalus with the spirit of the "dialogue of civilizations," and, in so doing, he presents al-Andalus as an antidote to Huntington's vision of an inevitable clash between the Muslim world and the West. Indeed, 'Ali pushes back against the notion that there is an irreconcilable separation between the Muslim world and the West. By calling al-Andalus "the gate through which Greek civilization entered what is today called Europe," 'Ali signals modern Europe's debt to al-Andalus and underlines the contributions that Muslims and Arabs have made to the civilization that we now know as Western civilization.

In *Rabi' Qurtuba,* there are several scenes and storylines that speak to this vision of al-Andalus as a site for the "dialogue among civilizations." Early in the series, we see that the caliph 'Abd al-Rahman III (played by Khalid Taja) surrounds himself with Jewish and Christian advisors. One of them, Hasdai ibn Shaprut, is the caliph's personal physician and is chosen by the caliph to lead an important diplomatic mission to Navarre in episode 3. After 'Abd al-Rahman III dies, his son and successor, al-Hakam II, follows his lead and continues to work closely with the leaders of Cordoba's Christian and Jewish communities. A sequence from episode 6 offers a striking example of this pattern. In that episode, Ordoño IV, the deposed king of León, comes to Cordoba to ask for al-Hakam II's support in his efforts to regain his throne. Al-Hakam agrees to support Ordoño's claim and assigns three of his ministers to accompany Ordoño back to León. All three ministers are Christians. One of them is Rabiʿ b. Zayd, who is identified, in the scene, as "the archbishop of the Christians of al-Andalus."[105] Ordoño is astonished to see that three Christians serve as ministers in a Muslim caliph's court. Ordoño's reaction provokes the following exchange with Rabiʿ b. Zayd:

> RABIʿ B. ZAYD: What is it that baffles you? This is our state, and he is
>   our caliph.
> ORDOÑO: But you are . . .
> RABIʿ B. ZAYD: Christians, yes . . . and Andalusis![106]

Rabiʿ b. Zayd's remark makes it clear that he sees no contradiction between being Christian and being Andalusi. He goes on to explain to Ordoño that the caliph gives Christians complete control over their religious affairs, and then he concludes: "I know that it is difficult for you, my lord, to understand this, but this is the Andalus that you're fighting against and about which you are ignorant."[107] The exchange between the Andalusi archbishop and the nobleman from León throws into relief competing understandings of cultural belonging. Ordoño cannot conceive of a pluralistic state, in which Muslims and Christians share a common identity. Rabiʿ b. Zayd, in contrast, articulates an Andalusi identity that is not predicated on religious affiliation.

What emerges from this scene—and others in ʿAli and Sayf's trilogy—is the implicit claim that the common dominator of al-Andalus is not Islam but Arabness, a cultural ideal that is rooted in a reverence for the language, culture, and customs of the Arabs. While Islam remains the unique domain of Muslims, Arabness is, in the trilogy, a cultural identity that is open to Christians and Jews. Indeed, *Rabiʿ Qurtuba* is full of non-Arab characters who "become Andalusi" through a cultural assimilation to Arabness. In other words, if becoming Andalusi requires a conversion, it is not a religious one but instead a linguistic and cultural one. As Rabiʿ b. Zayd indicates, there is no contradiction between being Andalusi and being Christian. In the narrative

world of 'Ali and Sayf's trilogy, the Andalusi identity is open to all who embrace Arabness, a cultural ideal embodied by the Arab elites of al-Andalus,
especially the Umayyad rulers.

Perhaps the best illustration of these ideas is a sequence of scenes, in episodes 4 and 5, in which we are introduced to one of the main characters in
the series: Subh, a singing slave girl (*jāriya*) of Basque origin who rises to
power when she becomes the favorite of al-Hakam II and bears him two sons,
including the future caliph Hisham II (b. 965).[108] Subh (played by Syrian actress Nasrin Tafish) first captures al-Hakam's attention when she performs
at an evening party at Madinat al-Zahra'. (Notably, she sings two poems
written by poets who lived in tenth-century Cordoba.) Although al-Hakam
is a reserved and studious man who, up until this scene, has shown little interest in love, he falls head over heels for Subh, sends her lavish gifts, and
summons her to return to the palace.

The scene of Subh's arrival at the palace, in episode 5, offers a look back at
Saqr Quraysh and weaves together many of the thematic strands that run
through 'Ali and Sayf's trilogy. As Subh enters the palace, there is a shift in
the background music. As a solo lute explores the notes of an unmetered
melody, an extradiegetic (off-camera) singer erupts in a rendition of 'Abd al-
Rahman I's poem for his palm tree in Rusafa. In particular, the singer sings
and then repeats the poem's third line: "You have sprung from soil in which
you are a stranger; and I, like you, am far from home."[109] In the original poem,
the grammatical subject of the main verb, "you have sprung," is the palm tree
(*nakhla*), a feminine noun in Arabic. Here, in contrast, it is Subh who occupies the grammatical position of the palm tree; it is Subh who has "sprung
up from soil in which" she is a "stranger" or a "foreigner." The line affords
many interpretations. It could be an allusion to Subh's roots in the Christian
Basque lands in the north of the Iberian Peninsula, or it could refer to the
fact that Subh has vaulted over class lines, moving from the residence for
singing slave girls to the heart of the caliph's palace. What is clear is that this
use of 'Abd al-Rahman's poem not only offers a glance back at the first part
in the trilogy but also indicates a surprising parallel between 'Abd al-
Rahman I, the Umayyad prince who left Syria and came to al-Andalus, and
Subh, a Basque girl who came to al-Andalus as a slave girl and rose to political power. The parallel is one of exile but also one of resilience: both 'Abd
al-Rahman and Subh are "strangers" who are far from home, but they are
also immigrants who have survived and thrived in a new land, al-Andalus.

Just as *Saqr Quraysh* links 'Abd al-Rahman I's successful transplantation in al-Andalus to his Umayyad roots in the Arab East, *Rabiʻ Qurtuba* links Subh's rise in Andalusi society to her assimilation in, and command of, elite Arabic culture. This point is made in Subh's first face-to-face encounter with al-Hakam, which occurs in the continuation of the scene described above. After servants lead Subh to a sumptuously appointed room, she gazes in wonder at her luxurious surroundings. The camera draws a full circle around her, inviting the audience to join in her wonder and identify with her reaction. Al-Hakam then shuffles into the room and begins an awkward conversation with Subh. She tells him that her name is "Aurora" and that she is Basque. This information leads to the following exchange between the two characters:

AL-HAKAM: Basque, then . . . But you are now Andalusi?
AURORA / SUBH: Yes, my tongue is Arabic, and all I know is the poetry and customs of the Arabs.
AL-HAKAM: But you still preserve your old name? [. . .] Aurora . . . What does it mean?
AURORA / SUBH: Something like the moment of dawn or the morning light.
AL-HAKAM: Ah, so, among us, you are Ṣubḥ.[110]

Neither here nor elsewhere is there any mention of Aurora / Subh's religious affiliation. Instead, the categories of identity that are in play are geographic and linguistic. The critical moment comes when both al-Hakam and Aurora equate "being Andalusi" with Arabness. When al-Hakam asks Aurora if she "is now Andalusi," she does not miss a beat; she immediately relates the question to her command of the Arabic language, Arabic poetry, and Arab customs. In response, al-Hakam affirms Aurora's new cultural identity by giving her an Arabic name, Ṣubḥ (dawn), the translation of her Spanish name. Indeed, translation, rather than conversion, seems to be the right paradigm for understanding how a character like Subh "becomes Andalusi." The proof of Subh's Andalusi identity is her mastery of the language and cultural codes of Arab society.

And yet, in *Rabiʻ Qurtuba* the edifice of the Arab al-Andalus is crumbling. The series portrays Arabness as the welcoming umbrella under which a culture of openness developed in al-Andalus, but the series also highlights several threats to the prevailing cultural order. As in *Saqr Quraysh,* the threats come from non-Arab groups and from intra-Arab factionalism. *Rabiʿ Qurtuba* depicts the Umayyad caliphs' increasing reliance on a private guard of northern European slaves known as *ṣaqāliba*—a word that literally means "Slavs," though it serves as a generic term to refer to all slaves of northern and central European origin.[111] In the series, the caliph's "Slav" guards torment the people of Cordoba by harassing women in the streets, stealing from stores in the market, and forcing craftspeople to pay arbitrary levies on their wares. The crisis posed by the tyranny of the *ṣaqāliba* is one of the main story lines of the series, and it plays a pivotal role in the downfall of the Umayyad caliphate.

The second half of *Rabiʿ Qurtuba* stages a series of power struggles in which various factions vie for control of the Umayyad court, backed by non-Arab mercenaries. In episode 18, al-Hakam II dies, leaving behind a power vacuum. The young age of the caliph's successor and only son, Hisham, leaves an opening for the caliph's chamberlain, Muhammad Ibn Abi ʿAmir (later known by the sobriquet *al-Manṣūr,* "the Victorious"), to usurp the caliph's power and to become the de facto ruler of al-Andalus. Ibn Abi ʿAmir recruits a private army of North African Berber soldiers to counterbalance the power of the *ṣaqāliba*. With the backing of his Berber guard, Ibn Abi ʿAmir succeeds in ousting the Slav troops from the caliph's palace, a move that angers the Slav leaders and eventually leads to a failed assassination attempt on the young caliph, Hisham.

These conflicts come to a head in the final episode of the series, in a sequence that foreshadows the eventual collapse of the Umayyad state. By this point, Subh, the mother of the caliph Hisham, realizes that Ibn Abi ʿAmir has succeeded in usurping her son's power and becoming the effective ruler of al-Andalus. In a scene set in the year 989, Subh sends a letter to a powerful Berber leader in Fez, Ziri b. ʿAtiyya, and offers him money to come to Hisham's aid and to fight for the caliph's rightful claim to rule over al-Andalus. Ibn Abi ʿAmir learns of Subh's plot, and in retaliation he sends his Berber guard to storm Madinat al-Zahra' and to seize the caliph's money. Dozens of al-Mansur's soldiers—dressed in the blue clothes that distinguish Berber characters in the series—swarm the palace, brandishing swords and shields. Subh tries desperately to stop them, but the Berber troops brush past her, enter the palace, and seize the money in the caliph's treasury. The scene confirms that the true center of power is no longer the Umayyad caliph,

Hisham, but instead his chamberlain, Ibn Abi 'Amir. More importantly, the image of al-Mansur's Berber guards storming the caliph's palace foreshadows an event that would take place just a few years later: the sacking of Madinat al-Zahra' by Berber troops during the civil war that ravaged al-Andalus in the early eleventh century, leading to the end of the Umayyad caliphate.

The specter of the lost Umayyad caliphate haunts the final installment of 'Ali and Sayf's trilogy, *Muluk al-tawa'if* (2005), which dramatizes the history of al-Andalus from 1036 to 1095, encompassing the emergence of the *taifa* kingdoms, the rising power of the Christian kings in the north, and the eventual conquest of al-Andalus by the North African Almoravid dynasty. From the opening credits, the phantom of the lost Umayyad caliphate looms over the series. In the opening credits, each of the main actors appears framed by an image of the famous red-and-white arches of the Umayyad Mosque of Cordoba. Building on this architectural allusion, the series title appears in-side an image of the interior of the Mosque of Cordoba, nestled among the mosque's columns and double arches (Figure 1.2). The choice of the Mosque of Cordoba, the most emblematic monument from Umayyad Cordoba, as the frame for the opening credits of the series is particularly striking because the series focuses on what happens in al-Andalus *after* the fall of the Umayyad caliphate and *after* the center of political power shifts away from Cordoba.

Figure 1.2. Image from the title sequence for *Muluk al-tawa'if. Muluk al-tawa'if,* Syrian Art Production International, 2005.

In the first episode of the series, several powerful families compete to fill the power vacuum left by the collapse of the Umayyad caliphate. The various competing claims to political power and authority all draw on (sometimes spurious) genealogical connections to the caliphate and to the Mashriq. At the beginning of the series, the main conflict is between the ʿAbbadids of Seville, who are the rulers of the most powerful *taifa* kingdom, and two North African rivals, the Hammudids and the Zirids, who migrated to al-Andalus at the end of the Umayyad period and went on to establish independent kingdoms with capitals in Málaga and Granada, respectively.

In episode 1 of *Muluk al-tawaʿif,* Abu al-Qasim b. ʿAbbad, the founder of the ʿAbbadid dynasty in Seville, learns that the ruler of the Hammudid clan, Yahya b. ʿAli b. Hammud, has declared himself caliph and conquered a city near Seville. In response to the news, Abu al-Qasim says:

Ha! Caliph! Yahya b. ʿAli b. Hammud . . . The Commander of the Faithful? Even though we've never heard that he and his people have any kinship with the caliphs! They're a bunch of upstarts [*qawm ṭari'ūn*]! As for us, the ʿAbbadids, we have been in the [Iberian] Peninsula since the very outset, and people know about our Lakhmid lineage, and that we can trace it back all the way to al-Nuʿman b. al-Mundhir b. Ma' al-Sama'![112]

Abu al-Qasim's comments have some coded references whose meaning might elude viewers in the United States and Europe, but the meaning would be clear for most viewers in the Middle East and North Africa. His defense of his family's right to rule and his rejection of the Hammudids' claim are both based on genealogical and ethnic criteria—ones that elevate Arabs and belittle Berbers. Abu al-Qasim not only points out that the ʿAbbadids have been in al-Andalus since the beginning of Muslim rule, but also claims that his family traces its lineage back to Lakhmids, one of the most influential Arab dynasties of the pre-Islamic period. In other words, Abu al-Qasim claims a family history that is both deeply rooted in al-Andalus and deeply rooted in the Arab culture of the Mashriq, going all the way back to the pre-Islamic period. The implied logic at work here seems to be that if al-Andalus cannot be ruled by the Arab Umayyads, then it should, at least, be ruled by an Arab dynasty whose roots stretch back to the Arabian Peninsula.

Abu al-Qasim's dismissal of his North African rivals is similarly grounded in genealogical claims. Abu al-Qasim mocks the Hammudids as "a bunch of upstarts" who have no "kinship" with the caliphs. The word that I have translated here as "upstarts" is *ṭāri'ūn,* a noun that is derived from a family of words that refer to sudden, unexpected, or unfamiliar occurrences. Another idiomatic translation of this noun would be "a bunch of nobodies." It is not a coincidence that, later in the series, the same noun and its derivatives are used by Abu al-Qasim's son, 'Abbad, to refer to the Almoravids, the new threat from North Africa.[113] This extended etymological pattern has the overall effect of presenting the conflict between the 'Abbadids and their North African rivals as a conflict between nobles and nobodies, between people who have deep Arab roots and people who come from nowhere (that is, North Africa) to seize power.

Within this Arab-centric social hierarchy, the 'Abbadids strengthen their position by hatching a plot that casts them as the restorers of the Umayyad state in al-Andalus. In episode 1 of *Muluk al-tawa'if,* the 'Abbadids find a humble mat-maker who bears an uncanny resemblance to the Umayyad caliph Hisham II (the son of al-Hakam II and Subh), who died or disappeared under mysterious circumstances in the early eleventh century. In a wink to the audience, the actor who plays the mat-maker is none other than Khalid Taja, the same actor who played an Umayyad caliph in Syria in *Saqr Quraysh* and the first Umayyad caliph in al-Andalus in *Rabi' Qurtuba.* In the third part of the trilogy, Taja's character is kidnapped and brought to the 'Abbadid palace. There, 'Abbad approaches the bewildered mat-maker and hails him as the long-lost Umayyad caliph, saying: "At last, we've found you, o Commander of the Faithful, o son of al-Hakam, grandson of al-Nasir, descendant of the Umayyad family tree, and the rightful ruler of all of al-Andalus."[114] This sequence mirrors events in the eleventh century, when the 'Abbadids propped up an imposter as the lost caliph Hisham.[115] The 'Abbadids' supposed "discovery" of a lost Umayyad caliph illustrates the extreme lengths to which the 'Abbadids and other *taifa* kings would go to align themselves with the memory of the caliphate. The cynical maneuver also reveals an underlying anxiety about the precariousness and the increasing erosion of a system that linked political authority in al-Andalus to clearly established genealogical linkages to the Mashriq. In this regard, it is noteworthy that both the 'Abbadids and their North African rivals, the Hammudids, stake their claims to political legitimacy on bogus connections to the caliphate.

In *Muluk al-tawa'if,* the other *taifa* kings suspect that the 'Abbadids' caliph is a fake, but they are obliged to recognize him because of popular support for the Umayyad dynasty and the institution of the caliphate. When
news of the 'Abbadids' maneuver reaches the ruler of Cordoba, Abu al-Hazm
b. Jahwar, he muses: "I feel sorry for that poor caliph. It wasn't enough for
people to rule in his name while he was alive, without giving him any share
of the power, but they even rule in his name when he is dead. For he is forever the absent present [*al-ḥāḍir al-ghā'ib*]."[116] Abu al-Hazm's comment points
to two different manipulations of the Umayyad caliph Hisham II: in his lifetime, Hisham was a puppet caliph who was overshadowed by his chamberlain, al-Mansur Ibn Abi 'Amir; after Hisham's mysterious death, his figure
was resurrected and used as a prop to legitimate the rise of the 'Abbadid
dynasty in Seville. In life and in death, Hisham was "the absent present"—a
presence that is absent but that continues to structure and condition the present moment.

Abu al-Hazm's striking yet paradoxical phrase—"the absent present"—is,
as we will see in Chapter 4, important for understanding Palestinian figura-
tions of al-Andalus. In the context of *Muluk al-tawa'if,* the phrase serves to
mark the Umayyad caliphate as a persistent past that continually exercises
influence on the present. This dynamic of the past in the present (or of a present that is always looking to the past) runs like a red thread through the
entirety of 'Ali and Sayf's trilogy about al-Andalus. In *Saqr Quraysh,* 'Abd
al-Rahman founds an Andalusi state "in the image of Syria"—a place whose
legitimacy is intimately tied to the Umayyad prince's lost home in Syria. In
Rabi' Qurtuba, the words of a poem written by an Umayyad prince in the
eighth century mirror the meteoric rise of a Basque slave girl in Arab Andalusi society in the tenth century. In *Muluk al-tawa'if,* the new *taifa* kings draw
on increasingly tenuous, and occasionally fictional, ties to the Umayyad past
in order to sustain an Andalusi project that is in crisis. At the dawn of the
twenty-first century, a Syrian director, a Syrian producer, and a cast of Syrian
actors came together to perform the story of Umayyad al-Andalus for a
pan-Arab audience whose members look to al-Andalus for inspiration,
entertainment, and a sign of collective identity. In all of these cases, the past
presents a paradox: it is, at once, absent and present, lost and found, ex-
pired and indispensable.

Conclusion: Choral Interventions

Muluk al-tawa'if carries forward many of the themes that were developed in the first two parts of the trilogy, but it also engages in more formal experimentation, such as the use of sepia-toned shots to mark flashbacks or important lines of dialogue. The most striking formal feature in the series is the use of a chorus that moves between the eleventh century and the year 2005 (when the series was released). As in the case of Greek tragedy, the chorus in *Muluk al-tawa'if* serves several purposes: it bears witness to the action and offers commentary; it advances the narrative by filling in missing information; and it even sings poems that were written by some of the characters in the series, such as the poets Ibn Zaydun and al-Mu'tamid. Most importantly, the chorus serves as a bridge between the present and the past, as well as between the audience and the narrative world of the series.

The chorus plays an integral role in the series from the very first scene of the first episode. The series opens, not in al-Andalus, but instead in Marrakesh (Morocco) in the year 2005. The first shot of the series is an aerial view of Marrakesh's emblematic Jemaa el-Fna (Jami' al-Fana) square, filled with pedestrians, open-air food stalls, and the steady hum of musicians playing drums, cymbals, and other percussive instruments. Amid this lively setting, the camera picks out a chorus of men and women of various ages, wearing long robes that distinguish them from the shoppers and tourists who mill around them without noticing them (Figure 1.3). As the chorus walks through the square, passing by stalls that hawk everything from cactus silks to Barcelona jerseys, it sings the following lyrics:

> Search for the tyrant!
> Search for the tyrant!
> For he is like the crow, foreboding devastation.
> This is the story of kingdoms that have passed
> and of kingdoms that remain present.[117]

After singing these lyrics, the chorus approaches a city wall in Marrakesh, passes through an archway in the wall, and reappears, on the other side, in a market in al-Andalus in the year 1036.

Figure 1.3. The chorus in *Muluk al-tawa'if*. *Muluk al-tawa'if,* episode 1, Syrian Art
Production International, 2005.

This enigmatic first scene not only introduces the chorus, a central feature
of the series, but also illustrates how the chorus straddles the past and the
present, the world of the plot and the world of the audience. The chorus signals this ambiguous temporal positioning when it announces that it (and, by
extension, the series) will tell "the story of kingdoms that have passed / and
of kingdoms that remain present." The meaning of these enigmatic lines
seems to be that the story of al-Andalus, like the chorus, moves fluidly between the past and the present: al-Andalus "has passed" and yet it "remains
present." Like the figure of the lost Umayyad caliph Hisham, al-Andalus is
an absence that remains present.

It is also noteworthy that the chorus's first lines are an imperative, addressed to an unidentified plural subject: "Search for the tyrant" (*ibḥathū ʿan
al-tāghiya*). To whom is this command addressed? And who is the "tyrant"
in question? The series does not offer clear answers to these questions—even
though the chorus's first lines become a refrain that is repeated in subsequent
episodes. The command to "search for the tyrant" is ambiguously directed
at a variety of subjects, including the people of al-Andalus, the viewers of
the series, and the people in Marrakesh's Jemaa el-Fna (where the action of
the series begins). Likewise, the identity of the tyrant remains elusive. He

could be one of the ʻAbbadid rulers who seize power in the name of the lost Umayyad caliphate, or perhaps one of the other Muslim or Christian rulers who outmaneuver and kill rivals in order to lay claim to the Iberian Peninsula. Moreover, it is hard not to associate the figure of the unnamed tyrant with the historical moment in which *Muluk al-tawa'if* was produced and consumed. The year 2005 witnessed the ongoing American military occupation of Iraq, the mounting crisis of Iraqi refugees in Syria and neighboring countries, as well as the assassination of the former Lebanese prime minister Rafiq al-Hariri, among other signs of turmoil in the region. In this sense, the unnamed tyrant is a figure that connects the story of eleventh-century al-Andalus to the present. The link to the American invasion of Iraq seems particularly pointed in the chorus's other main refrain, "Tyrants have always been the condition of invaders"—a refrain that the chorus first sings in episode 1 and then repeats at key moments throughout the series. Here again, the story of al-Andalus is one of "kingdoms that have passed / and of kingdoms that remain present."

Such entanglements of past and present are characteristic of Syrian television dramas, according to Christa Salamandra, a leading expert on the form. Salamandra argues that "chronopolitics" (the ideological deployment of time) are a defining feature of Syrian television dramas. In her words, "Syrian drama refracts time like a prism. Multiple pasts and presents brush against each other and often collide."[118] Building on Salamandra's insight, I would argue that the intricate relationship between the past and the present is at the core of *Muluk al-tawa'if.* The series suggests that the history of al-Andalus poses political problems that remain relevant today, but it also suggests that debates about the present are often debates about the unresolved meaning of the past. This complex temporal stance makes the role of the chorus all the more crucial, because the chorus is what articulates the relationship between the past and the present, between the characters in medieval al-Andalus and the viewers in the contemporary Arab world.

The two-way traffic between past and present is emphasized again in the very last sequence of the series, which serves as a bookend to the first scene described above. By the final episode (episode 30), al-Muʻtamid, the last ʻAbbadid ruler of Seville, and his family are languishing under house arrest in the desolate town of Aghmat, in southern Morocco. In one of the final scenes of the series, al-Muʻtamid asks his children for pen and paper and, after

having flashbacks to memories of al-Andalus, he composes a poem that the
historical al-Mu'tamid wrote at the end of his life as his own epitaph. The
Syrian actor Taym Hasan, who plays al-Mu'tamid, reads the first lines of
the poem in a voice-over:

> O, stranger's tomb,
>   may you be watered by those who come and go,
> Even though you've now taken possession
>   of Ibn 'Abbad's remains.[119]

In the series, al-Mu'tamid dies immediately after composing this poem,
and in the following scene, a funeral procession carries his body to be
buried on the outskirts of Aghmat. Along the way, the funeral procession
passes by the chorus, which observes the procession while singing an excerpt from al-Mu'tamid's epitaph poem, thus echoing the words that were
recited in the previous scene. After singing al-Mu'tamid's epitaph, the
chorus reappears in the streets of Aghmat in the year 2005. It approaches
the mausoleum that was built for al-Mu'tamid by the Moroccan government in the second half of the twentieth century. The chorus files into the
mausoleum, passing by tourists, and enters the small room that, for the past
few decades, has housed the tombs of al-Mu'tamid and his wife 'Itimad.
While looking at the tombs, the chorus sings a final reflection whose last
line echoes one of the main refrains from the series: "Tyrants were always the
reason for invaders!" The chorus then exits the mausoleum and disappears
into the streets of Aghmat, merging with the Moroccans who go about their
daily business on foot, mule, bicycle, and motorcycle. In other words, *Muluk
al-tawa'if* both begins and ends with time travel, marking the continuity
between the past and the present.

The first and last scenes of *Muluk al-tawa'if* signal a dense interweaving of
time and space. The chorus not only moves between the twenty-first century
and the eleventh century, but also moves between present-day Morocco and
medieval al-Andalus. These jumps are particularly apparent in the first
scene of the series, where the chorus moves seamlessly from twenty-first-
century Marrakesh to eleventh-century Seville. *Muluk al-tawa'if* thus portrays Morocco as a portal to the past, a place where moving from the present
to medieval al-Andalus is as simple as walking through a stone archway. This

artistic choice is surprising, and even a bit ironic, since for most of 'Ali and Sayf's trilogy, Morocco and North Africa serve as foils to al-Andalus.

'Ali and Sayf's Andalus trilogy emphasizes the Arabness (and the Syrianness) of al-Andalus, but it also suggests that contemporary Morocco is a time capsule where medieval al-Andalus remains alive—an idea whose genealogy and political career I have discussed elsewhere.[120] 'Ali and Sayf's decision to shot much of their trilogy on location in Morocco contributes to this view of Morocco as a time capsule for al-Andalus. Thus, for example, in *Rabi' Qurtuba* the Moroccan city of Chefchaouen serves as a stand-in for tenth-century Cordoba, and in *Muluk al-tawa'if* the Moroccan cities of Rabat and Meknes stand in for eleventh-century Seville.[121] As a result, 'Ali and Sayf's trilogy places Morocco in a vexed position—as the source of the greatest threats to the Arab al-Andalus in the Middle Ages and as a time-travel portal for al-Andalus in the present day. This tension is left unresolved in 'Ali and Sayf's trilogy, but it offers a helpful point of transition to Chapter 2, where I will take up North Africa's relationship to the contemporary legacy of al-Andalus—and, in particular, recent attempts to reimagine and celebrate the contributions that North Africans made to medieval Andalusi culture.

2

The Berber al-Andalus

On December 5, 2019, a cast of dignitaries that included Queen Letizia of Spain and the Moroccan billionaire philanthropist Dr. Leila Mezian descended upon the Alhambra in Granada to inaugurate a new exhibit called "Zirid Granada and the Berber Universe" (Figure 2.1).[1] The exhibit had two principal aims. The first was to document and highlight the contributions that the Berber peoples of North Africa—also known as Imazighen (sing. Amazigh)—made to al-Andalus in general and to Granada in particular. The second was to give the public a broad overview of Berber history and culture, from the pre-Islamic period to the present. The exhibit was the result of a collaboration between several local, national, and international institutions, including the Alhambra and Generalife Trust (the body that is in charge of the Alhambra), the Council of Europe, a foundation named The Andalusi Legacy (whose mission is to promote the cultural patrimony of al-Andalus), and the Dr. Leila Mezian Foundation (a Moroccan nonprofit that works to preserve and promote Moroccan culture). The temporary exhibit was the first step toward a larger project of creating a permanent museum of Berber culture in Granada, the first of its kind in Europe.[2] According to the exhibit's curator, Antonio Malpica Cuello, the goal was also to turn Granada "into the meeting place between the North African world and the European world."[3]

The Alhambra exhibit proposed a radical reimagining of Granadan, Iberian, and Mediterranean history, one that reoriented the story of al-Andalus southward toward North Africa—or, in the exhibit's language, toward "the Berber universe." In other words, the exhibit posed a challenge to a long and venerable tradition of cultural texts that have treated al-Andalus as a predominantly Arab phenomenon (a tradition that I explore in depth in Chapter 1).

Figure 2.1. Dr. Leila Mezian and Queen Letizia of Spain at the inauguration of "Zirid Granada and the Berber Universe." EFE / Miguel Ángel Molina.

The Alhambra exhibit countered the dominant Arab-centric view of al-Andalus and replaced it with another. Here, al-Andalus was not imagined as the creation of exiles from the Arab East but was, instead, imagined as the fruit of a vibrant exchange between the Iberian Peninsula and the Maghrib, an exchange that predated the rise of the Umayyad state in al-Andalus and survived, and even thrived, in the wake of the Umayyad caliphate's dissolution in the eleventh century. The exhibit centered on the Zirids, a Sanhaja Berber dynasty that founded an independent kingdom in Granada in the eleventh century, but the exhibit also suggested that the Zirids were part of a much longer process of exchange between North Africa and the Iberian Peninsula. Indeed, the exhibit argued that North African Berbers played a decisive role in shaping the culture of al-Andalus at every stage of its history—and especially after the fall of the Umayyad caliphate.

The focal point for this argument was Granada. The exhibit's curators presented the view that Granada, one of the most famous cities of al-Andalus, owes its very existence to Berbers, and that the city is a Berber (or Amazigh) creation, through and through. On this point, the exhibit brochure asserted that, with the arrival of the Zirids, "Amazigh and Granada fuse in an insoluble association for the rest of history. Indeed, today's Granada would not be conceivable as it is without the Zirids' imprint."[4] This idea was echoed in the gallery notes and in the official exhibition catalog, where the curator, Malpica Cuello, wrote: "The kingdom of Granada . . . is, thus, a political foundation (and not just a political one) of the Berbers."[5] What emerges from these statements is a sustained emphasis on the Amazigh / Berber identity of the Zirids and of the polity that they created in Granada.[6]

But the exhibit's emphasis on Berber identity did not end with its account of Zirid Granada. Instead, the exhibit positioned Zirid Granada (1013–1090) as the point of departure for a glorious span of four centuries in which al-Andalus benefited militarily, politically, and culturally from its fecund contacts with North Africa, and from the constant migration of Berber peoples between North Africa and al-Andalus. Through this process of constant exchange, al-Andalus became, in the words of the exhibit catalog, "a prolongation of North Africa."[7]

All of the gallery notes in the exhibit's main room contributed to this vision of a Berber or North African al-Andalus. For instance, a panel on the Almoravid and Almohad dynasties stated: "The 11th to 16th centuries are characterized by the strong resurgence of Berber dynasties, who become the main players in the defense of *Dār al-Islām* [the Muslim lands]. Much like the Turks in the East, in the Maghrib, the *Imazighen* would bring new vigor [*savia*] to Islamic civilization." Few historians would debate that the Almoravid and Almohad dynasties helped to prolong Islam's presence in the Iberian Peninsula and to stave off the military advance of the Christian kingdoms from the north. But the exhibit gave the North African dynasties credit for much more; it portrayed them as civilizing forces that infused al-Andalus with new cultural vigor. Along these lines, another panel in the main room suggested that Nasrid Granada (1237–1492), the last Muslim kingdom in the Iberian Peninsula, would not have existed, and cannot be understood, without examining Granada's intimate relationship with the Marinids, a Zanata Berber dynasty that ruled the western Maghrib from the middle of the thirteenth century to the middle of the fifteenth century.[8] The panel stated: "The Marinids, a Zanata dynasty with its capital in Fez, and the Nasrids do not only have in common the fact of being heirs of the Almohads, but they also nourished each other with mutual influences . . . Both entities appear to be mirrors of each other in art and architecture." Assertions like this one served to bring into focus a novel narrative about the cultural identity of al-Andalus—a narrative in which al-Andalus is not a mirror of Damascus and the Arab heartlands, but is instead a mirror and prolongation of Berber North Africa.

Indeed, the Alhambra exhibit flipped the script on some very common assumptions about al-Andalus, centering Berbers and North Africa as the source of some of the most visible expressions of Andalusi culture. A striking example of this move was the exhibit's analysis of one of the Alhambra's most emblematic spaces, the Courtyard of the Lions. The exhibit placed the Courtyard of the Lions within a distinctly *Berber* heritage of material culture. To this end, one of the exhibit's panels presented images of the Alhambra's Courtyard of the Lions alongside examples of similar lion imagery from two eleventh-century Berber polities: the Berber *taifa* in Badajoz and the Fortress (*Qalʿa*) of the Banu Hammad in the central Maghrib (today's Algeria) (Figure 2.2). The visual juxtaposition implied that the Alhambra's most famous courtyard is, in fact, the product of a long-standing Amazigh aesthetic tradition that goes back to North Africa.

The recent exhibit at the Alhambra is a prominent example of a process of historical recuperation that has been unfolding for almost a century. Since at least the 1930s, North African writers, scholars, artists, and public figures have worked to reassess and celebrate the contributions that Berbers made to al-Andalus. These modern celebrations of the Berber contributions to al-Andalus do have some medieval antecedents, but in general they represent a discursive tradition that has not been as widespread, as continuous, or as hegemonic as the one underwriting the "Arab al-Andalus."[9]

The modern recuperation of the "Berber al-Andalus" is a process that has unfolded in two waves, each of which reveals different understandings of Berber identity, Andalusi culture, and Moroccan national identity—and, crucially, the interrelations among the three. In the first wave, starting in the 1930s, writers and intellectuals associated with the Moroccan nationalist movement set out to revive the memory of famous Berber figures who contributed to the history of al-Andalus, from Tariq b. Ziyad to Yaʿqub al-Mansur (the third Almohad caliph). In particular, Moroccan nationalists sought to reevaluate and rehabilitate the Almoravid and Almohad dynasties, reimagining these dynasties as "Moroccan golden ages" characterized by cultural and political splendor. These efforts challenged a long-standing tendency, in

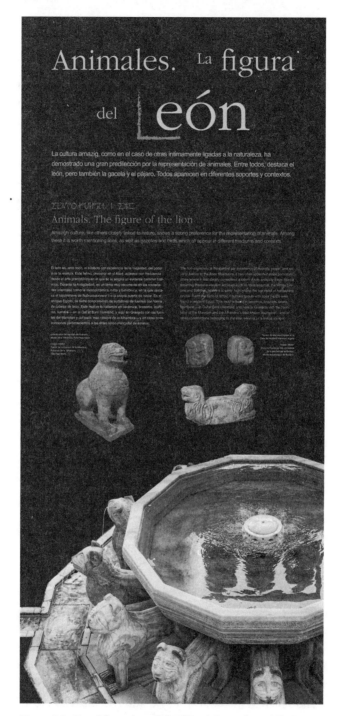

Figure 2.2. Panel from the exhibit "Zirid Granada and the Berber Universe." Photo by María de la Cruz Ruiz, © Patronato de la Alhambra y Generalife, 2020.

both Arab and European writings about al-Andalus, to vilify the Almoravids and the Almohads and to depict them as religious fanatics who were culturally backward and inimical to Andalusi culture.[10] In contrast with this widespread view, writers and thinkers associated with the Moroccan nationalist movement portrayed the Almoravids and the Almohads as revivers of Andalusi civilization, rather than as opponents to it. Furthermore, they credited the Almoravids and Almohads with unifying North Africa and al-Andalus into a single political and cultural territory whose center was in today's Morocco.

Crucially, Moroccan nationalists did not stress the Berber identity of the Almoravid and Almohad dynasties; instead they stressed the contributions these dynasties made to the promotion of Islamic and Arabic-language culture. As such, Moroccan nationalist intellectuals reclaimed the Almoravids and the Almohads by folding them into a unitary "Arab-Islamic" identity for Morocco. Their emphasis on Morocco's Arab-Islamic identity was largely a response to the French Protectorate's Berber policies, which—at least in the eyes of the Moroccan nationalist movement—sought to divide Moroccans along ethnic lines.[11] Many of the ideas about the Almoravids and the Almohads that originated in the Moroccan nationalist milieus of the 1930s have survived until the present, not only in scholarship and elite culture but also in cinema and other forms of popular culture. In recent decades, however, celebrations of the Berber contributions to al-Andalus have diversified as they have intersected with new cultural and political forces in North Africa—in particular, the Berber / Amazigh identity movement.

This point brings me to the second wave in the process of historical recuperation that I would like to trace in this chapter. In the final decades of the twentieth century, activists in North Africa and in the North African diaspora in Europe began to advocate for public and official recognition of the unique contributions that Berbers (or Imazighen, as they increasingly came to be known) had made to North Africa and the Mediterranean world. One facet of this diverse movement was a call for a reevaluation of the cultural legacy of al-Andalus, one that would lead to a new emphasis on the *Berberness* of al-Andalus as a historical and cultural phenomenon. These efforts took some of their inspiration from earlier attempts to revive and celebrate famous North African figures in al-Andalus. However, unlike their predecessors in the Moroccan nationalist movement, writers and public figures associated

with the contemporary Berber / Amazigh identity movement have not sub-
sumed Berber culture within a unitary Arab-Islamic identity; instead, they
have emphasized the cultural specificity of Berbers. That is, they have cast
Berbers as representatives of a unique cultural heritage, and not merely as
standard-bearers for a unitary Arab-Islamic cultural heritage in al-Andalus
and North Africa. This tendency has expressed itself in diverse forms, from
literary texts to scholarly conferences to public events. A particularly prominent example of this mode of thinking is the Alhambra exhibit "Zirid Granada
and the Berber Universe." But that exhibit does not stand alone. In the second
section of this chapter, I examine a selection of cultural texts and projects
that seek to imagine and claim a specifically *Berber* al-Andalus (and not just
an al-Andalus with Berbers). This tradition poses a challenge to forces from
outside North Africa but also from within it. It pushes back against Arab-
centric accounts of al-Andalus, such as the ones that I analyzed in Chapter 1;
at the same time, it also pushes back against the dominant discourse of
Moroccan nationalism, with its long-standing emphasis on Morocco's Arab-
Islamic identity.

Before closing this introductory section, I would like to address a thorny
issue of terminology: What term or terms should we use when referring to
the North African peoples who are at the center of this chapter? The term
Berber has a checkered past. It is not, as many scholars have noted, indigenous to North Africa and was not a name that the inhabitants of North Africa
used to describe themselves before the arrival of the Muslim Arab conquerors
in the seventh century.[12] In other words, *Berber* was, in its origins, a name imposed from the outside on people who did not identify as such. Compounding
this problem is the fact that the term *Berber* has derogatory connotations: it
derives from the Greek and Latin words for "barbarian" and conveys the
sense that Berbers are people who speak unintelligible languages.[13] In light
of these issues, many scholars prefer the term *Amazigh* (lit. "free person";
pl. *Imazighen*), a term that is indigenous to North Africa and free from the
derogatory associations of *Berber*.

Despite these considerations, the choice of terminology is not as straightforward as it would seem. Like many ethnic descriptors of dubious origin
(*American Indian* comes to mind), the term *Berber* has, in modern times,
gone through a process of "taking back," in which some North Africans have
reclaimed the term and used it to identify themselves. Another issue that

arises with the term *Amazigh* is that it was not in widespread use until very recently. Most of the texts I examine in this chapter use the term *Berber* to refer to the indigenous peoples of North Africa—and this pattern even holds in the work of authors who self-identify as "Berber." For these reasons, in what follows I will use the terms *Berber* and *Amazigh* somewhat interchangeably, as has become common practice in scholarship on North Africa.[14] In following this practice, I do not use the term *Berber* as a transparent and unproblematic ethnic description, but instead as an umbrella term (albeit a contested one) that encompasses various attempts to describe and assess the indigenous peoples of North Africa and, in particular, their contributions to the cultures and legacies of al-Andalus.

Al-Andalus from the South

Moroccan reassessments of the Almoravid and Almohad dynasties and, more broadly, of the Berber contributions to al-Andalus took off in the 1930s, a formative period for the Moroccan nationalist movement. On May 16, 1930, the French colonial authorities in Morocco issued a decree—commonly known as "the Berber *dahir*"—establishing separate judicial systems for Berbers and Arabs.[15] The controversial decree gave legal expression to a long-standing belief, among French colonial ethnographers and administrators, that Arabs and Berbers were two "races" with essentially different characteristics. In particular, many French writers asserted that Berbers, unlike Arabs, were only superficially attached to Islam, and that they were culturally and even racially closer to Europeans.[16] The so-called Berber *dahir* sparked massive protests in cities throughout Morocco. Behind the protests was a loosely connected network of young, urban, educated, Arabic-speaking activists who had grown up under colonial rule and who would emerge, in the wake of the Berber *dahir,* as the leaders of the nascent Moroccan nationalist movement. These emerging nationalist leaders saw the French Berber policy as an assault on Morocco's cultural, religious, and political unity. They countered the French policy by claiming the existence of a Moroccan national community that was unified in its commitment to Islam and Arabic-language culture.[17]

Not only was the Berber *dahir* episode an important catalyst for the Moroccan nationalist movement, but it also sparked a shift in how elite Moroccan intellectuals wrote about Berbers and their contributions to North African and Mediterranean cultures. In the face of French efforts to drive a wedge between Moroccan Berbers and Arabs, young Moroccan nationalists (most of whom came from urban, Arabic-speaking backgrounds) set out to claim Berbers as part of Moroccan culture, while, at the same time, subsuming Berbers within a unitary Arab-Islamic national identity.

Among the nationalists who led the charge to protest France's Berber policies in Morocco were two young Moroccan men studying in Paris: Ahmad Balafrij (1908–1990) and Muhammad al-Fasi (1908–1991).[18] These two men also played an important role in the process of rehabilitating the reputation of the Almoravid and Almohad dynasties. One of their first moves in this direction was their collaboration on a work about al-Andalus and the Maghrib under the Almoravid and Almohad dynasties. The work in question was a translation of and commentary on two lectures by the French writing duo Jean and Jérôme Tharaud, authors of numerous works on Morocco and Islam.[19] It was published in late 1930 or early 1931 in Salé by an outfit called the Nationalist Press (al-Matba'a al-Wataniyya), whose name reflected the rising nationalist sentiment among Moroccan urban intellectuals in the wake of the "Berber *dahir*" incident.[20]

In a foreword addressed to the reader, Balafrij and al-Fasi explained their decision to translate the Tharaud brothers' lectures into Arabic:

> We said: perhaps there is benefit in translating them because of how they bring to light some of the mighty secrets of this nation [*umma*] from which we descend. After all, a nation [*umma*] that was victorious in the Battle of Sagrajas [*al-Zallāqa*] and the Battle of Alarcos [*al-Arak*], and that sired the likes of 'Abd al-Mu'min and Ya'qub al-Mansur can only be regarded on the same level as the highest Islamic states—indeed, as the highest of all states. And what benefit is there in history if it does not serve as a lesson to those who would learn from it? We are now on the brink of our renaissance, and there are voices all around us telling us that our nation is nothing but a collective of tribes that has never known unity and political or moral sovereignty. And the response to all that is found in these two lectures. For we want our renaissance to be built in the present and to rest on our past glory.[21]

This statement draws a direct line from the glories of the Almoravid and Al-mohad dynasties to the rise of the Moroccan nationalist movement in the early 1930s. To elucidate this point, I should briefly unpack some of Balafrij and al-Fasi's historical allusions. The two young Moroccan writers allude to the first and third Almohad caliphs, ʿAbd al-Muʾmin (r. 1130–1163) and Yaʿqub al-Mansur (r. 1184–1199), who, as we shall see, would loom large in the Mo-roccan nationalist imaginary because of the role that they played in unifying al-Andalus and the Maghrib. Balafrij and al-Fasi also allude to the Battle of Sagrajas (1086) and the Battle of Alarcos (1195), in which the Almoravid and Almohad armies won decisive victories over the armies of Alfonso VI and Alfonso VIII of Castile, major setbacks in the Castilian efforts to conquer Muslim territories in the Iberian Peninsula.

Notably, Balafrij and al-Fasi claim all of these events and famous figures as integral parts of Moroccan national history. This claim hinges on their re-peated use of the word *umma* (nation, or people). In the Moroccan political lexicon of this period, *watan* (homeland) refers to the physical space of the nation, and *umma* refers to its people. Deploying the latter term, Balafrij and al-Fasi imagine themselves to be part of a Moroccan national community whose ancestors include the great Almohad caliphs and the victors in the major battles of eleventh- and twelfth-century Andalusi history.[22] In other words, the young Moroccan translators project the Moroccan nation back in time, endowing it with a history that includes the Almoravids and the Al-mohads. In a similar vein, Balafrij and al-Fasi lay claim to al-Andalus as part of Moroccan national history, when they refer to al-Andalus as "the land of our forefathers" in the foreword to their translation.[23] Such leaps across time are actually quite common in nationalist projects, which often seek to legiti-mize themselves by claiming a connection to a deep and prestigious past.[24]

Indeed, the intense traffic between past and present is what drives Balafrij and al-Fasi's interest in the Almoravids and the Almohads, and what pushes them to write about these dynasties at a critical moment in the development of the Moroccan nationalist movement. After all, the translators ask rhetori-cally: "What benefit is there in history if it does not serve as a lesson to those who would learn from it?"[25] In this regard, it is helpful to consider the two temporalities that structure their foreword: for Balafrij and al-Fasi, the Al-moravids and the Almohads represent a "glorious past" that should serve as

the foundation for the present—a present that they twice hail as a "renaissance" (*nahḍa*). Balafrij and al-Fasi unite past and present in one continuous
national story, running from the Almoravids in the eleventh century to the
Moroccan nationalists in the twentieth century.

The foreword to Balafrij and al-Fasi's 1930 translation indicates the foundational role that Moroccan nationalists would ascribe to the Almoravids and
the Almohads, but it skirts around the issue of Berber identity. However,
Balafrij would address that issue more explicitly in later writings—and especially in the articles that he wrote for some of the new journals that emerged
in the 1930s to represent the views of the Moroccan nationalist movement.
One such journal was *Maghreb,* which Balafrij launched with a group of
Moroccan and French colleagues in 1932.[26] Writing in *Maghreb* in May 1933,
Balafrij asserted the existence of a transcendent "Moroccan national spirit"
that had existed for centuries and that was defined by its commitments to
Islam and to Arabic-language culture.[27] Notably, he credited Moroccan Ber-
bers for the country's Islamization and Arabization:

> And, if Morocco is Muslim, it is thanks not to the Arabs (whose hasty
> expeditions did not have any serious influence), but rather to the Ber-
> bers themselves, first under the guidance of the Idrisids and then under
> the reign of the Almoravids and the Almohads, who are likewise the
> very ones who promoted the Arabization of our country . . .
>
> Let us remember the progress that Arabic culture made under the Al-
> mohad and Marinid dynasties. All these Berber dynasties that had
> power in Morocco could have destroyed Arabic culture and Islamic law
> if they had restricted them just a little bit. Instead, the Berber dynasties
> have done more for the Arabization of Morocco than the Arab dynas-
> ties themselves.[28]

Here Balafrij challenges the tendency in French colonial thought to treat
Islam and the Arabic language as foreign impositions on an indigenous
Berber culture. Instead, he presents Morocco's major Berber dynasties—the
Almoravids, the Almohads, and the Marinids—as champions of Islam and
the Arabic language, the twin pillars of the Arab-Islamic identity promoted
by the Moroccan nationalist movement.

Balafrij would build on these ideas in a two-part series that he published in November and December 1933 in the journal *al-Salam,* Morocco's first Arabic-language journal with an explicitly nationalist orientation.[29] The series traced the rise of the Almohad movement in the twelfth century. In the series, Balafrij did not shy away from identifying Ibn Tumart, the founder of the Almohad movement, and 'Abd al-Mu'min, the first Almohad caliph, as Berbers who spoke a variant of the Berber language.[30] The focus of his discussion, however, was on how the Almohads created an empire that united North Africa and al-Andalus, politically and culturally.

Balafrij stressed that the Almohad period was not only one of political power, but also one of cultural splendor and economic prosperity. He asserted that "Andalusi civilization returned to its flourishing" under Almohad rule.[31] To illustrate this point, Balafrij pointed to a host of industries that grew and prospered during this period: "The silk industry in Jaén in al-Andalus picked up . . . , the paper industry advanced and flourished in Fez and Ceuta, and the mines of iron, copper, silver, sulfur, lead, mercury, and other things were exploited in al-Andalus and in Morocco."[32] Continuing in this vein, Balafrij observed, "Trade was extremely brisk, and the markets of Alicante, Cordoba, Almería, Marrakesh, and Mahdiyya [Rabat] acquired worldwide fame in that period."[33] In these examples, Balafrij paints a picture of an Almohad realm in which people and goods traverse the Strait of Gibraltar, moving easily between al-Andalus and the Maghrib. Likewise, his description moves seamlessly between cities in the Iberian Peninsula (like Cordoba and Almería) and cities in North Africa (such as Fez and Marrakesh), uniting these cities into a single cultural and economic space.

A similar geographic imaginary undergirds Balafrij's description of literary life during the Almohad dynasty. While listing luminaries from the Almohad period, Balafrij makes no distinction between writers born in North Africa (such as the poet Muhammad b. Habbus) and writers born in al-Andalus (such as the poet al-Rusafi or the philosopher Ibn Tufayl).[34] All of these cultural figures were, in Balafrij's estimation, members of a single cultural realm whose capital was in the Maghrib and whose territories included al-Andalus. In Balafrij's account, the literature of al-Andalus and the literature of Morocco converge to form one continuous tradition, whose center of gravity shifts southward, over time, from the Iberian Peninsula to North Africa.

Like Balafrij's series on the Almohads, the earliest works of Moroccan literary historiography stressed the cultural unity of Morocco and al-Andalus
and highlighted the role that North African Berbers played in forging this
unity. This idea animated a book that is widely hailed as the first history of
Moroccan literature: 'Abd Allah Gannun's *al-Nubugh al-maghribi fi al-adab
al-'arabi* (Moroccan genius in Arabic literature, 1937).[35] Notably, Gannun
traced the origins of Moroccan literature back to the founding moment of
al-Andalus: the Muslim conquest of the Iberian Peninsula led by the North
African commander Tariq b. Ziyad in 711. As legend would have it, Tariq b.
Ziyad delivered a rousing speech that spurred his outnumbered troops to
victory in the battle against the forces of Visigoth ruler King Roderic.[36] In
al-Nubugh al-maghribi, Gannun cited Tariq's speech as the first example of
Moroccan oratory and one of the earliest examples of Moroccan literature.[37]
In the wake of Gannun's pioneering work, several other Moroccan writers
followed his lead by claiming Tariq b. Ziyad as one of the founding figures of
Moroccan literature. For example, in an essay on the history of Moroccan
literature published in 1940, Muhammad al-Fasi called Tariq's speech "the
oldest Moroccan literary text."[38]

'Abd Allah Gannun not only claimed Tariq's speech as a foundational work
of Moroccan literature; he also offered a sharp retort to scholars from the Arab
East (the Mashriq) who doubted that Tariq, a Berber, could have delivered
such an eloquent speech in Arabic. In response to these doubts, Gannun asserted, "Tariq b. Ziyad, though a Berber, grew up under the protection of
Arabness and Islam" and "grew up in an Arab Islamic house."[39] The Moroccan
scholar also argued, "In the speech, there are no rhetorical figures that pre-
vent [us] from attributing it to Tariq; and its eloquence, in our opinion, rests
first and foremost on its meaning. And meanings are not restricted to Arabs
or non-Arabs."[40] In his defense of the authenticity of Tariq's speech, Gannun
claims a famous Berber, Tariq b. Ziyad, as a crucial figure in Moroccan literary history; at the same time, he ties Tariq to the Arab-Islamic culture
that, for Moroccan nationalists of Gannun's generation, defined Moroccan
national identity. Through these moves, Gannun managed to incorporate the
Muslim conquest of al-Andalus into the history of Moroccan literature, while
also incorporating Berbers into the cultural history of al-Andalus.

The effort to interweave the history of Moroccan literature with the history of al-Andalus did not stop with the founding figure Tariq b. Ziyad. In

their pioneering surveys of "Moroccan literature," Gannun and al-Fasi cite many writers born in al-Andalus, such as Ibn Tufayl, Hafsa bint al-Hajj, and Ibn al-Murahhal.[41] Indeed, both Gannun and al-Fasi argue that the Almoravid and Almohad dynasties ushered in a period in which al-Andalus and Morocco merged to become a single territory. These Moroccan nationalist intellectuals envisioned an "Andalus from the south," an Andalus anchored in Morocco and kept alive by Moroccan dynasties, especially the Almohads and the Almoravids.

Gannun was particularly eager to rehabilitate the reputation of the Almoravids and to restore them to their rightful place in the history of al-Andalus. As I discussed in Chapter 1, Arab-centric accounts of Andalusi history have generally depicted the Almoravids and their leader, Yusuf b. Tashfin (d. 1106), as uncouth barbarians whose arrival in al-Andalus dealt a mortal blow to the culture of refinement and tolerance promoted by the Umayyads.[42] 'Abd Allah Gannun was well aware of this long-standing bias against the Almoravids when he set out to defend them in *al-Nubugh al-maghribi*. He complained that "our civilized writers" (the phase is sarcastic) had unfairly characterized Yusuf b. Tashfin as "a savage Berber king" (*malik barbari mutawaḥḥish*).[43] Along similar lines, Gannun lamented that writers and historians, driven by "bigotry and factionalism" (*al-taʻaṣṣub wa-l-taḥazzub*), "accused the great warrior Yusuf b. Tashfin . . . of savagery and brutality in his treatment of al-Muʻtamid ibn ʻAbbad," the last of the ʻAbbadid rulers of Seville.[44] As these examples illustrate, Gannun was acquainted with the long tradition of Arab and European writers who had depicted the confrontation between Yusuf b. Tashfin and al-Muʻtamid ibn ʻAbbad as a confrontation between barbarity and civilization, North Africa and al-Andalus, Berberness and Arabness.

Countering this deep-seated hostility toward Yusuf b. Tashfin and the Almoravids, Gannun argued that were it not for Yusuf b. Tashfin, there would be no al-Andalus after the eleventh century. On this point, he asserted:

In reality, Yusuf's action was lofty, very lofty—far beyond what is usually thought and beyond what those fanciful writers give him credit for. Indeed, Islam, civilization, and science are all indebted to Yusuf b. Tashfin . . . It is certain that if Yusuf had not hastened to rescue al-Andalus at that time, then there would be no Ibn Rushd, no Ibn

Tufayl, no Ibn Bajja, no Ibn 'Arabi, no Ibn Khaldun, no Ibn al-Khatib—
nor anyone else among those whom that Peninsula sired *in its second
life,* which Yusuf b. Tashfin granted to it.[45]

What Gannun proposes here is nothing short of an entirely new narrative
framework for understanding the evolution of Andalusi history. Gannun
takes the dominant "rise-and-fall" narrative, which is centered on Arab
Umayyad rule in al-Andalus, and replaces it with a narrative in which al-
Andalus experiences a first life of splendor under the Umayyads and then a
"second life" of splendor under the Moroccan Almoravid and Almohad
dynasties. Yusuf b. Tashfin's role, in this new narrative, is not merely that of
the military hero who led the Muslim forces to victory over the army of
Alfonso VI of Castile. Instead, Gannun casts the Almoravid leader as the champion of "Islam, civilization, and science." To back up this claim, Gannun
points to all of the luminaries who lived during and after the Almoravid
takeover of al-Andalus. The result is a veritable who's who of Andalusi cultural history, including such giants as the philosopher and musician Ibn
Bajja (Avempace, d. 1139), the philosophers Ibn Tufayl (d. 1185) and Ibn Rushd
(d. 1198), the mystic Ibn 'Arabi (d. 1240), and the polymath and historian Ibn
al-Khatib (d. 1375). Gannun's point here is that many of the greatest accomplishments associated with al-Andalus would never have happened, were it
not for the Almoravids.

Gannun not only credits Yusuf b. Tashfin and the Almoravids with
granting al-Andalus a "second life," but he also credits them with uniting al-
Andalus and the Maghrib:

Yusuf folded up the pages of history of the Maghrib and al-Andalus,
making them a single page, which is the page of the history of the unified
Maghrib. Political differences fell away, practical obstacles vanished, and
the people of the Maghrib and al-Andalus lived together with one another in a single homeland [*watan*] under the auspices of a single
state. They drew close to each other and came into contact as they never
had before.[46]

Gannun's claim, here, is that the Maghrib and al-Andalus became a single
nation under the auspices of the Almoravid dynasty. Driving this claim is a

book metaphor: Gannun represents al-Andalus and the Maghrib as two pages of a book, whose spine is the Strait of Gibraltar. In this metaphor, Gannun credits Yusuf b. Tashfin with binding (or folding) the two pages into a single book, with a shared story: the story of "the unified Maghrib"—a space that, for Gannun, includes al-Andalus.

Indeed, Gannun asserts that Yusuf b. Tashfin and the Almoravids unified al-Andalus and the Maghrib into a single *waṭan*. As I have already indicated, the term *waṭan,* in the lexicon of the Moroccan nationalists, refers to the physical space of the nation. The term is roughly equivalent to the Spanish *patria* and could be rendered into English as "homeland" or "nation." The idea of the *waṭan* is at the conceptual core of the Moroccan nationalist movement (which is known, in Arabic, as *al-ḥaraka al-waṭaniyya*). Gannun traces the origins of this idea back to the Almoravids and associates it with a realm whose cultural and political influence extends across the Strait of Gibraltar to encompass al-Andalus.

Gannun's vision of an expansive Maghrib, stretching across the Strait of Gibraltar, did not stop with the Almoravids. Like his contemporary Ahmad Balafrij, Gannun depicts the Almohad period as a moment of cultural splendor and of unity between al-Andalus and the Maghrib. Gannun's description of the Almohads abounds in metaphors of flourishing and renewal. For instance, Gannun calls the Almohad period a "flourishing age" (*'asr zāhir*) and frequently describes it as a "renaissance" (*nahḍa,* also translated as "awakening").[47] However, Gannun insists that it is impossible to understand the splendor of the Almohad period without taking into account what came before them: the Almoravids. Gannun goes so far as to call the Almoravid movement "the foundation stone for the building of the Almohad renaissance."[48] His argument is that the Almoravids' devotion to learning, even if mostly limited to religious topics, "pushed people to love research and study and to enter into close contact with the Andalusis."[49] Gannun thus suggests that the revival of religious learning that took place under the Almoravids was a necessary precursor that prepared the terrain for the flourishing of literature, philosophy, and science under the Almohads.

For Gannun and many other Moroccan intellectuals of his generation, Almohad architecture was one of the most eloquent symbols of the process of cultural unification that took place in al-Andalus and the Maghrib under the auspices of the North African dynasties. As Gannun noted, the third

Almohad caliph, Ya'qub al-Mansur, was a patron of architecture, commissioning major building projects throughout his realm:

> In the days of al-Mansur, civilization and urban life penetrated deeply
> in Morocco and blossomed. Architecture made advances alongside the
> advance of the building movement. Al-Mansur built the sweet-smelling
> city of Rabat, the magnificent Ibn Yusuf Mosque in Marrakesh, the
> mighty Kutubiyya minaret in the same city, the colossal Hassan min-
> aret in Rabat, and the Giralda minaret in Seville (which is one of the
> marvels of the world).[50]

This description, like many other passages analyzed in this chapter, moves seamlessly between the Maghrib and al-Andalus, evoking the imagined geography that I have dubbed "al-Andalus from the south." Gannun treats Ya'qub al-Mansur's building projects in Rabat, Marrakesh, and Seville as landmarks that trace the contours of this imagined geography.

Although Gannun certainly offers a full-throated defense of the Almoravids and the Almohads, it is important to keep in mind that he only celebrates these dynasties for their contributions to Islamic and Arabic-language culture in al-Andalus and the Maghrib. In other words, he valorizes the Almoravids and the Almohads only insofar as they can be associated with the promotion of a transcendent Arab-Islamic identity for Morocco. In fact, Gannun's only substantive criticism of the Almohads is that they showed, in his view, an excessive interest in cultivating the Berber language and promoting its use in religious and administrative contexts.[51] On this point, Gannun writes: "What is strange about this dynasty—which, as we have seen, went to great lengths to promote Arab-Islamic culture and to convey the Berber people from the depths of ignorance and lethargy to the peak of civilization and knowledge—is its excessive concern [i'tinā'uhā al-zā'id] for the Berber language and its failure to forget it."[52] Gannun is unable to reconcile the Almohad promotion of the Berber language with his view of the dynasty as champions of Arab-Islamic culture in al-Andalus and the Maghrib. Noting this tension, he writes: "The truth is that this is strange behavior, extremely strange, and it makes us stand before it in perplexity and bafflement, not knowing how to reconcile it with what we have already presented regarding the dynasty's vigilance over the general spread of learning and Arab-Andalusi culture."[53] As this comment illustrates, Gannun saw the Almohad promotion of the Berber language as a perplexing aberration that could not be reconciled with their contributions to "Arab-Andalusi culture." In another passage, he derides the Almohads' support for the Berber language as a "historical comedy" (*mahzala tārīkhiyya*).[54] It is therefore clear that Gannun's work aimed, not to reframe al-Andalus as the product of a specifically *Berber* culture, but instead to call attention to the contributions that the North African Berber dynasties made to Arabic-language and Islamic culture. By walking this fine line, Gannun was able to rehabilitate the Berber dynasties while upholding the Moroccan nationalist commitment to an Arab-Islamic identity.

From Yaʿqub al-Mansur to Muhammad V

The defense of the Almohads, advanced by Gannun and Balafrij, found echoes in the work of Muhammad al-Rashid Mulin (ca. 1916–2001), another Moroccan scholar with ties to the nationalist movement.[55] In 1946 Mulin published *ʿAsr al-Mansur al-muwahhidi* (The age of al-Mansur the Almohad), an influential study of the reign of the Almohad caliph Yaʿqub al-Mansur. Mulin saw the Almohad period—and especially the reign of Yaʿqub al-Mansur—as a model that Moroccans should follow in the present. On this point, he wrote:

> Al-Mansur spread the beams of science over his realm, awakening minds from their decline. The life of the mind took off among Moroccans, and the walls of the mosques and the schools resounded with the echo of the students' voices . . . They were lively students who understood, recorded, wrote, and showed us the path that we should follow if we want our glory to be revived. They left us a precious intellectual heritage that made the age of al-Mansur a golden age of which we can boast and be proud of.[56]

This passage starts in the twelfth century (in the age of al-Mansur) and ends in the twentieth century. In the space of a single paragraph, then, Mulin moves from the past to the present, holding up al-Mansur's reign as "a golden age" and as "the path that we should follow if we want our glory to be revived." Mulin's use of the first-person plural "we" is significant here. Through it,

Mulin conjures into being a collective Moroccan subject who must look to the Almohad past as a foundation on which to build the Moroccan present.

Just as Mulin's study bridges the past and the present, so too does it bridge the southern and northern shores of the Strait of Gibraltar, uniting the Maghrib and al-Andalus into a single Almohad realm. In his survey of intellectual life under Ya'qub al-Mansur, Mulin makes no distinction between figures born in Almohad North Africa and those born in Almohad al-Andalus. His survey draws attention to an impressive array of scholars and writers who were born in al-Andalus and who served in the caliph's entourage or in other parts of the Almohad administration. This list includes the doctor Ibn Zuhr, the poets Ibn Mujbar and Ibn Hariq, the religious scholar al-Suhayli, the philosopher Ibn Rushd, and many others.[57] In Mulin's view, all of these figures were integral parts of Almohad culture, a culture whose center was the Almohad court in Marrakesh and whose network spread across much of North Africa and the Iberian Peninsula.

While building on ideas that were already present in Moroccan texts from the 1930s, Mulin's study also added a new element to the mix: he portrayed Morocco's ruling 'Alawi dynasty—and, in particular, King Muhammad V (r. 1927–1961)—as the heirs to the Almohads and the restorers of the Almohad legacy in the modern era. This idea is particularly pronounced in the final paragraphs of Mulin's book, where the author directly addresses Ya'qub al-Mansur and draws out connections between the Almohad caliph and King Muhammad V:

> May God bless you, o al-Mansur . . . If only your pure spirit could fly today over the skies of your city . . . you would flutter with joy and delight. For your city is today the capital of a nation that is awake and aspiring to life with resolution and earnestness. It is led by an ingenious king, who has taken it from one great milestone to another . . .
>
> This young man is a son of your city. He grew up marveling at you. And he ventured, despite the obstacles, to devote his first efforts in the field of composition to reviving your memory, to spreading your feats, and to awakening the zeal for carrying out our duty toward you.[58]

This passage, the last in Mulin's book, casts Muhammad V's Morocco as the revival of Ya'qub al-Mansur's Morocco. Mulin unites the two rulers by drawing attention to their shared connection to Rabat, a city that was founded by the first Almohad caliph, 'Abd al-Mu'min, and developed under his successors, Yusuf and Ya'qub al-Mansur.[59] Mulin not only calls Muhammad V "a son" of the city that al-Mansur helped build, but he also points to Muhammad V's efforts to revive the memory of the Almohads in the twentieth century.

The final passage of Mulin's book is an early example of what would become, over the ensuing decades, a widespread effort to promote the symbolic connection between the Almohad dynasty and the 'Alawi dynasty (which has ruled Morocco since the seventeenth century). In the years leading up to Morocco's independence in 1956, and in the aftermath of independence, celebrations of the Almohad legacy would become increasingly intertwined with the legitimacy and visual identity of the ruling 'Alawi dynasty. This process unfolded in different arenas of public and cultural life and involved close collaborations between the 'Alawi monarchs, their powerful circle of advisors (often known collectively as the *makhzan*), and scholars and artists from Morocco and Europe. The most visible emblem of this vast project is, undoubtedly, the mausoleum complex for Muhammad V, erected in the 1960s on the site of a former Almohad mosque.

The Mausoleum of Muhammad V—today, one of Rabat's most famous landmarks—is an eloquent symbol of how the Moroccan state, especially under King Hassan II (r. 1961–1999), has made strategic use of the Almohad-Andalusi legacy in the post-independence era.[60] When King Muhammad V died in 1961, his son and successor, Hassan II, decided to build a mausoleum complex to honor his father's memory. To build the mausoleum complex, Hassan II hired the architect Vo Toan (born in Vietnam and educated in Paris), who worked with an army of Moroccan master craftsmen. Hassan II directed the architect to erect the mausoleum in front of Rabat's most famous Almohad monument, the Hassan Minaret (*ṣawma'at Ḥassān* or "Tour Hassan"). The site had both historical and contemporary significance. The Hassan Minaret is a remnant of a colossal mosque that Ya'qub al-Mansur ordered built in Rabat in the last years of the twelfth century. The site also had a much more recent resonance for Moroccans. In November 1955, when Muhammad V returned to Morocco after a two-year exile imposed by the French authorities, the Moroccan king led a crowd of thousands in Friday prayers on the esplanade in front of the Hassan Minaret. After the prayer, the king delivered a speech calling for the end of colonial rule and the coming of Moroccan independence.[61] In other words, the location that Hassan II chose for his father's mausoleum was not only a symbol of Almohad grandeur but also a landmark in the recent Moroccan struggle for independence.

Showcasing these links between past and present, the mausoleum complex for Muhammad V was designed as a continuation of the Almohad minaret that stands in front of it. The complex consists of three buildings: the mausoleum housing Muhammad V's tomb, an adjacent mosque, and a museum. The three buildings face the Hassan Minaret and form a line along the axis of the original Almohad mosque's *qibla* wall (indicating the direction of Mecca).[62] The main entrance to the mosque stands directly in front of the Hassan Minaret, as if the two structures, separated by eight centuries, were parts of the same project. This sense of continuity is further conveyed by the external design of the modern mosque and museum. Both buildings are made of ocher-colored stones that are very similar to the ones used in the Hassan Minaret and other major Almohad monuments in Rabat. Likewise, the external walls of the entire mausoleum complex feature the same interlacing honeycomb designs (known as *sebka*) that appear on all four sides of the Hassan Minaret and are a primary decorative element in many other Almohad monuments, including the Giralda in Seville.[63] Furthermore, the façade of the mosque features geometric shell designs that also appear in the monumental gateways that the Almohads built in Rabat, such as Bab Udaya and Bab Ruwah. Thus, the mausoleum complex for Muhammad V encloses many architectural allusions to Almohad monuments and, in so doing, suggests continuity between the Almohads and the 'Alawis, the medieval and the modern.

The mausoleum complex does not just blend temporal lines, but also spatial ones. Like many of the works analyzed in this chapter, the mausoleum conflates North Africa and al-Andalus and treats the Almohad Maghrib as the cultural heart of al-Andalus—an Andalus ruled from the south. Although the mausoleum complex's primary architectural model is the Hassan Minaret, it also incorporates allusions to several monuments located in today's Spain, including the Alhambra in Granada and the Alcázar and the Giralda in Seville.[64] In fact, the architect Vo traveled to Spain to find inspiration and models for the mausoleum project. He alludes to these travels in his guide to the mausoleum complex, where he writes: "[The architect] also had to visit Muslim Spain, where centuries of Islamic history and civilization have left in Cordoba, Seville, Granada, or Toledo prestigious palaces and mosques that are jewels of the art of an inventive and refined people who came, for the most part, from Morocco, either under the Almoravids, the Almohads, or the Marinids."[65] What I find most striking, in this passage, is that Vo gives credit to Moroccans—and especially to the three major Moroccan Berber dynasties, the Almoravids, the Almohads, and the Marinids—for creating the masterpieces of Andalusi architecture. In other words, for Vo, the art of Muslim Cordoba, Seville, and Granada is *Moroccan* art, and, by extension, the Mausoleum of Muhammad V represents the revival of that art on Moroccan soil. Vo's comments evoke a cultural genealogy that unfolds on a north-south axis, from North Africa to the Iberian Peninsula and back. The primary agents in this cultural relay are the Moroccan Berber dynasties and the 'Alawi rulers who have revived their heritage in the modern era.

A Moroccan in the Almohad Court

The Mausoleum of Muhammad V was a project built on ideas that originated in the elite milieu of Moroccan nationalist intellectuals. But today, these ideas are no longer limited to elite or official circles. Rather, they have seeped into many arenas of culture and public life, including tourism and film.[66] One of the most vibrant and popular expressions of this phenomenon is the box-office sensation *'Abdu 'inda al-muwahhidin* ('Abdu in the time of the Almohads, 2006), a historical comedy written and directed by Sa'id al-Nasiri (Said Naciri), one of Morocco's most famous comedians and entertainers.[67] Although the film has an outlandish plot, it is engaged in some serious debates about the relationship between the past and the present. In particular, the film illustrates the ongoing efforts, among Moroccan artists and writers, to refute negative portrayals of the Almohad dynasty and to claim the Almohads as the precursors of contemporary Moroccan identity.

The title character of al-Nasiri's film, 'Abdu (short for 'Abd al-Rahman), is a pot-smoking hustler from present-day Marrakesh who gets sent back in time to the age of Ya'qub al-Mansur. At the start of the film, 'Abdu is living with his mother and his brother in Marrakesh's casbah (which was built by the Almohads). 'Abdu's brother is a highly educated but unemployed bookworm who spends his days at home reading about al-Andalus, the Almoravids, and the Almohads. Unlike his brother, 'Abdu has no patience for history. He makes his living by peddling trinkets to tourists and landing the occasional petty drug deal. Early in the film, 'Abdu leaves his house in the casbah, drives his motorcycle past several Almohad monuments, and makes his way to Marrakesh's emblematic Jemaa el-Fna square. There, the police spot him buying pot from a friend and set out to arrest him, leading to a frantic chase scene through the streets of Marrakesh. 'Abdu eventually eludes the police by driving his motorcycle into an archaeological excavation site, where a group of scientists accidentally zap him with a laser, sending him back in time to the year 1198. 'Abdu reappears in a marketplace in twelfth-century Marrakesh, where he is immediately arrested by Almohad soldiers, who suspect him of being a spy for a group that is trying to overthrow the Almohad dynasty.

From this point on, much of the film's humor resides in the misunderstandings that arise from the encounter between an interloper from the twenty-first century and his compatriots from the twelfth century. Al-Nasiri's script makes effective use of the different levels of the Arabic language to signal the temporal gap between 'Abdu and the people he encounters in his new context. After arriving in twelfth-century Marrakesh, 'Abdu continues to speak in colloquial Moroccan Arabic (*dārija*), occasionally mixing French words with Arabic ones, while the other characters speak in Standard Arabic (*fuṣḥā*)—the language that is often used in Arabic-language historical dramas set in al-Andalus or in the early Islamic era.[68] The contrast between 'Abdu's colloquial and macaronic Arabic and the Almohad characters' Standard Arabic provides much comic fodder throughout the movie, but it also points to larger tensions within the Arab world and to debates about who gets to speak for al-Andalus and its cultural legacy.

These debates bubble underneath the surface of a humorous scene in which 'Abdu is hauled in front of the Almohad governor of Marrakesh for interrogation. 'Abdu tries to speak to the governor in Moroccan Arabic, but the governor and his advisers struggle to understand him. When 'Abdu hears them speaking to each other in Standard Arabic, he believes that he has stumbled onto the set of a historical film, and he asks them, in Moroccan Arabic: "You guys are Syrians, right?" In response, the Almohad governor asks, in stilted Standard Arabic: "What is this gibberish [*al-raṭāna*] that you're speaking?" The joke, here, revolves around two interconnected phenomena in contemporary Arab culture. On the one hand, Syrian actors have played leading roles in

many of the Arabic historical dramas that have aired during Ramadan in recent decades—including several high-profile dramas set in al-Andalus (such
as the ones I discuss in Chapter 1).[69] The preference for Syrian actors stems
largely from the fact that they receive a rigorous training in Standard Arabic, the predominant language in historical epics. As a result of the Syrian
dominance in historical television drama, Moroccan viewers have become
accustomed to seeing Syrian actors in the role of prominent figures from the
past and also to hearing Standard Arabic as the privileged language of the
past. At the same time, Moroccans have long faced criticism and mockery
for speaking an Arabic dialect that many Mashriqi Arabs have dismissed as
incomprehensible and "impure."[70] Al-Nasiri's script plays these common
stereotypes for laughs, but underneath the laughs, there are more serious
questions about how contemporary Moroccans, like 'Abdu, understand and
communicate with the Almohad past.

Although these language jokes emphasize the gap between a contemporary
Moroccan and the Arabic cultural heritage, the film's main message points
in another direction: to highlight 'Abdu's discovery of, and reconciliation
with, the Almohad past. In his journey back in time, 'Abdu encounters several luminaries from the Almohad era, such as the philosopher Ibn Rushd, a
female doctor from the Banu Zuhr family of Seville, and the engineer Abu
Ishaq Bazzar b. Muhammad. Through these encounters, 'Abdu learns about
many of the cultural and scientific achievements that took place in the
Maghrib and al-Andalus under Almohad rule: Ibn Rushd's commentaries
on Aristotle, the contributions that men and women made to the theory
and practice of medicine, and the marvelous innovations of Andalusi and
Maghribi engineers—such as the mobile *maqṣūra* (enclosure) that a team of
engineers designed for the Kutubiyya Mosque in Marrakesh. By highlighting
these accomplishments, al-Nasiri's film builds on ideas that have been central
to Moroccan representations of the Almohads since the 1930s. In particular,
al-Nasiri's film, like many of its Moroccan predecessors, portrays Almohad
Marrakesh as the vibrant center of a cultural network that spreads across
al-Andalus and much of North Africa.

In this vein, the film lays claim to Ibn Rushd (Averroes) as a paradigmatic
figure of the Almohad legacy. The fact that al-Nasiri's film insists on this point
is noteworthy, since Ibn Rushd is a figure who has often served as a litmus
test for competing views of the Almohad period. In particular, al-Nasiri's film

pushes back against the most famous cinematic representation of Ibn
Rushd's life: Egyptian director Youssef Chahine's *al-Masir* (Destiny), which
premiered at Cannes in 1997. Chahine's film portrays Ibn Rushd as a champion of free thought who suffers violent persecution from a sect of religious
fanatics. These religious fanatics gain the tacit support of the Almohad
caliph, Ya'qub al-Mansur, and convince him to ban Ibn Rushd's books and
to burn them in a bonfire in Cordoba's main square.[71] With this plot, Chahine's film joins a long line of Arab and European works that have dismissed
the Almohads as a group of religious fanatics who were inimical to the culture
of al-Andalus.

Sa'id al-Nasiri's film explicitly responds to Chahine's film—in particular,
to Chahine's negative portrayal of the Almohads. When al-Nasiri's protagonist, 'Abdu, meets Ibn Rushd in Marrakesh, his first reaction is to doubt
whether the Ibn Rushd that he is meeting is the real McCoy because this Ibn
Rushd does not look like the actor who plays the philosopher in Chahine's film.
'Abdu turns to another character in the scene and says: "Ibn Rushd . . . I've
heard of him! But he can't be this guy because I saw that film *Destiny* . . . It
wasn't this guy, and he doesn't look like him." In a later scene, 'Abdu asks Ibn
Rushd: "I want to get something straight because, honestly, I don't understand.
In that film *Destiny* . . . they said that al-Mansur is the one who burned
your books in al-Andalus. But now I don't understand anything because
here you are in Marrakesh, respected and honored, and [al-Mansur] is the one
looking after you." Another character then explains to 'Abdu that the caliph
pardoned Ibn Rushd and asked him to come to Marrakesh to teach philosophy.

'Abdu's repeated attempts to ask the twelfth-century Andalusi philosopher
to respond to a twentieth-century film about his life is one of many instances
of comic anachronism in al-Nasiri's film. Yet, once again, there is some serious business underneath the comedy. As these exchanges indicate, a twenty-
first-century Moroccan, like 'Abdu, encounters al-Andalus and its history as
highly mediated objects—as stories that have been told and retold many
times, but rarely from a North African perspective. Al-Nasiri's film vigor-
ously contradicts Chahine's film and, in so doing, makes the case for the need
to tell stories about al-Andalus and the Almohads from a Moroccan perspective. Al-Nasiri pressed this point when I interviewed him in Casablanca in
January 2020. The filmmaker told me that Chahine "lied about the history
of Morocco . . . He didn't give Morocco its due."[72]

My aim here is not to adjudicate whether Saʿid al-Nasiri or Youssef Chahine gave a more accurate representation of history in their respective films. Instead, I mean to suggest that the differences between the two films stem from competing stories about al-Andalus, stories that have divergent genealogies and political investments. As the clash between the two films illustrates, representations of Almohad al-Andalus—and of its most famous figure, Ibn Rushd—vary significantly based on where they are produced. Chahine's film builds on a long tradition that has represented the Almohads as an existential threat to Andalusi culture. Al-Nasiri's film, in contrast, emerges from a more recent tradition that has sought to celebrate the cultural achievements of the Almohads, to stress the cultural unity of North Africa and al-Andalus, and to claim the Almohad period as an important milestone in the emergence of Moroccan national identity.

A striking absence in al-Nasiri's film is the word *Berber*. Nowhere in the film is there any mention of the Almohad rulers' Berber / Amazigh origins or of the fact that many of them used the Berber language in public and religious contexts. Instead, al-Nasiri's characters from the Almohad era speak in Standard Arabic and use phrases like "Arab science" and "the Arab-Islamic world." At first glance, then, al-Nasiri's film appears to follow the rhetorical strategy of the Moroccan nationalist movement, which celebrated the Almohads by subsuming them in the category of Arab-Islamic culture. However, some of al-Nasiri's comments about the film in the press have indicated recent and significant shifts in the public conversation about Berber / Amazigh identities in Morocco and beyond. In an interview published in the newspaper *al-Quds al-ʿarabi* in March 2006, al-Nasiri said: "The film leans on an important subject, which is that the Almohads come from Amazigh origins, from the region of Tinmal, from which [their] leader Ibn Tumart originates, near Marrakesh. They embraced Islam and became Arabized, and they were able to rule the Arab world and to spread Islam."[73] In this comment, al-Nasiri attempts to walk a tightrope between recognizing the Almohads' Amazigh roots and underlining their embrace of Islam and the Arabic language. The director struck a similar note when I interviewed him in January 2020. He told me that Moroccan civilization is "a mixture between the Arabs, the Imazighen, and the other civilizations who came here." In a similar vein, he asserted: "The Almohads were Amazigh, but they spoke Arabic."[74]

Although al-Nasiri's comments may seem contradictory and at odds with his film, the apparent contradiction points to the overlap of two ways of talking about Berber / Amazigh identities in contemporary Morocco. On the one hand, many scholars and cultural figures have continued to emphasize the contributions that Berber groups have made to Morocco's Arab-Islamic identity—an emphasis that has been in play since at least the 1930s. On the other hand, Morocco has witnessed, in recent decades, a resurgence of interest in its Berber heritage and in the unique contributions that Berbers have made to Moroccan and North African history. Representations of al-Andalus have not been immune to these shifts in public conversations about Berber identity and history, as I illustrate in the next section.

Al-Andalus and the Amazigh Culture Movement

Since the late 1960s, and with increasing intensity since the 1990s, a broad and diverse group of scholars, artists, and activists who identify as Amazigh or Berber has worked to bring visibility to Amazigh culture in North Africa and in the North African diaspora.[75] This broad movement—which I will loosely refer to as the "Amazigh culture movement"—is multi-sited and ideologically diverse, but it has coalesced around some core goals and demands. Foremost among them is the demand that the independent North African states, particularly Morocco and Algeria, recognize the Amazigh people's existence and their myriad contributions to the formation of North African culture.[76] The Amazigh culture movement has posed challenges to many long-standing assumptions about national and regional identities in North Africa. Perhaps most acutely, it has called into question the homogeneous Arab-Islamic identity that was a central pillar of nationalist movements in North Africa during the colonial period and in the decades following independence.

The Amazigh culture movement has also led to a radical reassessment of the role that Imazighen (or Berbers) have played in North African and Mediterranean history—including the history of al-Andalus. In recent decades, artists and scholars have worked in concert with academic, cultural, and government institutions to center Berbers in the story of al-Andalus. A notable and visible example of this trend is the Alhambra's recent exhibit on Granada and the "Berber universe" (which I discussed at the beginning of this chapter).

But the Alhambra exhibit draws on cultural and political processes that have been developing in North Africa and the North African diaspora for several decades. In what follows, I examine some significant milestones in the ongoing efforts to rescue and celebrate a specifically *Berber* al-Andalus, one that diverges from the Arab-Islamic identity that has been a foundation of Moroccan national identity since at least the 1930s.

One of the first literary texts to reimagine the history of al-Andalus in a Berber key was Driss Chraïbi's novel *Naissance à l'aube* (1986, translated into English as *Birth at Dawn*), the final installment in Chraïbi's "Berber trilogy."[77] The novel's action unfolds on three timelines, each of which features a different member of the same extended Berber family, the Ait Yafelman (or Ayt Yafelman). The novel opens with a brief "Epilogue" set in the present (the year 1985), in which a Berber named Raho Ait Yafelman is dismissed from his job at the railway station in Sidi Kacem. The novel then jumps back in time thirteen centuries to the year 712 and follows the path of Tariq b. Ziyad as he leads the Muslim conquest of al-Andalus. One of the soldiers in Tariq's army is Azwaw Ait Yafelman, an ancestor of Raho Ait Yafelman. In the last chapter of the novel, the story jumps forward in time to the eleventh century and briefly follows the arrival of another member of the Ait Yafelman clan to Cordoba. In the novel's last paragraph, we learn that this individual is none other than 'Abd Allah ibn Yasin (d. 1059), one of the founders of the Almoravid movement, which would eventually conquer the Maghrib and al-Andalus. Thus, the novel traces an intricate web of relations between the past and the present, connecting the struggles of an impoverished Berber in post-independence Morocco to the exploits of his ancestors, who led the Muslim conquest of al-Andalus in the eighth century and then placed al-Andalus under Maghribi rule in the eleventh century.

We could say that *Birth at Dawn* marks a shift from an Andalus *with* Berbers to an Andalus *of* Berbers. Indeed, it is worth underlining that the novel's plot jumps from Tariq b. Ziyad in the eighth century to Ibn Yasin in the eleventh century, skipping over the period of Arab Umayyad rule, which has often been considered the zenith of Andalusi civilization. As this move illustrates, Chraïbi's novel seeks to sideline the Umayyads and to re-center the story of al-Andalus around North Africans—and, in particular, Berbers. It is, then, no coincidence that all of the novel's main characters are Berbers, from Raho Ait Yafelman in the late twentieth century to Tariq and his soldiers in the eighth century to Ibn Yasin in the eleventh century. These characters all identify themselves as Berber or are identified as such by the narrator. For instance, one of Tariq b. Ziyad's lieutenants compliments him by saying, "You are as sly as the most Berber among us." In response, Tariq says, "I am a Berber."[78] Likewise, when Ibn Yasin visits Cordoba in the last chapter, he introduces himself as "a Berber from over there"—signaling North Africa.[79] Such repeated assertions of Berber identity are not incidental to the novel's aims. In fact, *Birth at Dawn* offers something like a counter-history of al-Andalus, one that speaks back against a long tradition of scholars and writers who have silenced and marginalized Berbers. In this regard, it is noteworthy that one of the novel's main characters, Azwaw Ait Yafelman, is mute. Azwaw's tongue was cut out by an unnamed executioner who came with the conquering army that spread Islam in North Africa in the seventh century.[80] Azwaw is, therefore, both a participant in and a silent witness to the Muslim conquest of al-Andalus. Chraïbi's *Birth at Dawn* seeks to give voice to Berbers, like Azwaw, whose contributions to al-Andalus have been forgotten or minimized.

The primary spokesperson for the novel's assertive vision of a Berber-centered al-Andalus is none other than Tariq b. Ziyad. In the novel, Tariq not only embodies Berberness and the Maghrib, but also stands as a foil to Arabness and the Arab East. This dynamic emerges early in the novel, when Tariq addresses his army, composed primarily of Berbers, as they march on the road to Cordoba. Tariq says:

> Sons of the Levant and of Barbary, listen: the East is dying. It is behind you, with its Damascuses, its Baghdads, and its endless divisions that bloody the earth and corrupt God's word. Never again will you return there. You are here now, in the West, and it is as if you had just been born. Because I, I tell you that it is here, in the West, where the sun of the world will rise from now on . . . The past is over. All you have left is the future.[81]

In this passage, Tariq outlines the primary opposition that structures the novel: the one between Arabs and Berbers, the Levant and the Maghrib. Tariq refers to his homeland as "Barbary" (*Berbérie*), a toponym that derives from *Berber* and that highlights the primacy of Berbers in North Africa. His opposition between the Levant and the Maghrib is not only invested with ethnic connotations, but also with ethical and temporal ones. Tariq suggests that the Levant, the Umayyad heartlands, is the site of a moribund Islam in decline, and that "Barbary," the land of the Berbers, is the cradle of a nascent and future-oriented Islam. In a similar vein, he asserts that the Arab East— "with its Damascuses, its Baghdads"—is the past, and that the Islamic West is the future.

Throughout the novel, Tariq repeatedly asserts that his mission in al-Andalus is to restore the Prophet Muhammad's vision of an Islamic community, or *umma,* that is open and welcoming to all ethnicities, including Berbers.[82] This mission is not only framed as a restoration of the spirit of early Islam but also as a rebuke of the cultural and political legacy of the Umayyads. On this point, the novel's narrator says that Tariq was "tenaciously determined to succeed where the Muslims of the East, with their arrogance and verbosity [*tout en verbe et en verbiage*], had failed and had divided the *Umma* into a multitude of sects . . . General Tariq b. Ziyad had decided to conquer Spain to the limits of its borders and the end of the centuries and to establish there a young vigorous Islam, knowing neither decline nor death."[83] Chraïbi's novel thus calls out the Umayyads ("the Muslims of the East") for sowing division and Arab chauvinism, and it represents Tariq's conquest as a rejection of Umayyad culture and a revival of early Islam.

Emphasizing Tariq's role as the restorer of the Islamic *umma,* the narrator says that Tariq would "remake his own Hijra, a total emigration, in the company of true Berbers."[84] Chraïbi's word choice is important here. The term *hijra* means "emigration," but it also has a specialized meaning in Islamic history: it refers to the emigration of the Prophet Muhammad and his followers from Mecca to Medina in 622, an event that serves as the starting point of the Islamic (or *hijrī*) calendar. In other words, Chraïbi's novel depicts the conquest of al-Andalus, led by Tariq b. Ziyad, as a second *hijra,* a second beginning for Islam, and the novel depicts Tariq and his men as exemplary Muslims who follow in Muhammad's footsteps.

These efforts to underline Tariq's Muslim and Berber identities and to cast North African Muslims as the standard-bearers for the Islamic *umma* intervene in long-standing debates about the relationship between Berberness and Islam. One of the legacies of French colonialism in North Africa is that assertions of a distinctive Berber identity are often perceived as a threat to Islamic unity. The reason for this suspicion is that French colonial policies in

North Africa sought not only to codify the differences between Berbers and Arabs but also to distance Berbers from Islamic institutions. Behind these policies lay the conviction, widely articulated in French colonial literature, that Berbers, unlike Arabs, had only a superficial attachment to Islam and could easily be converted to Christianity.[85] In light of these precedents, many North African intellectuals and politicians in the post-independence period have dismissed claims of a distinctive Berber identity as relics of a colonial system whose aim was to divide North Africans along ethnic lines and to undermine North Africa's Islamic identity.[86] Chraïbi's novel wades into these debates by asserting Tariq's adhesion to the spirit of early Islam. The novel suggests that there is no tension between being Berber and being Muslim; indeed, it implies that Tariq's Berber identity is what led him to advocate for a more just and equitable Islam.

Chraïbi's novel not only underlines the Islamic identity of the Berber soldiers who conquered al-Andalus, but also challenges a long-standing tradition of thought that has upheld the cultural superiority of Arabs over Berbers. Upending these ethnic and cultural hierarchies, the novel stresses the contrast between Berber civilization and Arab barbarity. This idea emerges most explicitly in a scene where Tariq b. Ziyad savors a succulent dish alongside his fellow Berbers in North Africa:

> Savoring the delicacy in small mouthfuls . . . Tariq b. Ziyad thought of the unspeakable things that the Arabs consumed with delight, like those small balls of crushed camel hair held together with blood. To boil water or milk, they simply threw in a red-hot stone from the fire. Sons of Islam, he never ceased wondering at Providence, who had made Islam be born among them! Truly, if such a thing as civilization existed, it was here, in the country of savagery. He would carry the recipe of this succulent dish in his stomach's memory and would honor it in the palaces of the Andalusia of tomorrow.[87]

What makes this passage subversive is that it inverts the dichotomies that have governed representations of Arabs and Berbers since the days of Umayyad rule in al-Andalus. As I showed in Chapter 1, Arab-centric views of Andalusi history have, in general, associated Arab Umayyad culture with refinement and urbanity, while, in turn, associating Berbers with coarseness and violence. Chraïbi's novel subverts this tendency by reversing the roles of Berbers and Arabs. Chraïbi's Tariq vows to carry the splendor of Berber "civilization" to the palaces of al-Andalus. In this way, the novel places Tariq in the position that is normally reserved for Arabs in representations of al-Andalus: that of guardian of civilization.

In fact, Chraïbi's *Birth at Dawn* goes so far as to depict Tariq as the visionary who gave rise to the cultural splendor of Cordoba, the city that has traditionally been most closely associated with the Umayyad legacy. In the novel, after Tariq and his army take Cordoba, Tariq stands on Cordoba's ramparts and has a vision of the city that he plans to build there, with its splendid mosque, its abundant libraries, and its teeming markets.[88] Tariq imagines building a civilization where social harmony is so complete that "each inhabitant of the kingdom of al-Andalus, Muslim, Jewish, Christian, or atheist, would not wish to know any other world, neither here on earth nor in the hereafter."[89] In other words, Tariq envisions *convivencia,* the culture of interfaith tolerance and coexistence to which Umayyad Cordoba owes much of its fame today. As this passage shows, *Birth at Dawn* takes characteristics, such as *convivencia,* that have long been ascribed to Arab Umayyad culture and reassigns them to Tariq and the Berbers.

The novel's efforts to center Berbers in the story of al-Andalus do not end with the figure of Tariq. *Birth at Dawn* ties Tariq's story to that of 'Abd Allah ibn Yasin, the founder of the Almoravid movement. The novel weaves together the lives of these two famous Berber figures through a fictional family tree: a daughter of Tariq b. Ziyad marries Azwaw Ait Yafelman's grandson and from the marriage sprouts a family tree that eventually leads to 'Abd Allah ibn Yasin. The novel's narrator describes this genealogical chain in a passage that winds through time and space, making its way from eighth-century Cordoba to eleventh-century North Africa: "Through countless and subterranean branchings in space and time, Azwaw Ait Yafelman's spirit was reborn, and with it was reborn the Islam of the first days, naked and foreign amid the pomp of Arab civilization at its apogee. It happened in a Berber village of the Atlas, at the beginning of the eleventh century. His name was 'Abd Allah ibn Yasin."[90] Like Tariq b. Ziyad, Ibn Yasin is portrayed here as a figure of Islamic revival. And like Tariq, Ibn Yasin embodies a religious vision that is couched in ethnic terms: his religious revival emanates from "a Berber village of the Atlas" and stands in sharp contrast to "the pomp of Arab civilization." Thus, in the novel, Ibn Yasin represents a cyclical return to the past—both a return to the origins of Islam and a return to the ethno-religious vision of his supposed ancestor, Tariq b. Ziyad.

The last chapter of *Birth at Dawn* opens with Ibn Yasin's arrival at the gates of Cordoba in the year 1054.[91] In Cordoba, Ibn Yasin encounters several Andalusi characters who look down on him with a mixture of condescension and pity, driven by a profound sense of cultural superiority. As Ibn Yasin passes through Cordoba's gates, the Andalusi characters who observe him think: "Any son of Adam who lived outside Cordoba's walls—and perhaps even outside the borders of Andalusia—could only be a backward person [*sous-développé*]."[92] One of the Andalusi characters asks Ibn Yasin if he makes a living by teaching "the Qur'an to the barbarians."[93] The question pointedly draws out the etymological association between barbarians and Berbers. Although the Cordoban characters are convinced of their superiority, Ibn Yasin remains unmoved by their city's busy markets, sumptuous banquets, and stunning gardens. His sole wish is to visit the famous mosque of Cordoba. Once there, Ibn Yasin receives a divine revelation while standing in front of the mihrab. He hears a voice tell him, "Do not recite. Not one word. This is My command. Leave this place and act according to My voice."[94] This scene clearly mirrors the first revelation of the Qur'an, when Muhammad was instructed, "Recite! In the name of your Lord . . ."[95] Unlike Muhammad, however, Ibn Yasin is enjoined to act, not to recite. This revelation immediately precedes the last paragraph of the novel, which explains how Ibn Yasin carried it out: "He left and acted. Three seasons later, in the year one thousand fifty-five, he captured strongholds at the head of his commandos, conquered the Maghrib and the greater part of Spain, and founded the Berber dynasty of the Almoravids, which would last nearly a century—the space of a renewal, an infinitesimal spring of sidereal eternity."[96]

I want to pause here to take in the full meaning of the novel's stunning conclusion. It represents the Almoravid conquest of al-Andalus as a renewal of Muhammad's revelation—that is, as nothing less than a second Qur'an. This meaning is further emphasized by the last page of the novel, which features the Arabic text of the first sura of the Qur'an, the "Fatiha," arranged in an artful circle (Figure 2.3). Taking image and text together, the novel's conclusion suggests that Islamic history came full circle with the emergence of

Figure 2.3. Image from *Naissance à l'aube* by Driss Chraïbi, © Éditions du Seuil, 1986.

the Almoravids. In other words, the novel suggests that the Almoravids marked a return to Islam's origins, a move signaled by the parallels between Ibn Yasin's revelation and Muhammad's revelation, and by the use of the first chapter of the Qur'an on the last page of the novel.

The novel also ends with another stroke of circularity. In between the final paragraph and the final illustration, Chraïbi inserts the following postscript: "Dreamed in the Middle Ages, on the vestiges of a birth, in Cordoba, then in Fez; written in France in 1984–1985, at night, and sometimes in the afternoon, during the naps of my new-born: TARIQ."[97] The author's postscript carries the circular movement of history into the late twentieth century. Chraïbi's newborn son, Tariq, carries the same name as the novel's main character, Tariq b. Ziyad. The birth of Chraïbi's son reflects both the birth of the Almoravid movement (with which the novel ends) and the cycles of religious renewal spearheaded by Tariq b. Ziyad and Ibn Yasin. In short, the postscript traces another loop in a cyclical history that runs from the conquest of al-Andalus in the eighth century to the rise of the Almoravids in the eleventh century to the work of a Moroccan writer living in France in the 1980s. Each node on this trajectory is linked to North Africans who move between North Africa and Europe.

Chraïbi's *Birth at Dawn* is illustrative of a cultural and political moment in which artists, activists, and scholars in North Africa and in the North African diaspora began to assert their distinctive Berber identities and the Berberness of famous figures from North African history, such as Tariq b. Ziyad. These actors pushed for a broad reassessment of the Berber role in North African and western Mediterranean history. Their claims were counterhegemonic, though not necessarily revolutionary. Indeed, if we look at the case of contemporary Morocco, we see a surprising convergence between the interests of the Amazigh culture movement and those of the Moroccan state. It is, without a doubt, true that Amazigh- and Berber-identifying scholars and activists in Morocco have pushed back against the historical and cultural narratives that underpinned earlier formulations of Moroccan identity—and, in particular, against the vaunted Arab-Islamic identity that was championed by Moroccan nationalists in the colonial and post-independence periods. Nevertheless, it is also true that ideas that first emerged within the fold of the Amazigh culture movement have increasingly been adopted (some might even say coopted) by the Moroccan state, especially under the reign of King Muhammad VI, who ascended to the throne in 1999.

An interesting site for examining the convergence of the Amazigh culture movement and Moroccan state culture is the career and works of Muhammad Shafiq (Mohamed Chafik, b. 1926), often hailed as "the dean of the Amazigh culture movement."[98] As a young man, Shafiq received his secondary education at Tariq b. Ziyad High School (Lycée Tarik Ibn Ziyad) in Azrou, before pursuing higher education at the Collège d'Azrou, an institution founded by the French Protectorate to educate a new class of Francophone Berber elites.[99] Shafiq and other members of the first generation of graduates from the Collège d'Azrou would go on to play leading roles in the Amazigh movement in Morocco.[100] In the 1960s and 1970s, Shafiq held a number of prominent positions in the Moroccan government, eventually becoming the director of the

Royal College, where he taught future king Muhammad VI.[101] At the same time, Shafiq emerged as a leading advocate for the preservation of the Amazigh language and cultural heritage in Morocco. He contributed to this cause with scholarly articles on the Amazigh language and with a number of highly visible public initiatives.[102] In 1978, in the face of growing debates about the status of the Amazigh language in Morocco, the Moroccan Ministry of Interior commissioned Shafiq to write a report on the issue. In his report, Shafiq asserted that familiarity with the Amazigh language was a national necessity for all sectors of Moroccan society because the language was central to the heritage of all Moroccans.[103]

In November 1980, King Hassan II raised Shafiq's stature even further by naming him to Morocco's most prestigious scholarly body: the Moroccan Royal Academy (officially known as the Academy of the Kingdom of Morocco).[104] During the same year, Shafiq joined forces with a small group of fellow graduates from the Collège d'Azrou to found the Amazigh Cultural Association (Association Culturelle Amazighe), the first Moroccan association to carry the term *Amazigh* in its name.[105] The association's main activity was to publish the bimonthly journal *Amazigh,* devoted to discussions of Amazigh language and culture.[106] From his prominent perch as a member of Morocco's most prestigious academic body and as an editor of Morocco's first journal devoted to Amazigh issues, Shafiq quickly became the leading voice in public discussions about Amazigh identities and the Amazigh language in Morocco. These efforts culminated with Shafiq's appointment as the first director of Morocco's Royal Institute of Amazigh Culture (IRCAM, in its French acronym), which was created by King Muhammad VI in 2001.[107]

A brief survey of Shafiq's publications and activities between 1980 and 2001 brings into relief how Shafiq and his colleagues in the Amazigh culture movement have worked to reimagine the relationship between Amazigh identity and Moroccan identity and to propose new historical narratives that center Imazighen in Moroccan and Mediterranean history. Although al-Andalus is not usually front and center in these efforts, it is also not far from view. Indeed, Shafiq and other North African intellectuals have taken up the banner of the "Berber al-Andalus," propelling it into the twenty-first century with a bold and more assertive vision of the fundamental contributions that Berbers / Imazighen made to al-Andalus and its cultural legacy.

Shafiq piloted many of his ideas about Berber identity and Moroccan history in the lecture that he delivered upon his entry to the Moroccan Royal Academy in November 1980. The speech was later published in French translation in the journal *Amazigh* in 1981.[108] In the lecture, Shafiq threaded the needle of defending a proud and distinctive Berber identity, while stressing that such an identity does not pose a conflict to Islam, the ʿAlawi dynasty, or other pillars of contemporary Morocco's political order.

Shafiq's lecture placed particular emphasis on language as the central pillar of Berber identity. He said that Hassan II selected him for his seat in the Moroccan Royal Academy because the king wanted "to honor the Berber language, a fundamental element, if there is one, of our cultural personality." Likewise, Shafiq credited Hassan II with "the valorization and defense of our language and our Berber patrimony" and with safeguarding "our Moroccan authenticity."[109] All these statements suggest an intimate, almost essential, relationship between language and identity. They also revolve around an elastic use of the first-person plural possessive "our." Shafiq slips back and forth, in his speech, from imagining a Berber collective "we" to imagining a Moroccan collective "we." Indeed, the thrust of the speech was to assert that there should be little or no space between the Berber "we" and the Moroccan "we." In this spirit, Shafiq told his fellow members of the Royal Academy: "That the Berber language continues to live and prosper, gentlemen, is for *us* a subject of pride because it constitutes the oldest element of the cultural heritage that was bequeathed to *us* by *our* ancestors . . . Working in harmony with Arabic, it contributes to refining the religious conscience of *our* co-citizens, just as it once contributed to expanding the teachings of Islam in Europe and Africa."[110] Relying again on an elastic use of the first-person plural, Shafiq evokes Berber ancestors ("our ancestors") who have bequeathed a cultural heritage to all Moroccans, regardless of their ethnic identification. He calls on his Moroccan colleagues (many of whom identified as Arab) to claim the pre-Islamic Berber peoples as their ancestors and to claim the Berber language as part of their identity. Shafiq's call not only rests on the Berbers' long-standing presence in North Africa, but also on their fundamental contributions to Islam in North Africa. Indeed, he claims that the Berber language, working hand in hand with Arabic, helped spread "the teachings of Islam in Europe and Africa."

This last point allowed Shafiq to address the subject of al-Andalus head-on. Using the Berber language as his pivot, Shafiq turned to address the case of Tariq b. Ziyad, saying: "I lean strongly toward believing that Tariq b. Ziyad delivered his famous speech in Berber, since his soldiers were all neophytes of Islam who must only have had a very rudimentary knowledge of the language of the Prophet. It was the historians who were later responsible for transposing his famous harangue into Arabic."[111] With this assertion, Shafiq rescued Tariq b. Ziyad from a long tradition of Moroccan scholarship, going back to ʿAbd Allah Gannun, that had held up Tariq's speech as evidence of the cultural unity of Moroccans under the twin banners of Arabness and Islam. In contrast, Shafiq used Tariq's speech to place Morocco and al-Andalus under the banner of Berberness. That is, he held up Tariq's speech as a cultural document that attests to the long-standing importance of the Berber language on both sides of the Strait of Gibraltar.

Shafiq's lecture at the Moroccan Royal Academy laid the groundwork for the ideas that Shafiq would pursue in later works, including his groundbreaking study of Amazigh history, *Lamha ʿan thalatha wa-thalathin qarnan min tarikh al-Amazighiyyin* (*A Brief Survey of Thirty-Three Centuries of Amazigh History*), first published in Arabic in 1989 and then republished, with English and Spanish translations, by the Royal Institute of Amazigh Culture in the first decade of the twenty-first century. The book's title indicates Shafiq's gradual shift away from the term *Berber* and toward the term *Amazigh*.[112] Like his lecture at the Royal Academy, Shafiq's book on Amazigh history stresses that Imazighen have been present in North Africa, with a distinct cultural identity, for millennia. The book also underlines the centrality of language for Amazigh identity. In the book's introduction, Shafiq writes: "Today, an Amazigh's identification document is his ability to speak the language of Ẓ [i.e., the Amazigh language] or to sympathize with it."[113] Adhering to this focus on language, Shafiq surveys a long line of famous cultural figures who spoke variants of Amazigh.

Notably, many of the figures surveyed in Shafiq's book are ones who worked to bridge North Africa and the Iberian Peninsula, creating a zone of Amazigh cultural influence that extends across the Mediterranean. For instance, Shafiq repeats his claim, first advanced in his speech at the Moroccan Royal Academy, that Tariq b. Ziyad spoke in Amazigh when he delivered his famous speech on the eve of the conquest of al-Andalus.[114] Likewise, Shafiq notes that Yusuf b. Tashfin, who led the Almoravid conquest of al-Andalus, "spoke only Amazigh."[115] Continuing in this vein, Shafiq reminds the reader that Amazigh was the language of the court during the early Almohad period and that the first

Almohad caliph ʿAbd al-Muʾmin "would write his religious letters and would deliver his Friday sermons in Amazigh."[116] With these observations, Shafiq marks his distance from the work of any earlier generation of Moroccan scholars who had celebrated the Almoravids and the Almohads by highlighting their contributions to Arabic-language culture. Shafiq, in contrast, underlines their cultural and linguistic specificity as Imazighen who spoke Amazigh.[117]

For Shafiq, language is not the only point of contact between Imazighen and al-Andalus. His survey of the "Amazigh dynasties" includes both dynasties based in North Africa, such as the Almohads, and ones based in al-Andalus, such as the Zirids of Granada and the Banu Dhi al-Nun of Toledo (eleventh century CE).[118] Likewise, his survey of "Amazigh intellectual production" mentions cultural figures who were born in al-Andalus, such as Abu Hayyan al-Gharnati (d. 1344), a renowned grammarian born in Granada (to whose name Shafiq affixes the adjective *al-barbarī*, "the Berber").[119] In sum, Shafiq's work highlights the unique role that Imazighen played as the agents who unified North Africa and al-Andalus, from the time of Tariq b. Ziyad to the heyday of Nasrid Granada.

The publication of Shafiq's influential survey of Amazigh history came on the eve of a period of tectonic shifts in the relationship between the Amazigh culture movement and the North African states, especially Morocco. The 1990s witnessed the creation of several Amazigh-language journals and the emergence of various local and international organizations that advocated for Amazigh identity and culture—including the Paris-based World Amazigh Congress.[120] Riding this wave of Amazigh activism, a group of 229 writers, artists, professors, and businesspeople, led by Muhammad Shafiq, came together in March 2000 to issue a "Berber Manifesto," in French, calling on the Moroccan government and all Moroccans to recognize and affirm Morocco's Amazighness (*amazighité*). The manifesto is, in Bruce Maddy-Weitzman's assessment, "a core text for the modern Amazigh identity project, laying out a coherent historical narrative that stands in sharp contrast to the official Moroccan one."[121]

The central theme of the Berber Manifesto is that Morocco has undergone a systematic erasure of its Amazigh identity. The authors speak directly to this theme in the preamble to the Manifesto, where they write: "The disavowal, voluntary or involuntary, of Morocco's Amazighness—that is, of its Berberness—seriously compromises our future."[122] The preamble goes on to offer an account of the historical, political, and social conditions that made possible such a "disavowal" of Morocco's Amazighness, placing particular blame on the Arabization policies pursued by the Moroccan nationalist movement at the end of the colonial period and the beginning of the post-independence period. The authors of the Manifesto assert that, despite the long-standing efforts to suppress Morocco's Amazigh identity, "The Berbers will not renounce their Berberness [*sa berbérité*], nor will they stop until Morocco's Amazighness is officially recognized."[123] The Manifesto then concludes with nine demands for the Moroccan authorities, including the demand that the Berber language (described as "our original national language") be recognized as an official language in Morocco and that the Moroccan school curriculum be revised to include the Berber language and a new emphasis on Berber contributions to Moroccan history.

The Almoravid and Almohad dynasties figure prominently in the Berber Manifesto—both in its explicit demands and in the historical imaginary that underpins its defense of Morocco's *amazighité*. Under the demand that Moroccan schools offer instruction in the Amazigh language, the authors note that such a reform would have deep precedents in Morocco. "Morocco itself," they write, "at the apogee of its flowering, was not monolingual. If Arabic was the language of writing during the Almohad era, Amazigh continued to make its presence felt as the language of communication at the caliph's court and in daily life, and even as the language of the call to prayer."[124] In other words, the authors of the Manifesto align their demands for educational reform with the precedent of the Almohad empire, noting that Amazigh was the language of the court at the time of Morocco's maximum splendor.

The Manifesto's authors pursue a similar strategy when they demand that the history curriculum in Moroccan schools be revised to reflect a new emphasis on Amazigh contributions. Under this demand (the fifth in their Manifesto), they accuse "Moroccan pan-Arabists" of distorting Moroccan history in order "to belittle the historical role of the Imazighen . . . and to exalt excessively that of the Arabs."[125] The primary example that they adduce to illustrate this problem is the negative portrayal of Yusuf b. Tashfin, the Almoravid leader, in writings by Arab-identifying scholars. Regarding this issue, the Manifesto's authors write:

> Arabism, among us, has gone too far, alas, in falsifying our history. Its cultural proponents chose the city of Marrakesh, in 1995, as the place to convene in a conference and to curse the memory of Yusuf b. Tashfin,

the founder of Marrakesh, the very same person who bequeathed to us the first great outline of the political map of our country. The Middle Eastern champions of Arabism, spilling their bile, hurled every epithet at him, overjoying the Moroccan hosts, who shared their hostility toward Berbers. Yusuf's great crime, in their eyes, was that of tyrannizing Arabness in the person of al-Mu'tamid ibn 'Abbad, a little Andalusian king [*roitelet andalou*] who was deposed and exiled to Morocco because of his famous inability to stand up to the emerging Reconquista.[126]

The immediate target of this complaint is a conference held in Marrakesh. But the authors of the Manifesto are also tapping into a long tradition of writing about Berbers in al-Andalus, a tradition in which Yusuf b. Tashfin and the Almoravids have often been portrayed as the nadir of Andalusi history and as the enemies of the refined, urbane culture that emerged in al-Andalus under Arab rule. Responding defiantly to this tradition, the authors of the Berber Manifesto venture that if Yusuf had failed to intervene in al-Andalus, al-Mu'tamid and the other *taifa* kings would have delivered "a Muslim land to implacable enemies."[127] 'Abd Allah Gannun had already advanced a similar defense of Yusuf b. Tashfin in *al-Nubugh al-maghribi*. What is new here is that the authors of the Berber Manifesto, unlike Gannun, couch their defense of Yusuf in an assertive celebration of Amazigh identity and in a coherent narrative that places Imazighen at the center of Moroccan history and credits them with the survival of al-Andalus after the eleventh century.

The Berber Manifesto appeared during the first year of Muhammad VI's reign, a period in which the Amazigh culture movement has enjoyed increased support from the Moroccan government. An early and highly visible sign of this support was the creation of the Royal Institute of Amazigh Culture (IRCAM), whose mission is, in its own words, "to safeguard and promote Amazigh language and culture in all of its forms and expressions."[128] Among its many projects, the IRCAM has played a leading role in standardizing the Amazigh language, a process that has included the controversial decision to adopt the ancient Tifinagh alphabet as the official script for writing in Amazigh in public settings.[129] The IRCAM has also emerged as a major setting and patron for scholarship on Amazigh culture and history, organizing and funding numerous conferences and publications on the topic. As the IRCAM's public profile has grown, the Amazigh culture movement has continued to receive support and institutional backing from other corners. One indicator of this trend is the preamble to the new Moroccan constitution, ratified in 2011. It states that Moroccan national identity is "forged through the convergence of its Arab-Islamic, Amazigh, and Saharan-Hassani components," while being "nourished and enriched by its African, Andalusi, Hebraic, and Mediterranean tributaries."[130] As this statement indicates, Moroccan state discourse has shifted, in recent years, away from its earlier emphasis on a unitary Arab-Islamic identity and toward a new emphasis on cultural, ethnic, and linguistic pluralism. All of these political and institutional forces have converged to produce new understandings of how Amazigh history intersects with the history and cultural legacy of al-Andalus.

An eloquent illustration of this convergence is a conference that took place in Fez in July 2013 under the title "Amazighness and al-Andalus" (*al-Amāzīghiyya wa-l-Andalus*).[131] The conference was sponsored by the IRCAM along with several other local and national organizations. One of the co-sponsors, the BMCE Foundation, was represented at the conference by its president, Dr. Leila Mezian, who has also spearheaded several initiatives to promote the Amazigh heritage in Spain, including an endowed chair in Amazigh culture at Granada's Euro-Arab Foundation and the recent exhibit at the Alhambra on "Zirid Granada and the Berber Universe."[132] The main organizer of the Fez conference was Moha Ennaji (Muha al-Naji, b. 1953), a linguist who has published extensively on Amazigh and Arabic linguistics, as well as on issues related to gender in North Africa. In his introduction to the published proceedings of the conference, Ennaji writes that the purpose of the event "was not to cry over the ruins nor to return to the past, but rather to rehabilitate Amazigh culture in its relationship with al-Andalus."[133] The conference's aim was, thus, one of recovery work: to recover the cultural contributions of Imazighen to al-Andalus and to restore Amazigh culture to its rightful place in the story of al-Andalus.

The conference began with a provocative keynote lecture titled "The Berberness of al-Andalus" ("Berbérité d'al-Andalous") by the Tunisian French poet, novelist, and public intellectual Abdelwahab Meddeb (1946–2014).[134] At the beginning of the lecture, Meddeb signaled that his focus would be "the major role of the Berbers in the Andalusian feat [*le fait andalou*] and how it seems to me that this major role has been hidden."[135] Meddeb then acknowledged a major obstacle standing in the way of his focus: he noted that all of the expressions that are conventionally used to describe al-Andalus occlude the Berber contribution. To illustrate this point, he cited expressions like "Arabo-Islamic Andalusia" (*Andalousie arabo-islamique*), "Arabo-Andalusian music" (*musique arabo-andalouse*), and "the Spain of three cultures: Islamic, Christian, and Jewish." Taking stock of these expressions, Meddeb concluded, "In all these names, the Berber elements are hidden."[136] Meddeb's point, here, is simple but profound: the language that we have to talk about al-Andalus is inadequate; it systematically erases Berbers by subsuming them under other categories ("Islamic," "Arabic," and so on). The result of this practice, as Meddeb would suggest in his lecture, is a suppression of the Berber role in al-Andalus. Building from this point, Meddeb argued that Berbers played a "major role in the Andalusian adventure from the beginning," and that they played an especially prominent role under the Almoravid and Almohad empires, which he describes as "Berber glories."[137]

While acknowledging the importance of the Almoravids and the Almohads, Meddeb reserved his most effusive praise for another Berber polity in al-Andalus: Zirid Granada. He held up Zirid Granada as a landmark of Berber civilization and power in al-Andalus, calling it "the most spectacular principality of the *taifa* kingdoms" and "the most powerful *taifa* from the civilizational point of view, as well as from the military and political point of view."[138] The basis of this grandeur was, according to Meddeb, the Zirids' cultivation of culture and interfaith cooperation. On this point, Meddeb told the audience in Fez, "The reason I insist on this period is that this moment was not only one of high civilization but was also a witness to the period of the most spectacular glory that the Jews had known."[139] To back up this claim, Meddeb pointed to the case of "the famous Samuel b. Naghrila, the Jew and poet," who served as an important minister under the Zirids.[140] Meddeb remarked that the cultural and political achievements of Jewish figures in Zirid Granada, such as Samuel b. Naghrila, were not only "unheard of and astonishing" but were also "a unique case in what concerns the Jews of the diaspora before modern times."[141]

As these quotes illustrate, Meddeb identifies "high civilization" and interfaith cooperation as the touchstones of Zirid Granada and, more broadly, of Berber culture in al-Andalus. What is striking about his approach is that it largely mimics the ideas and attributes that have frequently been used to describe Umayyad Cordoba. In particular, Meddeb seems to evoke the idea of *convivencia,* while transferring it from Umayyad Cordoba to Zirid Granada—that is, from an Arab dynasty in al-Andalus to a Berber dynasty in al-Andalus. There are several indications that Meddeb had the idea of *convivencia* in mind. For example, in his description of Zirid Granada, Meddeb referred to the work of American scholar María Rosa Menocal, one of the foremost proponents of the *convivencia* narrative.[142] He also asserted that, "The Zirid of Granada represents the notion of the tolerant prince *par excellence.*"[143] In short, Meddeb depicted Zirid Granada as a place of exceptional tolerance. He insisted on this idea, despite acknowledging that the Jewish community of Zirid Granada suffered a massacre in 1066.[144] Through his positive portrayal of Jewish life in Zirid Granada, Meddeb appropriated a historical narrative that is commonly associated with Arab Umayyad culture and reassigned it to a Berber dynasty in al-Andalus. Several other participants at the Fez conference would follow Meddeb's lead, emphasizing that tolerance and openness to others were defining characteristics of Amazigh culture in al-Andalus.[145]

Meddeb also identified other elements of a specifically *Berber* cultural heritage in al-Andalus. In particular, he pointed to architecture, saying:

> I would add another element that is a symbol of civilization and that I think must dare to be called a Berber creation: it is Islamo-Moorish architecture, which is, before all else, Berber, and before all else, Amazigh, and that should absolutely be claimed as such by those who are looking to construct Amazigh identity—because it is an identity that is under construction and in the making [*en devenir*] and one that needs a memory and a history.[146]

According to Meddeb, the architecture of al-Andalus is "before all else, Berber." To substantiate this claim, Meddeb cites the examples of "the three sisters . . . the famous Giralda, the Hassan Tower, and the Kutubiyya of Marrakesh, which are pure masterpieces of the highest architectural intelligence."[147] For Meddeb, then, the three famous Almohad minarets are not merely signs of the cultural unity between North Africa and al-Andalus; they are also expressions of a specifically Berber or Amazigh cultural sensibility.

Meddeb evokes the three Almohad minarets (or "sisters") as emblems of a Berber-centered understanding of al-Andalus, but he also emphasizes their role in the construction of an Amazigh identity in the present. As Meddeb suggests, collective identity projects need "a memory and a history." Such projects look to the past to justify the claims of the present and to buttress the projects of the future. Meddeb's evocation of Almohad architecture illustrates this dynamic beautifully. Meddeb stresses that the minarets of Seville, Rabat, and Marrakesh are Amazigh and "should absolutely be claimed as such by those who are looking to construct Amazigh identity." In other words, he suggests that the Almohad minarets offer a usable past to the contemporary Amazigh culture movement. They are the materials from which the Amazigh culture movement can construct its identity, an identity whose foundations are, fittingly, architectural and monumental, and one whose full realization is on the horizon—or, in Meddeb's words, "en construction et en devenir."

Conclusion

Meddeb's lecture provides a helpful point of conclusion for this chapter because it illustrates the increasingly transnational dimension of the "Berber al-Andalus," a discourse that has transcended its original affiliation with the Moroccan nationalist movement and has morphed into an ideologically diverse project that unites heterogeneous actors and institutions in North Africa and Europe. In Meddeb's lecture, we find the case of a Tunisian-born writer speaking in French to an audience in Morocco about a cultural legacy that encompasses Granada, Seville, Rabat, and Marrakesh. Such a mapping eludes the gravitational pull of the Moroccan nationalist movement, with its emphasis on Morocco's Arab-Islamic identity. Yet the fact that Meddeb's lecture took place in a conference sponsored by the IRCAM indicates that the Moroccan state is also asserting its role in the ongoing efforts to remap the relationship between Amazighness and al-Andalus.

A similarly diverse and transnational map emerges if we return to the example with which this chapter opened: the recent Alhambra exhibit on "Zirid Granada and the Berber Universe." There, a team of Spanish and Moroccan scholars, working with the Dr. Leila Mezian Foundation and a host of Spanish and European institutions, organized a tribute to Berber culture in one of the most emblematic sites of the Andalusi heritage. Notably, Arabic was totally absent from the exhibit; all of the exhibit's signage was in Spanish, English, and Amazigh (in the Tifinagh script revived by the IRCAM). This curatorial choice was hardly neutral or haphazard. It must be interpreted as a nod to the Amazigh culture movement, which has placed supreme emphasis on the Amazigh language as the primary repository of Amazigh identity. Indeed, the curators echoed this emphasis when they wrote, in the exhibition brochure, "Amazigh identity(ies) take shape today, first and foremost, in language."[148] In other words, the exhibit highlighted the linguistic and cultural specificity of Imazighen, rejecting previous efforts to subsume Amazigh culture (and the Amazigh al-Andalus) under the umbrella of Arabic culture.

If the Arab al-Andalus is an imaginary that runs on an east-west axis, from Damascus to Cordoba, then the Berber al-Andalus is an imaginary that operates on a south-north loop, running a relay between North Africa and Europe. In the first wave of efforts to reimagine North African contributions to al-Andalus, the Moroccan nation, as embodied by the Moroccan nationalist movement, was the hero of the story. In the second wave, brought forth by the emergence of the Amazigh culture movement, the national imaginary has given way to an ethnolinguistic one, which prioritizes Amazighness. Though grounded in North Africa, the second wave is transnational in scope, with significant openings for the North African diaspora in Europe. Though rooted in a celebration of the Amazigh language, the second wave is multilingual and often speaks in French, Spanish, or other European languages. Though revisionist in its leanings, the Berber al-Andalus has often relied on long-standing ideas about al-Andalus, including the celebration of interfaith tolerance. Until recently, the "Berber al-Andalus" was a cultural vision that did not enjoy much representation in European and Middle Eastern institutions, which have historically placed more weight on the cultural legacy of Umayyad al-Andalus. The recent Alhambra exhibit, set in one of Spain's premier tourism destinations, is evidence that the debates that have been brewing in North Africa for nearly a century are now being reflected in Andalusi heritage sites in Spain. Likewise, the exhibit shows that Amazigh / Berber activists and scholars are increasingly demanding a place in public conversations about the legacy of al-Andalus.

3

The Feminist al-Andalus

In an upscale residential neighborhood in Casablanca, Morocco's bustling commercial capital, there is a high school named Wallada (Figure 3.1). Inside the front gate, in a paved courtyard with pruned eucalyptus trees, there is a marble plaque explaining that the school is named after "Wallada, the daughter of the Umayyad caliph al-Mustakfi bi-llah, the ruler of al-Andalus."[1] The plaque also offers a brief biographical sketch of Wallada: "She was born around the year 384 of the hijra [ca. 994 CE], and she was a literary princess and poet. She founded a literary salon where the writers of al-Andalus would gather for literary, creative, and intellectual competitions, in which she attained a great standing." Wallada High School, named after a famous female poet from al-Andalus, was founded in 1968 as a secondary school for girls. Its first director was Khanatha Binnuna (born ca. 1943), a writer and pioneer in the Moroccan feminist movement, who, a few years before assuming her role at the school, founded *Shuruq* (Dawn), the first Moroccan cultural journal for and by women.[2] Binnuna served as the director of Wallada High School from its foundation until the early 2000s. Under Binnuna's watch the school's enrollment grew to more than 2,000 female students. Today the school is co-ed and sits in a prosperous neighborhood alongside several cafés, a bookstore, a Pizza Hut, a Timberlake dealer, and a Moroccan taco chain called Tacos de Lyon. The neighborhood surrounding the school today reflects Casablanca's enmeshment in the tastes and brands of a globalized economy. But the school's name and the plaque in the school's courtyard outline a different form of transnational affiliation: they link the school and its students to al-Andalus—and, in particular, to Wallada, a "literary princess" from al-Andalus.

Half a world away, Wallada made another public appearance—this time, in the streets of Melbourne, Australia. There, on December 4, 2016, the Saudi

Figure 3.1. Entrance to Wallada High School in Casablanca. Eric Calderwood.

visual artist Ms. Saffaa debuted a mural titled "I Am My Own Guardian. Brunswick East. 2016" (Figure 3.2).[3] The work was part of an international protest campaign against Saudi Arabia's guardianship laws, which placed severe restrictions on Saudi women by requiring them to seek the permission of a male guardian before engaging in any of a wide range of activities, such as marriage or travel.[4] The mural "I Am My Own Guardian" was billed as "a tribute to Saudi women" and was the result of a collaboration between Ms. Saffaa and a handful of female artists scattered across the globe, including Saudi-born artist Balquis Al-Rashed and US artist Molly Crabapple. The work featured portraits of women, such as Saudi activist Samar Badawi, alongside short texts in Arabic and English. On the right side of the mural, there was a rectangular box of text in red Arabic calligraphy, reading, "I am a Saudi Citizen. I am free. I am independent." On the left side of the mural, above a bright pink stenciling of the words "Radical Muslim," there was an image of a young woman sporting a half-shaved head and a defiant look

Figure 3.2. *I Am My Own Guardian. Brunswick East. 2016.* Mural created by
Ms. Saffaa in collaboration with Khadija Wilson, Molly Crabapple, Dr. Janelle
Evans, Balquis AlRashed, Aseel Tayeh, Miniature Malekpour, Hayley
Pigram, Clancy Gibson, AliciaNArabia. Under the patronage of Hana Assafiri.
Ms. Saffaa.

(Figure 3.3). The image, based on a drawing by Molly Crabapple, came with
a caption in Arabic. The caption was none other than the first two lines of
a famous poem by Wallada:

> I am, by God, fit for lofty things,
> And I go my way with head held high.[5]

As legend would have it, Wallada had these lines embroidered in gold in the
right hem of her robe.[6] In modern times, many scholars have pointed to these
lines as evidence of Wallada's independent and rebellious spirit.[7] In the context of Ms. Saffaa's mural, Wallada's words were linked, by juxtaposition, to
the defiant actions of the female activists and artists who were standing in
opposition to Saudi Arabia's guardianship laws. In other words, Wallada's
poem served, in the mural, as an anthem for female activists—and, in

Figure 3.3. Detail from *I Am My Own Guardian. Brunswick East. 2016.* Ms. Saffaa.

particular, Saudi and Muslim female activists—fighting for women's rights in the twenty-first century.[8]

Here, then, are two scenes, separated by continents and united by a single figure, Wallada, a poet from medieval Cordoba. What ties these two scenes together? And how are they related to a broader network of ideas about al-Andalus? As will become clear over the course of this chapter, Wallada High School in Casablanca and the Wallada mural in Melbourne are both affiliated with a process of cultural memory that has been unfolding for over a century, linking stories about al-Andalus with debates about women in the Arab and Muslim worlds.

Since the late nineteenth century, a long line of female writers, scholars, and artists have turned to al-Andalus as a source of inspiration, imagining al-Andalus as a place of exceptional freedom, creativity, and cultural achievement for Muslim and Arab women. I call this wide-ranging discourse and imaginary "the feminist al-Andalus." In what follows, I trace its genealogy and evolution, placing particular emphasis on the voices of Arab and Muslim women who have used the memory of al-Andalus to debate gender politics in the present. As I introduce this phenomenon, I find myself oscillating between the adjectives "Muslim" and "Arab" for a few reasons. First, the diverse texts and projects that I'm grouping under the heading of the "feminist al-Andalus" have been framed in both religious and ethnic terms—that is, as stories about *Muslim* women or as stories about *Arab* women. Second, the texts analyzed in this chapter all share a focus on questions of gender, but many of them also place debates about gender into dialogue with other identity categories—primarily, though not exclusively, religion and ethnicity. As such, the "feminist al-Andalus," as case study, offers an opportunity to revisit some of the identity debates I explored in Chapters 1 and 2, but with a more explicit emphasis on questions of gender.

The cultural texts and projects that have, over the last century or so, contributed to building a feminist understanding of al-Andalus have come from a diverse range of ideological, cultural, and geographic positions. What they share in common, though, is the belief that the women of al-Andalus should serve as models for Muslim and Arab women living in the twentieth and twenty-first centuries. To study the diverse yet cohesive discourse that I'm calling the "feminist al-Andalus," I have adopted a broad and flexible definition of feminism. Following the lead of Lila Abu-Lughod and other scholars who have worked on feminism in the Middle East, I take the word *feminism* to refer not only to organized women's movements but also to a wide range of projects that have as an explicit goal or necessary foundation the social, political, and cultural advancement of women.[9]

One of the reasons al-Andalus has proven especially productive for feminist projects in the Middle East and North Africa is that it has helped writers and artists from these regions to articulate an indigenous or "authentic" Arab or Muslim feminism, independent from the history of feminist movements in Europe and the United States.[10] It has also helped them to counter long-standing European and American prejudices about the supposedly subordinate status of women in Muslim and Arab societies. To understand this point, one must keep in mind that women's rights served as one of the most common justifications for European (and, subsequently, American) imperialism in the Middle East and North Africa. From the missionaries and colonial officials of the nineteenth century to the technocrats and talking heads of the Bush-era "War on Terror," European and American writers and public figures have, as Abu-Lughod has shown, long proclaimed the need to "save" Muslim women—from oppression, from the veil, from Muslim men, and perhaps even from Islam itself.[11] In light of these precedents, feminism (at least in one of its Euro-American forms) has become, in many formerly colonized societies, intimately associated with the legacy of colonialism. Leila Ahmed has summed up this dilemma in the following terms: "Colonialism's use of feminism to promote the culture of the colonizers and undermine native culture has ever since imparted to feminism in non-Western societies the taint of having served as an instrument of colonial domination, rendering it suspect in Arab eyes and vulnerable to the charge of being an ally of colonial interests. That taint has undoubtedly hindered the feminist struggle within Muslim societies."[12] Following Ahmed, many scholars have echoed her assessment, noting that Western powers have, from the nineteenth century to the present, instrumentalized the discourses of feminism and women's rights to justify colonial and imperial enterprises in the Middle East, North Africa, and beyond.[13]

One way out of this bind is to imagine alternative histories and genealogies of feminism that circumvent the legacies and logics of colonialism. For many Muslim and Arab feminists, this has meant looking to the past for examples of women, such as the Cordoban poet Wallada, whose accomplishments demonstrate that there is no incompatibility between Islam and the social, cultural, and political advancement of women. Underlying these efforts is the implicit (and, at times, explicit) claim that feminism is not a program that needs to be imported to the Muslim world from Europe and the United States because feminism has always been stitched into the fabric of Muslim societies. Al-Andalus has played a significant role in this ongoing project of imagining an alternative genealogy of feminism because al-Andalus is one of the most frequently cited examples of a Muslim society that gave rise to an impressive array of female poets, scholars, thinkers, warriors, and rebels. Through imaginative recourse to the memory of al-Andalus, Muslim and Arab writers and artists have, over the past century, anchored their works in an indigenous cultural tradition that predates the history of European colonialism.

Before turning to specific examples of this phenomenon, I would like to acknowledge that there is a long-standing debate among scholars about whether or not women in al-Andalus did, in fact, enjoy a noteworthy or exceptional degree of freedom, social status, and cultural access.[14] Indeed, the position of women in Andalusi society has generated a steady stream of interest from Western scholars since the late nineteenth century.[15] Much of the early scholarship on this question suggested that women in al-Andalus enjoyed freedoms that they did not enjoy elsewhere in the Arab and Muslim worlds. Along these lines, the distinguished French Arabist Henri Pérès wrote in the 1930s: "The Andalusian woman was not the prisoner [recluse] that the rules of Islam would have us see in all Muslim women."[16] Pérès's comment is representative of a broader Orientalist tradition that characterized Islam as a religion that systematically oppresses women.[17]

In recent decades, several scholars have pushed back against the long-standing trope of the "free" or "emancipated" Andalusi woman. Their critique has taken a few forms. Some, like Manuela Marín, have argued that the concepts of "freedom" and "emancipation" are anachronistic and blunt instruments for understanding the diversity and complexity of women's experiences in medieval Andalusi society (a society that itself underwent several changes over eight centuries).[18] Others have observed pointedly that broad generalizations about women in al-Andalus have often hinged on limited and fragmentary evidence and on sources that are almost exclusively concerned with the lives of upper-class women.[19] Beyond this question of evidence, there is an even more pressing question of narrative. In modern scholarship, the women of al-Andalus have been saddled with a heavy burden of representation: their lives and writings are often marshaled as evidence for larger claims or narratives about Muslim women, Arab women, or the distinctions (or not) between Islam and the West. Kamila Shamsie has summed up this problem: "A great deal of the writing about women in al-Andalus is obscured by patriarchal narratives or by a skewed Islam versus the west argument in which al-Andalus is made to stand in for one or the other to further a political agenda."[20] In other words, scholarly debates about women in al-Andalus are often proxies (or smoke screens) for broader debates about the status of women in Islam. In this process, women in al-Andalus lose any glimpse of individuality and become a collective body of evidence whose sole purpose is to sustain larger historical narratives with deep political implications.

I am sympathetic to recent efforts by scholars in my field to push back against an earlier body of scholarship whose celebrations of Andalusi women often came at the expense of all other Muslim societies. I fear, though, that scholars in my field, in their rush to correct the record, might be missing an opportunity to ask a different, though equally valuable, set of questions, such as: Why do the writings and experiences of Andalusi women continue to exercise a hold on our imagination today? What political and cultural work do Andalusi women do in contemporary culture? I am not interested, here, in answering the question of whether or not al-Andalus was a place of exceptional freedom and cultural achievement for women. Instead, I want to know why this idea has proven so compelling and useful for modern-day writers and artists from the Middle East and North Africa—and, in particular, for many female writers and artists from these regions. Put succinctly: Why and how is the memory of al-Andalus productive for thinking about gender politics and feminism (broadly construed)?

In pursuing these questions, I turn to the diverse and far-flung corpus of writings on this topic by Arab and Muslim women writers, from the late nineteenth century to the present. My aim is not to offer an exhaustive account of this large body of work, but instead to identify some key trends within it. In particular, I want to arrive at a genealogy—what Foucault calls a "history of the present"—that allows me to understand and unpack the two scenes that I described at the beginning of this chapter.[21] In other words, I want to know: What are the cultural processes that have made it possible for Khanatha Binnuna, a Moroccan feminist pioneer, to become the principal of a high school named after the Andalusi poet Wallada, or that have made it possible for Ms. Saffaa to use Wallada's poetry in a mural that reflects the struggle for women's rights in twenty-first-century Saudi Arabia? Put differently, I'm asking: What are the histories, narratives, and hopes that these two examples tap in to? And what do they tell us about how al-Andalus functions in the present?

I turn here to genealogy not only as a method but also as a specific way of engaging with the past. Many of the authors and artists whose work I will analyze here have imagined themselves as descendants or metaphorical "daughters" of al-Andalus—they have imagined themselves as part of a cultural lineage that includes al-Andalus and that links the experiences and exploits of Andalusi women to the cultural and political ambitions of women in the present. This genealogical imagination takes several forms. One of the most common is for an author or artist to create a work that pays homage to a famous figure from al-Andalus, like Wallada. Such homages not only identify illustrious figures from the Andalusi past, but they also, in many cases, mold the illustrious women of al-Andalus into cultural matriarchs whose legacy stretches from al-Andalus to the present.

While many modern works revolve around the memory of a real figure from al-Andalus, there have also been many works, especially in recent decades, that have populated al-Andalus with a rich cast of fictional heroines who are scientists, rebels, poets, and adventurers. Perhaps the most famous example is the protagonist of Egyptian novelist Radwa 'Ashur's award-winning novel *Gharnata* (*Granada,* 1994), a work to which I will return later in the chapter. The benefit of such fictional approaches to al-Andalus is that they allow authors, like 'Ashur, to imagine experiences that remain occluded in the historical record. Andalusi sources, as I have already indicated, offer the modern reader, at best, a fragmentary view of women's lives. Literature and other imaginative forms, then, become important tools for understanding the past, responding to the gaps and silences in the archive by imagining stories of what might have been or could have been.[22] If the "feminist al-Andalus" is a project that, ultimately, entails a wholesale reimagining of who feminists are, where they operate, what languages they speak, what religions they practice, and how they live, then literature is a valuable tool for imagining this uncharted territory of feminism.

Daughters of al-Andalus

The feminist al-Andalus is as old as Arab feminism itself. In the 1890s, Egypt witnessed an eruption of writing in Arabic, by both women and men, about women and their position in society, a debate that saturated the public sphere and spilled over to the pages of newspapers, novels, and biographies, as Marilyn Booth has shown in her illuminating studies of the print culture of this period.[23] One of the earliest and most influential female voices in these debates was the writer Zaynab Fawwaz (ca. 1846 or 1860–1914), who was an active contributor to leading newspapers and magazines in Cairo and is best known as the author of a biographical compendium titled *al-Durr al-manthur fi tabaqat rabbat al-khudur* (Pearls scattered: Classes of ladies of cloistered spaces, ca. 1894 / 1895). Booth describes this work as "the very first lengthy work in Arabic of women's history" and "the first glimmer of Arab and Muslim feminist historiography."[24] Fawwaz's work (hereafter, *Pearls Scattered*) contains 453 biographical sketches of famous women (the "pearls" of the book's title), whose lives span a vast array of historical and cultural contexts. Her diverse subjects run the gamut from Cleopatra to Queen Victoria.[25] Fawwaz included, among her diverse cast of subjects, women from the Middle East, Central and South Asia, Europe, and North America, but she gave pride of place to Arab and Muslim women, who make up the majority of her "pearls."[26] Of particular interest for my argument is the fact that Fawwaz devoted more than two dozen of her biographical sketches to women from al-Andalus, all of them poets and many of them known for accomplishments in other fields of learning and culture.

Many of the Andalusi women profiled by Fawwaz would become, over the ensuing decades, protagonists in feminist and women-centered understandings of the Andalusi legacy. These figures include the ever-present Wallada; the Cordoban poet 'A'isha bint Ahmad (d. 1009 CE); Buthayna, the daughter of al-Mu'tamid ibn 'Abbad (eleventh century CE); and many others.[27] Most of Fawwaz's information about Andalusi women—and, indeed, much of her language in these biographical sketches—is copied directly from one source: al-Maqqari's seventeenth-century Andalusi compendium *Nafh al-tib*, which was circulating in fin de siècle Cairo thanks to an edition published by the government press at Bulaq, Cairo, in 1862.[28] Fawwaz, in other words, was not offering new information about women from al-Andalus. What she was doing, instead, was inserting the existing information in a new narrative framework, one that placed female figures from al-Andalus in a long line of illustrious women. Through this narrative framework, Fawwaz helped to create, among her readers, a female historical consciousness—an awareness of the significant role that women had played in Middle Eastern, Arab, and Muslim societies from antiquity until Fawwaz's lifetime in the late nineteenth century.[29]

Fawwaz's treatment of Wallada demonstrates how she connects the lives of Andalusi women to Arab and Muslim women who came before them, as well as to women living and working in the late nineteenth century. Fawwaz introduces Wallada with rhyming and rhythmic prose that she copies from al-Maqqari:

> She was unique in her age, the center of attention in her time [*kānat wāḥidat zamānihā, al-mushār ilayhā fī awānihā*], gracious in conversation, praised widely, and famous for her respectability and virtue. A woman of letters [*adība*] and poet, she was eloquent in diction and talented at poetry. She would vie with the poets and compete with the men of letters, surpassing the best of them. She lived a long life and never married.[30]

According to this sketch, Wallada was an accomplished poet and a model of eloquence and refinement. A keyword in Fawwaz's portrait of Wallada is *adab,* a polysemic term whose meanings include "literature," "etiquette," and "cultural refinement."[31] Wallada was, in Fawwaz's view, a woman who embodied the ideals of *adab,* in every sense of the word. Fawwaz also highlights the fact that Wallada did not rely on a powerful husband for her fame, a point that she repeats in other entries on women from al-Andalus.[32]

Crucially, Fawwaz depicts Wallada as a poet who could vie with, and even surpass, the best male writers of her day. Indeed, Fawwaz stresses that Wallada, at the peak of her fame, was the beacon for the men and women of Cordoba's cultural scene. On this point Fawwaz writes, "Her salon [*majlis*] in Cordoba was the gathering place for the city's nobles, and her courtyard was the racetrack for the steeds of poetry and prose. The literary set sought to be guided by the light of her forehead, and the poets and writers fought for the sweetness of her company."[33] Wallada is depicted here as both muse and master of ceremonies, an inspiration for her contemporaries and a cultural standard to which they should aspire. This portrait of Wallada's activities points to what might be a hint of irony in the title of Fawwaz's biographical compendium. Wallada, as described here, could hardly be confused for a "lady of cloistered spaces." On the contrary, Wallada, like many of Fawwaz's "pearls," is out in the public sphere, vying with her male counterparts for prestige and prominence.[34] This mode of conduct is one that Wallada shares with many of the Andalusi women profiled in Fawwaz's *Pearls Scattered.* For instance, in the entry on Maryam bint Ya'qub al-Ansari, a poet who was active in Seville in the eleventh century, Fawwaz writes: "She was at the head of [Seville's] eminences and people of letters . . . She crafted the finest rhetorical figures [*al-badī*] and ravished motifs [*al-maʿānī*] like a lion does its prey . . . She praised kings, encircling them with the necklaces of her panegyrics."[35] Fawwaz's Maryam, like her Wallada, is no meek flower, cowering behind a lattice partition. Instead, both women are, in this telling, plucky wordsmiths basking in the limelight.

After offering a brief sketch of Wallada's life, Fawwaz surveys Wallada's body of work, reproducing most of the Cordoban poet's extant verses, including her famous lines "I am, by God, fit for lofty things, / And I go my way with head held high."[36] In the entry on Wallada, as in the other entries on women from al-Andalus, Fawwaz gives priority to the poet's words, which are quoted at length and with minimal commentary. After all, Fawwaz was, much like al-Maqqari before her, a compiler. But while al-Maqqari's compilation creates a composite image of Andalusi culture, Fawwaz's compilation creates, in the composite, a narrative of female accomplishment. Though billed as a biographical compendium, *Pearls Scattered* is also an anthology of women's voices from across time. Because the work is organized in rough alphabetical order, rather than by chronology or region, it creates subtle juxtapositions and implicit connections between women whose lives were separated by time and space. For instance, Fawwaz's entry on Wallada is preceded by an entry on the poet Wuhayba bt. ʿAbd al-ʿUzza b. ʿAbd Qays (ca. seventh century) and followed by an entry on the Swedish opera singer Christina Nilsson (1843–1921). This organization places Wallada in a chain of creative women stretching from pre-Islamic Arabia to nineteenth-century Scandinavia.

Fawwaz's compendium outlines a vast array of accomplished women stretching across space and time, but it places emphasis on certain networks of affiliation, particularly those that connect Arab and Muslim women. In this vein, Wallada and the other notable women of al-Andalus emerge, in Fawwaz's book, as the standard-bearers for the cultural accomplishments of earlier Arab and Muslim women from the east. For example, Fawwaz compares Wallada favorably to Ulayya bint al-Mahdi (d. 825), a gifted poet from Abbasid Baghdad, when she writes: "It is said: [Wallada] was to the west what ʿUlayya bint al-Mahdi the Abbasid was to the east; but Wallada possessed more beauty, while in refinement, poetry, witty anecdotes [*nawādir*], and cleverness, she was not less than her."[37] This is not the only instance where Fawwaz draws an explicit comparison between a poet from al-Andalus and an illustrious predecessor from the Arab East. In a similar vein, Fawwaz compares the Andalusi poet Hamda bint Ziyad (ca. twelfth century) to al-Khansa', one of the most celebrated poets of the pre-Islamic and early Islamic periods. On this point, Fawwaz writes, in neat, rhyming prose, that Hamda bint Ziyad "was the Khansa' of the west and the poet of al-Andalus, the woman of letters of her age and the wonder of her time [adībat zamānihā wa-gharībat awānihā]."[38] Through these comparisons, Fawwaz draws a line of cultural continuity between pre-Islamic Arabia, Abbasid Baghdad, and al-Andalus, with women in each context passing the baton to their sisters in the next.

For Fawwaz, the women of al-Andalus were not only a bridge between east and west but also a bridge between past and present. Their accomplishments were a standard against which Fawwaz measured the accomplishments of her contemporaries. This movement between past and present is particularly notable in Fawwaz's biographical sketch of her contemporary 'A'isha Taymur (1840–1902), a Turkish-Egyptian poet and prose writer. Fawwaz writes that Taymur was

> a litterateuse virtuous and fine, a wise woman of rational mind, in brilliant skills most refined, writer of prose and the poetic line . . . She emerged as the extraordinary rarity of her age among the people of literary composition and recitation. She left to Wallada no utterance that proved her superior, and to al-Akhyaliyya no domain that showed her worthier. She out-Khansa'd Khansa'.[39]

In this passage Fawwaz extends the chain of cultural continuity to the present. She suggests that her contemporary, 'A'isha Taymur, builds on, and even surpasses, the accomplishments of predecessors from pre-Islamic Arabia (Khansa'), the early Umayyad period (al-Akhyaliyya), and al-Andalus (Wallada). In Fawwaz's women-centered narrative of history, al-Andalus stands, along with the pre-Islamic period and the period of early Islam, as one of the historical moments that gave rise to a host of learned and accomplished women, whose lives and works serve as inspirations for Fawwaz and her contemporaries in late-nineteenth-century Cairo.

Fawwaz's biographical compendium helped launch one of the most popular subgenres of women's writing in Arabic in the early twentieth century: biographies of illustrious women. Thanks in large part to the influence of

Fawwaz's work, biographical sketches of exemplary women became a common feature in the magazines created by and for women in early-twentieth-century Egypt, as Marilyn Booth has shown.[40] One of the leading periodicals to emerge in this scene was *Fatat al-sharq* (Young woman of the East, 1906–1939), a journal founded by Labiba Hashim (1882–1947), a Syrian Christian resident of Egypt.[41] Early in the journal's existence, Hashim launched a regular feature devoted to "Famous Women" (*shahīrāt al-nisā*'). Many of the profiles that appeared in this feature duplicated, or borrowed heavily, from the entries in Fawwaz's *Pearls Scattered*.[42] Given the emphasis that Fawwaz placed on illustrious women from al-Andalus, it is no surprise that Andalusi women also figured in the "Famous Women" column of *Fatat al-sharq,* as well as in similar features in other women's magazines of the period.

A notable example of this trend is an essay that the poet Warda al-Yaziji (1838–1924) published in *Fatat al-sharq* in March 1916, as part of the journal's regular feature on "Famous Women." Al-Yaziji opened the essay with the following straightforward assertion: "In al-Andalus, a number of women poets were famous, and they vied with men."[43] To back up this claim, al-Yaziji offered brief sketches of five distinguished female poets from al-Andalus—from Hassana al-Tamimiyya, who was active during the reign of 'Abd al-Rahman II (r. 822–852), to Umm al-Saʿd bint ʿIsam al-Humayri, who died in Málaga around 1242.[44] All of the Andalusi poets profiled by al-Yaziji also appear in Fawwaz's *Scattered Pearls*. Like her contemporary Fawwaz, al-Yaziji relied on al-Maqqari for her information about these Andalusi women.[45] And like Fawwaz, al-Yaziji reproduced poems by these Andalusi women, thus bringing their voices to the attention of a female readership in early-twentieth-century Cairo.

The sketch of the Cordoban poet ʿAʾisha bint Ahmad illustrates the approach al-Yaziji took to the subject of learned women in al-Andalus. Citing an Andalusi source, al-Yaziji writes of ʿAʾisha bint Ahmad: "There was no one among the noble women of al-Andalus who matched her in knowledge, refinement [*adaban*], eloquence, and poetry. She would write panegyrics to the kings of al-Andalus and would address them in whatever form the occasion demanded. She had beautiful handwriting and made copies of the Qurʾan."[46] For al-Yaziji, then, ʿAʾisha bint Ahmad was the epitome of *adab*—in the dual senses of "literature" and "refinement." She was also, notably, a learned woman of the public sphere who addressed her poetry to kings.

Al-Yaziji is more explicit than her contemporary Fawwaz in drawing a comparison between the women of al-Andalus and the women of her time. Along these lines, al-Yaziji writes:

> Whoever studies the books of history and biographies, and especially the history of al-Andalus, will find references to women poets and authors, and to women who had marvelous verses and prose . . . There is no doubt that if the women of our age were to occupy themselves with literary and intellectual matters, it would compensate for how they spend their lives in trivial matters, external appearances, and vacuous imitation. Geniuses would appear among them, achieving renown and great glory, and perpetuating their names on the pages of time. For, the women of that period [al-Andalus] were not endowed with a more elevated mind than them, or with a richer milieu than them, if only they wished to follow their lead.[47]

In this passage al-Yaziji highlights the accomplishments of Andalusi women and then pivots to the present in order to underline the contrast between the women of al-Andalus and the women of her time. Al-Yaziji does not claim that the women of al-Andalus were endowed with greater talent or sharper minds; instead she claims that Andalusi women were part of a society that encouraged them to turn their attention to *adab*. Al-Yaziji uses the stories of Andalusi women to hold a mirror to her society, and especially to her female peers, in order to decry their absorption in trivial and frivolous pursuits. Al-Yaziji's account of the female poets of al-Andalus is, then, equal parts homage and jeremiad. Al-Yaziji praises the women of al-Andalus, while scolding her contemporaries for not living up to their example.

Al-Yaziji's celebratory essay about the women poets of al-Andalus was noteworthy but not unique in its context. Just two months later, in May 1916, the editors of *Fatat al-sharq* devoted the monthly column on "Famous Women" to Subh (d. 999), the wife of the second Umayyad caliph of al-Andalus, al-Hakam II (r. 961–976).[48] The unsigned article (which is presumably by the journal's editor, Labiba Hashim) refers to Subh as "Sabiha," a variant spelling that appears in some sources.[49] The article praises Subh's learning and refinement (in short, her *adab*), while also highlighting her accomplishments in another domain: the exercise of political power.

Indeed, the article depicts Subh as the de facto ruler of al-Andalus at the time of its greatest cultural and political splendor. Under the title "Sabiha [Subh], queen of al-Andalus," the article begins:

> She [was] the wife of al-Hakam al-Mustansir bi-llah b. 'Abd al-Rahman al-Nasir, king of al-Andalus. And she [was] among the most famous Arab women . . . She possessed vast knowledge, copious refinement, and dazzling beauty. It did not take long before she won the trust and respect of her husband, and he elevated her status and began seeking her counsel on the gravest matters of politics and administration . . . He handed over the reins of power to his wife, Sabiha, when he saw her intelligence and sound judgment. And this mighty woman carried out the assignment exactly as it needed to be done. She worked to reform the condition of the nation [al-umma], to spread learning among all its classes, to organize the army and fleet, and to take all the necessary measures to check any movement that the princes of northern Spain might make.[50]

The Subh depicted here, much like the Andalusi women profiled by Fawwaz and al-Yaziji, is a paragon of knowledge, refinement, and beauty. But this biographical sketch of Subh places the Andalusi subject much more robustly in the public and political arenas. Here, the readers of *Fatat al-sharq* had a chance to marvel at an Andalusi woman who exercised leadership and influence in all spheres of society, from education to the military.

Subh's political acumen and power are, in fact, themes to which the author returns throughout the article. As the author explains, Subh was able to retain the reins of power after the premature death of al-Hakam II because she maneuvered to have her son, Hisham, proclaimed caliph, even though he was not next in line for the position. Subh was appointed Hisham's regent, and in that role, as the article explains, "she began to preside over the councils, participate in negotiations, emit orders, enact laws, organize the armies of land and sea, and work toward spreading learning and developing industry and agriculture throughout the land."[51] Through a string of active verbs, the passage conjures up an image of a Subh who is all action and poise, commanding councils, giving orders, and generally being (as we would say today) "a boss." This portrait of Subh foreshadows another prominent trend in

modern celebrations of Andalusi women: stories that emphasize the political power and leadership that women exercised in al-Andalus.

Fatat al-sharq's profile of Subh also brings to the fore an element that was
present, but more muted, in the works by Fawwaz and al-Yaziji: the cultural
Arabness of Andalusi women. According to the author of the profile in *Fatat
al-sharq*, Subh was "among the most famous Arab women" (*min ashhar nisa'
al-'arab*).[52] This description is noteworthy because Subh was actually of Basque
origin.[53] The author's attribution of an Arab identity to Subh is, in part, an
indication that the author had limited access to sources about the history of
al-Andalus. But it is also a sign of the author's systematic efforts to ascribe
an Arab identity to al-Andalus and its people. In this spirit, the author describes al-Hakam II as a ruler who "strengthened the pillars of the Arab
kingdom in the [Iberian] peninsula."[54] In a similar vein, the author describes
Ibn Abi 'Amir, Subh's powerful ally and rumored lover, as a leader who "raised
the affairs of the Arabs in al-Andalus."[55] Such repeated insistence on the *Arabness* of al-Andalus—even when the claim flies in the face of al-Andalus's
ethnic diversity—is a symptom of *Fatat al-sharq*'s political orientation and
its position within Egyptian society. The journal's editor was, as I have indicated, a Syrian Christian residing in Muslim-majority Egypt. The journal's
articles often emphasized unity among Muslims and Christians.[56] Putting
aside the specific situation of the journal *Fatat al-sharq*, the biographical
sketch of Subh illustrates, more broadly, that the "feminist al-Andalus" is a
political and cultural project that intersects, at times, with the discourse that
I have described as the "Arab al-Andalus" in Chapter 1.

The examples discussed thus far do not, by any means, represent an exhaustive account of the presence of Andalusi women in the emergent women's
press in Egypt at the turn of the twentieth century.[57] Instead, what I hope to
have shown with this selection of examples is that by the early twentieth
century, a certain way of writing about the women of al-Andalus had coalesced among literary elites in the eastern Arab world. This discourse about
Andalusi women would persist and grow over the following decades, taking
on new details but maintaining its core idea: namely, that al-Andalus was a
site of extraordinary achievement for women and an inspiration for Arab and
Muslim women living in the modern period. Over the course of the last
century, this discourse has, at times, been inflected through the lens of Arabness and, at other times, through the lens of Islam. In other words, stories

about women in al-Andalus are sometimes interpreted as stories about Arab women and other times interpreted as stories about Muslim women. (And sometimes the distinction between "Arab" and "Muslim" is blurred.) This ambiguity has proven productive, because it has allowed the discourse about Andalusi women to take hold in a broad range of geographic and cultural contexts, while maintaining distinct emphases and inflections in each context.

The Feminist al-Andalus between Arab and Muslim Identities

Carrying the banner of a pan-Arab identity, Syrian author Salma al-Haffar al-Kuzbari (1923–2006) was one of the writers who led the charge to depict the women of al-Andalus as models for Arab women at the middle of the twentieth century. Al-Haffar al-Kuzbari was born to a wealthy family in Damascus in 1923.[58] Her father was a prominent politician who was exiled from Syria because of his vocal opposition to the French mandate. Al-Haffar al-Kuzbari spent much of her childhood in Beirut, where she received a cosmopolitan education in Arabic and French. Over the course of her career, she would publish in both languages, as well as in Spanish. Her interest in al-Andalus and Spain took off in the early 1960s and persisted until the end of the author's career, leaving a mark on her poetry, her fiction, and her public lectures.[59] Al-Haffar al-Kuzbari moved to Madrid in 1962, when her husband was named the Syrian ambassador to Spain. She arrived in Spain at a moment when the Franco regime was actively promoting Spain's Andalusi heritage in order to forge cultural and political ties with the Arab world.[60] The author's stint in Spain overlapped with that of Syrian poet Nizar Qabbani, who at the time was a counselor to the Syrian embassy in Madrid. Both Syrian writers participated in the World Festival of Arabic Poetry held in Cordoba in 1963, and both worked to link the Andalusi heritage to a pan-Arab cultural identity whose lineage ran from Umayyad Syria to Umayyad Cordoba.[61] Al-Haffar al-Kuzbari was one of many Arab writers of her generation to contribute to this cultural imaginary, but she took it a step further, extending it to debates about Arab women in the past and present.

Al-Haffar al-Kuzbari's ideas about the women of al-Andalus came into focus in a public lecture that she delivered on February 18, 1963, at Madrid's Ateneo, a prestigious cultural institution (Figure 3.4). The lecture was titled

EL ALMA DE NARDO DEL ARABE AN-
DALUZ.—Esta frase de Manuel Machado tiene
mucho que hacer, en la voz y en el aspecto físi-
co, en la manera de decir, de la señora Salma
Haffar de Kuzbari, Embajadora de Siria en España, que ha dado, en el Ateneo, una charla
sobre «La mujer árabe».

Morena, esbelta, de graciosa estatura y vivacidad, Salma Haffar podía pasar por una de esas
andaluzas que tienen la alegre vivacidad del pa-
jarito, y también su ligereza. Ha terminado, pa-
ra mayor similitud bética, hablándonos de la
opinión de su marido. No quería aburrirle.

La conferencia trae un perfume de poetisas.
De la España árabe y del árabe hispánico. Al-
guna anécdota prodigiosa. La de los mamelucos
en Egipto, eligiendo una reina. ¡Oh manes de
Cleopatra! Y los duros abasíes protestando. La
voluntad de Dios —el Islam es un pueblo funda-
mentalmente religioso— ha colocado, cultural-
mente, a la mujer árabe en el mismo camino que
el hombre. Había un perfume delicadamente fe-
menino, quintaesenciadamente femenil, en la
conferencia, tan feminista, pero tan respetuosa
con el varón, señor casi exclusivo de la cultura
y la vida activa, hasta pocos años ha. En Madrid
ha caído muy bien.   ES.

Figure 3.4.   Salma al-Haffar al-Kuzbari at the Ateneo de Madrid. Photograph
published in *La estafeta literaria,* March 2, 1963. Courtesy of the Ateneo de Madrid.

"Influencia de la mujer árabe en nuestra historia" (Influence of the Arab
woman in our history). The lecture was published in Spanish by the Ateneo
in 1963 and was later published in Arabic translation as part of al-Haffar
al-Kuzbari's collection *Fi zilal al-Andalus* (Under the auspices of al-Andalus,
or, more literally, In the shade of al-Andalus, ca. 1971).[62] Early in the lecture,
al-Haffar al-Kuzbari identified her topic as "the Arab woman, her senti-
ments and her unending struggle, from the most distant times, to achieve a

life worthy of her ideals."[63] As this sentence illustrates, al-Haffar al-Kuzbari spoke, in her lecture, of Arab women in the singular—as "the Arab woman." Although the grammatical singular can be used in Spanish (as in Arabic) to talk about an abstract or collective entity, its use in this context also highlights one of al-Haffar al-Kubzari's central contentions: namely, that there is a line of cultural continuity that connects Arab women across time, from antiquity to the present.

In her lecture, al-Haffar al-Kuzbari traced a historical narrative that began in the ancient Near East and worked its way up to twentieth-century Syria and Egypt, with stops along the way in pre-Islamic Arabia, the early period of Islam, Umayyad-era Damascus, and al-Andalus. In fact, her lineage of illustrious women bore a striking resemblance to the one that emerged from Fawwaz's biographical compendium and the "Famous Women" columns published in the women's magazines of early-twentieth-century Egypt. Like her predecessors, al-Haffar al-Kuzbari paid homage to the female poets of pre-Islamic Arabia, such as al-Khansa', to several of the Prophet Muhammad's female relatives, to Andalusi poets like Wallada and 'A'isha bint Ahmad, and to female luminaries of the late nineteenth and early twentieth centuries, including 'A'isha Taymur.[64]

Her lecture placed particular emphasis on Syria as a major center of Arab culture (including Arab women's culture) in the past and the present. Indeed, it is through the Syrian Umayyad connection that al-Haffar al-Kuzbari made the transition, in her lecture, from the Arab heartlands to al-Andalus. She argued that the collapse of the Umayyad dynasty in Damascus and the rise of the Abbasid dynasty in Iraq marked a moment of crisis and decline for Arab women—a moment when, in her words, "woman was thrown to the shadowy abyss of reclusion and illiteracy."[65] According to al-Haffar al-Kuzbari, while the status of women declined in the East, Arab women found in al-Andalus a new arena for intellectual and political splendor. She narrated that shift in the following terms: "While Damascus and Baghdad were in decline, Cordoba flourished. When Arab civilization reached its apogee in al-Andalus, toward the end of the eighth century [*sic*], the cultural and artistic flourishing was reflected in the Arabo-Spanish woman [*la mujer arábigo-española*]."[66] Al-Haffar al-Kuzbari went on to detail the diverse accomplishments of women in al-Andalus—particularly those who lived during the period of Umayyad rule: "It is evident that many women of the era of the emirate and the caliphate in Cordoba [756–1031] devoted themselves to science, letters, and the arts, and they were, for almost three centuries, ardent enthusiasts of study."[67] She then highlighted the achievements of famous women poets from al-Andalus, such as Wallada, 'A'isha bint Ahmad, Hafsa bint al-Hajj, and others.

But al-Haffar al-Kuzbari also stressed women's accomplishments in other spheres, such as education and politics. On the latter she asserted, "We have to recognize that the woman in al-Andalus had a broad influence on the course of political events, not only under the caliphate but also in the following periods."[68] In this part of the lecture, al-Haffar al-Kuzbari gave snapshots of a handful of notable women who were at the center of political life at the Umayyad court in Cordoba. She mentioned, for example, Nizam, "the famous palace secretary in Cordoba during the period of Hisham b. al-Hakam, who left a splendid trace of her collaboration in the administration, thanks to her perspicacity and her eloquence, since she was an excellent composer of political documents."[69] In a similar vein, al-Haffar al-Kuzbari cited the case of Lubna, "an expert in arithmetic and grammar" who worked in the palace of al-Hakam II.[70] Through such sketches, al-Haffar al-Kuzbari created an overall image of an al-Andalus where women exceled in all spheres of knowledge while exercising influence in politics and public life.

At the end of her lecture, al-Haffar al-Kuzbari made a leap across time and space, jumping from medieval al-Andalus to Egypt and Syria at the turn of the twentieth century. Through this leap, al-Haffar al-Kuzbari was able to bring her historical narrative up until the present, wrapping up a story of cultural continuity that went from pre-Islamic Arab women, to Arab women in the formative period of Islam, to Arab women in al-Andalus, and finally to women in the Arab "Awakening" (or Nahda) of the nineteenth century. In this narrative, al-Andalus served not only as a bridge between the eastern and western edges of the Arab world, but also as a link between the past and the present, especially for Arab women. For al-Haffar al-Kuzbari, the women of al-Andalus were not only the successors to the notable women of the ancient Near East, but also the predecessors to the learned women who spearheaded the women's movements in the Arab world in the twentieth century.

The fact that I have dwelled at some length on a lecture delivered in Spanish (and in Madrid) might lead some to wonder whether the views that al-Haffar

al-Kuzbari expressed in her lecture at the Ateneo were intended primarily
for a Spanish (that is, non-Arab) audience. Undoubtedly, al-Haffar al-Kuzbari
was an important point of contact between Spanish audiences and Syrian
(and, more broadly, Arabic-speaking) audiences, a role that she continued to
play until the end of her career.[71] It is also important to keep in mind, however, that the Syrian author translated and published her lecture from the
Ateneo in Arabic.

Moreover, al-Haffar al-Kuzbari touched on similar themes in later essays
and public lectures aimed at audiences in the Arab world. For instance, in a
lecture that she gave in Damascus in 1965 and then published in 1971, she
asserted that al-Andalus experienced its "golden age" under the Umayyad caliphs 'Abd al-Rahman III and al-Hakam II, whose reigns led to a period of
cultural splendor for Arab women.[72] Elaborating on this point, she said:

> Arab civilization in al-Andalus radiated, and its fame rang out in the
> West and East. Women, from noble women to female slave performers
> [*jawārin*], had a deep influence in that radiance . . . Just as Arab thought
> found in al-Andalus a fertile ground that helped it to grow and flourish,
> we see that the Hispano-Arab woman [*al-mar'a al-'arabiyya al-isbāniyya*]
> found there a great launch pad for her talents, a stimulus for perfecting
> her personality, and, indeed, an exciting setting for creativity under its
> auspices. There is no doubt that woman is deeply influenced by the mi-
> lieu in which she grows up and lives. And it is inescapable that the factors
> of flourishing and decline that leave a stamp on that milieu will be
> reflected in her life. So, when Arab civilization reached its apex in al-
> Andalus, it was inescapable that woman would make progress in
> thought and artistry. And that is, indeed, what happened, because she
> learned and taught, coming to occupy a notable place in society and in
> the court. The Muslim woman in al-Andalus attained a deep culture and
> enjoyed a broad freedom.[73]

In this account of women's accomplishments in al-Andalus, al-Haffar al-
Kuzbari echoed an idea that frequently surfaced in debates about women in
the late nineteenth and early twentieth centuries: namely, the idea that the
status of women in a society is a gauge of that society's overall civilizational
progress.[74] Building from this premise, al-Haffar al-Kuzbari suggests that

women's widespread accomplishments in al-Andalus were a reflection of the cultural splendor that al-Andalus enjoyed under the rule of the Arab Umayyad caliphs.

As the last quoted passage illustrates, al-Haffar al-Kuzbari would occasionally oscillate between the terms "Arab" and "Muslim" when talking about the women of al-Andalus. However, the Syrian author placed far greater emphasis on the Arabness of Andalusi women, an emphasis that she signaled by her focus on the period of Arab Umayyad rule and by her repetition of phrases like "Arab civilization," "Arab thought," and "the Hispano-Arab woman."[75] Although al-Haffar al-Kuzbari was certainly one of the most prominent champions for this way of talking about the women of al-Andalus, she was by no means acting alone. She was preceded, as we have already seen, by the likes of Warda al-Yaziji, and has been followed by a number of Arab authors who have espoused similar views about women in al-Andalus.[76]

While al-Haffar al-Kuzbari's work from the 1960s and 1970s exemplifies an approach to the feminist al-Andalus that is inflected by an emphasis on Arabness, the work of Moroccan sociologist and feminist Fatima Mernissi (1940–2015) shifts the emphasis to the question of women in Islam. Mernissi takes up this question in her book *Sultanes oubliées: Femmes chefs d'État en Islam* (1990; translated into English as *The Forgotten Queens of Islam*, 1993).[77] In that work, Mernissi explores the political role of women in Muslim societies across the sweep of Islamic history. The catalyst for Mernissi's work was Benazir Bhutto's election as prime minister of Pakistan in 1988. As Mernissi explains in the introduction to *Sultanes oubliées*, some of Bhutto's political opponents in Pakistan, and many in the Western media, claimed that Bhutto was the first woman head of state in a Muslim society.[78] In response to this oft-repeated (though erroneous) claim, Mernissi turned to the past to recover the stories of Muslim women who had occupied positions of power in Muslim societies since Islam's emergence in the seventh century. Mernissi describes her role in the book as that of "playing the detective"— that is, as someone who uncovers a hidden truth.[79] The question that underpins her investigation is: Under what conditions and under what titles have women exercised political power in Muslim contexts? Mernissi acknowledges that no Muslim woman has held the title of "caliph," but she argues that many have exercised power under other titles, such as *sulṭāna*, *malika* (queen), and *ḥurra* (lit. "free woman").[80] While Mernissi draws on examples from a vast array of contexts, many of her case studies center on women from al-Andalus.

In contrast with al-Haffar al-Kuzbari, Mernissi does not limit her account of Andalusi women to those who identified as Arab, and she places particular emphasis on women who played a prominent role in tying together the histories of North Africa and the Iberian Peninsula. It is noteworthy, for example, that one of her first case studies is Zaynab al-Nafzawiyya, an eleventh-century Berber princess who was the wife and, by some accounts, political adviser of Yusuf b. Tashfin, the Moroccan commander who led the Almoravid conquest of al-Andalus. Mernissi cites Zaynab as a prototype for Muslim women who have held the title of *malika*, noting:

> We might say that *malika* is bit like the title bandied about for any woman who has obtained a bit of power anywhere in the Muslim world, from New Delhi to North Africa. Many Berber queens had the right to this title. The most famous is Zaynab al-Nafzawiyya, who shared power with her husband, Yusuf b. Tashfin. She is described by the historian [Ibn] Abi Zar' al-Fasi as "*al-qā'ima bi-mulkihi*"—she who disposed of his authority. And what an authority it was, since it covered one of the two empires created by Moroccan sovereigns whose authority extended to Spain.[81]

It is worth underlining that Mernissi's point of entry to Andalusi history is not the Umayyad court but instead a Berber queen who is associated with the Almoravid conquest of al-Andalus—an event that, in Arab-centered accounts of Andalusi history, is often depicted as a tragic moment of decline (as I discuss in Chapters 1 and 2). Speaking back against Arab-centric historical accounts that have effaced the Berbers and their contributions to Maghribi and Andalusi culture, Mernissi rescues a prominent Berber woman, Zaynab al-Nafzawiyya, and places her at the center of a history of powerful Muslim women across time. Mernissi's move is one that has been adopted by many Moroccan feminists who have followed in her footsteps. Indeed, Zaynab al-Nafzawiyya has become something of a feminist icon in contemporary Morocco, where she has come to stand as a symbol for the power and status that women—and, in particular, Berber women—supposedly enjoyed during the Almoravid period.[82]

Turning from Zaynab al-Nafzawiyya to the stories of other powerful women, Mernissi introduces the term *hurra* to talk about women who exercised power in al-Andalus. The literal meaning of *hurra* is "free woman," but, as Mernissi explains in her book, the term also denotes an aristocratic birth and can be used as a synonym for *malika* or *sulṭāna*.[83] According to Mernissi, one of the most famous women to carry this title was the woman known as "ʿAʾisha al-Hurra," the mother of the last Muslim ruler of Granada, Abu ʿAbd Allah Muhammad b. ʿAli (known in Western sources as "Boabdil"). Mernissi portrays ʿAʾisha al-Hurra as the center of power in the Nasrid court during the final years of Muslim rule in al-Andalus.[84] As Mernissi tells the story, ʿAʾisha al-Hurra worked behind the scenes to help her son ascend to the throne, snatching power from a rival claimant. Yet in Mernissi's account, ʿAʾisha al-Hurra is no mere court schemer; rather, she is a shrewd political strategist who imposed her will on her son and commanded respect among the people of Nasrid Granada. In Mernissi's words, ʿAʾisha al-Hurra "was a remarkable leader who took heroic action at a tragic moment."[85] The "tragic moment" referenced here is none other than the conquest of Muslim Granada. Pointing to ʿAʾisha al-Hurra's central role in that event, Mernissi calls ʿAʾisha al-Hurra a "witness of and actor in one of the most traumatizing periods in the history of Islam."[86]

According to Mernissi, the fall of Granada in 1492 was both a trauma for the Muslim world and a catalyst for Muslim women to enter the political arena:

> The fall of Granada propelled other *hurras* on to the political scene, women of the elite who would otherwise have led a sleepy life in the harem and whom the debacle pitched into the melee, obliging them to take charge and to participate in the momentous events the community was living through. Freed from the iron grip of tradition that paralyzed them and relegated them to the domestic sphere, women revealed themselves to be, despite their inexperience, astute strategists—at any rate, just as brilliant as men. One of them, a Moroccan of Andalusian origin, found no better way of forgetting the defeat than to launch herself into piracy. She displayed such talent for it that she soon became *'hakimat Titwan'* (the governor of Tetouan).[87]

This passage serves as the transition to Mernissi's sketch of the figure known as "al-Sayyida al-Hurra" (lit. "The Free Lady"), a Moroccan woman of Andalusi descent who governed the northern Moroccan city of Tetouan in the early sixteenth century, a period when Tetouan became one of the major hubs for piracy in the Mediterranean.[88] Through the story of "al-Sayyida al-Hurra," Mernissi is able to pivot from al-Andalus to North Africa while shining a light on the people—and especially the women—whose lives bridged the two lands. Coming on the heels of her sketch of 'A'isha al-Hurra, Mernissi's sketch of "al-Sayyida al-Hurra" places this Moroccan figure in a cultural lineage that goes back to al-Andalus and that migrates to North Africa after the fall of Muslim Granada.

Here, then, is an imaginary that is genealogical in quite a literal sense: al-Sayyida al-Hurra is one of many famous figures from modern Moroccan history who traces her family roots back to al-Andalus.[89] Al-Sayyida al-Hurra embodies the intertwined histories of the two shores of the Strait of Gibraltar, and, in this particular context, she embodies the continuity between the "free" or "noble" women of al-Andalus and their descendants in Morocco. Unlike Zaynab Fawwaz and Salma al-Haffar al-Kuzbari, Mernissi's feminist imagining of al-Andalus does not work on an east-west axis, connecting al-Andalus to the Middle East; instead, it runs on a north-south axis, connecting al-Andalus to North Africa. Moreover, the larger history in which Mernissi inserts the stories of Andalusi women is not that of Arab women but instead that of Muslim women—and, in particular, that of Muslim women who have exercised political power.

Andalusi Doubles

For much of the twentieth century, the figures at the forefront of the cultural and discursive project that I've dubbed "the feminist al-Andalus" were primarily educated and literary women from the Levant, Egypt, and, to a lesser extent, the Maghrib. Women from these contexts have continued to play a leading role in the conversation in the twenty-first century, but, with the rise of the new millennium, new actors have come on the scene to expand the map of contexts where the feminist al-Andalus operates. This process of geographic expansion has been driven by a number of factors, including the increasing visibility of Arab diasporic artists who are based outside the Middle East, the growth of the Arab and Muslim communities in Europe and the United States, as well as the emergence of new centers of cultural activity within the Middle East, especially in the Gulf region. As a result, the feminist al-Andalus has become, in recent decades, a multi-sited and multilingual endeavor. Despite this diversity and dispersion, the feminist al-Andalus, as a cultural and political discourse, has preserved certain core ideas that have been in circulation since the late nineteenth century, such as the emphasis on the relevance of Andalusi women's lives to the lives of Arab and Muslim women today. Today, the feminist al-Andalus operates in a number of cultural forms, from literature to street art to blogs. It is no coincidence, for example, that one of the most prominent female cyberactivists during the 2010–2011 uprisings in Tunisia went by the handle "Wallada."[90] Amid this vibrant cultural scene, a handful of prominent Arabic-language poets have picked up the baton from earlier generations and imagined themselves as "daughters of al-Andalus"—that is, as members of a cultural tradition that harkens back to the women of al-Andalus.

One of the most interesting voices to emerge in this space is that of Emirati poet, playwright, and novelist Saliha Ghabish (b. 1960). In 2002 Ghabish published a collection of poetry titled *Bi-man ya Buthayn taludhin?* (With whom do you seek refuge, Buthayna?).[91] The collection's title poem is actually a thirteen-part suite of poems devoted to famous figures from al-Andalus—and especially to Buthayna (or Buthayn), an Andalusi poet who was the daughter of al-Mu'tamid ibn 'Abbad (d. 1095), himself an accomplished poet as well as the ruler of Seville in the period leading up to the Almoravid conquest of al-Andalus.

Ghabish explains her choice of subject in two prefaces to her collection. In the first preface, titled "Why Her?" ("Li-madha hiya?"), Ghabish responds:

Because her story has a bit of myth, a lot of values, and a part of me. There arose an unseen interval at whose beginning I stand. And she stands at the end of it. Or perhaps I stand at the end of it, and she stands at the beginning of it. Between the beginning and the end, there is a single story that makes us similar and shapes the bonds of friendship and kinship, but not with their customary and traditional characteristics. This resemblance is not in the details of our life stories, but rather in a stance and a conviction that, on the strength of its presence, is on the verge of being a single identity for some woman.[92]

Here, the first-person speaker (Ghabish's persona) imagines that she and Buthayna stand at opposite ends of an invisible trajectory that connects them and "shapes the bonds of friendship and kinship" between them. In other words, the speaker envisions Buthayna as her double and, in the last sentence of the passage, suggests that their two identities converge into "a single identity." This doubling sets up Buthayna, the eleventh-century Andalusi poet, as a mirror or mask for Ghabish, the twenty-first-century Emirati poet.

The first preface also foreshadows the dialogic structure of the thirteen poems that make up the collection's title suite, "Bi-man ya Buthayn taludhin?" Throughout the suite, a first-person speaker engages in intimate dialogues, in the second person, with famous figures from al-Andalus. The speaker's main interlocutor is Buthayna, but she also addresses, or adopts the voice of, other notable figures from Andalusi history, including 'Abd al-Rahman I (the founder of the Umayyad state in al-Andalus), al-Mu'tamid (Buthayna's father), I'timad (Buthayna's mother), and 'A'isha al-Hurra (the mother of the last Muslim ruler of al-Andalus). Through these imagined dialogues, the speaker gives voice to, and engages with, figures whose lives represent nearly the entire scope of Andalusi history, from the rise of the Umayyad emirate in the eighth century to the conquest of Muslim Granada in 1492.

In the second preface, titled "Her Poem," Ghabish recounts Buthayna's story, drawing on the details that have been preserved in al-Maqqari's *Nafh al-tib,* where the portrait of Buthayna appears in the section on the famous women poets of al-Andalus.[93] As Ghabish tells the story, Buthayna was "an Andalusi princess" whose father, al-Mu'tamid, spent the last years of his life in exile in Aghmat, Morocco.[94] At the moment of the Almoravid conquest of Seville, Buthayna got separated from her family and was eventually sold into slavery. She was bought by a merchant from Seville who, believing her to be one of the slaves from al-Mu'tamid's palace, offered her to his son as a gift. Refusing to serve as a concubine, Buthayna revealed her noble lineage and declared that she would not marry the merchant's son without her father's blessing. Buthayna then resolved to write to her father, sending him a poem in which she explained her situation and asked for his permission to marry the merchant's son, despite the fact that the merchant's family was of a lower station than her own. When Buthayna's poem reached al-Mu'tamid in Morocco, he rejoiced to learn that his daughter was still alive, and he gave her his blessing to marry.

In the second preface, Ghabish not only narrates Buthayna's story but also reproduces the bulk of Buthayna's only extant poem.[95] Thus, like her predecessor Zaynab Fawwaz, Saliha Ghabish engages in recovery work, preserving the words of female Andalusi poets and transmitting them to readers in the present. Yet Ghabish, like Fawwaz, does not limit herself to recycling the past; rather, she pursues a program of creative adaptation, using the past to create something new.[96] Indeed, Buthayna's words form the foundation on which Ghabish builds her own poetic edifice. Many of the poems in Ghabish's collection take their titles from lines in Buthayna's poem. As a result, Buthayna's words are woven into Ghabish's poetic suite, just as the figure of Buthayna is woven into Ghabish's poetic persona.

One such example is the second poem in the suite, titled "Fa-ʿasaka ya abati" (Perhaps you might, oh father . . .). The poem's title comes from the penultimate line of Buthayna's poem to her father al-Muʿtamid: "Perhaps you might, oh father, present me to him / if he is one who can hope for my affections."[97] This line and Ghabish's poem in response to it both begin with the particle ʿasāka ("perhaps," "could it be that . . ."), which introduces the subjunctive mode and denotes a degree of doubt or uncertainty. The use of this particle is fitting, since Ghabish's suite probes the uncertain terrain of an impossible conversation between a poetic speaker and an Andalusi woman who are separated by nine centuries.

Throughout the poem "Fa-ʿasaka ya abati," the speaker apostrophizes Buthayna, conjuring her into being and addressing her as an intimate companion. For instance, at the conclusion of the poem, the first-person speaker addresses Buthayna in the following terms:

> You lost your father,
> as were lost the notebooks that he would read to his city.
> You were the favorite among his words,
> until the context lost your features,
> and the pulpits of Seville went along
> wetting their pens in the saliva of the late morning
> and waiting for al-Muʿtamid.
> So perhaps he might save your name for the coming sermon.
> He is not yet aware that the auction platform has exhibited you,
> and that you have thrown your name into the furnace of fear.[98]

The grammar of these lines is significant, as it helps to decode Ghabish's creative engagement with the Andalusi poet Buthayna. Buthayna's poem, which provides the title for Ghabish's poem, stages a dialogue between the poet and her parents—and especially with her father, al-Muʻtamid. In contrast, Ghabish's riff on Buthayna's poem dislodges al-Muʻtamid from the grammatical position of the second person (the "you") and relegates him to the margins of a conversation between the first-person speaker and Buthayna. Ghabish's poem, then, opens up a space for dialogue with the poet's Andalusi double, Buthayna.

Crucially, the speaker in Ghabish's poem imagines that she is addressing Buthayna at a moment after Buthayna has been sold into captivity but before Buthayna has written to her father. In other words, the speaker imagines herself in contact with Buthayna at the moment of creation, at the moment when the poem is about to spring from Buthayna's pen. The time of Ghabish's poem thus converges with the time of Buthayna's writing, as if both poets were engaged in simultaneous and overlapping acts of writing. While the distinction between the speaker and Buthayna remains fairly clear in "Fa-ʻasaka ya abati," it becomes increasingly murky as the suite progresses. In the penultimate poem in the suite, "Qabla al-suqut al-akhir" (Before the final fall), the speaker refers to herself repeatedly as "another Buthayna" and "your second Buthayna."[99] Ghabish's speaker thus gradually assumes the identity of her Andalusi double.

As I have already indicated, Buthayna is not the only Andalusi mask that Ghabish's speaker adopts. In the poem "Ibki ka-l-nisa'" (Cry like a woman), Ghabish's speaker adopts the perspective of ʻA'isha al-Hurra. The poem's title echoes a statement that ʻA'isha al-Hurra supposedly made to her son, Boabdil, after the conquest of Granada in 1492. As legend would have it, when Boabdil and his entourage departed from Granada, the deposed ruler took a final look back at the Alhambra and wept for the city that he had lost—a scene that has become immortalized in European writings as "the Moor's last sigh."[100] The conclusion to this (likely apocryphal) story is that Boabdil's mother, ʻA'isha al-Hurra, turned to her son and told him that he should not "cry like a woman" for a place that he could not defend like a man.[101] This story and, in particular, the figure of Boabdil have long captivated the European imagination, where the ousted ruler of the Alhambra has stood as a tragic figure of loss and exile.[102]

In *Bi-man ya Buthayn taludhin,* Ghabish reimagines the final days of Muslim Granada, reframing the story around 'A'isha al-Hurra. The poem begins:

> To you goes my shivering under the windows of a palace
> which is visited by the fever of defeat.
> Since the spears of your hands fenced you in,
> throw me its keys.[103]

Neither the speaker nor the second-person male interlocutor are named, but their identities are clear enough from the allusion in the poem's title. Ghabish's speaker, adopting the perspective of 'A'isha al-Hurra, entreats Boabdil to throw her the keys of the Alhambra ("a palace / which is visited by the fever of defeat"). This opening suggests a counterfactual history, in which Boabdil handed over the keys of the Alhambra to his mother, rather than handing them over to the Catholic Monarchs, Ferdinand and Isabella. While Ghabish's poem does not pursue this alternate history, it does portray 'A'isha al-Hurra as a figure of resistance, who stands ready to seize the keys of Granada when her son prepares for defeat. It also portrays 'A'isha al-Hurra and her double, Ghabish's speaker, as actors who have preserved the memory of al-Andalus long after its fall.

This fluid movement between past and present comes into full focus in the poem's last stanza, where the speaker says:

> I love you, al-Andalus,
> but union with you [*waṣlaki*] is the story of a people whose
>   daughter I am.
> They shattered your name in a night
> that blocked my feet on its bridge.
> They came searching for its remains in me,
> and your *s* flows like spent blood
> in your broken name.[104]

Here, as in many moments in Ghabish's collection, the speaker's identity is ambiguously poised between a historical figure, 'A'isha al-Hurra, and a female speaker who gives voice to that historical figure in the present. The speaker frames her relationship to al-Andalus in genealogical terms, identifying herself as the "daughter" of a people whose story is al-Andalus.

While proclaiming her identity as a cultural descendant (or "daughter") of al-Andalus, the speaker also nods subtly to one of the most famous poems from al-Andalus: Ibn al-Khatib's "Jadaka al-ghayth." The most famous lines from Ibn al-Khatib's poem are, as I have discussed elsewhere in this book, the following:

> May the rain cloud shower you when the rain cloud pours,
>   O time of union [*yā zamān al-waṣl*] in al-Andalus!
> Union with you [*waṣluka*] was but a dream
>   in slumber, or the deception of a deceiver.[105]

These lines revolve around the repeated use of the noun *al-waṣl,* whose meanings include "union," "connection," and the reunion of lovers. Through the repeated use of this noun, Ibn al-Khatib's speaker suggests that his separation from al-Andalus is like the separation between two lovers. In Ghabish's poem, the speaker echoes Ibn al-Khatib's famous words, placing them in the mouth of a female speaker who floats between the time of al-Andalus's conquest and the remembrance of al-Andalus in the present. The words that Ghabish's speaker uses to express her connection to al-Andalus are built on the words that a previous poet, Ibn al-Khatib, used to talk about his separation from al-Andalus in the fourteenth century. Here, then, memories are layered upon earlier memories, just as Ghabish's poems are built with the material of earlier poems.

In the final stanza of "Ibki ka-l-nisa'," the speaker personifies and apostrophizes al-Andalus; that is, she treats al-Andalus as a lover whom she can address directly. Yet the reunion with this lover—the moment of *waṣl*—is one that is inexorably linked to communal processes of storytelling: the reunion with al-Andalus is, for the speaker, "the story of a people whose daughter I am." That is, when the speaker reunites with al-Andalus, she also narrates, and lays claim to, the story of the community from which she descends. The poem's final stanza blurs the distinction between al-Andalus's status as a specific place and time and its status as a discourse that is useful for thinking about collective identity. Indeed, in the final two lines of the poem, al-Andalus is transformed from lover to letter, when the speaker says,

"And your *s* flows like spent blood / in your broken name."[106] In these lines, al-Andalus becomes a string of letters, ending in *s*, which are on the verge of collapsing and flowing away, "like spent blood." In the face of this peril, language emerges as the terrain on which the speaker can reestablish union with al-Andalus. Through a poetic practice of adaptation, weaving new poems from the strands left behind by earlier Andalusi poets, the speaker sets out to preserve the story of al-Andalus and, in so doing, to claim her identity as the metaphorical "daughter" of the Andalusi cultural tradition.

While gender is the primary grounds on which Ghabish's speaker asserts her claim on al-Andalus, the speaker's gendered identity is often inflected through other affiliations and collective imaginaries. In particular, Arabness offers the speaker another channel for making connections across time and space. Like Salma al-Haffar al-Kuzbari, Saliha Ghabish attempts to insert the story of al-Andalus into the broader history of the Arab world, a history that includes pre-Islamic Arabia and that extends to the present-day Middle East, including the Gulf states. Throughout the title suite, "Bi-man ya Buthayn ta-ludhin?," Ghabish's speaker imagines herself as part of a collective Arab subject that looks westward to al-Andalus from its historical homeland in the Middle East. This spatial imaginary is apparent, for instance, in the poem "Wa-kadha al-zaman ya'ul . . ." (And so time turns . . .), whose title is taken from another line in Buthayna's poem. In Ghabish's poem, the speaker says:

> I examine the Arab tear for its salt,
> and for evidence of its faith . . .
> There, *at our western door,* your olive tree has the scent of all
>   seasons,
> the fragrance of those who reap with song,
> the sand dancing in its water.
> And the orange tree *in our east* has a taste of freedom
> brought to us
> by the promise of the Lord of heaven.[107]

The speaker uses the plural first-person possessive "our" to inscribe herself within a collective Arab subject who is located in "our east" and looks to al-Andalus, "at our western door." These spatial coordinates appear alongside cultural allusions that firmly place Ghabish's poems in the Arab East. For example, the speaker refers, on two occasions, to the pre-Islamic Arabian storm god Quzah.[108]

One of the key figures in Ghabish's pan-Arab imaginary is Buthayna, the title character of *Bi-man ya Buthayn taludhin*. Although Ghabish initially identifies the titular Buthayna as Buthayna bint al-Mu'tamid, the Andalusi poet, she later suggests that there are, in fact, many Buthaynas who populate her work. In particular, Ghabish plays with the story of Jamil b. Ma'mar (ca. 660–701) and his cousin Buthayna, two legendary lovers who lived in the Hijaz (the westernmost region of today's Saudi Arabia) in the seventh century. Their relationship was immortalized in the passionate love poems that Jamil wrote for Buthayna.[109] In *Bi-man ya Buthayn taludhin*, Ghabish makes several allusions to the story of Jamil and Buthayna, and in so doing, she suggests an implicit connection between Buthayna, the lover of the seventh-century Hijaz, and the eleventh-century Andalusi poet who shares her name.

Indeed, Ghabish's poems move easily between these two Buthaynas without signaling any jump in time or space. For instance, the sixth poem in Ghabish's suite, "Fa-kharajtu haribatan" (So, I left in flight), takes its title from a line in Buthayna bint al-Mu'tamid's poem and contains several allusions to the Buthayna from al-Andalus. Yet, by the next poem in the suite, Buthayna's identity has shifted, as illustrated by the following lines:

> With whom do you seek refuge, Buthayna,
> while the evening is a long spear in the palm of a Jamil
> who defends thousands and thousands of Buthaynas?[110]

These lines (which also provide the title for Ghabish's collection) allude to the story of Jamil and Buthayna; they also conjure up the image of a long line of Buthaynas, originating with the seventh-century lover and extending to the present.

Ghabish would later elaborate on this idea in a 2016 interview with Sharjah TV's program *Manarat* (Beacons), where she said that there are three Buthaynas in her collection: Buthayna, the Andalusi poet; Buthayna, the seventh-century lover; and Buthayna Khidr Makki, a contemporary Sudanese novelist who is the founder of the Sudanese League of Women Writers and a friend of Ghabish. Ghabish told the interviewer from Sharjah TV, "Each of the three Buthaynas has a story, a story that is connected with women, that is connected with history, that is connected with poetry, knowledge, writing, and literature."[111] Ghabish's statement illustrates the triangulation that is at the heart of her collection, *Bi-man ya Buthayn taludhin?* Through the figure of Buthayna, Ghabish triangulates between a female poet from al-Andalus, a famous woman from seventh-century Arabia, and a generation of contemporary Arab women writers that includes Buthayna Khidr Makki and Saliha Ghabish herself.[112] This identification between the Buthaynas of the past and the Buthaynas of the present is bolstered by Ghabish's preface to the collection, where she establishes the intimate relationship between her speaker and Buthayna bint al-Muʿtamid. The poetic and cultural lineage that Ghabish traces in *Bi-man ya Buthayn taludhin?* is, therefore, one that originates in the Arabian Peninsula, with the figure of Buthayna, travels west to al-Andalus, with the figure of Buthayna bint al-Muʿtamid, and then returns to the Middle East in the twenty-first century. Although this lineage bears a clear resemblance to the one that emerged from the work of Levantine writers in the early twentieth century, Ghabish's take on this story is more Arabian than Umayyad, more Hijazi than Damascene. It centers on a lesser-known figure from al-Andalus, Buthayna bint al-Muʿtamid, and places her in dialogue with women writers who are based in cultural contexts that were barely on the radar for earlier generations of Arab women writers.

Even as the feminist al-Andalus has expanded to encompass new voices and new contexts, it has continued to circle back to familiar figures and themes, especially the figure of Wallada. Wallada lives on in street art, blogs, and zines.[113] And she lives on in literature, in many genres and many languages, including Arabic, Spanish, and English.[114] Of Wallada's many returns, one of the most striking is the one staged in the work of Maram al-Masri (b. 1962), a Syrian-born poet who has lived in France since the 1980s. Al-Masri rose to international acclaim in 1998, when her book *Karaza hamra' ʿala balat abyad* (*A Red Cherry on a White-Tile Floor*), won the Adonis Prize for Arabic literature. In 2007 al-Masri was an artist in residence at the Carmen de la Victoria, a historic building in the environs of the Alhambra that is run by the University of Granada as a residence for visiting artists and scholars. The result of al-Masri's stay in Granada was a bilingual volume of poetry titled *al-ʿAwda / El Retorno* (The return, 2007). The "return" evoked in the collection's title is none other than the return of Wallada, an event that is dramatized in the collection's first and longest poem, "ʿAwdat Wallada / El regreso de Wallada" (Wallada's return). The poem would later provide the title for the French edition of this collection, *Le retour de Wallada* (2010), a collaboration between al-Masri and a French translator.

In a 2010 interview with the Spanish newspaper *ABC*, al-Masri explained why she decided to devote a collection of poetry to the Cordoban poet Wallada:

> For me, Wallada is a model, an archetype, and a very current character. At a time when many Muslim women feel attracted to the obscurantism of a certain fundamentalist tradition, it seemed to me that it was very urgent to speak of the "return" of Wallada, since she, the Andalusi poet, is still an archetype of freedom, conquered through the word and through the charms of poetry and love.[115]

As this statement illustrates, al-Masri holds up Wallada as a model for twenty-first-century Muslim women. In particular, al-Masri positions Wallada as a counterweight to the forces of religious fundamentalism and as "an archetype of freedom, conquered through the word." For al-Masri, then, Wallada not only represents a model of female freedom that is indigenous to the Muslim world, but also embodies the power that language, and especially poetic language, holds in the struggle for women's rights.

These same themes come to the surface in al-Masri's poem "'Awdat Wallada" (Wallada's return). In it, the speaker assumes the voice of Wallada, who returns to al-Andalus after a long absence. The poem begins:

> I am the queen of this place
> I return to it without crowns
> A sultana without a scepter
> A slave performer [*jāriya*] with a garland of jasmine from Damascus,
> I dance and sing.
>
> The sun's body, I
> am warm
> Like the tears of a man who has lost his kingdom
> Like the blood of childbirth [*ka-dam al-wilāda*].[116]

The first word of the poem is the pronoun *anā* (I), an opening that draws attention to the speaker's voice and subjectivity. This focus on the first-person speaker is sustained throughout the first stanza by the repeated use of first-person verbs, such as "I return" and "I dance." The pattern continues in the first verse of the second stanza, where the poet inverts the subject and predicate ("The sun's body, I") so that the first-person "I" stands prominently at the end of the line, like a bookend or echo to the "I" that appears at the beginning of the poem.

Although emphatically individualized, the speaker also contains multitudes. For starters, al-Masri's poem playfully blurs the line between two perspectives: that of Wallada and that of an unidentified female speaker who visits Granada in the twenty-first century (a clear stand-in for al-Masri herself). The speaker's multitudinous identities do not stop there. The second stanza of the poem contains an allusion to Boabdil, the man who sheds tears after losing his kingdom. The stanza then ends with a pun on Wallada's name, which means "fertile" (*wallāda*) and which, when written, is visually identical to the Arabic word for "childbirth" (*wilāda*). Through such allusions and puns, the speaker aligns herself with several moments in Andalusi history. She is a figure of finality and loss, like Boabdil, but also one of renewal or rebirth, like Wallada. In other words, the speaker carries the memory of al-Andalus's loss, while also holding out the promise of al-Andalus's return. Such cycles of departure and return are woven through the poem, as when the speaker says, "Fleeing I was from you, and today I'm returning to you."[117] Al-Andalus is both origin and destination for the speaker's wanderings, wanderings that disperse her voice across different times, places, and people.

While the poem opens as a monologue, it develops into a dialogue between the first-person speaker and al-Andalus. Al-Masri's main rhetorical tools in this poem are personification and apostrophe, and she combines them to turn al-Andalus into a living and present being. Such is the case with the following stanzas, where the speaker addresses al-Andalus in the second person:

I, who have no house, reside in your house,
I, who, since the day I departed from you, roam the alleys of
     memory,
wandering aimlessly like a shepherd who has lost his sheep.

I, who no longer have any homeland [*waṭan*] except
paper and words,

I, who no longer have any bed
except the sidewalks of hope,
I return to you so that you might grant me solace,
so that you might revive me from the excess of grief.[118]

Like the first stanza of the poem, these stanzas begin with the pronoun "I,"
underlining once more the speaker's voice and perspective. Here, though, the
speaker's tone is more vulnerable and less self-assured. She identifies herself
as a vagabond who wanders aimlessly without house or home. The only homeland left to her is that of writing, of "paper and words."

Yet this homeland is not as meager as it might seem at first glance. What
is left unsaid in these verses is that "paper and words" are the very tools that
allow al-Masri to imagine a return to al-Andalus. If, as al-Masri suggested
in her interview with *ABC*, words are the weapons that Wallada used to "conquer" her freedom, then words are also the bridge that connects al-Masri
and other contemporary Arab women poets to Wallada and other notable
women from al-Andalus. Al-Masri's poetic homage to Wallada is a meditation on the power of words: their power to give voice, to bear witness, and
to remember and evoke bygone people and places, such as Wallada and
al-Andalus.

Like al-Andalus itself, al-Masri's collection of poetry for Wallada lives in
translation. It originated as a bilingual Arabic-Spanish edition and was later
published as a French text, which is, today, more widely available than the
Arabic-Spanish original. To date, there is no monolingual Arabic-language
edition of this work. This state of affairs says something about the global
market for literature and, in particular, about the uneven ways that the work
of contemporary Arab poets circulates inside and outside of the Arab world.
But the story of al-Masri's book also says something about the *translatability*
of Wallada and other Andalusi women. The lives and works of Andalusi
women (and especially of Andalusi women poets) have shown a remarkable
capacity for cultural translation—that is, for traveling across geographic and
temporal lines. Genealogy—broadly understood as an imagined cultural lineage extending from the past to the present—has been the dominant mode
for establishing a link between the women of al-Andalus and Arab and
Muslim women in the twentieth and twenty-first centuries. Yet, genealogy
is not the only way of imagining or enacting a "feminist al-Andalus." In the

next section, I will turn to another strategy: stories based on fictional Andalusi women who serve as models for women in the present.

Radical Conservation

The figure of the learned woman—the *ʿālima* (scholar) or *adība* (woman of
letters)—has been a fixture of fictional reimaginings of al-Andalus since the
early twentieth century. Literature and, more recently, film and television
have brought into being an Andalus that is populated with female scientists,
storytellers, and scholars, as well as singers, rebels, and warriors. An early
example of this leitmotif comes from Jurji Zaydan's novel *ʿAbd al-Rahman
al-Nasir* (1910), which is set in tenth-century Cordoba, during the reign of the
Umayyad caliph ʿAbd al-Rahman III.[119] One of the novel's main characters is
an *adība* named ʿAbida, who dazzles the Umayyad court with her eloquence,
knowledge of poetry, beautiful calligraphy, and prodigious memory. Over the
course of the novel, ʿAbida recites poetry, sings, plays musical instruments,
copies scholarly books with an elegant hand, and engages in witty and erudite
exchanges with her male peers. While Zaydan's ʿAbida engages in intellectual
jousts with her male peers, some of the Andalusi characters who have come
in her wake engage in literal combat. For instance, the title character of the
Tunisian comic *Jamila al-Qayrawaniyya* (1982) is a young arms maker from
the North African city of Qayrawan who leaves her hometown in the late
fifteenth century to join the armed struggle to defend Granada, the last bastion of Muslim rule in al-Andalus.[120] As the cases of ʿAbida and Jamila illustrate, fictional heroines from al-Andalus exercise their talents in a number of
arenas, from intellectual inquiry to armed struggle. These heroines are symbols
of power—power that is exercised through the mind, the body, or both.

In the long line of texts that have conjured up powerful women (real and
imagined) from al-Andalus, arguably the most influential is the award-
winning *Granada Trilogy* by Egyptian writer and scholar Radwa ʿAshur
(Radwa Ashour, 1946–2014). ʿAshur was born in Cairo in 1946, studied English literature at Cairo University, earned a doctorate in African American
literature from the University of Massachusetts, and then taught as a professor of English literature at Ain Shams University in Egypt until her death
in 2014.[121] Alongside her distinguished academic career, ʿAshur published
several works of fiction, the most famous of which is *The Granada Trilogy*

(1994–1995). The trilogy traces the saga of several generations of a Muslim Arab family from Granada, in the period between the Christian conquest of Granada and the expulsion in 1609 of the so-called Moriscos, the descendants of the Muslims who remained in Spain after 1492 and were forced to convert to Christianity. The first part of the trilogy, *Gharnata* (1994, translated into English as *Granada*), won the Cairo International Book Fair's Book of the Year Award in 1994; the whole trilogy—comprising *Gharnata, Maryama* (Maryama, 1995), and *al-Rahil* (The departure, 1995)—won first prize at the first Arab Women's Book Fair in 1995.[122]

The first part of the trilogy, *Granada,* covers the period between 1491 and 1527 and centers on the family of a bookbinder named Abu Ja'far, and especially on his granddaughter, Salima. Through the story of Salima and her family, the reader witnesses the tragic consequences of the Castilian conquest for Granada's Muslim community, which struggles to preserve its culture, identity, and freedom in the face of violent pressure from Granada's new rulers. Over the course of the novel, Salima grows from being a precocious and free-spirited girl into being a brilliant and fearless scientist and healer who refuses to bow to the pressures from the new Castilian government. Thus, in the lineage of female protagonists from al-Andalus, 'Ashur's Salima lands somewhere in the middle of the spectrum between 'Abida, Zaydan's literary woman, and Jamila, the warrior who is the title character of *Jamila al-Qayrawaniyya*. Salima, the protagonist of 'Ashur's *Granada,* is a warrior of knowledge, a character whose struggles on behalf of her community take the form of reading, writing, and teaching. My reading of 'Ashur's novel will focus on Salima's role as a figure of resistance—and, in particular, as someone who enacts resistance through knowledge and learning.[123]

Salima's mode of resistance derives its energy from Granada's book culture, a central theme in 'Ashur's novel. Salima's grandfather, Abu Ja'far, is a *warrāq,* a papermaker or bookbinder. In the novel's first chapter, there is a detailed description of how Abu Ja'far teaches an apprentice to bind a book and to decorate its cover with intricate geometric patterns.[124] Abu Ja'far's profession is a nod to Granada's thriving book trade, but it is also, more importantly, a metaphor for cultural preservation. To bind a book is to protect it for posterity. In the context of 'Ashur's novel, bookbinding—and especially the binding of Arabic books—is an act of preservation for a culture that is facing an existential threat.

Through the story of Abu Ja'far and his descendants (especially Salima), 'Ashur's *Granada Trilogy* mounts a defense of preservation as a form of cultural resistance. The trilogy suggests that bookbinding, manuscript copying, record-keeping, and other efforts to preserve the past are not necessarily reactionary, past-oriented pursuits; they can also be radical, forward-looking enterprises. Indeed, 'Ashur spoke to this point in a lecture she delivered in 1999 at her alma mater, the University of Massachusetts. There, in a reflection on her work, 'Ashur said, "I had also opted for the role of scribe, a copier of valuable manuscripts; the only difference is that, unlike the scribes of old, I appropriated the canonical texts in an effort which one might call radical conservation."[125] 'Ashur's phrase, "radical conservation," encapsulates the form of resistance that Abu Ja'far and his descendants enact in *The Granada Trilogy*. Their struggles are not just about preserving the past; they are also about creating the conditions for the future.

In *Granada,* Abu Ja'far's efforts to preserve al-Andalus's imperiled book culture are not limited to his workshop; they also extend to his grandchildren, Salima and Hasan. Abu Ja'far invests all of his money and his hope in his grandchildren's education, hoping that they will grow up to become eminent scholars. Of the two grandchildren, it is Salima who shows the greatest intellectual promise and who eventually emerges, over the course of the novel, as the scholar in the family. Salima's keen intelligence is paired with a rebellious streak that leads her to buck the expectations that her female relatives have of a girl of her age. For instance, although Salima excels in her studies, she shirks her chores at home. This state of affairs causes consternation in Salima's grandmother, Umm Ja'far, while eliciting indulgence and even pride in her grandfather, as the following passage shows:

> Umm Ja'far was concerned that her granddaughter didn't even know how to fry an egg, and unlike other girls of her age from the neighborhood, she didn't help her mother at all with the housework . . .
>
> Abu Ja'far on the other hand didn't share his wife's and his daughter-in-law's concern. For he knew that the girl's laziness was completely compensated by a different kind of activity. Her mind was like a mill in constant motion, and she never stopped poking around, observing, studying, and asking questions. She was only nine but had already learned by heart a third of the Qur'an and could recite it effortlessly

and write in a clear and elegant hand. Her teacher marveled at how quickly she understood and readily grasped the complexities of Arabic grammar.[126]

This passage not only highlights Salima's precocious intelligence but also indicates that her intellectual pursuits allow her to defy gender conventions—and, in particular, the expectations of her mother and grandmother.[127]

While Salima bucks the expectations of her female relatives, she embraces the path of her Andalusi foremothers. Indeed, the hope that Abu Ja'far deposits in his granddaughter's education is not framed as a rupture from tradition but, instead, as an homage to the example set by female Andalusi luminaries from the past. On this point, the narrator observes: "Abu Ja'far, although he never revealed this to anyone, hoped in the depth of his heart that Salima would become like 'A'isha bint Ahmad, the pride and joy of Cordoba's women and also its men, whom she surpassed in intellect, learning, and refinement [*adab*]."[128] As a model for Salima's education, Abu Ja'far looks to the example of 'A'isha bint Ahmad, one of the illustrious *adība*s of al-Andalus. Salima thus emerges as a figure of "radical conservation": she defies gender conventions in the present by following in the footsteps of her Andalusi predecessors.

'Ashur's Salima is not only an homage to illustrious women from earlier periods of Andalusi history; she is also the product of a modern tradition of writing about women in al-Andalus. It bears noting, for example, that 'Ashur's description of 'A'isha bint Ahmad closely resembles Zaynab Fawwaz's description of the same figure from the late nineteenth century. Fawwaz wrote of 'A'isha bint Ahmad: "In her age, there was no one among the noblewomen of al-Andalus who matched her in learning, intellect, refinement, eloquence, and poetry."[129] I do not know if 'Ashur was familiar with Fawwaz's biographical compendium, but the point that I am making does not hinge on any direct connection between the two writers. Instead, what I'm driving at is that 'Ashur and Fawwaz are both drawing from the same discursive tradition, one that has celebrated the intellectual accomplishments of Andalusi women and envisioned a continuous cultural lineage that runs from Umayyad Cordoba to the modern-day Middle East.

Early in 'Ashur's *Granada,* Abu Ja'far succumbs to a premature death, and his granddaughter, Salima, must fill his shoes as the family's custodian of

Andalusi book culture. This turn of events hinges on the novel's portrayal of a real historical event: a bonfire of Islamic books that took place in Granada's Bibarrambla Square in 1499.[130] In the novel, Abu Ja'far dies from the shock of seeing the public burning of precious religious books. Fortunately, his own books are spared from the flames because he had taken the precaution to hide them in the basement of the family's country house outside Granada. In response to Abu Ja'far's untimely death, Salima goes to the family's country house and makes a detailed inventory of the books that her grandfather had stored there.[131] In other words, Salima's response to her grandfather's death—her mourning for him—is a bibliographic and curatorial act: to honor her grandfather's memory, she must record and preserve his books. With this act, Salima picks up the baton from her grandfather, becoming the caretaker of the family's books and, more broadly, of the intellectual and scientific heritage of al-Andalus.

As the novel's action progresses, Salima's commitment to her grandfather's books, and to Arabic books in general, becomes an increasingly defiant act of resistance. The Spanish authorities issue a decree outlawing the possession of Arabic books. Despite this decree, Salima continues to study her grandfather's books and to acquire new ones on the black market. At one point, she even spends all of her savings to buy a medical compendium by the Andalusi botanist and pharmacologist Ibn al-Baytar (d. 1248).[132]

For Salima, reading is not only an act of resistance against the forces of cultural assimilation but is also an act of liberation, one that allows her to transcend her oppressive circumstances. For that reason, the novel's descriptions of Salima's studies are often laden with metaphors of imprisonment and liberation. Such is the case in the following passage: "She waited until the dark of night when everyone went to bed to light the lantern and read. And the narrow confines of her prison would gradually expand, and the iron bars of her cell would be pried open to the sunlight that shone from the book and from her mind."[133] As this passage illustrates, Salima's studies are not just aimed at preserving her grandfather's memory and, with it, the memory of Andalusi book culture; they are also aimed at survival and resilience in the face of cultural oppression.

Salima is not only a custodian of knowledge, but also a creator of it. Her studies of scientific works from al-Andalus and the Middle East inspire her to design her own medical experiments at home. These experiments, in turn, lead her to withdraw gradually from her husband Saʿd and to immerse herself in the life of the mind, as the narrator explains:

> She withdrew from Saʿd and immersed herself in reading books, mixing herbs, and concocting blends, ointments, and potions. At first it was only the books that held her attention, and she would stay up all night poring over them, underlining the important passages, and writing notes in the margins. Then she took great interest in asking women savants [*al-ʿārifāt*] for the ancient remedies they used to cure different kinds of pain. She began to purchase pots, jars, vessels, and vials, and she mixed herbs both fresh and dry, making infusions, powders, and salves that she boiled, froze, and distilled. The women of the neighborhood came seeking her advice about curing one illness or another. Umm Hasan couldn't bear any of this and quarreled with her so vehemently that all the neighbors could hear. But Umm Hasan's incessant protestations and her attempts to bring her daughter back into the fold of proper housewives who please their husbands with sons and daughters, with kohl-painted eyes, made-up faces, and bodies perfumed with musk and jasmine, fell on deaf ears.[134]

Salima's medical training, as the passage indicates, straddles different gendered spheres of Andalusi intellectual life: she learns from the writings of illustrious Andalusi men but also benefits from the knowledge of female healers in her community. Her devotion to medicine and research is portrayed here as a challenge to gender norms—and, in particular, to the norms governing the behavior of wives in Muslim Granadan society. Yet Salima's work does not lead to a rupture with her husband Saʿd. In fact, Saʿd comes to accept Salima's medical research and, along the way, to take up his own form of resistance, by joining the armed struggle against Granada's new Christian rulers. Thus, even as ʿAshur's novel stages a conflict over gender norms, it ultimately sides with Salima, who follows in the footsteps of a long line of learned Andalusi women.

Like her grandfather Abu Jaʿfar, Salima pursues a line of work that has an allegorical resonance. Salima attends to the wounds and ailments of her neighbors and community. In the context of a novel about the struggles of Granada's Muslim community in the wake of the events of 1492, Salima's work functions as a response to collective trauma. For what is collective

trauma if not a communal wound that demands healing? Salima quite literally heals the wounds of the present, and she does so by turning to knowledge inherited from the past. I have called such an approach (adopting 'Ashur's
phrase) "radical conservation" because it is one that envisions a path forward
by, paradoxically, looking to the past. Salima's research into the scholarly and
popular knowledge of her Andalusi peers is not, fundamentally, about
clinging to the past, but rather about nourishing life in the present and the
future. For this reason, Salima's scholarly pursuits do not lead her to a state
of monastic isolation but rather to one of deep engagement with her neighbors and her community. Salima's neighbors begin to flock to her house
because, as the narrator explains, "she had the power of healing, and her treat-
ments cured both the body and the soul—at least that's what people were
saying."[135] Salima's cures bring fame and sustenance to her family—and they
continue to do so even after Salima's death. In the second part of 'Ashur's
trilogy, a rich Granadan merchant gives Salima's grandson a job because the
merchant remembers that Salima had long ago cured his mother of a life-
threatening disease.[136]

While Salima's medical experiments garner her admiration among her
neighbors, they also land her on the radar of the Inquisition. Toward the end
of the novel, the Inquisition authorities detain Salima and accuse her of witch-
craft. The last three chapters of *Granada* center on Salima's trial before the
Inquisition, an ordeal that concludes in her being condemned to death by
burning at the stake. Salima's Inquisitors accuse her of sorcery and of consorting with the devil. In their interrogation, they demand an explanation
for the herbs, concoctions, and books that were found in Salima's house. Pursuing this line of interrogation, one of the Inquisitors asks Salima: "Do you
not believe in the existence of black magic and witches who have the power
to induce storms, kill livestock, or infect people with deadly illnesses?"[137] In
response, Salima says, "I believe that all those things, I mean storms and the
death of livestock and people, have natural causes that we don't know about
because our knowledge as human beings is insufficient. No, my lord, I do not
believe in witches."[138]

As this exchange illustrates, Salima's confrontation with the Inquisition
stages a battle between science and religion, reason and faith. But in its portrayal of this battle, 'Ashur's novel inverts the misogynist convention that associates reason with masculinity and irrational emotion with femininity.[139]

It also challenges the long-standing Orientalist trope of the "fanatical Muslim." In defiance of these pernicious stereotypes, 'Ashur's novel pits an educated and rational Muslim woman against a panel of fanatical and superstitious male zealots. Read against the backdrop of the entire novel, Salima's confrontation with the Inquisition (the novel's culminating scene) recasts the Christian conquest of Granada and the attendant loss of al-Andalus as the story of a fanatical, patriarchal, Christian society that overturned a Muslim society committed to scientific inquiry and the intellectual and social advancement of women.

It is no coincidence, then, that as Salima faces impending death, her thoughts turn to her grandfather, Abu Ja'far, who championed her education and modeled it on the memory of famous women from al-Andalus. In the novel's last chapter, the narrator traces Salima's thoughts as they wind their way from Abu Ja'far to the learned women of Cordoba: "She conjured the image of her grandfather, Abu Ja'far, the grown-up who inscribed the first word in her book. It wasn't her father or mother who did that, but the grandfather who announced that he would provide her with an education just as he would for Hasan, and who whispered to his wife that Salima would be like the learned women of Cordoba [*ka-nisā' Qurṭuba al-'ālimāt*]."[140] In an astute analysis of this passage, Christina Civantos notes that Salima, when confronting death, imagines herself as a book.[141] Indeed, Salima is a book on which are inscribed not only the hopes and dreams of her grandfather, but also the collected knowledge of the women and men of al-Andalus, stretching from postconquest Granada back to Umayyad Cordoba.

Like the Andalusi knowledge that she embodies, Salima eventually faces the wrath and destruction of the Spanish Inquisition. In one of the novel's last scenes, Salima is led in shackles to Granada's Bibarrambla Square, where the Inquisition authorities have set up the woodpile where she will burn. This scene echoes the earlier scene of the bonfire of Islamic books in Bibarrambla Square. Through this repetition of bonfire imagery, 'Ashur's novel reinforces the idea that Salima is the embodiment of Andalusi book culture, a culture that both threatens, and is threatened by, the Spanish authorities.

Although Salima dies at the hands of the Inquisition, she leaves behind a legacy that lasts for generations, nourishing her descendants. The books that Salima inherits, catalogs, preserves, and annotates become, after her death, central characters in her family's unfolding saga. In the second part of 'Ashur's trilogy, Salima's brother introduces her grandson, 'Ali, to the hidden library of books that Salima inherited from her grandfather. Those books then become the foundation of 'Ali's clandestine education in Arabic. When 'Ali is forced to depart from Granada at the end of the novel, he places the books in a trunk that he has inherited from his aunt Maryama and buries the trunk in the courtyard of the family's house in the Albayzín neighborhood of Granada. In the third and final part of the trilogy, 'Ali takes refuge in a village near Valencia among a community of fellow Moriscos (crypto-Muslims). 'Ali serves the community by teaching Arabic to its children, thus keeping alive the link between the Moriscos and the language and culture of their Andalusi ancestors.

At the end of the trilogy, 'Ali and his neighbors, along with all of the remaining Moriscos in Spain, face deportation because of the expulsion decrees issued by King Philip III. As 'Ali stands on the Spanish coast, preparing to depart on a boat for North Africa, his mind turns to the books that he has left behind, buried in a trunk in the courtyard of his family's house in Granada. At that moment, he resolves to defy the expulsion order and to remain in Spain. In this pivotal scene, the narrator tracks 'Ali's thoughts as he comes to his bold decision to stay:

> Why leave then? Perhaps death might come in departing, not in remaining. He needed to know the meaning and details of the story, and what his ancestors had done. The question pressed him with burning urgency, and where would the answer come from? From a strange land or from here? Perhaps it was buried like the books preserved in Maryama's trunk. He would remain.[142]

'Ali's refusal to depart is framed as a need to understand the story of his ancestors—a story that is not across the sea in North Africa but rather is buried in the very soil of Granada, like Salima's books. Those books, then, are the link that connect 'Ali back to his family's heritage, just as they had previously served as a link between Salima and the illustrious female scholars of Umayyad Cordoba. The books carry the story of a culture that goes underground, but does not perish, after the expulsion decree of 1609.

We could even say that 'Ashur's trilogy extends Salima's legacy beyond 1609, connecting the story of Salima's family to the present. Indeed, the concerns of the present are never far from 'Ashur's engagements with the Andalusi past. In the lecture that 'Ashur delivered at the University of Massachusetts in 1999, she called history a "pervading presence" in her work and remarked, "I don't think that there is a clear demarcating line between the present and the past . . . The past is too much of a present and the present is too imbued with the past to make any sense without it."[143] Pursuing this line of thought, 'Ashur compared Granada, the setting of her trilogy, to Cairo's Manial el-Rawda neighborhood, which is built on a strip of land in the middle of the Nile River. "Like Manial el-Rawda which knits the two sides of the river," 'Ashur said, "Granada attempts to connect past and present by means of a metaphorical image of loss and resistance."[144] The meaning of this comparison is that Granada, like the neighborhood built in the middle of the Nile, stands in between the banks of past and present, guiding the two-way traffic between one and the other.

This two-way traffic between past and present has ramifications that cannot be reduced to a single political or cultural project. In this chapter, I have sought to trace the imprint that real and fictional Andalusi women, from Wallada to Salima, have had on feminist and women-centered projects in the modern period. 'Ashur's trilogy plays an important role in this story; yet it also points to other questions, hopes, and struggles that are embedded in the far-flung and heterogeneous project of imagining al-Andalus in the present. For instance, in 'Ashur's lecture at the University of Massachusetts, she referred to Granada as "a metaphorical image of loss and resistance" and gave the following explanation of the city's symbolism:

> To me Granada was the Granada of the Moriscos, defeated men and women whose resistance was doomed to failure. It was a correlative of my experience of the bombing of Baghdad, a bombing which brought with it the 1967 bombing of Sinai, the 1982 bombing of Beirut, and the persistent bombing of Southern Lebanon. It was a means to explore my fears, impotence and also the chances of survival through resistance.[145]

'Ashur draws a line, here, from the Granada of the Moriscos to the bombing of Baghdad during the First Gulf War, an event that, for the Egyptian writer, evoked the memory of other experiences of loss and suffering from her lifetime. Lurking in the background of these associations is, of course, the struggle for Palestine and its ongoing ramifications for Egypt, Lebanon, and the broader region. In fact, in her lecture at the University of Massachusetts, 'Ashur spoke of "the major formative influence" that the war of June 1967 had on her and her work. "I now realize," 'Ashur summed up, "that all my novels are attempts to cope with defeat."[146]

What emerges from these statements is the implicit, though clear, suggestion that the Palestinians are the Andalusis of the twentieth century—or, to adopt one of 'Ashur's metaphors, that Palestine and al-Andalus are two banks of the same river, which flows between interconnected experiences of loss and resistance. 'Ashur is far from the only modern writer to articulate this point. Within the variegated cultural afterlife of al-Andalus, the metaphorical pairing of Palestine and al-Andalus is one of the most persistent tropes, especially for Arab writers who, like 'Ashur, came of age between 1948 and 1967. But the Palestinian al-Andalus is a story that predates 1948 and that persists until the present. I take up that story in Chapter 4.

4

The Palestinian al-Andalus

On November 5, 1932, the Jaffa-based newspaper *Filastin*, the most widely read Palestinian newspaper of the time, published an article titled "Sister of Andalus, Greetings!" ("Ya ukht Andalus, 'alayki salam").[1] The article's author was Yusuf al-'Isa (1870–1948), a journalist and newspaper entrepreneur who edited *Filastin* with his cousin.[2] The occasion for al-'Isa's article was the fifteenth anniversary of the Balfour Declaration (November 2, 1917), in which Lord Balfour, Britain's foreign minister, pledged his country's support for the establishment of a Jewish homeland in Palestine. Addressing the Balfour Declaration and its nefarious consequences for Palestine, al-'Isa wrote:

> The sister of Andalus is none other than Palestine, the sacrificial animal of Britain, the victim of its policy in the twentieth century. The Arabs of the first al-Andalus had some sort of consolation because they did not leave their country until the sword dangled over their bodies. As for the Arabs of the new al-Andalus, Palestine, one stroke of the pen from Balfour was enough to sell their homeland and make them guests of their adversary.[3]

Al-'Isa's article thus opened with an explicit comparison between al-Andalus and its "sister," Palestine. With this comparison, al-'Isa traced a direct line from the loss of al-Andalus in the fifteenth century to the threat of losing Palestine in the twentieth century. In the eyes of the Palestinian journalist, al-Andalus and Palestine were two Arab homelands facing existential threats from foreign adversaries.

Al-'Isa's allusions to Palestine as "the sister of Andalus" and "the new al-Andalus," as striking as they might seem, were actually part of a broad

phenomenon in Palestinian print culture during the British Mandate period (1920–1948). Starting as far back as 1921, the newspaper *Filastin* began
publishing articles that compared Palestine to al-Andalus.[4] In June 1933
Filastin even ran a twelve-part series titled "The Andalus of the Twentieth
Century in Palestine" ("Andalus al-qarn al-'ashrin bi-Filastin"). Such explicit
comparisons between Palestine and al-Andalus were not limited to the pages
of *Filastin*. In fact, they abounded in the Palestinian press of the 1920s and
1930s, where it was not uncommon to find descriptions of Palestine as "the
second al-Andalus" and "the new al-Andalus."[5]

The question is: What did all of these comparisons to al-Andalus mean to
Palestinian writers and readers living through the turbulent decades of the
1920s and 1930s, when tensions between Palestinian Arabs and Zionist set-
tlers were on the rise? One answer may be found in an article that 'Abd al-
Ghani al-Karmi (1906–1974), a prominent Palestinian journalist, published
in *Filastin* in December 1934. The article was titled "We Want a Rigorous
National Literature Today—Who Will Bemoan the Second al-Andalus in the
Near Future?" ("Nurid al-yawm adaban qawmiyyan 'anifan: Man yandab al-
Andalus al-thaniyya 'amma qarib?"). In it, al-Karmi scolded leading writers
of his generation, such as the poet Ibrahim Tuqan, for failing to produce a
literature that reflected the plight and struggles of the Palestinian people
in the 1930s. He then issued the following call to his contemporaries:

> It is incumbent on our writers to reform that which has been corrupted
> by politics and to bring forth to the public sphere a rigorous nationalist
> literature to keep people from their errors and to revive their dead hopes.
>
> If they don't do that, then I fear that we will turn our attention to one
> of them—and it could be soon—and find him composing a poem in
> which he bemoans the second al-Andalus, bringing back to us the
> memory of the poet who bemoaned the first al-Andalus in his tearful and
> bloody poem:
>
> > *Everything declines after reaching perfection*
> > *So let no man be deceived by the sweetness of a pleasant life.*[6]

Here, the memory of al-Andalus serves as a cautionary tale. Al-Karmi warns
his contemporaries that if Palestinian writers are not able to find a literature

that captures the Palestinian reality and that inspires Palestinians to take action, then he and his readers could soon find their writers elegizing the loss of Palestine, just as the poets of al-Andalus once elegized the loss of their homeland. To drive home this point, al-Karmi cites the first line of one of the most famous poems from al-Andalus: an elegy that al-Rundi (d. 1285) wrote for Seville and the other Andalusi cities that were conquered by Christian forces in the thirteenth century.[7]

Al-Karmi's comparison between al-Andalus and Palestine hinges on familiarity and legibility. Al-Karmi assumes that his readers will be familiar with the story of al-Andalus and even with al-Rundi's elegy, which he quotes without naming the author or source. The ease and speed with which the Palestinian writer moves from the first al-Andalus to "the second al-Andalus" (that is, Palestine) suggests that he is working with cultural referents that are, if not yet hackneyed, then certainly legible for his readership. Al-Karmi's article suggests, then, that by the middle of the 1930s al-Andalus had become a recognizable and readily available point of reference for understanding and debating the plight of Palestine in the face of the dual threats of colonial rule and Zionist encroachment.

Al-Karmi was just one of many writers who used the memory of al-Andalus to sound the alarm about Palestine's precarious situation, as the country careened toward the war of 1948, an event known as the *Nakba* (or "calamity") in Palestinian historiography. Indeed, the comparison between al-Andalus and Palestine was a widespread idiom that was shared by Palestinian writers and their counterparts throughout the Arab world. Al-Andalus offered Arab writers of this period a shared point of reference for thinking about Palestine and for placing its struggles in a broader historical framework, one that resonated with readers inside Palestine and beyond its borders. Among the most famous figures to participate in this discourse was the renowned Iraqi poet Muhammad Mahdi al-Jawahiri (1901–1997), who, in the period between 1929 and 1948, wrote at least two poems that expressed concern for Palestine by comparing the country to al-Andalus.[8]

Al-Jawahiri's work would find echoes in Palestinian poetry from the same period. For example, at a meeting of the Arab National Fund in Haifa in 1945, Palestinian writer Burhan al-Din al-'Abbushi (1911–1995) recited a rousing poem in which he called on his compatriots to fight for Palestine in order to avoid the fate of al-Andalus:

O son of the land, you who are its only hope,
On the day of eviction, listen to the crow's caw!
What befell al-Andalus grips its peer.
So sacrifice on its behalf before it is too late [lit. "before its
    departure"].[9]

Here again al-Andalus serves as a cautionary tale. This message is reinforced
by the image of the crow, a common symbol of foreboding.[10] In the original
Arabic, al-ʿAbbushi rhymes the "crow" (*ghurāb*) with "departure" (*dhahāb*),
foreshadowing the imminent collapse of Palestine, a repetition of the fate that
befell al-Andalus.

But al-Andalus is much more than a cautionary tale for Palestinian
writers and their allies. Long after the *Nakba* of 1948, al-Andalus remained
a potent site for reflecting on the past, present, and future of Palestine. From
1948 until the present, al-Andalus has been a persistent presence in Palestinian
literature—primarily in poetry but also in other genres, such as theater and
speculative fiction. In a book-length study addressing this phenomenon,
Palestinian scholar Muhammad ʿAbd Allah al-Juʿaydi has observed, "In general, the concept of al-Andalus in Palestinian literature carries the meaning
of loss and of sighing over what is lost."[11] I am indebted to al-Juʿaydi, Spanish
scholar Pedro Martínez Montávez, and others for helping me to build the
corpus for this chapter.[12] However, I think that many of the scholars who have
addressed this topic have underestimated its historical range, semantic elas-
ticity, and political possibilities. In the long discursive tradition that I am
calling the "Palestinian al-Andalus," the meanings of al-Andalus are varied
and supple. In this tradition, al-Andalus is not only a symbol of loss and occupation but also a vehicle for thinking about resistance and resilience. It
is not only a means of lamenting a lost past but also a platform for imagining
a possible future.

In fact, one of my main claims in this chapter is that al-Andalus is useful
for thinking about various forms of Palestinian time. Some of these forms
might seem obvious. For instance, the "Palestinian al-Andalus" can evoke a
sense of nostalgic time, one that finds its meaning in a longing look to the
past. Another form that this imaginary can adopt is that of cyclical time,
where a writer, such as al-Karmi or al-ʿAbbushi, imagines a repetition of past
losses in the present. Yet these temporal modes do not exhaust the possibilities

of thinking about Palestinian time—or of thinking about how Palestinian time intersects with Andalusi time.

In an interview with French newspaper *Le Monde* in 1983, Palestinian poet Mahmud Darwish (1942–2008) said, "Palestine is not a memory, but rather an existence; not a past, but rather a future. Palestine, it is the aesthetics of al-Andalus; it is the Andalus of the possible."[13] Later in the chapter I will return to this quote in order to place it within Darwish's extensive meditations on al-Andalus. For now, I want to draw attention to Darwish's description of Palestine as "the Andalus of the possible" (*l'Andalousie possible*). The "possibility" that fuels Darwish's thinking is not the same one that motivated his predecessors al-'Abbushi and al-Karmi: Darwish is referring, not to the possibility that Palestine could become lost like al-Andalus, but instead to the possibility that Palestine could return in the future. He suggests that the power of Palestine, like the power of al-Andalus, resides not in the past but instead in the future—in a future that is possible, if not yet fully articulated.

As the quote from Darwish illustrates, Palestinian reflections on al-Andalus are often curiously poised between past, present, and future.[14] Their temporality is split in multiple directions. They open up onto alternative timescapes in which the past is open for debate and the future is subject to ongoing negotiation. In this arena, history repeats itself, but with each repetition, it leaves open the possibility of revision and reimagination. This chapter, then, will explore the long and ongoing story of how Palestinian writers have turned to al-Andalus as a source of meaning and inspiration, as a narrative structure for thinking about Palestinian history, and as a vehicle for imagining Palestinian futures.

The Palestinian al-Andalus between *Nakba* and *Naksa,* 1948–1967

In the crucial period between the establishment of the state of Israel in 1948 and the June 1967 war, in which Israel occupied the West Bank and the Gaza strip, al-Andalus continued to take shape as a trope for talking about Palestine. Whereas before 1948, comparisons between Palestine and al-Andalus usually came in the conditional (as in "Palestine *could become* al-Andalus"), after 1948 the mood and temporality of such comparisons took on new complexity. The Palestinian al-Andalus would become, at once, retrospective and prospective, elegiac and visionary. For many Palestinian writers and activists working in this period, the turn to the memory of al-Andalus was not an admission of defeat; rather, it was an attempt to learn from the past and, in so doing, to call for resistance in the present.

One of the first and most influential writers from this period to imagine a Palestinian al-Andalus was Burhan al-Din al-ʿAbbushi, a poet and playwright from the city of Jenin. As I have already noted, al-ʿAbbushi made an early allusion to al-Andalus in a poem he recited in Haifa in 1945. But his most enduring contribution to the Palestinian al-Andalus was his 1949 play in verse *The Specter of al-Andalus* (*Shabah al-Andalus*), written in the wake of the *Nakba* of 1948. The play centers on the battle for Jenin (1948), a battle in which al-ʿAbbushi himself fought alongside a contingent of Iraqi volunteers. The play's main character is an unnamed "Poet"—clearly an alter ego for al-ʿAbbushi—who participates in the battle of Jenin and provides commentary for the audience.

In his introduction to the play, al-ʿAbbushi places the war of 1948 in a long historical trajectory that harkens back to al-Andalus. In particular, he compares Palestine to the situation of al-Andalus in the middle of the eleventh century, when the Umayyad caliphate splintered into a number of rival kingdoms known as the *taifa* kings. In present-day scholarship on al-Andalus, the term *taifa* (or *ṭāʾifa*) is generally reserved for referring to a specific moment in the political history of al-Andalus: the period between the collapse of the Umayyad caliphate in 1031 and the Almoravid conquest of al-Andalus at the end of the eleventh century. Al-ʿAbbushi, however, takes a much broader view of the *taifa* period: he uses the term *ṭāʾifa* to refer to the long period of political instability, internal strife, and territorial loss that begins in the eleventh century and stretches to the conquest of the kingdom of Granada in 1492. In other words, al-ʿAbbushi treats the term *ṭāʾifa* as a shorthand for referring to political division in al-Andalus—and for linking political division to the eventual fall of al-Andalus.

It is this cycle of political division and territorial loss that al-ʿAbbushi sees as the link between medieval al-Andalus and modern Palestine. On this point, he writes in the introduction to *The Specter of al-Andalus:*

> And look how history repeats itself! For the authority of the Arab state in al-Andalus dwindled during the dynasty of the Banu al-Ahmar [1232–1492], and that resembles what we see today in the Arab Triangle and what

remains of the mountains in the region of Jerusalem, Hebron, and Gaza. And even this piece will get away from us if our leaders do not learn a lesson from the fate of the *ṭā'ifa* kings, and if the Arabs from these tiny countries do not hasten to join ranks, to mobilize thousands, to give up division, to renounce hypocrisy, and to learn the lesson of what happened to the Arabs of the Banu al-Ahmar and their obliteration.[15]

In this passage, al-'Abbushi compares the Muslim kingdom of Granada, ruled by the Banu al-Ahmar dynasty until 1492, to the "Arab Triangle," the region between the Palestinian cities of Jenin, Tulkarm, and Nablus. Taking the comparison a step further, al-'Abbushi compares the small and fractured Arab states that opposed Israel in the war of 1948 to the *taifa* kings who divided up al-Andalus in the eleventh century. The playwright calls on the leaders of the Arab world to "learn the lesson of what happened to the Arabs" of al-Andalus. That lesson is, for al-'Abbushi, straightforward: a divided Arab world cannot stand and will eventually succumb to foreign occupation.

Building on these ideas, al-'Abbushi goes on to address the title that he chose for his play:

I named this book of mine *The Sister of al-Andalus* [*Ukht al-Andalus*], but another writer was appalled by this name, thinking it a harbinger of misfortune. So I substituted it for *The Specter of al-Andalus* [*Shabah al-Andalus*] . . .

With the title *The Specter of al-Andalus,* I wanted to draw the attention of the Arabs—people, kings, and governments—to the fact that our current state of disagreement and strife is sufficient to lose Palestine and the Arab lands, just as al-Andalus was lost. This title, *The Specter of al-Andalus,* brings back to the Arabs' memory the story of *The Arabs' Exit from al-Andalus,* which we often performed in our theaters so that people would learn a lesson from it. And here we are in these times performing the story of the Arabs' exit from Palestine. So when will the Arabs perform the story of the Arabs' entry in Palestine and liberation of it? Certainly this story will be performed on the day in which all foreign influence vanishes from our land and from the company of our life, since it is the foundation of all tribulation and the source of all malady.[16]

In the move from the original title to the definitive one, al-ʿAbbushi traded a sisterly metaphor for a spectral one. The play's original title, *The Sister of al-Andalus,* suggested kinship and intergenerational transmission—a family history that repeats itself. In contrast, the second and definitive title, *The Specter of al-Andalus,* evokes an image of al-Andalus as a specter that hovers over and haunts the Palestinian present. In the second title, the Andalusi past is very much present, but it is not inevitable. Rather, it serves as a "lesson" for learning from the past and, perhaps, for intervening in the present to build a different future. Indeed, it is important to note that al-ʿAbbushi, in this passage and throughout his introduction to the play, uses didactic metaphors to talk about his understanding of al-Andalus. Here, then, al-Andalus is not a story about loss but rather a story that teaches you how to avoid it.

Al-ʿAbbushi does not only understand al-Andalus as a lesson but also, crucially, as a story. In this regard, it is noteworthy that his main point of reference in the previous passage is not actually al-Andalus itself but rather a play about al-Andalus, one that he and his peers would "perform in our theaters so that people would learn a lesson from it."[17] For al-ʿAbbushi, then, the comparison between Palestine and al-Andalus is not an operation that involves a direct leap from 1948 to 1492. Instead, it is a comparison that is mediated by many interposed layers of storytelling. Al-ʿAbbushi suggests that al-Andalus is a story that repeats itself, but he also suggests that each repetition holds out a potential for revision, for creating new outcomes and new meanings. In other words, the story of "the Arabs' exit from al-Andalus" could lead, over time, to the story of the Arabs' entry in Palestine.

While al-ʿAbbushi looked to the *taifa* kings as a precedent for thinking about political division in Palestine, his compatriot, the poet and literary critic Salma al-Khadraʾ al-Jayyusi (b. 1925), took inspiration from a different facet of Andalusi history: the great Umayyad mosque of Cordoba. That building, the most famous monument constructed by the Umayyad state in al-Andalus, is at the center of al-Jayyusi's poem "The Mosque of Cordoba" ("Jamiʿ Qurtuba"). Al-Jayyusi first published this work in 1955 in the Lebanese literary journal *Adab* and later included it in her first collection, *al-ʿAwda min al-nabʿ al-halim* (The return from the dreamy fountain, 1960). The collection, published in the heyday of pan-Arab political rhetoric, contained several poems that addressed the Palestinian crisis. Most notably, the poem "Bi-la judhur" (Rootless) was a long free-verse meditation on the *Nakba* and the exodus of Palestinian refugees from Palestine.[18] Although the allusions to Palestine in "The Mosque of Cordoba" are, in comparison, more muted, the poem, nonetheless, works to mobilize pan-Arab support for the Palestinian struggle. Crucially, the poem treats the Mosque of Cordoba as a source of inspiration for such political action.

Al-Jayyusi wrote "The Mosque of Cordoba" after a visit to the mosque in the 1950s, in a period when she was living in Spain with her husband, the Jordanian diplomat Burhan al-Jayyusi.[19] The Palestinian poet is thus part of a long tradition of Arab writers who have used a sojourn in Spain as an opportunity for reflecting on the past, present, and future of the Arab world. Al-Jayyusi nods to this tradition in the poem's opening lines:

> Behold the place of circumambulation [*al-maṭāf*]! For it is God's
>> house: our mosque
>>> *God is great!*
> From our spirit, it attained immortality and lived to immortalize us
>>> *God is great!*
> It is an Arab fragment in the land of Andalus, which I see
> remaining throughout time as monuments to good fortune on its soil.
> And, as long as time wishes, the echo of its muezzin flashes from its
>> heights.
> Listen to the voice of the colossal mosque that calls out, proclaiming:
>> "I am here, I am here
>> a symbol, I am
>> despite the trials and tribulations,
>> I continue to disdain time."[20]

As these lines illustrate, the poem stages an encounter between the Mosque of Cordoba and a speaker who oscillates between an individual perspective ("I") and a collective one ("we"). Indeed, all three actors—the mosque, the individual speaker, and the collective identity—are present from the first line of the poem. By placing the word *masjadnā* ("our mosque") at the end of the first line, the poet draws attention to the first-person plural possessive, "our." But who, I ask, is the collective "we" invoked in this line? And what is the relationship between this "we" and the Mosque of Cordoba?

Al-Jayyusi has left us some helpful hints for responding to these questions. The first line of her poem places the Mosque of Cordoba in a pan-Islamic imaginary. The speaker calls the mosque *al-maṭāf*, which I have translated as "the place of circumambulation." The term *al-maṭāf* usually refers to the mosque of Mecca, where Muslim pilgrims perform seven ritual circumambulations around the Ka'ba as part of the hajj. By using this term, the poet associates the Mosque of Cordoba with the holy sites in Mecca, suggesting that Cordoba is a second Mecca for Muslims. This association is reinforced by the following phrase, "God's house" (*bayt Allah*), another name for the sacred mosque of Mecca. Through this opening, the poem casts the Mosque of Cordoba as a holy pilgrimage site for all Muslims. The Islamic framework continues to be showcased in the next three lines, where the speaker echoes the call to prayer, "God is great!" The muezzin's call to prayer thus resounds across time, from the period of Umayyad Cordoba to the twentieth century.

While the poem's first four lines underline the mosque's Islamic identity, the speaker soon shifts her focus to highlight the building's Arab identity. In this move, al-Jayyusi follows the example of many other writers from the Mashriq (the Arab East)—writers who, as I discussed in Chapter 1, have tended to emphasize the Arabness of al-Andalus. This way of talking about the legacy of al-Andalus comes to the fore in the poem's fifth line, where the speaker refers to the mosque as "an Arab fragment in the land of Andalus" (*qiṭ'a 'arabiyya fī arḍ Andalus*). For the rest of the poem, Arabness predominates as the collective identity uniting the speaker, her audience, and the Mosque of Cordoba. This identity is particularly explicit in the poem's third stanza, which circles around the repeated assertion of a collective "we" whose identity is revealed in the stanza's last line: "We are the Arabs: so let the world bow before us!"[21]

Up until this point, al-Jayyusi's poem, while elegant and erudite, is virtually indistinguishable in its themes from the works of earlier Arab and Muslim writers who visited Spain in the modern period and composed poems that celebrated the monuments of al-Andalus, treating them as springboards for meditations on the past grandeur of Arab or Muslim civilization.[22] In the second half of the poem, however, al-Jayyusi's speaker pivots from the glories of the past to the struggles of the present, making repeated allusions to "our struggle" (*niḍālnā*) and "our fight" (*kifāḥnā*). One such allusion comes in a section where the speaker addresses 'Abd al-Rahman I (d. 788), the founder of the Umayyad state in al-Andalus, and repeatedly hails him as the "builder" (*bannā*') of al-Andalus. At the end of that section, the speaker says:

> Builder, o builder of ours!
> The nations feared our bloc [*takattulanā*]
> and the world shook, by wind, sea, and ocean
> because of our fight [*li-kifāḥinā*]![23]

With these lines, the speaker evokes a moment of political unity ("our bloc"), forged from communal struggle ("our fight"). These lines could be a reference to the political unity that 'Abd al-Rahman I brought to al-Andalus with the foundation of the Umayyad state in the eighth century. Yet, it is hard not to see some connection between these verses and the political struggles that roiled the Arab world in the 1950s, in the wake of the 1948 *Nakba*. Like al-'Abbushi in the prologue to *Shabah al-Andalus,* al-Jayyusi underlines the need for unity—that is, for Arabs to form a united bloc (the meaning of the verbal noun *al-takattul*). The poet also calls for *kifāḥ* (fight, or struggle), a word that she uses elsewhere in the same collection to refer to the fight for Palestine.[24]

The interplay between past and present remains subtle for much of the poem but becomes much more pronounced in the poem's final stanza. There, the speaker shifts her focus from a bygone past to a brilliant and imminent future:

> Tomorrow is ours
> There is no doubt that tomorrow is ours.
> Time turned and returned to kiss our separation
> And time in its turning
> is like the stars running their course.
> Yesterday, it radiated with our dawn
> and rose to the highest heights . . . and then it dropped and fell to
>   our horizon.
> There where it fell . . . the masters of light toppled us
> And evening enveloped us, and the wings of life folded up on us

The mighty giants fell
And the great geniuses fell
The chisel broke to pieces, and rust took possession of the sword.
And hope extinguished from our eyes!
Today, a first trace of light returned to our eyelids
Today, a first trace of brightness returned to our blade
Tomorrow, our stars will break forth
Tomorrow, our resolve will shine
Tomorrow is our greatest day
For tomorrow is ours
There is no doubt that tomorrow is ours![25]

The final stanza revolves around the refrain "Tomorrow is ours," an assertion that is repeated at the beginning and the end of the stanza. In between, the speaker traces the long circular movement of history, as it turns from a radiant "yesterday" to a period of decline and loss, and from there to a "today," where hope ("a first trace of light") has returned. But the stanza's focus is decidedly future-oriented, pushing the reader inexorably toward a "tomorrow" that will surpass the glories of "yesterday." If we connect the poem's conclusion to its beginning, we could say that the speaker's reunion with the Mosque of Cordoba does not ultimately lead to a nostalgic meditation on the past but rather to an energetic claim on the future. In this work, Cordoba is not (or not merely) a site of nostalgic longing, nor is it a cautionary tale about the dangers of political disunity; rather, it is a horizon for imagining the future, a future inspired by the past but built from the collective struggles of the present.

In al-Jayyusi's poem about the Mosque of Cordoba, the references to the Palestinian struggle are muted but hard to miss. In the work of her contemporary Harun Hashim Rashid (1927–2020), these references become much more explicit and forceful, as does the poet's call to arms. Rashid was born and educated in Gaza and garnered acclaim in the 1950s as a poet whose work was firmly committed to the Palestinian cause. Al-Jayyusi would later describe Rashid as "the first poet to address himself to the question of the physical and spiritual alienation of the Palestinians."[26] In the period between the wars of 1948 and 1967, Rashid remained in Gaza, working as a teacher and as the director of the local broadcasting station of "Sawt al-'Arab" (Voice of the Arabs). In the June 1967 war, Israeli forces occupied Gaza and eventually compelled Rashid to flee the region.[27]

In the wake of those events, Rashid published his poem "La mafarr" (No escape, or, Nowhere to flee) in 1968. The poem is an extended riff on a famous speech that is attributed to Tariq b. Ziyad, the North African general who led the Muslim conquest of the Iberian Peninsula in 711. As the story goes, Tariq and his men were vastly outnumbered by the forces of the Visigoth king Roderic. Undaunted by this challenge, Tariq chose to burn the ships that he and his army had used to cross the Strait of Gibraltar so that his men would not be tempted to retreat. The North African general then delivered a rousing speech to his soldiers, urging them to stand their ground against the superior Visigoth army. Tariq's speech (which is of dubious authenticity) has come down to us as one of the most celebrated examples of Arabic oratory.[28] Of particular fame is the speech's opening: "People! Where will you flee [*ayna al-mafarr*]? The sea is behind you, and the enemy is front. By God, there is nothing for you now but courage and endurance."[29] These famous lines are the inspiration for Harun Hashim Rashid's poem, "La mafarr."

Rashid's poem harvests the words, themes, and rhetorical features of Tariq's speech to launch a call for Palestinian resistance in the wake of the June 1967 war. The poem's speaker adopts the position of Tariq b. Ziyad, exhorting his comrades to stand their ground and fight against all odds. In the poem, the most famous words from Tariq's speech become the building blocks upon which Rashid mounts his call to arms. Echoing Tariq, Rashid's speaker says:

> For today is your day
> The sea is behind you
> and the adversary is in front of you.
> By God, there is nothing for you now . . .
> but endurance
> By God, there is nothing for you now . . .
> but the grave.[30]

In these lines, the speaker replicates Tariq's memorable image of an army caught between the sea and the enemy. The poet returns to this image multiple times in the poem, developing it like a musical motif that recurs throughout the text.

In the second appearance of the motif, the speaker even makes an explicit allusion to Tariq, thus highlighting the relationship between the poem and Tariq's speech. The allusion to Tariq comes on the heels of a string of imperatives that the speaker addresses to his audience:

> So crush what lies in front of you
> and destroy the obstacles.
> Seek inspiration, my loved ones
> in the darkest straits.
> You are on the path
> Forge ahead . . .
> And follow . . .
> Your history . . .
> Your glory . . .
> Wests and Easts
> Clamor in your ears
> Like thunder, like lightning
> Just like what Tariq said to the conquerors
> The sea is behind you
> The adversary is in front of you
> By God, there is nothing for you now
> but endurance
> By God, there is nothing for you now
> but the grave.[31]

This passage not only cites Tariq by name and echoes his words but also mimics two of the main rhetorical features of Tariq's speech: imperatives and parallel structures. The passage culminates with a parallel structure ("By God, there is nothing for you . . .") that draws attention to the rhyme between "endurance" (*al-ṣabr*) and "the grave" (*al-qabr*). With this rhyme, the poem's speaker, like Tariq speaking on the eve of the conquest of al-Andalus, stresses to his audience that their only options are struggle or death.

In 711, Tariq used this message to spur his army to the conquest of al-Andalus; in 1968, the poet Harun Hashim Rashid revived Tariq's words to exhort his compatriots to take back Palestine. This goal is outlined in the poem's final stanza, where the speaker says:

The signs of the road
Are laid out before you
Struggle . . . struggle
The aim of all aims
War . . .
Pitched battle . . .
Blazing
And violent rebellion
Bellows out the earthquake
Saying:
There is no doubt about it . . . no doubt
So come forth
So that the mountains may clamor
In Jerusalem . . .
In Nablus . . .
In Jarizim . . .
In 'Aybal . . .
Rebellion . . .
Rebellion . . .
O men . . .
O men . . .
The sea is behind you
And the adversary is in your homes
By God, there is nothing for you now
But endurance
By God, there is nothing for you now
But the grave
There is no escape
From the necessity of combat
No escape
So fight . . .
And fight . . .
Until there is . . .
Victory . . . [32]

Calling for "struggle" (al-niḍāl) and "rebellion" (al-thawra), the speaker invokes the names of four Palestinian places that were occupied by Israeli forces in the 1967 war: Jerusalem, Nablus, Jarizim, and 'Aybal. (The last two are the mountains that surround Nablus.) This invocation of conquered places is reminiscent of a similar move in Andalusi city elegies, where poets would often list place names to revive and preserve the memory of the conquered cities of al-Andalus.[33] In Rashid's poem, however, the invocation of place names does not serve an elegiac function but rather an exhortatory one: the speaker calls on his compatriots to take back these places. To signal this call, the speaker turns one last time to the words from Tariq's speech. In the final reprise of the motif, however, the speaker introduces subtle variations that adapt Tariq's speech to the context of post-1967 Palestine. The speaker and his audience are still caught between the sea and the enemy, but now, the enemy is not "in front of you" but rather "in your homes" (fī diyārikum). This variation calls to mind the Israeli occupation of Palestinian lands and homes in the wars of 1948 and 1967. It also places the Israeli occupying forces in the position of the Visigoth forces that opposed Tariq b. Ziyad's army in 711. Reaching across time from 1967 to 711, Rashid's speaker appropriates Tariq's words, but he also alters them so that they lead to an image of imminent "victory" (al-naṣr), instead of a vision of certain death ("the grave"). Harun Hashim Rashid's "La mafarr" is, thus, a Palestinian poem crafted in the mold of an Andalusi speech. By drawing a line from the conquest of al-Andalus in the eighth century to the fight for Palestine in the twentieth century, the poem suggests a cyclical history of struggles that repeat over time. However, in Rashid's poem, the echo of al-Andalus in Palestine is not a harbinger of loss and occupation; on the contrary, it is a memory that ignites a call to reclaim Palestine.

When read together, the works by Rashid, al-Jayyusi, and al-'Abbushi illustrate both the diversity and the coherence of the discourse that I am calling the "Palestinian al-Andalus." The three Palestinian writers invoke the full run of Andalusi history: from Tariq b. Ziyad's conquest in 711, to the apogee of Umayyad Cordoba, to the disintegration of the Umayyad caliphate into taifa kingdoms, and finally to the conquest of Granada in 1492. Although looking to different moments in Andalusi history, all three writers find in al-Andalus not only a historical analogue for post-Nakba Palestine but also an inspiration for imagining a Palestinian future.

The Andalus of the Possible

The list of Palestinian poets and authors who, in the long wake of the 1967 war, wrote about al-Andalus reads like a veritable "who's who" of modern Palestinian literature. That list includes such names as Mu'in Bsisu (1927–1984), Samih al-Qasim (b. 1939), Khalid Abu Khalid (b. 1937), Muhammad al-Qaysi (b. 1944)—and, most famously, Mahmud Darwish (1942–2008), who is widely regarded as the leading Palestinian poet of his generation.[34] Salma al-Khadra' al-Jayyusi has called Darwish "the poet of Palestinian identity par excellence" and "the finest Arab lyrical poet" of his time.[35] In this section, I will focus on Darwish's writings, not only because of the poet's prominent place in the canon of Palestinian literature but also because of the breadth and depth of his engagements with the memory of al-Andalus. From the early 1970s until the early 1990s, Darwish scattered allusions to al-Andalus, like breadcrumbs, throughout his poetry and prose works. Over this twenty-year period, al-Andalus became one of the primary metaphors and referents that Darwish used to reflect on the past, present, and future of Palestine.

Darwish was born in 1942 in the Palestinian village of al-Birwa, near the coastal city Acre ('Akka).[36] In 1948, when Darwish was still a young child, Israeli forces razed his home village, pushing Darwish and his family to flee to Lebanon. The following year, Darwish and his family snuck back across the border and became internal refugees in the newly created state of Israel.[37] They were classified as "present-absentees," a legal category that the Israeli government established to describe the Palestinian refugees who wandered within the state of Israel, without homes or citizenship.[38] This paradoxical condition of "present-absence" shaped Darwish's young life as a Palestinian refugee growing up in Israel, a state that did not recognize the existence of Palestine. Over the course of his career, Darwish would often return to the paradox of the "present-absentee" and use it as a vehicle for talking about Palestine and Palestinians—a place and a people that insist on remaining present, despite efforts to make them absent. This tension between presence and absence also pertains to Darwish's treatment of al-Andalus. Like Palestine, al-Andalus is an absence that remains very present in Darwish's writings.

Darwish's earliest writings about al-Andalus are from the early 1970s, when the poet left his homeland for a long period of exile. By this time, Darwish had already established a name for himself as a poet and journalist whose writings sought to give voice to Palestinians living under Israeli rule.[39] His early work led to several clashes with the Israeli authorities. In the 1960s, Darwish was imprisoned five times for such offenses as traveling without permission to recite his poetry in public or publishing a nationalist poem in a newspaper.[40] After an extended house arrest in Haifa in 1969, Darwish decided to leave Israel in 1970. He first traveled to Moscow with a delegation from the Israeli Communist Party. After a brief stint in the Russian capital, the poet moved to Cairo, where he joined the staff of *al-Ahram*, Egypt's leading newspaper. Less than two years later, in 1973, he moved to Beirut to work for the Palestinian Liberation Organization (PLO). Darwish would remain in Beirut until the Israeli invasion of the city in 1982.[41]

The earliest allusion to al-Andalus that I have found in Darwish's work dates to this period of exile and, in particular, to the first volume of poetry that Darwish published after leaving Israel / Palestine: *Uhibbuki aw la uhibbuki* (I love you or I don't love you, 1972). That volume includes a suite of poems titled "Psalms" ("Mazamir"). The sixteenth psalm goes as follows:

> I toy with time
> As a prince caresses a horse
> And I play with the days
> As children play with colorful marbles.
>
> Today I celebrate
> The passing of a day on the previous one
> And tomorrow I will celebrate
> The passing of two days on yesterday.
> I drink to yesterday's health
> In remembrance of the coming day.
> And thus I carry on my life!
>
> When I fell from my indomitable horse
> And broke my arm,
> I felt pain in my finger, which was wounded
> a thousand years ago!

When I commemorated the passing of forty days on the city of
   Acre's death,
I burst into tears for Granada.

And when the hangman's noose encircled my neck,
I felt a deep hatred for my enemies
Because they stole my tie![42]

Although only featuring a passing reference to Granada, the poem anticipates two elements of Darwish's subsequent engagements with the legacy of al-Andalus: temporal playfulness and spatial slippage. In this and future works, Darwish plays with, and eventually elides, the temporal and spatial gaps that separate al-Andalus from Palestine. Such play is evident from the poem's first stanza, in which the speaker boasts: "I toy with time [*udāʿib al-zaman*] / As a prince caresses a horse / And I play with the days / As children play with colorful marbles." Time, here, is the speaker's plaything; it is malleable in the speaker's hands. The speaker toggles easily between today, yesterday, and tomorrow—celebrating in one moment the passing of another. As the events of one day bleed into those of another, the speaker perceives that an accident in the present resonates with an injury from the deep past ("I felt pain in my finger, which was wounded / a thousand years ago!"). It is in this slippery terrain, where past bleeds into present, that the poem makes its allusion to al-Andalus. The speaker commemorates the loss of Acre on the fortieth day of its passing (a time of ritual mourning in Islam), and his mourning for Acre leads seamlessly to his weeping for the loss of Granada. Thus, for the speaker, the occupation of Acre in 1948 resonates with a wound suffered far away and long ago in al-Andalus.

Even as Darwish set out, in the early 1970s, to probe the comparison between Palestine and al-Andalus, he was also quick to signal the limitations of this comparison. This point emerges clearly in the first of the three major works of autobiographical prose that he wrote over the course of his career: *Yawmiyyat al-huzn al-ʿadi* (*Journal of an Ordinary Grief*), published in Beirut in 1973. One of the book's first chapters, titled "The Moon Did Not Fall into the Well," is an extended dialogue between two characters whose identities are not revealed until the end of the chapter. In the last lines of the chapter, we discover that the dialogue is between the narrator and his childhood self.

The narrative voice is thus doubled and split across two times. The older speaker shares memories of his childhood with the younger speaker and explains the circumstances under which he and his family fled from al-Birwa to Lebanon during the 1948 war.

The younger speaker asks the older speaker if Palestine is "the lost paradise" (*al-firdaws al-mafqūd*), a phrase that has, since the early twentieth century, served as a popular nickname for al-Andalus in Arabic.[43] The child narrator's use of the phrase leads the older narrator to an extended reflection on the differences between al-Andalus and Palestine:

> As long as the struggle continues, the paradise is not lost but remains occupied and subject to being regained . . . Palestinians cannot look at their homeland from the perspective of the lost paradise, as the Arabs look back on al-Andalus or as the faithful look forward to their reward [in heaven]. Between Palestine and al-Andalus there is a difference that resembles death . . . The idea of the lost paradise is alluring to poets in need of a moving topic, but it inflicts on the Palestinian condition an accumulation of tears and weakness in the blood. This is how my homeland surpasses paradise: it resembles paradise but is possible.[44]

In this passage, Darwish's narrator (an alter ego for Darwish himself) seems to reject outright the comparison between al-Andalus and Palestine, asserting that between the two there is "a difference that resembles death." To equate Palestine with the "lost paradise" of al-Andalus is, in the older narrator's view, to accept Palestine's defeat and demise. The narrator avows that, "as long as the struggle" continues, Palestine, unlike al-Andalus, "remains occupied and subject to being regained." The narrator's main point of contention, here, is not so much with the metaphorical possibilities of al-Andalus as it is with a specific and widespread vision of al-Andalus as the "lost paradise." The narrator associates this phrase with a sense of irrevocable loss. In the narrator's eyes, Palestine resembles the "paradise" of al-Andalus but also surpasses it because, unlike al-Andalus, Palestine is a paradise that remains "possible." In other words, Darwish replaces the paradigm of the "lost paradise" with another paradigm: that of the "possible" paradise, whose horizon is the future, not the past.

Judging from this passage in Darwish's autobiography, it would be easy to suppose that the Palestinian writer would abandon any comparison between

Palestine and al-Andalus in his future writings. On the contrary, however, Darwish's allusions to al-Andalus would become even more insistent and polyvalent over the subsequent two decades. A metaphor that refuses to go quietly, al-Andalus rises to the surface, time and time again, in Darwish's poetry, prose, and interviews from the 1980s and 1990s. It is not that Darwish retracts his earlier assertions and succumbs to a vision of Palestine as a "lost paradise." What happens, instead, is that Darwish's vision of al-Andalus, like his vision of Palestine, evolves toward a horizon of possibility and futurity—toward what he would call "the Andalus of the possible." Along the way, Darwish conjures an Andalus futurism that goes hand in hand with a Palestinian futurism.[45]

Darwish would elaborate on these ideas in several of his writings and interviews from the 1980s and early 1990s—culminating in the eleven-part poetic suite "Ahad 'ashar kawkaban 'ala akhir al-mashhad al-andalusi" (Eleven stars over the last Andalusi scene, 1992). The work from this period emerged from an experience of intense and prolonged itinerancy. In the summer of 1982, during the Israeli invasion of Lebanon, Darwish fled Beirut along with the rest of the PLO leadership. The poet then began a long period of wandering in which he moved between different cities in Europe and the Middle East, residing primarily in Paris. This peripatetic period, between Darwish's flight from Beirut in 1982 and his eventual return to Palestine in 1996, was one of the poet's most fecund and led to some of his most celebrated works. It was also a period in which Darwish turned, again and again, to the memory of al-Andalus, using it to think about the aftermath of the 1982 war and about the future of Palestine.[46]

In January 1983, a few months after fleeing from Beirut, Darwish gave an interview to *Le Monde*. Responding to a question about his childhood, Darwish told the interviewer from the French newspaper:

My childhood, it's not just mine; it's a collective childhood. Its place does not evoke al-Andalus because this has been lost forever. Al-Andalus is no longer a place; it is a psychological state. As for Palestine, it is my childhood; it is an achievable paradise, not a lost paradise. When I speak about it (and I speak about it a lot), it is to get my hands back on that which was the origin of my existence. In this sense, Palestine is not a memory, but rather an existence; not a past, but rather a future. Palestine, it is the aesthetics of al-Andalus; it is the Andalus of the possible.[47]

Here again, Darwish refuses to equate Palestine with the "lost paradise" of al-Andalus. Yet, at the same time, he leaves open the possibility of finding another way of relating Palestine to al-Andalus. In particular, he emphasizes the distinction between al-Andalus as a place and al-Andalus as "a psychological state." While the former is lost, the latter resides, for Darwish, in the domain of the aesthetic and the possible.

Darwish's comments bring to mind a famous passage from Aristotle's *Poetics,* where the Greek philosopher draws a distinction between history and poetry. Aristotle claims that the difference between the historian and the poet "is that the former relates things that have happened, the latter things that may happen . . . Poetry tends to speak in universals, history of particulars."[48] Without citing this passage from Aristotle, Darwish lands on a similar set of conclusions. His comments to the interviewer from *Le Monde* suggest that he does not want to equate Palestine to the *place* of al-Andalus, a place that was lost in 1492; he does, however, want to retain the idea, or "psychological state," of al-Andalus. Adopting Aristotle's terms, we could say that Darwish is more interested in the *poetry* of al-Andalus than he is in the history of al-Andalus. That is, he is interested in al-Andalus's potential to transcend a particular time and place and to speak to people living in different contexts. It is for this reason, I think, that Darwish calls Palestine "the aesthetics of al-Andalus" and "the Andalus of the possible." For Darwish, Palestine is not the Andalus that *was* or *is* but rather the Andalus that *could be.*

Perhaps the right way to think about Darwish's approach to al-Andalus is not to focus on the question of verbal tense but rather on the question of mood. Darwish's Andalus is not indicative but rather subjunctive: it is the Andalus of *could* and *might,* the Andalus of potentiality and desire. It is no coincidence, then, that the subjunctive mood governs Darwish's allusions to Cordoba in one of his most famous poems from the 1980s: "Idha kana li an u'id al-bidaya" (Were it up to me to begin again), published in the collection *Ward aqall* (Fewer roses, 1986). The poem begins:

> Were it up to me to begin again, I would choose what I chose: the
> roses on the fence
> I would travel again on the paths that might and might not lead to
> Cordoba.[49]

These lines are prominently displayed today on a plaque in the Mahmud
Darwish Museum in Ramallah (Figure 4.1). In the poem, they set in motion
a series of conditional statements that are predicated on the hypothetical
possibility of return to an unspecified origin ("Were it up to me to begin again").
It is in this domain of hypotheticals and conditionals where the speaker
mentions a return trip to Cordoba. Yet even this statement is shrouded in
additional uncertainty. In the second line of the poem, the speaker twice
uses the Arabic particle *qad*, which connotes uncertainty and translates
roughly into English as "might" (as in "might and might not lead to Cordoba").

Figure 4.1. Plaque at Mahmud Darwish Foundation (Ramallah).
Photograph by Eric Calderwood.

In other words, the speaker's journey to Cordoba is twice thrown into doubt: because it is predicated on an ability to start over that might not materialize and because it follows a trajectory that might or might not lead to Cordoba. And yet, even in the face of such emphatic uncertainty, the path to Cordoba remains open, if only in the realm of possibility. What I discern, in these lines, is a poet who is looking for a grammar for talking about al-Andalus (and Palestine), a grammar that does not relegate al-Andalus to the past and yet also does not guarantee its future existence. In this poem, Cordoba and al-Andalus persist but only in the realm governed by the particle *qad*. Indeed, the particle *qad* offers an avenue, a linguistic structure, for understanding Darwish's Andalus, which is, after all, "the Andalus of the possible."

All of these ideas come to a head in Darwish's most famous work about al-Andalus: the eleven-part suite of poems titled "Ahad 'ashar kawkaban 'ala akhir al-mashhad al-andalusi" (Eleven stars over the last Andalusi scene), which Darwish published in 1992, on the fifth centennial of the conquest of Muslim Granada. The work's title contains an allusion to the story of the prophet Joseph. In the Qur'anic telling of this story, Joseph (Yusuf) tells his father: "Father, I dreamed of eleven stars and the sun and the moon: I saw them all bow down before me."[50] Joseph is an archetypal figure of fraternal betrayal in the Abrahamic traditions. His brothers, jealous of the favor he enjoys with their father, conspire to abandon him in a well. Joseph is later sold into slavery in Egypt. In a poem from the collection *Ward aqall* (1986), published after the PLO's evacuation from Beirut, Darwish draws on the Joseph story to lament the betrayal and abandonment of the Palestinians at the hands of their Arab brothers.[51] The specter of fraternal betrayal likewise hovers over Darwish's suite "Ahad 'ashar kawkaban 'ala akhir al-mashhad al-andalusi," but the work also plumbs other themes from the Joseph story, including visions of the future, the struggles of exile, and the yearning for a return to the place of origin.

The title of "Eleven Stars over the Last Andalusi Scene" (hereafter, "Eleven Stars") not only connects the work to the Joseph story but also highlights al-Andalus's ambivalent position between history and representation. Darwish's suite centers on the last days of Muslim Granada, and the title refers to Muslim Granada as "the last Andalusi scene" (*ākhir al-mashhad al-andalusī*). Darwish's word choice here underlines the theatricality of al-Andalus; that is, it draws attention to the fact that Granada is a "scene" in a drama that has unfolded on the stage of collective memory. In this work, as the title would suggest, al-Andalus is not so much a historical period as it is a story that has been told and retold over time.

The idea that al-Andalus is a stage for stories is present from the very beginning of Darwish's suite. In the first poem of the suite, the speaker is situated in Granada on the eve of the city's occupation by the new Castilian rulers. The poem introduces many of the suite's main themes, including the plight of the conquered, the cyclical repetitions of history, and the fragile line that separates the past from the present. I will translate the poem in its entirety here:

On the last evening in this land, we cut our days off
From our shrubs and count the ribs we will carry with us,
And the ribs we will leave behind, here . . . On the last evening
We do not bid farewell to anything, and we do not find the time to
    finish . . .
Everything remains as it is. The place changes our dreams
And changes its visitors. Suddenly, we are no longer capable of irony.
The place is prepared to play host to the abyss . . . Here on the last
    evening
We enjoy the mountains surrounded by clouds: conquest . . . and
    counter-conquest
And an ancient age hands this new age the keys to our doors.
So enter our homes, o conquerors! And drink our wine
From our simple *muwashshaḥ!* For we are night at midnight. There
    is no
Dawn carried forth by a horseman coming from the direction of
    the last call to prayer . . .
Our green tea is hot, so drink it! And our pistachios are fresh, so eat
    them!
And the beds are green, made of cedar wood, so give yourself over
    to slumber
After this long siege, and sleep on the feathers of our dreams.
The sheets are ready, the perfumes on the door are ready, and the
    mirrors are many,

So come in so we can leave once and for all. Before long, we will
    search for what
Was our history around your history in distant lands.
And in the end we will ask ourselves: Was al-Andalus
Here or there? On earth . . . or in poems?[52]

In the last lines of the poem, the speaker poses a rhetorical question that underlines the tension between al-Andalus's dual status as a place in history ("on earth") and a place in discourse ("in poems"). The speaker's question implies that it is difficult to disentangle the Andalus that existed in history from the one that has persisted in poetry.

The distinction between historical experience and representation—"earth" and "poems"—is not the only point of ambiguity in this poem. Likewise, it is difficult to locate the speaker in place or time or to pin down the speaker's identity. The speaker repeats the adverb "here" throughout the poem, but the speaker also seems to occupy a position that straddles "here" and "there"—one that is both in al-Andalus and looking at al-Andalus. In a similar vein, the speaker uses the first-person plural "we" but does not identity the referent for the pronoun. From the allusion to the *muwashshah* (a form of poetry that originated in al-Andalus) and from the reference to al-Andalus in the penultimate line, we can deduce that the speaker is one of the last Muslim inhabitants of Granada and speaks for that community. And yet the poem also sketches a cyclical view of history, one that unfolds in movements of "conquest . . . and counter-conquest." This emphasis on the cycles of conquest through history suggests that the poem's speaker inhabits an ambiguous position between a particular historical situation and a broader historical predicament: he is, on the one hand, aligned with the inhabitants of Muslim Granada and, on the other, part of a long lineage of exiles and conquered peoples. Darwish would later underline this idea when, in a 1996 interview with Israeli poet Helit Yeshurun, he explained that his aim in "Eleven Stars" was "to establish a dialogue with the exiles on earth."[53]

Darwish's suite deploys an arsenal of rhetorical tools that give expression to this cyclical view of history. Among those tools is anaphora, or poetic repetition, one of the main rhetorical figures used throughout the suite. In the first poem in the suite, the speaker repeats the adverb "here" and the phrase "on the last evening" to identify and commemorate a place and a time that are on the verge of extinction. The remaining poems in the suite also rely heavily on anaphora, and many of them feature refrains (that is, lines that are repeated, like a chorus, throughout the text). The most emphatic example comes in the last poem in the suite, "al-Kamanjat" (Violins), where every line begins with the word *al-kamanjāt* ("the violins"), and where the following refrain is repeated at the beginning, middle, and end of the poem:

> The violins weep with the Gypsies going to al-Andalus
> The violins weep over the Arabs leaving from al-Andalus.[54]

This refrain suggests a circular movement in which one marginalized group replaces another: as the conquered Arabs depart al-Andalus, the "Gypsies" (*al-ghajar*) come to take their place. These lines are actually not the first or only place where Darwish sought to posit an affinity between Gypsies and Andalusi Arabs. Comparisons between the two groups pop up a handful of times in Darwish's poems from the 1980s.[55] In these earlier examples, as in the previously quoted lines from "Eleven Stars," the figure of the Gypsy is associated with exile, wandering, and a lost homeland—themes that connect the Gypsies to the Andalusi diaspora and also, of course, to the post-1948 Palestinian diaspora. In a similar spirit, Darwish draws parallels between Native Americans and Palestinians in his poem "Khutbat 'al-hindi al-ahmar'—ma qabla al-akhira—amama al-rajul al-abyad" (The "red Indian's" penultimate speech before the white man), which appears in the same collection as "Eleven Stars."[56] The thread connecting these various poems is Darwish's desire to imagine networks of solidarity that connect colonized and exiled peoples living in different places and times. Darwish uses tropes of repetition—such as anaphora and refrain—to dramatize and give voice to these cycles of oppression, linking the story of al-Andalus to the experiences of other cultural and ethnic groups, including Palestinians.

Another strategy that Darwish uses to trace these cyclical movements of history is to vary the speaker's identity and temporal location throughout "Eleven Stars." For instance, in the fourth poem in the suite, the speaker adopts the perspective of the last Muslim ruler of Granada, Abu 'Abd Allah Muhammad b. 'Ali (ca. 1461–1534), commonly known as "Boabdil" in Western historiography. In contrast, in the fifth poem in the suite, the speaker adopts the perspective of an Arab visitor who returns to Granada in 1992, five hundred years after the city's conquest. In other poems, the speaker seems to straddle different perspectives—1492 and 1992, Boabdil and Darwish, and so on. These shifts and conflations of perspective contribute to the sense that there is a two-way traffic between the past and the present: the present bleeds into the speaker's vision of the past, just as the past hovers over and shapes the speaker's present.

These dynamics come to the fore in the eighth poem in the suite, "Kun li-jitarati wataran, ayyuha al-ma'" (Be a string for my guitar, o water!). Here is my translation of the poem in its entirety:

> Be a string for my guitar, o water! The conquerors have arrived
> And the old conquerors have departed. It is difficult for me to
>   remember my face
> In the mirrors. So you be my memory so that I might see what I
>   have lost . . .
> Who am I after this collective exodus? I have a rock
> Carrying my name on the hills that overlook what has departed
> And elapsed . . . Seven hundred years bid farewell to me behind the
>   city's walls . . .
> In vain, time revolves so that I may rescue my past from an
>   instant
> That gives birth now to the history of my exile in myself . . . in the
>   others . . .
> Be a string for my guitar, o water. The conquerors have arrived
> And the former conquerors have departed to the south, as people
>   who restore their days
> In the heap of transformation: I know who I was yesterday.
>   So what am I
> Tomorrow, beneath Columbus's Atlantic banners? Be a string,
> Be a string for my guitar, o water! There is no Egypt in Egypt, no
> Fez in Fez, and Syria is far away. There is no hawk in
> The people's banner, no river to the east of the palms besieged
> By the Mongols' swift horses. In which Andalus do I come to an
>   end? Here
> Or there? I will know that I perished, and that I left here
> The best of me: my past. I have nothing left but my guitar.
> Be a string for my guitar, o water. The conquerors have gone,
> And the conquerors have come . . . [57]

The poem's speaker appears to be Boabdil. According to legend, when Boabdil departed Granada with his entourage, the deposed ruler took a final look back at the city and wept. This scene is known as "the Moor's last sigh" and is the origin for the name of an overpass in the mountains near Granada. Darwish's speaker seems to have this story in mind when he alludes to "exodus" from Granada and "a rock / Carrying my name on the hills that overlook what has departed."

Yet here, again, the speaker's identity and location are ambiguous. He inhabits Boabdil's perspective at the moment of the conquest of Granada in 1492, but his gaze also takes in the full run of Andalusi history ("Seven hundred years bid farewell to me") and even a future in which Boabdil's departure from Granada would be commemorated by a rock named after him. These slippery movements across times are articulated and dramatized by the poem's verbal tenses, which shift between past, present, and future. At times, these temporal shifts come in quick succession, as when the speaker asks, "I know who I was yesterday. So what am I / Tomorrow?" At other times, the poem's tenses verge on something like a future anterior—a time that "will have been." Such is the case when the speaker imagines a future in which he will understand the past: "I will know that I perished, and that I left here / The best of me: my past." This slippery sense of time is also present in one of the poem's refrains: "The conquerors have arrived / And the old conquerors have departed." The refrain, repeated three times in the poem, reiterates the suite's sustained concern with the cycles of history—and, in particular, the repetitions of conquest over history. Notably, the final appearance of the refrain, at the end of the poem, is followed by ellipses, which suggest that the cycles of conquest are open and ongoing.

While noting the cycles of conquest and defeat, the poem also gestures toward the possibility of resilience through poetry and song. A glimpse of this resilience comes through in the poem's other refrain, "Be a string for my guitar, o water." This refrain combines apostrophe and imperative, two figures of speech that recur throughout "Eleven Stars." Both figures are, in some sense, centered on the same target: to summon into presence that which is inanimate, absent, or in peril. They are figures that refuse absence through language. It is no coincidence, then, that apostrophe is one of the most common rhetorical features in the Arabic elegiac tradition, where it serves to preserve the memory of the dead and departed.[58] But what is apostrophized in Darwish's poem is not a dead person but rather water, a substance whose symbolism is famously fluid (pun intended). Among water's many meanings is that of change or the passage of time, often symbolized by images of flowing water. In Darwish's poem, the speaker commands water to be "a string for my guitar." The speaker thus pairs water, a symbol of fluid transformation, with the guitar, a symbol of music—and, in particular, of the musical traditions of the Iberian Peninsula, from the lutes of Andalusi court music to the guitars of contemporary flamenco. The pairing of the two symbols, water and the guitar, suggests that change, transformation, and perhaps even violent upheaval can be confronted, processed, and surmounted through song. Amid the ongoing flux of conquest and counter-conquest, the speaker appeals to the power of songs, songs that bears witness to conquest and exile, songs that outlast the lifespan of one conqueror or another. Indeed, this turn to song is a gesture repeated elsewhere in "Eleven Stars." The second poem in the suite ends with a litany of phrases that begin with the imperative "Sing!" and the final words of the poem are, "Granada is for singing, so sing!"[59]

What I glean from Darwish's "Eleven Stars" is the idea that there are multiple *Andaluses*—one that existed "on earth" and came to an end with the conquest of 1492, and another, or perhaps many others, which have come into being in poetry and song. The speaker of the eighth poem in the suite confronts the multiplicity of al-Andalus when he asks: "In which Andalus do I come to an end? Here / Or there?"[60] This question echoes the one that the speaker poses at the end of the first poem in the suite. In both questions, the adverbs "here" and "there" point to locations whose definition is equivocal. The "here" and the "there" of these poems, like Darwish's Andalus itself, exist in the tension between history and its representation in poetry and song. Darwish's Boabdil is both a deposed ruler who left Granada in 1492 and the human subject of a story that resonates far beyond Granada and 1492.

Of the many Andaluses that are evoked in "Eleven Stars," the one that most interests Darwish is the Andalus of Palestine, the Andalus of the possible. Palestine lurks just beneath the surface of the entire suite, asserting its presence, or absence, in subtle but unmissable ways. The first subtle nods to Palestine come in the suite's first poem (translated above). In addition to the poem's meditation on exile, the poem also uses a specific image that suggests an affiliation between Palestine and al-Andalus. I'm referring to the moment when the speaker says:

Here on the last evening
We enjoy the mountains surrounded by clouds: conquest . . . and
    counter-conquest
And an ancient age hands over to this new age the keys to our
    doors.[61]

The key imagery has a particular resonance and poignancy for Palestinians and North Africans of Andalusi descent. In both communities, it is a common practice to hold on to the keys to the ancestral homes that were left behind in Palestine and al-Andalus.[62] These keys serve dual functions, as links to the past and as claims on the future. They allow Palestinians and North Africans of Andalusi descent to mourn a lost homeland but also to stake a claim of ownership over it.

While the key imagery is subtle, the links between Palestine and al-Andalus become more forceful in the suite's third poem. There, the speaker makes two allusions to the Spanish poet Federico García Lorca (1898–1936), a native of Granada, a famous champion of southern Spain's Andalusi heritage, and a revered figure for modern Arab poets writing about Spain.[63] The allusions to Lorca would seem to place the speaker in the twentieth century, after Lorca's death. Nevertheless, as is usually the case with Darwish's sense of time, things are not as simple as they seem. The speaker occupies a liminal position that straddles present and past, Palestine and al-Andalus. This bifurcation of time and place comes into relief in the poem's final lines:

. . . The stranger [*al-gharīb*] passed through
Carrying seven hundred years of horses. The stranger passed
    through
Here so that the stranger could pass through there. I will soon exit
From the wrinkles of my time, a stranger to Syria and al-Andalus.
This land is not my sky, but this evening is my evening.
The keys are mine, the minarets are mine, the lamps are mine, and I
Am mine, too. I am the Adam of two paradises, twice lost to me.
So banish me slowly,
And kill me slowly,
Under my olive tree,
With Lorca . . . [64]

These lines allude repeatedly to the figure of *al-gharīb,* "the stranger" or "the foreigner." The word is etymologically linked to *ghurba,* separation from one's homeland or exile. These lines, then, trace the stranger's cyclical movements from "here" to "there"—from the exiles of the past to the exiles of the present.

What links the speaker to the figure of the wandering Andalusi is the shared experience of estrangement, of separation from the homeland. Capturing these links, the speaker pronounces, "I am the Adam of two paradises, twice lost to me." Here, the speaker uses the grammatical dual form to express his division or doubling across two paradises (*al-jannatayn,* literally "two gardens" but also "two gardens of paradise") and two times (*al-marratayn*). The invocation of the twice lost "paradises" suggests a parallel between the conquest of al-Andalus in 1492 and the Palestinian *Nakba* of 1948. It also resonates, of course, with the long-standing trope of al-Andalus as the "lost paradise" and with the related tropes of Palestine as the "second al-Andalus." The speaker seems to assert that, through his status as a *gharīb,* he belongs to both paradises, al-Andalus and Palestine, and to both moments of loss, 1492 and 1948.

While the third poem in the suite centers on cycles of loss, the final poem in the suite, "al-Kamanjat" (Violins), moves from the repetition of loss to the possibility of return. Darwish noted this move when he discussed "Eleven Stars" in his 1996 interview with Helit Yeshurun, where he explained: "Popular poetry from the 50s and 60s about Palestine made the comparison: we lost Palestine just as we had lost Andalusia. But that's not how I see things. I've always said that Andalusia could be refound."[65] One can glimpse this shift, from the "lost paradise" to paradise found, in the opening lines of "al-Kamanjat":

The violins weep with the Gypsies going to al-Andalus
The violins weep over the Arabs leaving from al-Andalus

The violins weep over a time lost that will not return
The violins weep over a homeland lost that might return [*qad yaʿūd*].[66]

The meaning of the last line was not lost on Darwish's readers. When Darwish would recite this famous poem in public, his audiences would often cheer at his allusion to "a homeland lost that might return."[67] This allusion not only rescues al-Andalus from a fate of irrevocable loss; it also envisions a possible return to (and of) Palestine, another homeland that was lost and that "might return." It is worth noting that this line lands Darwish, once again, in the realm of the *qad,* of the "might," of the possible and the desired— in short, the Andalus of the possible. Darwish's Andalus is neither nostalgic nor elegiac nor naively optimistic; it is, rather, one that is caught between these competing impulses, just as it is caught between the memory of the past, the struggles of the present, and the promises of the future.

The Palestinian al-Andalus in the Post-Oslo Era

I consider Darwish's work to be the zenith of the discourse that I have dubbed "the Palestinian al-Andalus." I base this assessment on several factors, including Darwish's fame as the modern Palestinian poet par excellence, the longevity of his engagements with the memory of al-Andalus, and the sensitivity with which the poet intertwined the stories of al-Andalus and Palestine. All of the Palestinian writers who have dealt with the topic of al-Andalus since 1992 have, in some sense, been forced to confront the long shadow of Darwish's writings on this topic. Despite this challenge, a number of Palestinian writers have picked up the baton from Darwish and taken the "Palestinian al-Andalus" into the twenty-first century. Writers working in this arena have had to contend with a long tradition of Palestinian writing about al-Andalus but have also had to respond to ongoing developments in the Palestinian-Israeli conflict, including (but not limited to) the Oslo agreement of 1993, the expansion of Israeli settlements in the West Bank, the second intifada (2000–2005), and the ongoing daily struggles of life under Israeli occupation.[68] Amid these contentious events and processes, al-Andalus has continued to serve as a useful metaphor for thinking about Palestine as a place and a project that have both a past and a future. Some of the writings from the past thirty years have revived the militant spirit that characterized works from the middle of the twentieth century.[69] Other works have focused less on political or armed struggle and more on the themes that occupied Darwish's later writings about al-Andalus, especially the fate of exiles, the search for home, and the intricate relations between past and present.

Among the writers who have followed in Darwish's footsteps is the poet Musa Hawamida (b. 1959), who, from 1999 to 2015, published a handful of poems that celebrated the cultural legacy of al-Andalus and drew parallels between al-Andalus and Palestine.[70] For Hawamida, as for Darwish before him, the Andalusi is a figure who travels across space and time, finding company with other exiles and wanderers. This theme is particularly evident in Hawamida's poem "Rihlat al-andalusi al-akhir" (Journey of the last Andalusi, 2004), where the first-person speaker, the "last Andalusi" of the poem's title, is an anonymous wanderer who journeys from the Middle East to the Maghrib before eventually arriving in al-Andalus. There, the speaker rubs elbows with poets and princes, dances flamenco with Gypsies, and communes with famous figures from al-Andalus, including Ibn Hazm (994–1064) and Ibn Rushd (1126–1198).[71]

Hawamida's speaker is a witness to the splendor of al-Andalus but also to its disintegration, which reverberates across space and time. The speaker traces those reverberations in the following stanza:

> The *taifa* wars broke out
> Seville fell
> Granada
> Baghdad fell
> And Jerusalem [*bayt al-muqaddas*]
> The kingdoms of al-Andalus came to nothing
> And I remained suspended in Ibn Zaydun's poems
> And in the threads of Damascene silk in the robes of Wallada bint
>   al-Mustakfi
> I could not forfeit the last of my forts
> On account of a cockfight.[72]

At the beginning of this stanza, Hawamida uses the phrase "*taifa* wars" (*ḥurūb al-ṭawā'if*), which evokes the conflicts between the rival Muslim kingdoms that emerged in al-Andalus after the collapse of the Umayyad caliphate in the eleventh century. However, Hawamida, like his predecessor al-'Abbushi, does not reserve the term *ṭawā'if* (factions) for describing a specific period in Andalusi history; rather, he uses it to refer to a broader problem of political division and instability. For Hawamida, the phrase "*taifa* wars" encompasses a long history of defeats and setbacks, from the conquest of Seville in the thirteenth century, through the conquest of Granada in the fifteenth century, and on to the occupation of Jerusalem in the present. The poem suggests that political factionalism—in short, *ṭawā'if*—led to the fall of al-Andalus and to the fall of Palestine. Both events are, in this poem, part of one continuous story that runs from medieval al-Andalus to the present. Amid this temporal flux, the poem's speaker finds a refuge or, at least, a perch in poetry. After the kingdoms of al-Andalus "came to nothing," the speaker remains "suspended" (*'āliqan*) in the works of two illustrious Andalusi poets: Ibn Zaydun (1003–1070) and Wallada bint al-Mustakfi. These lines carry echoes of Darwish, since they suggest that al-Andalus persists in the domain of poetry, which resists the linear progression of history and erodes the boundary between past and present.

While several Palestinian writers have explored the entanglement between Andalusi time and Palestinian time, the most inventive take on this theme in recent years is the one found in 'Adwan Nimr 'Adwan's (b. 1969) novel *'Awdat al-muriski min tanahhudatihi* (The Morisco's return from his sighs, 2010). The novel's innovation resides primarily in its narrative structure, which dramatizes the fluid movements between Palestine and al-Andalus. The novel's plot begins in fifteenth-century Granada, moves to the modern-day West Bank and from there to Granada, where it toggles between the present and the fifteenth century, before returning to the West Bank at the time of the second intifada. The novel is, in other words, one in which time gives way to other times, and space gives way to other spaces. These slippages are dramatized not only by shifts in temporal setting but also by shifts in narrative perspective, as the following plot synopsis will elucidate.

The novel's first two chapters are set in fifteenth-century Granada, during the reign of the last Muslim ruler of the city, Boabdil (known here by another of his nicknames, Abu 'Abd Allah al-Saghir). At the beginning of the novel, an omniscient third-person narrator explains that Boabdil is facing a revolt led by a blacksmith named Bazmat. To counter this threat, Boabdil decides to release one of his rivals, Musa b. Abi al-Ghassan (hereafter, Ibn Abi al-Ghassan), from prison in order to neutralize the influence of the charismatic rebel leader Bazmat. This section of the novel ends with Ibn Abi al-Ghassan's release from prison and his journey to visit his dying father.

The novel then makes an abrupt shift in setting and narrative perspective. The third chapter is set in the present-day West Bank and features a first-person narrator named Musa, a Palestinian from a village near the city of

Nablus. Musa narrates his childhood in the village, his move to Nablus for education, and his increasing involvement in the Palestinian resistance against the Israeli occupation, an activity that lands him in jail. Facing oppression and few opportunities at home, Musa eventually wins a scholarship to pursue a master's degree in history at the University of Granada. Upon arrival in Granada, in the fourth chapter, Musa experiences an intense sensation of déjà vu. In one of his classes at the history department, Musa learns about Ibn Abi al-Ghassan and soon begins to have visions of Ibn Abi al-Ghassan's life in late-fifteenth-century Granada.

At this point in the story, the novel makes another shift in narrative perspective. The fifth chapter is narrated by a Moroccan doctor named al-Tahir b. 'Allun, who lives in Granada and specializes in hypnosis. Dr. Ibn 'Allun gives a report on one of his patients, a Palestinian student named Musa, who has come to believe that he is Ibn Abi al-Ghassan, a knight from medieval Granada. Through the doctor's report on his treatment of Musa, the novel offers an account of the turbulent final years of Muslim rule in Granada. As the novel tells the story, Ibn Abi al-Ghassan is one of a group of Granadan leaders who reject the terms of the peace treaty that Boabdil and his allies negotiate with King Ferdinand and Queen Isabella. Refusing to surrender to Castilian rule, Ibn Abi al-Ghassan bids farewell to Granada, exits the city on his horse, confronts a group of Castilian knights, and then ends his own life by riding his horse into the Genil River, where he drowns. After Dr. Ibn 'Allun narrates Ibn Abi al-Ghassan's dramatic death, he concludes his report with a brief history of the so-called Moriscos, the Muslims who remained in Spain after 1492, were forced to convert to Christianity, faced persecution from the Spanish Inquisition, and were ultimately expelled from Spain in 1609.

After the report from the Moroccan doctor, the novel makes a final shift in narrative perspective, returning to the first-person narration of Musa, the Palestinian student. In the last two chapters of the novel, Musa narrates his return from Granada to the West Bank, where he navigates the hassles and humiliations of checkpoints, military surveillance, and the other challenges of daily life under occupation. Musa eventually joins an armed uprising against the Israeli occupation. (There are allusions in the novel that place these events in the early 2000s, during the second intifada.) When Israeli forces lay siege to Nablus, Musa refuses to surrender, and he eventually takes his own life in a manner that mirrors Ibn Abi al-Ghassan's suicide in fifteenth-century Granada.

As this plot synopsis illustrates, 'Adwan's novel plays with the slippage between Granada and Palestine, and between past and present. These slippages and conflations are, as we have seen, common themes in the Palestinian treatment of al-Andalus—particularly in Darwish's "Eleven Stars." One of the new ingredients that 'Adwan brings to these themes is an intricate narrative structure that throws into question the possibility of separating Palestinian time from Andalusi time, and of separating Palestinian voices from Andalusi voices. Over the course of the novel, the story of Musa b. Abi al-Ghassan, the Granadan knight, merges with the story of Musa, the eponymous student from Nablus; likewise, the struggle to defend Muslim Granada merges with the struggle for Palestine. With these conflations, 'Adwan's novel, like Darwish's poetry, probes the porous borders between historical events, their representation in writing, and their afterlife in politics and memory.

These blurred boundaries are front and center from the very beginning of the novel. The novel opens with a one-paragraph preface from an unidentified first-person narrator (likely Musa, the Palestinian), who says:

> I'll start by recording my story for you, this story that is overflowing with marvels and that might possibly be true. Forgive me for that! It is possible that I have the honor of writing, the writing of this story, but not only that of being a recorder, like an instrument for writing down. At times, esteemed audience, I will work against the literal recording or writing down of the events. And that is because I write, for writing is a bulldozer against recording and truth.[73]

The speaker presents himself, here, as an unreliable narrator who confesses, and even relishes in, the tension between his story and "the literal recording" of events. Twice in the first two lines of the preface, the narrator uses the phrase *min al-mumkin an* (meaning "it is possible that" or "possibly"). With this repetition, the narrator places his story in the realm of the *mumkin,* "the possible"—the very same realm that Darwish envisioned for the Palestinian al-Andalus.

The narrator also refers to his writing as a bulldozer or, literally, an "excavating tool" (*ālat ḥafr*). This phrase is striking because metaphors of excavation recur throughout the novel. For instance, the Moroccan hypnotist Dr. Ibn 'Allun describes his line of work as "human geology, each layer leading to another until we arrive at the spiritual core and the collective memory."[74] In another iteration of this theme, Musa observes, "History means exhuming the tombs of the dead."[75] The excavating metaphors, in the aggregate, suggest that if we peel off one layer of history—say, the history of post-1948 Palestine—we will find another layer underlying it and, to some extent, structuring its meaning. The narrator's journey is not so much to move from the past to the present but rather to excavate the intricate bonds between them.

This archaeological sense of time, where one layer rests on another, is at work in the novel's many shifts between settings and narrative perspectives, but the effect is particularly forceful in the section where Musa travels to Spain to study history. On the flight to Spain, Musa imagines that he is 'Abbas b. Firnas (b. 887), an Andalusi scientist who famously designed a gadget with wings in an (unsuccessful) attempt to fly.[76] Once in Madrid, Musa fancies that he is following in the path of famous figures from al-Andalus, musing, "Perhaps Tariq b. Ziyad was here, and perhaps many of the poets of al-Andalus stood over this river or over that lake."[77] These musings are but a prelude to Musa's arrival in Granada, where the lines separating al-Andalus from Palestine, and past from present, dissolve and vanish. As Musa approaches Granada by train, he notes "a very strong resemblance between this land and Palestine."[78] He also registers a disquieting feeling of déjà vu, as if his arrival in Granada were actually a return. "I began to imagine," Musa says, "that I had seen this view before."[79]

This uncanny feeling of familiarity haunts Musa as he starts to explore Granada. One of his first excursions in the city takes him to a park that affords a view of the nearby mountains:

> I sat on a wooden step and stared far, far away: It was the famous Sierra Nevada mountains that surround Granada and are lined with the remains of snow. I continued to look and look and look toward the mountains that resembled the pictures that I had seen. And then I began to swivel my head in a circular motion. I was anticipating the shape of the mountains and hills that surrounded me, as if I were looking at the mountains of Nablus. I began to bring back the view, time and time

again, and my agitation grew. For Granada, which the Arabs inhabited for several centuries, appeared familiar to me, perhaps even more so than cities that are near to me and that I have visited many times.[80]

As Musa scans Granada's surroundings, he is surprised to discover a familiar landscape, one that reminds him of home. This sensation of familiarity is mirrored at the level of language. 'Adwan uses repetition to mirror the doubling of Granada and Nablus and the echoes of shared history rippling across time: Musa stared "far, far away" (*fī al-baʿīd al-baʿīd*); he continued "to look and look and look" (*baqaytu anẓur wa-anẓur wa-anẓur*); and he brings back the view "time and time again" (*marra ithra marra*). With each of these circular phrases, Granada draws closer to Nablus, and the present draws closer to the past.

Indeed, as Musa continues to explore Granada, the city's past erupts to overtake the present. When Musa visits the Alhambra for the first time, he notes, "I was startled by the sight of the building, and I was even more startled that I knew parts of it, stone by stone."[81] Likewise, when he visits Granada's Albayzín neighborhood, his intuition leads him to a church built on the ruins of a former mosque. There, he feels an intense personal sense of loss, "as if," he explains, "I had prayed there hundreds of times."[82]

These episodes of déjà vu foreshadow Musa's impending crisis, in which his identity merges with that of Ibn Abi al-Ghassan. Musa becomes obsessed with Ibn Abi al-Ghassan after learning about him in a lecture at the University of Granada. Musa then scours the Internet and local archives for information about this figure. At the same time, he experiences increasingly frequent visions of Ibn Abi al-Ghassan's life in medieval Granada. These experiences push Musa to the brink of insanity, as he loses his grip on the boundary between his life and Ibn Abi al-Ghassan's life. Musa's roommate and his Spanish girlfriend eventually intervene and convince him to seek treatment with Dr. Ibn 'Allun, the Moroccan hypnotist. It is only through his work with the hypnotist that Musa, the Palestinian, is able to disentangle himself from Musa, the Granadan.

At the end of his treatment with Dr. Ibn 'Allun, Musa resolves to leave Spain in order to free himself from his Andalusi double, Ibn Abi al-Ghassan. He explains the rationale for his departure by pointing to the exploits of another figure from al-Andalus, Tariq b. Ziyad:

We are poets who compose poems that nullify those of our forefathers, the master poets. Tariq b. Ziyad, when he arrived with his army at Spain's shores, burned the ships that had conveyed him there and addressed his soldiers, saying: 'The sea is behind you, and the enemy is in front of you. By God, there is nothing for you now but courage and endurance!' Is it not that burning the ships entails burning the past and the return to it? I will do as Tariq did, but in reverse: I will depart al-Andalus and burn my past in it. I will not leave behind a boat for me to return to it. I sympathize with you, o Ibn al-Ghassan, but I implore you to give me my freedom, my life, and my Nablus-ness.[83]

Musa presents himself as a Tariq b. Ziyad in reverse: burning his ships to *leave* al-Andalus, rather than to conquer it. He refuses to get stuck in the past, in the "lost paradise" of al-Andalus. However, the passage also illustrates the tangled web that the novel weaves between past and present. Even as the novel's narrator announces his intention to leave behind al-Andalus, he refers to Tariq b. Ziyad as the model for his actions. The passage suggests, paradoxically, that the narrator must find inspiration in one figure from Andalusi history in order to leave behind another.

As Musa prepares to leave Granada and return to the West Bank, he receives final words of caution from Dr. Ibn 'Allun, words that lay bare the historical analogy between al-Andalus and Palestine. The doctor tells Musa: "I fear that you, in your summoning of the historical figure of Ibn al-Ghassan, will spread repetition . . . suicidal repetition: The Jews are the Moriscos of the Nazis, and the Palestinians are the Moriscos of Jewish Zionism in the modern age. The roles are swapped on the tragic stage of life."[84] Dr. Ibn 'Allun's parting words make explicit a comparison that is implicit for much of the novel: namely, that the fate that befell the Moriscos after the conquest of Granada is analogous to the fate that has befallen the Palestinian people since the *Nakba*. Dr. Ibn 'Allun also introduces another group into this cyclical history of oppression: the victims of the Holocaust. Such fast and facile analogies across different contexts might make some readers uncomfortable. What 'Adwan's novel seems to be driving at, however, is a vision similar to the one that emerges in Darwish's "Eleven Stars." Both texts place the history of the last Andalusis in a longer narrative framework whose aim is to establish parallels, and even solidarities, among different victims of violence, displacement, and cultural erasure. In ʿAdwan's novel, the term "Morisco" refers not only to the specific meaning that the term has in the Iberian context but also to a structural position within recurring patterns of violence and cultural erasure.

In the last section of ʿAdwan's novel, the story of Musa's return to the West Bank bears out this cyclical understanding of the "Morisco" as a figure (or a predicament) that pops up cyclically in different historical contexts. Although Musa had resolved, upon leaving Granada, to leave behind the figure of Ibn Abi al-Ghassan, he nonetheless meets a fate that closely mirrors the fate of the knight from fifteenth-century Granada. Like Ibn Abi al-Ghassan, Musa chooses struggle over surrender, joining a desperate fight to defend his city against an occupying army. As Musa makes his last stand against the Israeli forces in Nablus, his thoughts turn to Granada, and he imagines himself following in Ibn Abi al-Ghassan's footsteps:

> I continued shooting bullets, struggling to breathe, until I had run out of ammunition. I felt that I was leaping into the waters of the Genil River in Granada, plunging beneath its waters, the armor pushing me down, deeper and deeper to the bottom of the river, to the river of death. And I perceived (with what little perception remained to me) that I was the prodigal son, and that I was duty bound to return to my father and to make contact with the ancient ancestors, whose echo reverberates in my heart and my soul forever.
>
> I wished that I had a sword with me so that I could plant it in the ground and lean into it, allowing its blade to slip into my heart, as was the custom of the ancient Arabs. But in the end, I took out my revolver and sighed the last sighs of the Andalusis. I shot a bullet in my head and was content to live far off in another land.[85]

Here, as Musa prepares for death in twenty-first-century Nablus, he imagines himself as a knight riding to his death in Granada's Genil River.

This scene not only reprises the scene of Ibn Abi al-Ghassan's suicide but also evokes the legend of the "Moor's last sigh" and the title of ʿAdwan's novel (*The Morisco's Return from His Sighs*). While the title might seem, at first glance, to refer to Boabdil or to Ibn Abi al-Ghassan, the final scene of the novel reveals that the title is also an allusion to Musa, a Palestinian resistance fighter whose dying breaths extend "the last sighs of the Andalusis." ʿAdwan further highlights these rippling echoes of history by packing the scene of Musa's death with metaphors of echo and return, as when Musa says, "I was duty bound to return to my father and to make contact with the ancient ancestors, whose echo reverberates in my heart." With this comment, Musa claims the Andalusis as "ancestors" whose actions (or "echo") reverberate in the present, sustaining Palestinian resistance.

Musa's suicide, despite its apparent finality, does not mark an end to the cycles of history that are the central theme of 'Adwan's novel. As Musa lays dying, he addresses the reader one last time, vowing, "I will return to you one day, free and renewed. I will let my body burn in the kiln of this war. And some day, in some place, I will come back to life and will rise from beneath the ashes, and my spirit will return as another phoenix in another body. So await me [*fa-intaẓirū-nī*]."[86] Musa's final word is an imperative enjoining readers to expect his future return. He compares his spirit to the mythic phoenix, rising from the ashes. In fact, the phoenix is a suitable metaphor for how al-Andalus operates in 'Adwan's novel: al-Andalus is a death that offers new life, a past that rises from the ashes to become the future.

These temporal paradoxes align 'Adwan's novel with Darwish's writings about al-Andalus but also with many other Palestinian cultural texts of the post-Oslo period. During this period, as Hoda El Shakry has argued, the politics and aesthetics of time have become central concerns for Palestinian artists and cultural producers.[87] One of the artists studied by El Shakry, visual artist Larissa Sansour (b. 1973), said in a 2018 interview: "It is hard to talk about the Palestinian trauma without addressing several tenses. The Palestinian psyche seems to be planted in the catastrophic events of 1948 and is tied to a constant projection of the future, yet the present is in a constant limbo."[88] Although this remark was not addressed to the question of al-Andalus, it could easily be adapted to describe the workings of al-Andalus in contemporary Palestinian culture. After all, it is hard to talk about the Palestinian al-Andalus without addressing several tenses. The Palestinian al-Andalus is a project that exists in the tension between past, present, and future—or, to use some of Darwish's terms, in the tension between presence and absence, between a "here" and a "there" whose coordinates are in flux and under debate.

It is no coincidence that 'Adwan adopted the form of speculative fiction to work through a story that bridges the past and the present and holds out the promise of the future. After all, science fiction and other forms of speculative art have allowed many Palestinian writers and artists in recent years to imagine a viable and even vibrant future for Palestine.[89] But what is science fiction if not another name for that domain that Darwish calls "poetry," the space of possibility, of what could be? Whether it be speculative fiction or poetry, the Palestinian al-Andalus is a long-standing discourse and cultural practice that, since the early twentieth century, has engaged with the unfolding relationship between a past that was and a future that could be.

Coda: The Israeli al-Andalus

Just as al-Andalus has proven a resonant site of memory for Palestinian writers, it has also served a wide range of cultural and ideological needs in Israeli society. I cannot do full justice to this part of the story, since telling it demands a much better command of Hebrew than I have. Nonetheless, I would like to point briefly, in this concluding section, to some of the meanings and uses that al-Andalus has accrued in contemporary Israeli culture. Doing so will not only offer an interesting counterpoint to Palestinian writings about al-Andalus, but will also further illustrate the extreme plasticity of the Andalusi legacy, which has served to undergird and legitimate competing political projects and narratives of belonging in Palestine / Israel.[90]

If one of the names for the Andalusi legacy is "poetry" (in the broad Darwishian sense of the term), then another is translation—translation across temporal, spatial, linguistic, and religious lines.[91] It is no coincidence, then, that the first major project to translate Arabic literature into Hebrew did so under the aegis of al-Andalus. At the turn of the twenty-first century, Israeli actress and activist Yael Lerer (b. 1967) founded Andalus Publishing, a project devoted to translating Arabic literature and introducing it to Israeli readers.[92] The publisher's "Declaration of Intentions," written in 1999, explained the link between al-Andalus and its namesake, Andalus Publishing:

> Andalus is a new publishing house that specializes in the translation of Arabic literature and prose into Hebrew. Andalus, the site of the "golden age" of Islamic and Jewish thought, was also an era during which Jewish and Arabic cultures fed and fertilized one another; an epoch known for

its literary and intellectual output by some of the greatest Moslem [*sic*] and Jewish philosophers, theologians, and poets. It was a period during which materials were translated from Arabic to Hebrew and vice versa.[93]

As this statement illustrates, the publishing initiative was conceived as a tribute to a historical era, al-Andalus, in which texts and ideas circulated freely between Jewish and Muslim readers, and between Arabic and Hebrew. In a first step toward reviving the spirit of al-Andalus, Andalus Publishing released its first book in 2000: a Hebrew translation of a collection of poetry by Mahmud Darwish (Figure 4.2). From 2000 to 2009, Andalus published more than twenty Hebrew translations of Arabic literature, including two more works by Mahmud Darwish.

A translation project of this nature went against the prevailing winds of Israeli politics in the early 2000s, a period that saw the collapse of the peace process, the rise of the second intifada, and the expansion of the Israeli occupation. Lerer, the founder of Andalus Publishing, was acutely aware of these political developments and was no stranger to Israeli politics. Before launching Andalus Publishing, she helped found Balad, a political party that represented the views of Palestinian citizens of Israel and supported, in her words, "the national identity of the Palestinians."[94] In her "Declaration of Intentions" for Andalus Publishing, Lerer not only celebrated Jewish-Muslim coexistence in al-Andalus but also underscored the contrast between interfaith relations in al-Andalus and intercommunal conflict in contemporary Israel. "Israeli attitudes about Arabs," she wrote, "have regressed into the basest forms of racism and xenophobia."[95] Lerer and her collaborators viewed translating Arabic literature into Hebrew as a tool to combat mounting anti-Arab racism in Israeli society and the widespread effacement of Arabic-language culture in the Israeli public sphere. They also viewed Andalus Publishing as an act of resistance against the Israeli occupation regime. On this last point, Lerer would later write, "I have searched for ways to make the translation of Arabic literature into Hebrew a means of resisting the occupation. In our racist reality, where the walls of 'separation' loom larger by the day, making Arabic language and culture present in everyday Hebrew life is itself a form of resistance to the rhyme and reason of occupation."[96] Lerer suggests, here, that translating Arabic literature into Hebrew is not only an homage to the fluid exchanges that took place in al-Andalus but is also a form of resistance against

Figure 4.2. Book cover of the Hebrew translation of Mahmud Darwish's *Why Did You Leave the Horse Alone?* (Andalus Publishing, 2000). Andalus Publishing.

an occupation regime that is bent on policing the borders between Hebrew and Arabic, Israelis and Palestinians.

As significant as Andalus Publishing was as a cultural enterprise, it was not a total anomaly in Israel; rather, it was the outgrowth of long-standing debates about al-Andalus, debates that predate the creation of the state of Israel in 1948. During the early years of the British Mandate in Palestine, a handful of prominent Arabic-speaking Jewish scholars of Sephardic and Middle Eastern origin—among them, the Jerusalemite Abraham Shalom Yahuda (1877–1951)—held up al-Andalus as a model for Jewish-Arab coexistence and cultural revival in Palestine.[97] As Yuval Evri has documented, when Yahuda addressed a mixed audience of Muslim, Jewish, and Christian dignitaries in Jerusalem in 1920, he called on them to revive "the spirit of tolerance and freedom that prevailed in the golden age of Arab thought in al-Andalus."[98] Yahuda's call would find echoes in the work of some of the Jewish intellectuals who immigrated to Israel from Arab- and Muslim-majority countries in the middle of the twentieth century. One such case is Salim Sha'shu', an Iraqi Jew who immigrated to Israel in 1951 and later published a book, in Arabic, about "the golden age" of "Jewish-Arab cooperation in al-Andalus."[99]

Building on these precedents, al-Andalus has become, in recent years, an important symbol of cultural identity for Mizrahi Jews in Israel. *Mizrahi* (lit. "Easterner," pl. *Mizrahim*) is a catchall term that is used to describe the Jews who immigrated to Israel from North African and Middle Eastern countries, as well as those who claim descent from the Jewish communities expelled from Spain in the fifteenth century (the Sephardim).[100] Since their mass arrival in Israel in the 1950s and 1960s, Mizrahi Jews have often suffered from social exclusion and cultural marginalization at the hands of the country's ruling elites, who have primarily been Ashkenazim (Jews of European descent).[101] The social and cultural marginalization of Mizrahi Jews in Israeli society is a problem with a complex history, but one of its main roots is undoubtedly what Yael Lerer (herself an Ashkenazi Jew) has called "the dominant Ashkenazi-Zionist ideology that conceives of Israel as a European 'bastion of the West in the East.'"[102] The fact that Israel's Mizrahi Jews descend from communities where Arabic was, for many centuries, the main language of culture and daily life has, for most of Israel's history, worked to disempower them in mainstream Israeli culture. In recent decades, many Mizrahi scholars, artists, and public figures have turned to the cultural legacy of al-Andalus as a source of pride and collective mobilization, and as a tool for combatting the hegemony of Eurocentric Ashkenazi culture in Israel.

An illustrative example of this trend is an open letter that a group of young Mizrahi intellectuals and activists published in 2011 to express their solidarity with the political uprisings sweeping the Middle East—the so-called Arab spring. The open letter carried an Arabic title—"Ruh jadida" (New spirit)—and was published online in four languages: Hebrew, Arabic, English, and Spanish. The letter's authors described themselves as follows:

> We are Israelis, the children and grandchildren of Jews who lived in the Middle East and North Africa for hundreds and thousands of years. Our forefathers and mothers contributed to the development of this region's culture, and were part and parcel of it. Thus the culture of the Islamic world and the multigenerational connection and identification with this region is an inseparable part of our own identity.[103]

Having affirmed their "connection" and "identification" with the Arab and Islamic worlds, the authors then drew a comparison between the Arab uprisings of 2010–2011 and the struggle for freedom and justice in Israel, whose government, according to the authors, "is in an ongoing process of minimizing democratic liberties, and constructs racist barriers against Arab-Jews, the Arab people, and Arabic culture."[104] After signaling the parallels between the political struggles in Israel and those taking place elsewhere in the Middle East, the letter's authors called for dialogue and cooperation with their generational peers in the Arab world. Notably, their model for such dialogue was none other than al-Andalus. Alluding to this model, the authors wrote, "We have faith in intra-regional dialogue—whose purpose is to repair and rehabilitate what was destroyed in recent generations—as a catalyst towards renewing the Andalusian model of Muslim-Jewish-Christian partnership, God willing, Insha'Allah, and as a pathway to a cultural and historical golden era for our countries."[105] In this letter, then, the memory of al-Andalus performs at least three functions: it is a testimony of the long-standing connection between Jews and the Arab-Islamic world; a sign of solidarity between

Mizrahi Jews and their generational peers in Arab countries; and a symbol of Mizrahi pride and struggle in contemporary Israeli society. Finally, it is also "a pathway" to a different future for Arab-Jewish relations—"for a cultural and historical golden era," a future built on the model of al-Andalus.

Perhaps the most visible connection between the Andalusi legacy and contemporary Mizrahi politics is the ongoing work of the Israeli Andalusian Orchestra, founded in 1994 by Motti Malka and Yehiel Lasri, both children of Moroccan immigrants to Israel.[106] In 2006, the orchestra won the Israel Prize, the most prestigious prize for a cultural enterprise in Israel.[107] Since then, the orchestra has continued to build its international profile by performing regularly in festivals and concerts in Israel, Europe, and Morocco. The orchestra performs a diverse repertoire of North African music, including twentieth-century popular music sung in Maghribi Arabic and French, Judeo-Spanish songs (liturgical and secular), and pieces from the suite-based musical tradition commonly known as "Andalusi music" or *gharnāṭī* (Granadan).[108] The orchestra's leaders organize all of these diverse musics under the loose heading of "Andalusi(an)" (in Hebrew, *andalusit*), thereby tying the memory of al-Andalus to a wide range of cultural expressions linking Mizrahi Jews to modern North Africa and medieval Iberia. The "Andalusi" label, as Meirav Aharon has argued, lends an aura of prestige and authenticity to the orchestra, associating the group with a glorious past and portraying the orchestra's Mizrahi musicians as a living bridge between al-Andalus and Israel.[109]

This malleable understanding of the links between the Andalusi past and the Mizrahi present was on stage in a performance that I caught in March 2019 in Ashdod, a port city that is home to the Israeli Andalusian Orchestra and to one of Israel's oldest and largest North African communities.[110] When I took my seat at the Performing Arts Center in Ashdod, I found myself sitting next to three older women who were speaking in a mixture of French and Hebrew. Their code-switching reminded me of the French-Arabic mash-ups that one often finds in affluent settings in Morocco; it was a sign that the women probably came from the Francophone Jewish bourgeoisie that migrated to Israel in large numbers in the 1950s and 1960s.

The show we attended, called "Alger, Alger," was a tribute to the music of Algiers. The program was printed in French and described the first part of the show in the following terms: "We will open with some pieces of Algerian classical music called Garnati, a tradition coming straight from Granada in Spain and that was particularly appreciated in the northwest of Algeria."[111] The second part of the program featured popular songs from mid-twentieth-century Algeria—songs that the program described as "popular Andalusian music." The show concluded with a rousing rendition of "L'Oriental," a 1962 hit by Enrico Macias (b. 1938), a French-Algerian singer of Sephardic descent.[112] The song brought the house down. The audience clapped and sang along to the French lyrics performed by Benjamin Bouzaglo and Josette Kalifa, two vocalists of North African Jewish descent. Everyone joined forces to belt out the song's most famous line, "They call me the Oriental!" (*Et l'on m'appelle l'oriental*). In Ashdod, this line was not only a reminder of the popular music that many in the audience had consumed in their youth; it was also an affirmation of a Mizrahi (or "Oriental") Jewish identity rooted in North Africa, transplanted to Israel, and built on the long and malleable memory of al-Andalus.

The Israeli Andalusian Orchestra has also pursued a number of high-profile collaborations with Muslim and Jewish artists from North Africa and Europe. For example, the orchestra inaugurated its 2015–2016 season with a series of concerts featuring guest appearances by Jalal Chekara (Jalal Shaqara, b. 1974), a Moroccan Muslim violinist and vocalist who leads an acclaimed flamenco fusion group based in southern Spain.[113] Chekara and the orchestra joined forces again in November 2017 to perform at the Royal Palace of El Pardo, near Madrid, for an audience of Spanish and Israeli dignitaries, including King Felipe V and Israeli president Reuven Rivlin. As this example illustrates, the Israeli Andalusian Orchestra has become something of a cultural ambassador for Israel and has helped to create a triangular network of exchange between Israel, Morocco, and Europe (especially Spain and France).

The Israeli Andalusian Orchestra is just one of many musical ensembles that have, in recent decades, used the legacy of al-Andalus as a platform for promoting artistic exchange across religious, ethnic, linguistic, or geographic lines. The orchestra's leaders have often asserted that the music they play is not only a product of Jewish-Muslim coexistence in the past but also a vehicle for promoting intercultural tolerance in the present. The current director, Jacob Ben Simon, underscored this point in a 2018 interview with a program aired on Spanish national television, where he said: "Perhaps the most interesting thing and what I like the most is that Andalusi music is much more than music. It is born in the values of coexistence and tolerance. It is born in the dialogue between communities and peoples."[114] This comment will serve as my segue to Chapter 5, where I will explore how a number of artists from diverse backgrounds have used music as an avenue for engaging with the memory of al-Andalus and for promoting different narratives about al-Andalus in the public sphere.

5

The Harmonious al-Andalus

On a cool April morning in 2019, a few hundred middle school and high school students filed into the auditorium at Chicago's Old Town School of Folk Music for a performance titled *The Andalusian Trail*.[1] The performance was the brainchild of Ronnie Malley, a Chicago-born musician and educator of Palestinian descent. In recent years, Malley has created a number of theatrical productions that celebrate the musical and cultural legacies of al-Andalus.[2] In his performance at the Old Town School of Folk Music, Malley and his ensemble introduced the student audience to the history and heritage of al-Andalus through a program that blended a diverse range of musical traditions from the Mediterranean, along with lyrics sung in Spanish, Ladino (Judeo-Spanish), and Arabic.

The performance began with a famous story of migration. While strumming his lute, Malley told the audience: "In the ninth century, during the Islamic ʿAbbāsī reign, the musical legend Ziryab left Baghdad and traversed Greater Syria, Egypt, North Africa, and finally landed in al-Andalus, a land where Jews, Christians, and Muslims would coexist for over seven centuries, creating a unique and diverse society." This story is one that has been told many times before. It is the story of Ziryab (ca. 789–857), a musician who left his native Iraq in the early ninth century, fleeing a jealous rival, and made his way across the Middle East and North Africa to al-Andalus, where he settled, bringing with him the music and fashions of the Abbasid court in Baghdad. Ziryab would go on to establish a famous music conservatory in Cordoba and to pioneer a style of court music that would, over the course of many centuries, shape a variety of musical traditions in the Iberian Peninsula, North Africa, and the Middle East—traditions that all claim some connection to al-Andalus.[3] Evoking Ziryab's fateful journey from Baghdad to

Cordoba, Ronnie Malley used Ziryab as a point of departure for telling a larger story about al-Andalus, one that emphasized the movements of people and culture between the Iberian Peninsula and the Middle East. Malley's story also highlighted the coexistence of Jews, Christians, and Muslims in al-Andalus and credited this interfaith coexistence with giving rise to al-Andalus's cultural splendor.

Malley repeated these points at the end of his introduction to *The Andalusian Trail*, telling his audience: "Spain has been host to one of the most influential and culturally rich periods in history, largely due to its religious and ethnic diversity. Together, we take a musical journey across time, from past to present, to pay homage to a tradition of cross-cultural collaboration and coexistence." Malley's invitation to his audience to join him on "a musical journey across time" points to the unique role that music plays in his engagement with the Andalusi heritage. In Malley's approach, music is both an expression of al-Andalus's unique heritage and a vehicle for interacting with that heritage. It is a tool that allows him and his audience to sound the depths of the past.

In *The Andalusian Trail*, Malley was engaging in a form of storytelling through music that has become quite common in recent decades. It is an approach that harkens back to al-Andalus but that draws on musical practices and cultural narratives of much more recent vintage. The program for *The Andalusian Trail* illustrated this complex interplay between past and present. After the opening narration about Ziryab's journey to al-Andalus, Malley and his ensemble played "Arji'i ya alfa layla," a mid-twentieth-century composition by the Lebanese composing duo 'Asi and Mansur Rahbani, who wrote the song in the style of a *muwashshah,* a song-form that originated in al-Andalus.[4] The song was the first track on Fayruz's hit album, *Andalusiyyat* (1966), one of the most popular musical tributes to al-Andalus from the modern era.[5] Like Fayruz, Malley and his ensemble also performed a musical arrangement of the poem "Jadaka al-ghayth" by the Andalusi writer Ibn al-Khatib (d. 1375). The poem's most famous line is "O time of union in al-Andalus!" (*yā zamān al-waṣl bi-l-Andalus*). Fayruz sang these words over a composition by the Rahbani brothers. Ronnie Malley, in turn, sang them over an original flamenco composition titled "Seville at Night," written by Carlo Basile, the guitarist in Malley's ensemble. When Malley introduced the piece, he told the audience that Ibn al-Khatib's poem "speaks of the golden age of enlightenment in al-Andalus, the Arabic name for Andalusia." Malley then asked the audience to practice saying *al-Andalus.* Three hundred students shouted back, "al-Andalus!" As the name reverberated through the auditorium, Basile struck up a slow and melancholy guitar melody. Malley soon joined in, singing Ibn al-Khatib's poem in Arabic and lingering on the line: "O time of union in al-Andalus." While Malley sang, Leticia Aravena, the ensemble's flamenco dancer, stamped her feet and played the castanets.

This piece was not the only one that suggested an intimate relationship between al-Andalus, flamenco, and other popular music traditions that have emerged in Spain and the western Mediterranean in the modern era. In one of the most rousing moments of *The Andalusian Trail,* Malley and his ensemble performed a lively mash-up of the Moroccan folk song "Bint bladi" (Daughter of my country), made popular by Moroccan musician 'Abd al-Sadiq Shaqara (Abdessadek Chekara, 1931–1998), and the Spanish folk song "La tarara," collected and set to music by the Spanish writer Federico García Lorca in the 1930s. Malley introduced the piece with the following explanation: "Similar to America, as artistic traditions mingled and developed in al-Andalus, so did the pluralistic Andalusian culture. Folk musical styles and poetic forms were explored and reconstructed. The following piece blends a folk Andalusian melody in Arabic with 'La tarara,' a poem by the Spanish writer Federico [García] Lorca." With these remarks, Malley drew a line from the music of al-Andalus to a melody that became popular in Morocco in the twentieth century. He also suggested that his group's fusion of a Moroccan song and a Spanish song evoked the "pluralistic" culture that developed in medieval al-Andalus, where different musical styles and poetic forms mingled and merged. Finally, he hinted at a parallel between al-Andalus and the United States, two places where the blending of cultures has given rise to new forms of cultural expression.

Malley returned to these ideas throughout the performance and in conversations with me on the day of performance. During the sound check before the show, he told me: "We're living in a modern-day Andalusia here in America, in a sense. You know? Many religions, many different faiths, centers of learning."[6] For Ronnie Malley, then, the path of al-Andalus—the "Andalusian trail," if you will—not only connects Baghdad to Cordoba, but also stretches to Chicago. It is a past that remains present, living on in musical traditions that flourished in al-Andalus and then resonated across the globe.

As Ronnie Malley's work illustrates, music has become one of the primary platforms for engaging with al-Andalus in contemporary culture. Malley's work excavates deep layers of history and memory, but it also leans heavily on musical practices and projects that are quite modern and have risen to prominence in recent decades. Turning to this cultural phenomenon, this chapter will examine how contemporary artists perform, imagine, or engage with the legacy of al-Andalus through music. Many of the artists whose work I will discuss here claim to recreate the sound or the spirit of al-Andalus through their music. These claims take a variety of forms. For instance, a performer might attribute lyrics or a melody to al-Andalus, or a performer might claim to blend musical styles in a way that evokes or pays homage to the multicultural environment of al-Andalus. (Ronnie Malley does all of these things.) My aim will not be to assess the veracity of these claims, but rather to figure out what kind of political or cultural work they are doing. In other words, rather than asking, "Does this music come from al-Andalus?", I ask: What does it mean when a performer claims to embody or represent al-Andalus through music? What political or social needs do such claims satisfy? And how do these claims vary across different contexts, from Cordoba to Chicago, from Tetouan to Granada, and from Fez to Barcelona?

As I pursue these questions, I will treat music as both an object of study and a method—as something to study and something to study *with*.[7] By that, I mean to say that I will examine musical evocations of al-Andalus while also thinking about how musical transmission and performance are themselves metaphors for how the memory of al-Andalus operates in contemporary culture. Like the legacy of al-Andalus, music is promiscuous, traveling across cultural, spatial, and temporal lines. There is not much of a leap from the notion of *convivencia,* the coexistence of the Abrahamic faiths in al-Andalus, to the notion of *fusion,* the blending of musical genres or styles that come from distinct cultural spheres. What is musical fusion if not a harmonious *convivencia* of musical traditions that often live separately? It is no surprise, then, that many of the projects under consideration in this chapter take the form of musical fusion, and that these fusion projects often align themselves with ideas about religious and cultural coexistence in al-Andalus. Nevertheless, "fusion" does not exhaust the range of musical practices I examine in this chapter, nor does *convivencia* exhaust their political meanings or their interpretations of al-Andalus. My aim, then, will be to explore a variety of contemporary musical evocations of al-Andalus, while, at the same time, considering how music offers a model for thinking about the memory of al-Andalus and its movements across space and time.

At the heart of this chapter is a set of deceptively simple questions. Where does the memory of al-Andalus reside? Where did al-Andalus go after 1492, and where should we look for its traces today? In posing these questions, my aim is to attend to what the Spanish choreographer Patricia Álvarez has called "the living remains" of al-Andalus.[8] When I interviewed Álvarez in Madrid in January 2020, she told me that the Andalusi patrimony does not reside in texts but rather in rituals, gestures, and quotidian experience. Álvarez has pursued this idea through a recent series of performances, public lectures, and classes that she has organized under the title of *Alandalusa*. In a similar vein, many of the performers whose work I will examine here propose that the memory of al-Andalus resides in music, and that it is through performance that musicians and audiences can most deeply engage with the Andalusi past and its living heritage.

Layered Listening

Since the early 1980s, one of the most popular ways of staging al-Andalus is through performances and recordings that bring together musicians from Europe and North Africa. These projects have taken many forms, from so-called early music to hip hop, but several of the most prominent ones have explored the possibilities of fusion between Spanish flamenco and a North African musical tradition commonly known as "Andalusi music" (an umbrella term that covers an array of vocal and instrumental traditions found in many North African cities).[9] Both the names and the origins for flamenco and Andalusi music were hotly contested over the course of the twentieth century; what the two traditions have in common is that they have both been linked to the musical legacy of al-Andalus. For that reason, as Spanish and Maghribi performers have worked to combine the two traditions in recent decades, these efforts have often been understood, by performers and audiences alike, as attempts to reconstruct a cultural heritage that is common to Spain and North Africa and rooted in medieval Muslim Iberia.

Performers, audiences, and critics have often turned to the metaphors of "encounters" and "bridges" to describe collaborative projects between Spanish and North African performers. Behind these metaphors stands the belief that musical exchange between Spanish and North African artists can serve as a means to make deep connections across space and time—from the past to the present, and from one side of the Strait of Gibraltar to the other. "Fusion" is another common description of these intercultural music projects, though the term, common in discussions of world music, takes on a particular valence in this context. A repeated claim that runs through many of these projects is that Spanish flamenco and North African Andalusi music share a common origin in al-Andalus and that they are both the products of the diverse cultural exchanges that took place in the Iberian Peninsula in the Middle Ages. In some sense, then, both musical traditions are already "fusion" projects, insofar as they draw on cultural elements from diverse ethnic and religious groups. As a result, the musical collaborations that I explore here can also be understood, paradoxically, as fusions of traditions that are already fused.

An early and influential landmark in these efforts is a work titled *Macama jonda* (1983), a collaboration between the renowned Moroccan violinist and vocalist ʿAbd al-Sadiq Shaqara, one of the most famous Moroccan musicians of the second half of the twentieth century, and the Spanish playwright, poet, and activist José Heredia Maya (1947–2010), one of the leading figures in the modern *Gitano* (Roma) rights movement in Spain.[10] Since its premiere in 1983, *Macama jonda* has served as an inspiration and template for future collaborations between Spanish and North African musicians. To take just one example, Shaqara and Heredia Maya's work was the first to stage the mash-up of the Moroccan song "Bint bladi" and the Spanish song "La tarara," a combination that has become a standard in the repertoire of flamenco-Andalusi fusion projects (and that was reprised in Ronnie Malley's *The Andalusian Trail*).

Yet, despite *Macama jonda*'s significant innovations, the work was also indebted to cultural forces that had been brewing for many years. Over the preceding decades, Spanish and North African writers and performers had been plumbing the connections between musical traditions on both sides of the Strait of Gibraltar. Much of this work took place in Andalucía, Spain's southernmost region (which takes its name from al-Andalus), as well as in northern Morocco, the site of the Spanish Protectorate in Morocco (1912–1956). As a result, conversations about Spanish and North African music became wrapped up with debates about Andalusian regional identity, Spanish colonial practices in Morocco, and Moroccan responses to Spanish colonialism.

Since the middle of the nineteenth century, Spanish writers, particularly those from Andalucía, have postulated that the popular musical traditions of southern Spain and Morocco share a common origin in al-Andalus.[11] By the early twentieth century, these ideas coalesced into a coherent narrative that underpinned two distinct but intertwined projects: *andalucismo* and Spanish colonialism in Morocco.[12] The first of these projects, *andalucismo* (sometimes translated as "Andalusian regionalism"), is a political and cultural movement that emerged in the nineteenth century and has survived until the present day. Its proponents have sought to define and defend a distinct Andalusian regional identity. A core claim of *andalucismo* is that the modern-day region of Andalucía is the heir to the cultural legacy of medieval al-Andalus, and that the survival of this cultural heritage in modern-day Andalucía has made the region distinct from the other regions of Spain. Since the early twentieth century, several proponents of *andalucismo* have celebrated flamenco and related musical traditions as vibrant signs of Andalucía's unique cultural identity—and also as vestiges of the blending of cultures that has taken place in southern Spain over time. Furthermore, many of the prominent figures associated with early twentieth-century *andalucismo* were also defenders of Spanish colonialism in Morocco, as I have explored in depth elsewhere.[13] The point of convergence between these two projects, *andalucismo* and Spanish colonialism, was none other than al-Andalus. Proponents of Spanish colonialism often argued that Spain was the European nation that was best equipped to colonize Morocco because Spain and Morocco share a common cultural heritage that originated in al-Andalus. Music—both Spanish flamenco and North African Andalusi music—was a common illustration of this assertion of common cultural origins.

The vexing upshot of this story is that the effort to locate a common origin for Spanish and Moroccan music served, by the early part of the twentieth century, two goals that might, at first glance, seem to be at odds with each other: the strengthening of cultural ties between Spain and Morocco and the advancement of Spain's colonial interests in Morocco. The challenge, then, is for us to find a framework for understanding contemporary musical collaborations between Spanish and Moroccan musicians that takes into account this colonial backstory without allowing these colonial precedents to exhaust the potential meanings and implications of musical collaboration today. In other words, I'm asking: Can ideas that once served colonialism be rehabilitated today in the service of productive intercultural dialogue? However we might respond to this thorny question, I think that it is incumbent upon us to attend to the layers of history, both deep and recent, that are nestled within contemporary flamenco-Andalusi fusion projects. These projects proclaim a connection to medieval al-Andalus but also mobilize ideas and stories that were central to political projects of the early twentieth century. In a similar spirit, as we listen to these projects and think about them, we need to keep our ears tuned to multiple historical moments: medieval al-Andalus, twentieth-century Andalucía, colonial Morocco, and current events. With this practice of layered listening in mind, I would like to turn, briefly, to some of the early-twentieth-century antecedents to contemporary Spanish-Maghribi fusion projects. These antecedents are both theoretical and experiential: that is, they include both theoretical writings about music and also performances and experiences of music.

The music that is known today as flamenco is a repertoire that was largely standardized in the nineteenth century. The name *flamenco* was not in common use until the second half of the nineteenth century. Since then, the origins of this music and the names for describing it have been the topics of contentious debate.[14] In the 1920s and 1930s, a handful of prominent Andalusian intellectuals and composers entered the fray of these debates, pushing back against earlier attempts to associate the word *flamenco* (whose literal meaning in standard Castilian is "Flemish") with Flanders and northern Europe. These intellectuals and composers argued that flamenco was the musical expression of the diverse peoples and cultures that had interacted in the region of Andalucía over several centuries. They also held up flamenco as one of the most vibrant symbols of Andalusian regional identity—an identity that was, as I've indicated, under construction at that time.

A major milestone in these efforts was a music contest organized in Granada in 1922 by the composer Manuel de Falla (1876–1946) and the writer Federico García Lorca (1898–1936). The event was called the First Contest of Deep Song (*I Concurso de Cante Jondo*)—named after a style of song, the *cante jondo* (lit. "deep song"), that Falla and Lorca viewed as the most authentic expression of flamenco music.[15] In preparation for the contest, Falla wrote an influential essay about the origins and significance of the *cante jondo*.[16] In the essay, Falla attributed the emergence of the *cante jondo* to the confluence of three historical factors in Spain: the Spanish church's adoption of Byzantine chants; the settlement of large *Gitano* communities in Spain; and the Muslim conquest of the Iberian Peninsula (an event that he calls "the Arab invasion").[17] On the last point, Falla criticized previous Spanish musicologists for their failure to account for the significant influence that medieval Muslim culture in Iberia had exercised on the development of the *cante jondo*. Regarding this influence, Falla wrote:

> What leaves no room for doubt is that the music that is still known in Morocco, Algeria, and Tunisia with the name of "Andalusian music of the Moors of Granada" not only has a particular character that distinguishes it from other [musics] of Arab origin, but also that in its rhythmic forms of dance we can easily recognize the origin of many of our Andalusian ones: *sevillanas, zapateados, seguidillas,* etc.[18]

Building on this assertion, Falla speculated that the earliest forms of the *cante jondo* and of related Andalusian dances must have originated in Granada, the capital of the last Muslim kingdom in the Iberian Peninsula.[19] Falla thus sketched out a family tree of music whose roots stretched back to al-Andalus and whose branches extended across modern Andalucía and Morocco.

Falla's ideas were soon taken up by another major Andalusian thinker of the same period, Blas Infante (1885–1936), who is widely recognized today as a founding father of *andalucismo*.[20] In a series of writings from the 1920s and early 1930s, Blas Infante explored the common links between flamenco and North African Andalusi music. He would eventually develop the argument that flamenco is the music that emerged from the communities of displaced Spanish Muslims who were forced to convert to Christianity in the sixteenth century, after the Castilian conquest of Granada.[21] According to Infante, the forced converts to Christianity fled their Castilian oppressors and took refuge among *Gitano* communities in the rural and mountainous regions of Andalucía. These mixed communities of crypto-Muslims and *Gitanos* were, in Infante's view, the birthplace of flamenco, a music that expressed the dislocation and oppression experienced by Spanish Muslims after the fall of al-Andalus. In fact, Infante went so far as to assert that the word *flamenco* itself bore witness to this origin story. He postulated that *flamenco* derived from the Arabic phrase "felah-mengu," which he translated as "expelled peasant" (*campesino expulsado*).[22] The word, Infante insisted, had nothing to do with Flanders but, instead, referred to the Spanish Muslim laborers who were expelled from their lands in the sixteenth century. Infante's etymology of *flamenco* is dubious, but it has, nonetheless, exercised a significant influence on many Andalusian intellectuals, who have frequently repeated Infante's claim that the word *flamenco* refers to the displaced and impoverished Muslims who were forced to convert to Christianity in sixteenth-century Spain.[23]

Infante developed these ideas into a robust narrative about the relationship between modern flamenco and Spain's Muslim past. He referred to the sixteenth century as the beginning of the "flamenco era"—the period in which the spirit of al-Andalus and its displaced people found expression in a new musical style: flamenco and its variant, the *cante jondo*. On this point, Infante wrote in 1931:

> FLAMENCO or FELAH-MENCO era. Of contempt for the defeated race, of the Moorish race converted into a day-laborer . . . Era of subterranean flows, hidden or unspoken, of the Andalusian style, creating its cultural deeds like a thief who hides in shadows; continuing the original fluence of al-Andalus [*la fluencia original de Al-Andalus*], through hostile centuries. FLAMENCO ERA! The continuer of the authenticity of Andalucía, despite the European tyranny that Spain exercised and developed against us . . . Here, we still remain alive. The terrible and age-old tragedy has been presided over by a dirge: the *cante jondo*.[24]

In this exultant passage, Infante weaves together his speculative Arabic etymology of *flamenco* with a larger story about how flamenco carries forward the spirit and culture of al-Andalus, whose expelled inhabitants crafted the music as they fled from persecution. In this view, flamenco is not just a vestige of Spain's Muslim present; it is a cipher that bears the traces that al-Andalus has left on Spanish culture.

The emerging body of Andalusian writing that posited a link between flamenco and al-Andalus would also reverberate across the Strait of Gibraltar and shape Spanish colonial discourses and practices in Morocco. Blas Infante was no stranger to this process, as he would become, over the course of his life, an aficionado of North African music as well as a prominent voice advocating for Spanish colonialism in Morocco under the banner of *andalucismo*.[25] While traveling in Morocco in 1924, Infante attended a performance of a *nūba*, one of the eleven suites that make up the repertoire of Andalusi music in Morocco.[26] In his unpublished notes about the experience, Infante described the *nūba* as "the lyrical nostalgia of Andalucía in exile."[27] Infante thus contended that the Moroccan *nūbas*, like Spanish flamenco, gave voice to an experience of collective displacement that was set in motion by the conquest of al-Andalus. In Infante's view, the *nūba* and flamenco were related musical forms that connect Andalusians on both sides of the Strait of Gibraltar. This idea was shared by many Spanish intellectuals working in colonial Morocco. Among them was Infante's colleague, Rodolfo Gil Benumeya (1901–1975), a prominent advocate for Andalusian identity as well as for Spain's colonial interests in North Africa. Writing in 1932, Gil Benumeya called Moroccan Andalusi music "the oldest *cante jondo*."[28]

Colonial Morocco was also the context that gave rise to some of the earliest documented collaborations between Spanish musicians and Moroccan musicians in the modern era. Some of them developed under the aegis of Spanish colonial institutions, such as the Hispano-Moroccan Conservatory of Music in Tetouan, where Spanish and Moroccan musicians worked together to transcribe suites from the Moroccan Andalusi repertoire.[29] But such collaborations were not limited to the walls of colonial institutions; rather, they spilled out onto the stage and the radio waves. Colonial Tetouan had a vibrant flamenco scene, featuring frequent performances in the city's numerous theaters, bars, and *cafés cantantes*.[30] The biggest names in flamenco— such as Manolo Caracol, Lola Flores, and Pepe Marchena—regularly went on tour in colonial Morocco, making stops throughout the Spanish Protectorate zone.[31] Tetouan was not just a stop for flamenco artists from Spain; it also produced its own homegrown flamenco scene, in which both Spaniards and Moroccans participated.

A notable figure to emerge from this scene was Tuhami al-Dad al-Qasri (Touhami Kasri, ca. 1932–2017), a versatile artist and performer whose career illustrates the close collaboration between Spanish and Moroccan artists during the Protectorate period.[32] Al-Qasri was one of the first Moroccan students to receive a scholarship from the Spanish colonial authorities to attend

Tetouan's School of Fine Arts. During his student days, al-Qasri frequented the flamenco shows on offer in Tetouan's theaters and bars, where he would eventually cut his teeth as a singer. His passion for flamenco blossomed when he moved to Seville in 1953 to pursue his art studies. In 1954, al-Qasri took second prize in a *cante jondo* contest organized by Radio Nacional in Seville. Around this time, he landed a spot in the flamenco troupe led by legendary singer Pepe Pinto and his contemporary Manolo Caracol. Al-Qasri performed in the troupe under the artistic name "El Niño de Alcázar" (a nod to his birth city of al-Qasr al-Kabir). According to al-Qasri's biographer, Pepe Pinto and Manolo Caracol once shocked an audience in Spain by revealing that their singer, "El Niño de Alcázar," hailed from Morocco. Al-Qasri convinced the incredulous audience that he was Moroccan by performing a *mawwāl*, one of the vocal improvisations that are a common element in the repertoire of Moroccan Andalusi music.[33] This anecdote from al-Qasri's career is striking but not unique. Historians Rubén Gutiérrez Mate and Amin Chaachoo have uncovered similar attempts to marry flamenco and Andalusi music on the stages of colonial Tetouan in the 1930s and 1940s.[34]

Perhaps the most famous musician to emerge from this environment of intense artistic exchange between Morocco and Spain was none other than 'Abd al-Sadiq Shaqara. In fact, one of the performances that cemented Shaqara's fame on the national stage was a collaboration with Clara Eugenia Sabarezi, a Spanish choreographer who taught both Spanish and Moroccan students at the Hispano-Moroccan Conservatory of Music in Tetouan.[35] In 1957 Shaqara was invited to perform at the inauguration of Rabat's Muhammad V Theater. According to an account from one of Shaqara's contemporaries, the musician electrified the audience (which included King Muhammad V himself) with a rousing rendition of a popular song that he had collected in his travels through the mountainous regions surrounding Tetouan, "Hbiba w-jarahtini" (You've wounded me, darling). Shaqara was accompanied on stage by a group of dancers trained and led by Sabarezi.[36]

It is no surprise that Shaqara would end up collaborating with Sabarezi, since both artists came from the milieu of Tetouan's Hispano-Moroccan Conservatory. Shaqara was accepted to the conservatory as a violin student in 1947, when he was sixteen.[37] When his teacher died in 1956, Shaqara took over as the professor of violin at the conservatory.[38] In his new professorial role, Shaqara became a founding member of the conservatory's orchestra, which would quickly become one of the leading interpreters of the Andalusi repertoire in post-independence Morocco, performing throughout the country.[39] At the same time, Shaqara gained a wide following in Morocco on account of his renditions of popular songs that he collected on his travels through the country—songs that Moroccan connoisseurs variously describe as "popular" (*sha'biyya*), "heritage" (*turāthiyya*), or "authentic" (*aṣīla*).[40]

In the 1960s, Shaqara also embarked on a long career of recording and touring in Europe. In 1968, Shaqara and members of his ensemble traveled to Spain to collaborate with the Spanish group Atrium Musicae, led by Early Music pioneer Gregorio Paniagua. In a fifteenth-century church in the province of Burgos, Shaqara and his ensemble recorded excerpts from the Moroccan Andalusi repertoire. The recording was released as part of Atrium Musicae's multipart anthology of early Spanish music.[41] It was, as Dwight Reynolds has noted, "the first recording overtly designed to introduce Arabo-Andalusian music to Western audiences as a musical tradition contemporary with, and indeed related to, European Early Music."[42] The recording consolidated Shaqara's status as one of the primary ambassadors for Moroccan Andalusi music in Europe, a status that was reinforced by Shaqara's performances in Europe throughout the 1970s.[43]

What I hope to have illustrated here is that Shaqara's famous collaborations with José Heredia Maya in the early 1980s—collaborations that led to their work *Macama jonda* (1983)—came on the back of several decades of cultural interactions between Spanish and Moroccan artists and scholars, interactions that often highlighted the common cultural origins of Spanish and Moroccan music, in general, and Andalusi and flamenco music, in particular. As such, any analysis of Shaqara and Heredia Maya's work (and of the body of music that it has inspired) demands an approach that I have dubbed "layered listening"—a mode of listening that attends to the various layers of history that are embedded in this kind of intercultural music-making in contemporary Spain and Morocco. Indeed, as I hope to show, Shaqara and Heredia Maya were aware of, and adroit with, the layers of history embedded in their musical performance.

Encounters

The collaboration between the two artists took off in 1980 when Heredia Maya invited the orchestra of the Conservatory of Tetouan (of which Shaqara was a founding member) to perform in the First Encounter of Andalusi Music in

Granada. The event took place on the Paseo de los Tristes, at the foot of the Alhambra, the most visible symbol of Granada's Andalusi heritage.[44] In an interview with the newspaper *El País,* Heredia Maya described the event as "the first serious attempt at bringing together flamenco and Arab music."[45] He went on to explain that the aim of the event was "to spread and popularize knowledge of Andalusi folklore and of flamenco, as well as to facilitate the in-depth study of the musical similarities and identities between both cultural manifestations of different eras in Andalucía."[46] In other words, Heredia Maya described flamenco and Andalusi music as two manifestations of Andalusian culture, dating from different periods of Andalucía's history. His statements, like those of Blas Infante, enclosed a broad conception of "Andalusian" history and culture, one that encapsulated medieval al-Andalus, the modern-day region of Andalucía, and the cultural remnants of al-Andalus that remain alive in modern Morocco. The event in Granada was thus conceived as an encounter across space and time, between the music of medieval al-Andalus and the music of contemporary Andalucía, as well as between musicians from contemporary Granada and musicians from the region of Morocco where Andalusi exiles took refuge after the conquest of Granada in the fifteenth century.

This spirit of encounter was carried on, notably, in Heredia Maya and Shaqara's most famous collaboration: the theatrical production *Macama jonda* (1983). In fact, the notion of "encounter" was inscribed in the work's bilingual title. As Heredia Maya explained in an interview with the Spanish newspaper *ABC* in April 1983, he chose the Arabic word *Macama* (*maqāma*) for the title because it can be roughly translated as "meeting" or "encounter."[47] The second word of the title, *jonda* (masc. *jondo*), is an Andalusian variant of the adjective *honda* (deep). In the flamenco lexicon, *jondo* refers to a style of song, the *cante jondo,* and, more broadly, to the affective state that the song produces. The title *Macama jonda* thus invites the audience to a "deep encounter," an encounter between two peoples and two musical traditions that share deep roots.[48] Heredia Maya indicated as much when he told the newspaper *ABC,* "I was aiming for this possibility of union to be present from the title itself. The title is onomatopoeic and even musical. In it are gathered all the keys to the show."[49] For Heredia Maya, the work's title was "onomatopoeic" in the sense that its sound echoed its meaning. By joining together an Arabic word and a colloquial Andalusian musical term, the title signaled the marriage between two cultures that were, in the view of the work's creators, united through their common origin in the area of today's Andalucía. By all accounts, Heredia Maya's Moroccan collaborators shared his understanding of the project's aims and scope. One of them told the Spanish newspaper *El País* that *Macama jonda* "sets out to unite, for the first time in five hundred years, that which was already united."[50] Both the Spanish and the Moroccan contributors to *Macama jonda,* then, viewed the work as an encounter across national, cultural, and temporal lines—a marriage of Spanish and Moroccan musicians through the legacy of al-Andalus.

Macama jonda premiered in Granada in February 1983 at the Manuel de Falla Auditorium—fittingly named after the Andalusian composer who had led the revival of interest in the *cante jondo* in the early twentieth century. The show was then staged at major venues in Seville and Madrid.[51] The music from the Granada production was later released on an album published by the label Ariola-Eurodisc. My discussion of *Macama jonda* is based on the Seville production, which was filmed and broadcast on Spanish National Television.[52]

Given the work's emphasis on unions and "encounters," it is no coincidence that the plot of *Macama jonda* centers on the marriage between a Muslim girl from Tetouan and a *Gitano* from Granada. The political symbolism of this marriage plot was front and center for the work's creators. On the eve of the performance in Seville, Heredia Maya told the newspaper *ABC,* "*Macama jonda* is a show in which we've sought to unite Arabo-Andalusian music with modern-day flamenco, [as well as] to push for unity and fraternity, symbolized in the wedding of a Moorish woman [*mora*] from Tetouan and an Andalusian from Granada."[53] A similar sentiment was expressed in the voiceover narration that introduced the television broadcast of the show in 1983. At the beginning of broadcast, the narrator explained: "The show that we're going to see, *Macama jonda,* seeks to push the spectator toward coexistence [*convivencia*] and solidarity, starting from a concrete deed: the wedding of a Moorish woman from Tetouan and an Andalusian *Gitano*."[54] The narrator thus explicitly associated the work's plot with the goal of *convivencia.*

While the term *convivencia* often refers to the coexistence of different religious groups in al-Andalus, it has also been used, in recent decades, to talk about North African immigration to Spain and to call for a multicultural Spanish society that is welcoming of cultural difference.[55] All of these associations were at work in the staging of *Macama jonda*. For the television narrator, as well as for Heredia Maya, *Macama jonda* was a metaphor for cultural coexistence in the past and the present. They both suggested that the work's fusion of Spanish and Moroccan music would recreate the cultural coexistence that once flourished in al-Andalus.

At the beginning of the show, Shaqara and his ensemble performed a brief lyrical fragment from the Moroccan Andalusi repertoire, a *muwashshah* taken from the suite known as *Nubat al-Hijaz al-Kabir*. The lyrics, sung by Shaqara in Arabic, evoked a joyous encounter with the beloved, a motif that foreshadowed the marriage plot at the center of *Macama jonda*. Shaqara and his bandmates performed the short piece while sitting at stage right on a raised platform that was decorated with leather poufs, a tea set, and other objects that conjured up a domestic setting in Morocco. The musicians were dressed in elegant djellabas and red fezzes. For a Moroccan audience, the scene would have been legible as a representation of the elegance and refinement frequently associated with Andalusi music in Morocco, traits that are, in turn, associated with the music's prestigious roots in al-Andalus. For a Spanish audience, however, these signs would have been more difficult to decipher. Neither the melody nor the lyrics of the song would have been easily recognizable for most Spanish listeners. As a result, the opening scene might well have struck many Spanish viewers as a display of cultural difference, rather than a representation of cultural encounter. Yet *Macama jonda* would work to challenge this reaction. What the work reveals is that two things that might appear different at first glance could turn out to have much in common.

After the opening scene, the action shifted to stage left (and, by extension, to Andalucía), where Enrique Morente (1942–2010), arguably the most famous flamenco vocalist of his generation, performed a virtuosic solo about two lovers meeting at dawn. The theme is a common one in both the flamenco and Andalusi traditions. The musical commonalities did not stop at the level of lyrics. In the solo, Morente made extensive use of melisma, a form of vocal ornamentation that consists of assigning many notes to a single syllable. Melisma is also a common form of vocal ornamentation in Moroccan Andalusi music. As Morente performed his solo, the strings of Shaqara's ensemble accompanied him with tremolos in a compatible mode. This moment of exchange exemplified some of the strategies of musical fusion pursued in *Macama jonda*. Throughout the work, the Moroccan and Spanish musicians mirrored each other by exploring melodies, modes, or ornamentation techniques that had first been performed by their counterparts. There were also several moments in which instrumentalists from one of the ensembles would accompany vocalists from the other ensemble. These convergences intensified in tandem with the story of the two lovers, whose courtship and marriage formed the nucleus of the work, symbolizing the union of Spanish and Moroccan culture.

All these elements came to a head in the show's final scene, in which the Moroccan and Spanish musicians mingled on stage, bridging the spatial division of the set and blending their musical styles. At the beginning of the scene, the performers moved downstage and sat together in a festive arrangement that conjured up a wedding scene. Amid this festive scene, Morente and Shaqara met at center stage to sing together. Their exchange highlighted the theme of cultural union, with nods to the deep past and to the more recent past of relations between Spain and Morocco.

Morente opened the exchange by singing the following line (in Spanish) over a soft guitar accompaniment: "A man has his brother / in another man whose / hands are just as clean as his." Morente then passed the baton to Shaqara, who sang a line, in Arabic, from Ibn al-Khatib's "Jadaka al-ghayth." As I have noted before, Ibn al-Khatib's poem is one of the most famous from al-Andalus and has become a mainstay in modern musical tributes to al-Andalus. When Shaqara sang an excerpt from the poem in *Macama jonda,* he faced the flamenco guitarists who accompanied him from the other side of the stage. In other words, the fourteenth-century Andalusi poem bridged the stage, connecting one side of the set to the other. After this lyrical nod to al-Andalus, set to flamenco, Shaqara handed off to Morente, who repeated the lines from the beginning of the exchange. Morente then sang the word "brother" (*hermano*) three times, stretching out the syllables across several notes. Shaqara picked up the line, joining Morente in repeating the word, "brother." Finally, all of the other performers, Spanish and Moroccan, joined the duo, singing the word "brother."

This scene, in which Spanish and Moroccan musicians joined forces to sing about brotherhood, is a fitting snapshot of *Macama jonda,* which was a tribute to the possibility of Spanish-Moroccan union. Through the use of Ibn al-Khatib's poem, the scene pointed to al-Andalus as the foundation for building Spanish-Moroccan brotherhood in the present. Yet, the scene also drew on much more recent precedents—ones drawn from Spanish colonial history. After all, one of the most common rhetorical justifications for Spain's colonial projects in Morocco was the assertion that Spaniards and Moroccans are "brothers" who share a common cultural heritage. Advocates for Spanish colonialism in Morocco used the "brotherhood" discourse to distinguish Spain from its colonial rivals and to argue that Spain's colonial presence in Morocco was not, in fact, colonialism but was, instead, the restoration of the long-standing cultural and historic bonds between Spaniards and Moroccans.[56] This colonial backstory demonstrates just how tricky it is to get our arms around the form of cultural memory at work in a project like *Macama jonda*. The show couched its approach to cross-cultural musical collaboration in terms that explicitly evoked the heritage of al-Andalus. Yet, at the same time, the show's evocation of al-Andalus drew heavily on practices and tropes that had emerged in the context of Spanish colonialism in Morocco. This matrix produces a kind of musical stratigraphy, in which different layers of history are superimposed in the same performance.[57]

Macama jonda concluded with the piece that has become the most famous fragment from the show: a lively mash-up of the Moroccan folk song "Bint bladi," sung in colloquial Moroccan Arabic, and the Spanish folk song "La tarara," sung in Spanish. It is curious that this particular piece has had such a lasting influence on contemporary musical evocations of al-Andalus, since its Moroccan component, "Bint bladi," is the only piece from *Macama jonda* that 'Abd al-Sadiq Shaqara did not draw from the *nūba* repertoire or from the poetry of al-Andalus. Instead, "Bint bladi" is one of the many *sha'bī* (popular) tunes that Shaqara adapted and brought to fame in the middle of the twentieth century. Once again, then, this piece illustrates that contemporary fusion projects often make reference to al-Andalus while drawing on cultural phenomena that are quite modern. Yet, in some way, the famous mash-up of "Bint bladi" and "La tarara" realizes the premise that Blas Infante had floated in the early twentieth century. Like Infante's work on flamenco, the final piece in *Macama jonda* suggests that popular music is a repository where the memory of al-Andalus remains alive. The piece insinuates that the two main facets of Shaqara's career—the "popular" repertoire and the more formal *nūba* repertoire—might come from the same root, al-Andalus, and that this root has given rise to a musical lineage with descendants in the popular musical traditions of contemporary Spain and Morocco.

Macama jonda has exerted tremendous influence over the musical collaborations that have come in its wake. Since the work's premiere in 1983, there
have been dozens of high-profile collaborations between Spanish flamenco
artists and North African (primarily Moroccan) musicians.[58] While these
projects are admittedly diverse, many of the performers behind them have
explicitly cited *Macama jonda* as an inspiration for their work.[59] Many of
these performers have also adopted musical, lyrical, and discursive strategies
that *Macama jonda* helped to put into wide circulation. Thus, *Macama jonda*
helped create a vocabulary (both musical and conceptual) for practicing musical fusion, as well for understanding it.

For example, in many of the collaborative projects, the primary approach
to fusion is the one adopted by the performers in the final scene of *Macama
jonda*: the Spanish and Moroccan musicians trade verses in Spanish and Arabic over a common rhythmic framework and a shared musical mode, using
instruments from both the flamenco tradition (such as guitar, voice, clapping,
and cajón) and the North African Andalusi tradition (such as lute, violin,
tambourine, and darbouka).[60] The songs might incorporate lyrics from
Spanish and North African popular music (such as the case of the famous
mash-up of "Bint bladi" and "La tarara"), or they might incorporate lyrics
from Andalusi literary texts (such as the poem by Ibn al-Khatib). Many
flamenco-North African collaborations adopt these formal and stylistic traits.
Most importantly, though, they almost always nod to al-Andalus as the discursive framework that undergirds, motivates, and makes legible the music
that arises from these exchanges. While gesturing back to al-Andalus, these
projects also revive and promote ideas about music that emerged in the early
twentieth century—particularly Blas Infante's ideas about the deep connections between flamenco and North African Andalusi music. Such ideas, as I
have noted, arose from the context of Spanish colonialism in Morocco, but
they have since been adapted to address new political and social forces shaping
relations across the Strait of Gibraltar.

In particular, the musical fusion projects that have followed in *Macama
jonda*'s wake have coincided with a boom in Moroccan immigration to Spain,
a phenomenon that took off in the 1980s and 1990s, when Spain joined the
European Economic Community (now the European Union) and became
one of the main points of entry for migrants from North and West Africa to
Europe.[61] As a result, the musical collaborations that have emerged in this

period (and the public responses to them) have often woven together debates about al-Andalus and debates about immigration to contemporary Spain. A common theme in these projects is that collaborations between Spanish and North African artists not only pay homage to the cultural fusions that took place in al-Andalus but also work to revive the Andalusi cultural legacy in the present with the aim of building a multicultural Spanish society that is open to the new migrant communities from North Africa and elsewhere.[62] In other words, debates about al-Andalus have increasingly become entangled with debates about immigration, and music has become an important tool for articulating and understanding this relationship between past and present. Many of the performers working in this space are themselves migrants from North Africa, often from Spain's former colonial territories in northern Morocco.

A notable example is Jalal Chekara (Jalal Shaqara, b. 1974), the nephew of 'Abd al-Sadiq Shaqara and a leading voice in flamenco fusion projects today.[63] Jalal's father, 'Abd Allah, was the lute player in 'Abd al-Sadiq Shaqara's ensemble and one of the performers in the original production of *Macama jonda*. Jalal studied violin at Tetouan's music conservatory, where his uncle was a professor. In 1987, at the age of thirteen, Jalal joined his uncle's famous ensemble. With the ensemble, Jalal performed throughout Morocco and eventually participated in a few high-profile collaborations with musicians in Europe, including a performance with British composer Michael Nyman at the Seville Expo in 1992.[64] As 'Abd al-Sadiq Shaqara's health declined in the 1990s, he began to groom Jalal as his successor. After 'Abd al-Sadiq Shaqara's death in 1998, Jalal took over as the director of the orchestra named after his uncle. One of his first projects as the ensemble's director was a collaboration with Enrique Morente called "Sonidos de Al Andalus" (Sounds of al-Andalus), which premiered at the Pirineos-Sur festival in Spain in 1997. The two joined forces again in 2000 for a new project titled "Voces de Al-Andalus" (Voices of al-Andalus).[65] Around that time, Morente encouraged Jalal Chekara to migrate to Spain, where he still lives today.[66] Morente and Chekara continued to perform and record together until Morente's death in 2010. Since Enrique Morente's death, Chekara has collaborated with Morente's daughter, Estrella Morente, herself a major figure in the contemporary flamenco scene.[67] Chekara has also performed and recorded with the likes of Carmen Linares, Segundo Falcón, and Ángeles Gabaldón.

Many of these collaborations have revived ideas that can be traced back to 'Abd al-Sadiq Shaqara's groundbreaking work with Spanish artists in the 1980s. In particular, Jalal Chekara and his collaborators have drawn inspiration from the idea that Spanish and Moroccan music share a family relationship that is rooted in their shared Andalusi heritage. Chekara's work has built on the notions of musical "encounters" across the two shores of the Strait of Gibraltar, and of the family or "fraternal" relationship between flamenco and North African music (especially Andalusi music). At the same time, it has woven these long-standing ideas into new debates about immigration—and, in particular, about the place of North African and Muslim immigrants in contemporary Spanish society.

Debates about immigration shaped many of Chekara's projects in the early 2000s, while also shaping the responses to Chekara's work among Spanish critics and musicians. For example, in 2001, Chekara began a new project with flamenco singers Segundo Falcón (b. 1970) and Arcángel (b. 1977). The project's title was "Flamenco Couscous" ("Cus-cús Flamenco"), a cheeky allusion to Morocco's most famous dish. The project's first public performance was a show at Granada's Teatro Isabel la Católica—named, ironically, after one of the Spanish monarchs who led the conquest of Muslim Granada. In contrast with the venue's namesake, "Flamenco Couscous" heralded the return of Muslims to Granada and the marriage of two musical cultures that claim connections to medieval Muslim Granada. The performance inspired the following review in the major Spanish daily *El País*:

> While politicians insist on making immigration a problem and cultural differences a stigma, artists approach the issue from another angle and find something much more valuable: the richness that exists in the exchange of cultures. That is what some Spanish and Moroccan musicians demonstrated last night in a concert in which—without mixing, without any kind of fusion—their respective musical styles, flamenco and Andalusi music, were woven together, joining hands. Arabic sounded to the tune of bulerías [*sonó por bulerías*], and the nubas seemed to be from the Sacromonte.[68]

The review hailed the performance as a rebuttal to divisive political rhetoric about immigration to Spain. The implication—one that is often present in reviews of musical collaborations of this type—was that exchanges between Spanish and Moroccan musicians have the potential to overcome cultural divisions in contemporary Spain. Jalal Chekara hammered home this point when he told *El Pais,* for the same article, "Between artists, the concept of racism doesn't exist . . . For us, this has all come easily because both musics have things in common."[69] The newspaper's review also suggested that "Flamenco Couscous" was not a work of "fusion," because the show brought together two musical traditions that were already fused. According to the reviewer, the performance made Arabic speak flamenco, while making the *nubas* seem like they came from the Sacromonte, a neighborhood in Granada that is a famous center for flamenco and *Gitano* culture. In other words, the show, like Heredia Maya's *Macama jonda,* staged a family reunion between flamenco and Andalusi music, and between Moroccans and Spanish *Gitanos.* Blas Infante would have been proud.

"Flamenco Couscous" helped launch Chekara's career in Spain. The show led to Chekara's first album in Spain, numerous performances throughout Spain (including at the prestigious Bienal de Flamenco in Seville), and a tour of Latin America.[70] In "Flamenco Couscous," Chekara also crafted the approach to musical fusion—and even some of the arrangements—that he has since used in the two studio albums that he has released under his own name: *La Chekara y el flamenco* (Chekara and flamenco, 2008) and *Tan cerca, tan lejos* (So close, so far, 2014). In these albums, and in the many stage shows that have emerged around them, Chekara blends flamenco with *sha'bī* ("popular") music from Tetouan, especially the songs that were made famous by his uncle. Chekara also occasionally draws on lyrics or melodies from the Moroccan Andalusi repertoire, though he leans much more heavily on popular music from northern Morocco. The resulting blend is a style that Chekara and his collaborators call "Andalusi flamenco" (*flamenco andalusí*).[71]

In many of the tracks on *La Chekara y el flamenco,* Chekara takes a song that his uncle wrote or made famous and combines it with a classic from the flamenco repertoire. For example, the album includes Chekara's rendition of his uncle's hit "Hbiba w-jarahtini," the same song that 'Abd al-Sadiq Shaqara performed to the choreography of Clara Eugenia Sabarezi in the 1950s. Chekara's rendition is woven together with a *soleá* (a form of flamenco), performed by Segundo Falcón, with lyrics that pay tribute to the legends of Seville's flamenco scene.[72] This track and others like it are not only linguistically bilingual but also musically so: they feature Spanish and Moroccan musicians, using instruments that are commonly associated with flamenco or Andalusi performance, such as the guitar and the lute. At the end of each track, the tempo picks up, and all of the musicians play together. In other words, the tracks tend to follow a pattern in which they begin with two separate components (a Moroccan song and a Spanish song) and then work toward a moment of convergence or union.

These traits are well illustrated in Chekara's collaborations with the Seville-born singer Alicia Acuña (b. 1978), collaborations that led to two tracks on *La Chekara y el flamenco* and the 2008 stage show *Multaka* (from the Arabic *multaqā*, "meeting place").[73] On a track titled "Amulati," Chekara and Acuña blend "Amulati" (Oh, my lady), a love song attributed to 'Abd al-Sadiq Shaqara, with "Ábreme la puerta verde" (Open the green door), a popular love song from Andalucía. Chekara and Acuña perform the songs over a *tanguillo*, a 6/8 rhythm that is often used in fusion projects because it can be adapted to both flamenco and North African *sha'bī* music.[74] In both of the songs that make up this track, a first-person speaker addresses a lover in the second person. Chekara sings in Arabic, "Oh, my lady, for God's sake, have mercy on me!" Acuña, for her part, sings in Spanish, "Come to the window / for I'm here with my arms full of flowers / . . . Open the green door for me!" The two singers continue in this vein, exchanging verses addressed to an unnamed lover. When Acuña sings in her rich alto, Chekara occasionally echoes her with wordless cries or with quick embellishments on his violin. The resulting effect is that the two singers seem to be addressing and mirroring each other, each one becoming the object of the other's love song. The track, then, recreates in song the love allegory that was a central component of *Macama jonda*. In the track, the flirtatious courtship between the speaker of "Amulati" (embodied by Chekara) and the speaker of "Ábreme la puerta verde" (embodied by Acuña) mirrors the marriage of Moroccan and Spanish culture. As this example illustrates, in Chekara's "Andalusi flamenco," al-Andalus serves less as a historical point of origin than as a narrative framework for describing how Chekara and his collaborators interweave musical traditions from Morocco and Spain.

Bridges

While the Shaqara and Morente families have played a prominent role in the practice and conceptualization of flamenco fusion over the past four decades, they are not, by a long shot, the only artists working in this space. Another major figure in this scene is Amina Alaoui (Amina al-'Alawi, b. 1964), a Moroccan-born vocalist who has been based in Europe since the 1980s. A notable difference between Alaoui and Jalal Chekara is that Alaoui is not only a distinguished performer but is also a scholar of North African and Iberian music. She has published her writings on music in academic journals as well as in the lyrical essays that appear in the liner notes for her albums *Alcántara* (1998) and *Arco Iris* (2011). If we look at Alaoui's writings and recordings together, as two parts of a unitary project, then the thesis that emerges from them is that North African Andalusi music and the popular musical traditions of modern Spain and Portugal are all part of the same musical family, whose roots go back to al-Andalus.

Alaoui was born in Fez, Morocco, to an elite family that claims descent from al-Andalus.[75] In an introductory essay to her first solo album, *Alcántara* (1998), Alaoui recalls that at family gatherings and celebrations during her childhood, her family would sing the poetry of Ibn Zamrak (ca. 1333–1393), whose works adorn the walls of the Alhambra.[76] In this family milieu, imbued with reverence for the Andalusi heritage, Alaoui was initiated in Moroccan Andalusi music. She told me, in an interview in October 2020, that she grew up "with the *nūbas* in her ears."[77] One of the relatives who influenced her early music education was her grandmother's cousin Mouley Ahmed Loukili (Ahmad al-Wukili, 1909–1988), a distinguished performer who taught Andalusi music at the Conservatory of Tetouan and served, for three decades, as the director of Moroccan national radio's orchestra. Loukili would host musical soirees at Alaoui's childhood home, giving her early exposure to the Moroccan Andalusi repertoire.[78] Alaoui later continued her musical education in Rabat, where she studied piano and European classical music with a private teacher and then at the Rabat Conservatory. In 1982, she moved to Spain to pursue a university degree. After a year in Madrid, she moved to Granada, where she studied Spanish and Arabic philology at the University of Granada. Alaoui describes her encounter with Granada as the "spark" that reignited her interest in Andalusi music and put her on the professional path that she is on today.[79]

Over the course of the past four decades, Alaoui has built a reputation as a leading interpreter of the North African art music known as *gharnāṭī* (lit. "Granadan"), a school of Andalusi music that is found in Morocco and

Algeria, especially in the Algerian-Moroccan borderlands.[80] Her interest in *gharnāṭī* music led her to work with Ahmed Piro (Ahmad Biru, b. 1932), one of the preeminent performers of that repertoire. In 1995, the two artists joined forces to produce a critically acclaimed album of *gharnāṭī* music.[81] Three years later, Alaoui released her first album as a solo artist, *Alcantara*. The album's title comes from the Arabic word for "bridge," *al-qanṭara*. Yet, as Alaoui explained in her introductory essay to the album, the title also evokes the Spanish verb for singing, *cantar*. As a result, Alaoui playfully translated the album's title as "a bridge of song."[82] This play on words articulates the main idea that has driven Alaoui's work over the past few decades: namely, the idea that music and songs form a bridge that unites the past and the present, the Iberian Peninsula and North Africa, as well as the various peoples and faiths of the Mediterranean world.

This idea is not limited to Alaoui's recording career but also extends to her scholarship, where she has persistently argued for the underlying unity of Iberian and North African music. One of her approaches to this question has been to look for a common link between the Spanish term *duende* and the Arabic term *ṭarab,* which are among the most common (and charged) terms used to describe flamenco and Andalusi music, respectively. The first term, *duende* (spirit), was popularized by Federico García Lorca and refers to the mysterious and ineffable spirit that inspires flamenco artists.[83] The second term, *ṭarab* (ecstasy), refers to the pleasure that Andalusi music induces in the listener, and the term also serves, by extension, as one of the names for Andalusi music (*al-ṭarab al-andalusī*).[84] In many of her writings, Alaoui has asserted that *duende* and *ṭarab* are interrelated terms that refer to a shared cultural experience. For example, in an article published in a Spanish journal in 2006, Alaoui wrote, "In the Arab tradition, when a singer is recognized as having talent, he is called a *muṭrib*—that is, an accomplished performer who is capable of provoking *ṭarab*. I remember hearing in Morocco, during my childhood there, the expression *ṭarab andalusī* or *ṭarab gharnāṭī* to define Andalusi music and its schools. A beautiful way of describing the Andalusi *duende*."[85] Continuing in this vein, Alaoui declares, "All I'll say is that *ṭarab* is, in essence, *duende*."[86] Although these terminological considerations might seem like insider baseball, they have helped Alaoui to posit a deep connection between North African and Iberian music. Her strategy has been to identify the two terms that are most intimately associated with flamenco and

Andalusi music (indeed, the two terms that are thought to represent what is untranslatable about these musics), and then to suggest that the two terms are, in fact, one and the same, pointing to a quality that is common to North African and Spanish music.

Alaoui is not the first scholar or performer to explore the possible connections between flamenco and North African music, but, for the past two decades, she has taken this long-standing project in a new direction by connecting it to another musical genre: fado, which has long been regarded as a quintessential expression of Portuguese culture, "the sound and soul of Portugal."[87] Like flamenco, fado has many competing origin stories. The standard view among scholars is that fado emerged in the early 1800s in Lisbon's socially marginalized communities, drawing on Afro-Brazilian influences that came to the city via the slave trade and other forms of contact across Portugal's colonial networks.[88] Although this view holds sway among scholars, there is another origin story that carries significant weight among fado practitioners and enthusiasts. Many of them believe that fado draws on sounds and memories that are vestiges of the long presence of Muslims and Arabs in medieval Iberia. (It is worth noting, here, that much of today's Portugal was part of al-Andalus.) In particular, as Lila Ellen Gray has documented, many fado enthusiasts point to the common practice of using extended vocal ornaments (voltinhas) as evidence of fado's "Arabness" and as "proof of fado's Moorish origins."[89]

In recent years, Amina Alaoui has waded into these debates, arguing for fado's Arab origins and placing fado in an Iberian family tree that includes flamenco and North African Andalusi music. As Alaoui tells the story, her interest in fado took off in 1999, when a fan approached her after one of her concerts and told her that he sensed a link between her work and the work of fado legend Amália Rodrigues.[90] Intrigued by this suggestion, Alaoui obtained a grant from the French government to pursue research on possible connections between fado and gharnāṭī music.[91] This research would eventually lead to Alaoui's writings about fado and to her album, Arco Iris, which draws on influences from fado, flamenco, and Andalusi music.

In a 2003 essay titled "Réminiscences de la culture arabe dans le fado" (Reminiscences of Arab culture in fado), Alaoui argues that fado descends from the culture of the marginalized and oppressed Iberian Muslims who were forced to convert to Christianity in the sixteenth century after the fall of al-Andalus. This argument bears a clear resemblance to Infante's influential work on the origins of flamenco—work that Alaoui cites in her essay on fado.[92] Another move that Alaoui borrows from Infante's playbook is that she offers an Arabic etymology for the word *fado*. While most scholars have argued that *fado* derives from the Latin *fatum* (fate), Alaoui contends that *fado* derives from the Arabic *ḥaẓẓ* (or *al-ḥaẓẓu,* with case inflection), also meaning "fate" or "fortune."[93] But, for Alaoui, fado's affiliations with the Arab world do not stop there. She also claims that fado's lyrics descend from poetic traditions that trace back to al-Andalus—and, in particular, to the *zajal,* a genre of poetry in colloquial Arabic that originated in al-Andalus.[94] Finally, Alaoui points to the sound of fado as the ultimate proof of the music's affiliation with Arab and Muslim cultures. In particular, she catalogues several similarities between fado and *gharnāṭī,* similarities that include techniques of vocal ornamentation (such as melisma), forms of improvisation that are common to both musical traditions, as well as practices of call-and-response among the performers and between the performers and the audience.[95] Alaoui concludes that fado is the most vibrant illustration of a much larger process of cultural transmission, through which the legacy of al-Andalus found its way into many facets of Portuguese culture, including poetry, tilework, daily gestures, and the Portuguese language (which, like Spanish, has many words of Arabic origin).[96]

Alaoui had an opportunity to put these ideas into practice in her album *Arco Iris,* her first solo project with the European label ECM.[97] On the album, she sings in Arabic, Spanish, and Portuguese, performing musical arrangements of lyrics taken from a broad range of Iberian authors, including al-Muʿtamid ibn ʿAbbad (d. 1095), Ibn Khafaja (d. 1139), Teresa de Ávila (d. 1582), and António Sousa Freitas (d. 2004). In a similar spirit, Alaoui's musical arrangements draw on a diverse array of Iberian and Mediterranean musical traditions, including fado, flamenco, and North African Andalusi music. In an introductory essay to *Arco Iris,* Alaoui writes that the music on the album probes "the common crucible" of fado, flamenco, and Andalusi music and "transcribes an Iberian Peninsula reaching towards dialogue."[98] With echoes of Blas Infante, Alaoui suggests that the album—with its nods to fado, flamenco, and *gharnāṭī*—is a tribute to the cultural legacy of the Moriscos, the Muslims who remained in the Iberian peninsula after 1492 and were eventually forced to convert to Christianity. Invoking these predecessors, Alaoui writes: "The drama of history is the ghost of the past. I venture forth on the traces of the Morisco of the sixteenth century."[99] In other words, Alaoui suggests that the album is a work of excavation, one that reveals the "traces" that the past has left on the music of the present. She also suggests that the album is a work of cultural mapping, one that stages a dialogue between interrelated musical traditions in order to map out the far-reaching legacy of al-Andalus, a legacy that cuts across geographic, linguistic, and religious lines.

These intersecting dimensions are at work in the track "Oh Andaluces" (O Andalusians), where Alaoui takes lyrics from an Andalusi source and sets them to a musical arrangement that evokes the Andalusi and flamenco traditions. The song's lyrics come from one of the most beloved poems from al-Andalus: "Ya ahl Andalus" (O people of al-Andalus) by Ibn Khafaja, a poet born in the area of Valencia in the eleventh century. The poem is a canonical text in the *nūba* tradition—and one of a just a handful of texts in that tradition to mention al-Andalus explicitly.[100] In Alaoui's rendition of the song, the Moroccan vocalist sings the poem's first four hemistiches:

> O people of al-Andalus! How God showered you
>   with water, shade, rivers, and trees!
> The Garden of Paradise is nowhere if not in your land,
>   and if given the choice, I would have chosen it myself.[101]

These famous lines evoke a time of abundance and ease in al-Andalus. Yet, as Jonathan Glasser has argued, contemporary performances of Ibn Khafaja's poem not only pay tribute to al-Andalus but also invite audiences to identify with al-Andalus and to imagine themselves as part of a living chain of memory that goes back to al-Andalus. In this reading, the meaning of Ibn Khafaja's line, "O people of al-Andalus," expands to include not only the inhabitants of medieval al-Andalus but also the people who keep the memory of al-Andalus alive in the present.[102] Translating this insight to Alaoui's performance, we might say that, by using Ibn Khafaja's words, Alaoui and her collaborators both evoke the "people of al-Andalus" and assert their place among them.

While the lyrics indicate a bridge across time, the track's musical arrangement enacts a bridge across space, uniting musical traditions from modern-day North Africa and Spain. The track opens with an unmetered improvisation by Tunisian lute-player Sofiane Negra, who explores the piece's melodic mode.

Such instrumental introductions are common in North African Andalusi music, where they are known as an *istikhbār* (lit. "inquiry").[103] Amina Alaoui then joins in, singing the first three hemistiches of Ibn Khafaja's poem, lingering on each phrase and emphasizing words with extensive melismas (such as when she attributes dozens of notes to the phrase "people of al-Andalus"). As Alaoui sings, Negra responds, filling in the silences between Alaoui's phrases with improvised runs that mirror the vocalist's inflections and embellishments. The two musicians proceed in this manner, with call and response, until Alaoui reaches the poem's third hemistich: "The Garden of Paradise is nowhere if not in your land."

Up until this point, Alaoui and Negra are firmly in the terrain of North African Andalusi music, by dint of the choice of text, the instrumentation, and the style of improvisation. At the midway point in the song, however, Alaoui pivots to a different musical idiom. Negra's lute falls away, and Alaoui sings a plaintive "Ah." She ascends and then descends three notes (E-F-G), a nod to the Phrygian mode that is a hallmark of Spanish flamenco. As if on cue, a Spanish flamenco guitarist, José Luis Montón, joins in and echoes Alaoui as she repeats her ascending and descending "Ah." As Montón plays along with Alaoui, he marks the beat by tapping on the body of his guitar, a common percussive technique in flamenco. Montón then performs an unmetered improvisation that harkens back to Negra's solo from the beginning of the track. Finally, Alaoui returns to Ibn Khafaja's poem, repeating the third hemistich and then singing through to the end of the poem's second line. As Alaoui sings the poem, Montón improvises responses to her inflections and embellishments. In other words, the track begins as a piece of North African Andalusi music and then becomes a flamenco song. Ibn Khafaja's poem and Alaoui's voice are the anchors holding the two parts together. Alaoui takes Ibn Khafaja's words, which originated in medieval Iberia, and passes them, like a baton, from a North African musician to a Spanish musician, enacting a cultural relay that moves back and forth between the Iberian Peninsula and North Africa.

While in "Oh Andaluces" Alaoui sings lyrics that originated in al-Andalus, on another track, "Las Morillas de Jaén," Alaoui performs lyrics that traveled from Arabic to Spanish, and from medieval al-Andalus to modern Spain. The track's lyrics, sung by Alaoui over a flamenco arrangement, adopt the perspective of a first-person speaker who has fallen in love with "three

Moorish girls from Jaén" (*tres morillas de Jaén*). These lyrics come from a popular poem whose transmission history stretches from Spain to the Middle East, with several stops in between.[104] Indeed, the poem's travels, adaptations, and translations exemplify the cross-cultural connections that animate Alaoui's work.

The earliest version of the poem emerged in ninth-century Iraq and migrated from there to al-Andalus, along with the waves of musicians and scholars who moved from the Abbasid court in Baghdad to the Umayyad court in Cordoba. The poem enjoyed great popularity in al-Andalus, where there were several variants of it, dating from tenth-century Cordoba to fourteenth-century Granada. Sometime around the end of the period of Muslim rule in the Iberian Peninsula, a version of the poem made the leap into the Castilian language, likely through the work of poets and performers who lived on the frontier between the Muslim and Christian territories in the Iberian Peninsula. The Arabic poem that directly inspired the Castilian adaptation was likely a *zajal*, a genre of poetry composed in the Andalusi Arabic dialect, sometimes mixed with Romance expressions. The earliest extant version of the Castilian poem appears in the *Cancionero Musical de Palacio*, a Spanish manuscript containing songs from the late fifteenth and early sixteenth century—that is, from the period immediately before and after the conquest of Granada. The *Cancionero* manuscript was rediscovered in the late nineteenth century and published by Spanish composer and musicologist Francisco Asenjo Barbieri (1823–1894). Barbieri's edition contained two versions of the poem about the "three Moorish girls from Jaén." The poem reached international fame in the twentieth century when it was set to music and performed by a number of Spanish artists, including, most famously, Federico García Lorca. The Granadan poet adapted the poem from the *Cancionero*, wrote music for it, and recorded it with singer Encarnación López, better known by her artistic name "La Argentinita."[105] The recording was released as part of their acclaimed *Colección de canciones populares* (Collection of popular songs, 1931), a project that both reflected and spurred a growing interest in Spanish popular music. Amina Alaoui's 2011 rendition of the song follows in the footsteps of this performance tradition; her lyrics are the ones that Lorca prepared for his recording with La Argentinita.

The backstory for "Tres Morillas de Jaén" reads like an allegory for Alaoui's entire musical project. On the track, Alaoui sings a popular Castilian poem that originated in ninth-century Iraq, traveled from the Middle East to al-Andalus, and then made its way into Castilian culture in the fifteenth century through the work of poets and performers who traversed the border between Muslim and Christian Iberia. In another turn in this saga, the poem in question owes much of its current fame to Federico García Lorca, a writer who famously celebrated flamenco and southern Spain's Andalusi heritage.[106] What more, the poetic genre that served as the bridge between the Arabic versions of the poem and the Castilian versions of the poem was likely the *zajal,* a genre that, according to Alaoui, gave rise to a number of popular lyrical traditions in Spain and Portugal, including fado. (In one of her articles, Alaoui calls the *zajal* "a veritable hyphen between all the communities" in medieval Iberia.[107]) The lyrics that Alaoui sings are, then, words that bear witness to the imprint that al-Andalus has left on popular culture in present-day Spain and Portugal. The track's original music, written by Alaoui and arranged by Montón, also points to the traces of al-Andalus. The music has a strong air of flamenco, with the percussive strumming (*rasgueado*) of Montón's guitar and the use of cajón to mark the rhythm; but the music also has some nods to fado, through the incorporation of Eduardo Miranda's mandolin, whose timbre resembles that of the Portuguese *guitarra,* the most common instrument in fado performance.

It is worth pausing to reflect on Amina Alaoui's position within these circuits of cultural exchange, stacked on top of each other like Russian dolls. Alaoui is, as I've noted, a Moroccan-born vocalist who made her name as a performer of *gharnāṭī,* a North African musical tradition that claims direct descent from al-Andalus. She is also a Moroccan Muslim immigrant residing today in Granada, a city closely associated with Spain's Andalusi heritage. In "Tres Morillas de Jaén," Alaoui's performance crosses gender lines and adopts the position of a Christian speaker who has fallen in love with three Muslim ("Moorish") women. At the very end of the song, there is an exchange between the first-person speaker and the three *moras:*

> I said to them: "Who are you, ladies,
> who have robbed me of my life?"
> "We are Christians who were Moors in Jaén" [*Cristianas que éramos
>   moras en Jaén*].

As Alaoui sings these lines, the last of the song, she voices multiple perspectives—that of the first-person speaker (presumably a Christian man) as well as that of the three women, "Christians who were Moors in Jaén." At this moment, Alaoui's performance straddles multiple identities: male and female, lover and beloved, Christian and Muslim. The moment is a fitting conclusion to a song that illustrates the cultural traffic between the Middle East and the Iberian Peninsula through the mediation of al-Andalus. Like Alaoui in her performance, the poem about "the three Moorish girls" has straddled Arabic and Spanish, Muslim and Christian actors, and the past and the present. The poem epitomizes the traces that al-Andalus has left on Spanish popular culture, just as flamenco, fado, and *gharnāṭī* epitomize (for Alaoui, her collaborators, and many of their predecessors) the long afterlife of al-Andalus in music. Alaoui's song leads you, like a treasure map, along lyrical and musical pathways that stretch back to al-Andalus and across present-day Spain, Portugal, and Morocco.

Strait Flow

While contemporary performers of flamenco, *nūbas,* fado, and North African *sha'bī* music can claim a direct (albeit contested) link between their work and the musical heritage of al-Andalus, such a claim would seem, at first glance, to be less accessible to performers who work in genres that have only taken shape in recent decades, such as hip hop. Nonetheless, a survey of global hip hop reveals a vast and surprising array of allusions to al-Andalus, a cultural symbol that has remained relevant for hip-hop artists around the world, from Atlanta to Barcelona, and from Tangier to Paris.[108] Although hip-hop evocations of al-Andalus criss-cross the Atlantic and the Mediterranean, they have found a particular density of meaning in the contemporary Spanish and Moroccan rap scenes. Just as rappers around the world speak of "street flow," it is possible to speak of a "Strait flow" that has emerged from the work of hip-hop artists living on both sides of the Strait of Gibraltar.[109] The lyrical flow that has emerged in this area is one that draws its energy from the movement of people, languages, and sounds across the Strait of Gibraltar. It gives expression to contemporary migrations from Morocco to Spain, while carrying the echoes of earlier exchanges between North Africa and the Iberian Peninsula.

Not surprisingly, al-Andalus has figured prominently in this musical milieu, and especially in recent collaborations between Spanish and Moroccan hip-hop artists. The meanings attached to al-Andalus in this context are diverse. At times, allusions to al-Andalus in hip hop serve to highlight cultural affinities between Spain and Morocco, affinities that are grounded in a shared historical experience. At other times, allusions to al-Andalus bring into relief alliances that are not grounded in the historical or cultural specificity of the area surrounding the Strait of Gibraltar; al-Andalus has also served, as we will see, to articulate expressions of solidarity with the urban poor in Europe, North Africa, and the Americas. In this sense, the hip-hop al-Andalus invites an intersectional analysis, one that takes into account diverse and overlapping affiliations of nationality, ethnicity, religion, and class.[110] Through this dense web of meanings, al-Andalus has offered hip-hop artists a historical symbol for talking about relations between Spain and Morocco, while also allowing them to reflect on experiences of social marginalization and political action that connect Spanish and Moroccan hip-hop artists to networks of allies in Europe and the Americas.

In recent years, there have been a handful of high-profile collaborations between Spanish and Moroccan hip-hop artists. Some of them have developed under the aegis of Spanish musical festivals that promote exchange with artists from North and sub-Saharan Africa. An early example of this trend is the track "Hip Hop Exchange," a collaboration between two of the leading figures in the Spanish and Moroccan rap scenes: ToteKing, a rapper from Seville, and H-Kayne, a group from Meknes.[111] The song premiered in July 2009 at the festival La Mar de Músicas (based in Cartagena, Spain) and later appeared on a compilation album issued by the multinational retail chain FNAC. It featured a catchy hook by Moroccan vocalist Oum, who sang:

Jīnā, jīnā, jīnā mnayn wa-layn
Ṣawtnā fī al-Andalus bayn

We've come, we've come, we've come back and forth [lit. "from
    where and to where"]
Our voice in al-Andalus is clear![112]

In this hook, Oum repeats the verb "we've come" [*jīnā*], emphasizing the movements back and forth between the Iberian Peninsula and North Africa. These circular movements seem to encompass a broad range of historical actors, from the North Africans who traveled to al-Andalus in the eighth century, to the Andalusis who sought refuge in North Africa after the fall of Muslim Granada, to the present-day North African migrants who cross the Strait of Gibraltar to start a new life in Europe. The collective memory of these movements has left a visible mark on Spain, where, as Oum sings, "Our voice in al-Andalus is clear."

Oum's hook revolves around a first-person plural subject whose identity is left ambiguous. Since Oum delivers these lyrics in Moroccan Arabic, she appears to be laying claim to the Moroccan contributions to al-Andalus and its heritage in today's Spain. Yet, given the song's emphasis on "exchange"—a theme that comes up in nearly every verse in the track—it does not seem too much of a stretch to think that Oum's lyrics are meant to evoke a collective "we" that encompasses Moroccans and Spaniards. In this reading, al-Andalus becomes the cultural ground on which Moroccan and Spanish artists can affirm their shared roots and engage in an exchange that cuts across national, cultural, and linguistic lines.

While Spanish music festivals have created spaces for Spanish and Moroccan artists to collaborate, they are not the only avenues for pursuing this kind of artistic exchange. Outside the festival circuit, rappers from southern Spain and northern Morocco have come together to produce some memorable tracks. One of the most fruitful collaborations is the one that has emerged between Seville-born rapper Haze and Tangier-born rapper Sayflhak. Haze has built a reputation as one of the leading proponents of a style that he calls "flamenco rap," which blends rap lyrics and flamenco sounds (such as clapping, percussive guitar strumming, and beats on the cajón).[113] Haze's collaboration with Sayflhak took off in 2013, when the two rappers met in Tangier to shoot the video for "Air and Sea" ("Sma O Bhar" / "Aire y Mar"). The video has received 3.8 million views on YouTube, cementing the song's status as a touchstone of Spanish-Moroccan rap exchange.[114]

The video for "Air and Sea" was shot in Tangier's casbah, which offers views of the Strait of Gibraltar and the nearby coast of Spain. As befits this setting, the song and its video explore the proximity between Morocco and Spain, making frequent allusions to al-Andalus and its influence on contemporary Spanish and Moroccan culture. The video opens with a shot of Haze and

Sayflhak walking side by side through the narrow streets of the casbah. Accompanying this image, the track opens with a short unmetered improvisation by a lute, a sound that evokes North Africa and, specifically, the instrumental improvisations that often introduce pieces from the Andalusi music repertoire. After this brief instrumental introduction, Spanish vocalist Elena Vargas belts out the song's hook in Spanish:

> When I wake up in the morning,
> The sunlight through my window,
> Comes to speak to me from Andalucía.
> I put a foot in the street, and to the Giralda
> I send a letter from Tangier.
> Give me a poem of freedom.

In the hook, Vargas adopts the perspective of a speaker who straddles Tangier and Seville, blurring the lines between the two cities. Standing in the streets of Tangier, she sends a greeting to the Giralda, which is currently the bell tower of Seville's cathedral and was formerly an Almohad minaret from the twelfth century. Like the allusion to the Giralda, Vargas's hook outlines a palimpsest, where various layers of history stack on top of each other: Tangier's streets evoke Seville's buildings, which are, in turn, testaments to the city's former life as the Andalusi capital of a North African empire.

These interconnected histories have not only left a mark on Spanish and Moroccan cities but also on the music and dance traditions from both countries, as "Air and Sea" works to illustrate. While Vargas sings the hook in the video, Haze, Sayflhak, and another collaborator, Tangier-based rai singer Ibra Rai, dance in a festive scene shot on a rooftop in Tangier. The three men, along with the other people at the party, clap their hands and adopt dramatic poses that are clearly reminiscent of *sevillanas,* a form of popular dance derived from flamenco (Figure 5.1). These are not the only allusions to flamenco. Vargas sings the hook over a sample of flamenco-style handclapping, and the somewhat strident timbre of her voice is indebted to flamenco performance. In this song, as in other examples discussed in this chapter, flamenco serves as a sonic sign of Spain's Andalusi heritage—and as a sound that transcends borders and fuses Spain and Morocco.

Figure 5.1. Sayflhak, Ibra Rai, and Haze in "Sma O Bhar (Aire y Mar)." "Sma O Bhar (Aire y Mar)," Aflam Bla Flous, 2013.

Such movements across space and time are at the heart of Haze's verse on "Air and Sea." The Seville-born artist raps the following lines in Spanish:

I'm sensitive, irreplaceable,
I was born in the city of the Invincible Armada.
In Moroccan land—at attention! [¡firme!]
Reminds me of a Nasrid kingdom,
I feel an Andalusi essence, undeniable . . .
From the Guadalquivir River.
History carries an echo,
Arabic poetry, hand-in-hand Andalucía and Morocco,
To the rhythm of rap,
Flamenco and rai greet each other,
As do Arabic and Castilian,
There's no racism here.
Two continents and a single content, right on! [¡Razón!]
I write from my mind what is dictated by my heart [corazón].

Haze's lyrics are an emphatic tribute to a Spanish-Moroccan unity grounded in the legacy of al-Andalus. Like Vargas's hook, Haze's verse moves easily between Seville (described here as "the city of the Invincible Armada") and Tangier.[115] The latter, according to Haze, has an undeniable "Andalusi essence" and evokes "a Nasrid kingdom" (that is, Muslim Granada). Yet, for Haze, the echoes of al-Andalus are not limited to Morocco; rather, they unite his hometown and Tangier, his native tongue and Arabic. Asserting that "History carries an echo," Haze enacts this idea at the level of rhyme: he rhymes *arábiga poesía* ("Arabic poetry") with *Andalucía,* associating the poetry of al-Andalus with the name of the region where he comes from in southern Spain. Likewise, Haze raps that he is coming "from the Guadalquivir River" ("desde el río Guadalquivir"), a line that not only alludes to largest river in southern Spain but also illustrates how the Arabic language is woven into the fabric of Spanish. After all, the river's name, Guadalquivir, comes from the Arabic for "big river" (*al-wādī al-kabīr*). Drawing on these etymological connections, Haze juxtaposes the Spanish word for river with a Spanish toponym derived from the Arabic word for river, just as he juxtaposes Seville and Tangier.

Toward the end of the verse, Haze gestures to the political project that is inscribed in this song. According to his lyrics, his collaboration with his Moroccan colleagues signals that "There's no racism here," and that Spain and Morocco represent "two continents and a single content." Such proclamations of tolerance and cultural unity are, as we've seen in this chapter, quite common in contemporary fusion projects that bring together performers from Europe and North Africa. The musical traditions that have carried the banner for this message have often been ones that claim descent from al-Andalus, such as flamenco and North African Andalusi music. In the case of "Air and Sea," however, it is hip hop that provides the musical framework for enacting the memory of al-Andalus, with its imagined legacies of tolerance. What more, Haze frames the spirit of Andalusi tolerance in racial terms, instead of religious ones. His lyrics do not invoke the well-worn *convivencia* of the three Abrahamic faiths but rather the *convivencia* of people from different racial backgrounds. The lyrics thus draw on long-standing ideas about al-Andalus but adapt them to new musical practices and to a new focus on race as a major category of identity politics in contemporary Spain and Morocco.[116]

Sayflhak and Ibra Rai, for their part, contribute to the track with shorter verses that center on the phenomenon of migration from northern Morocco to Spain. Saylfhak raps about those who "cross over seas and mountains," and he gives shout-outs to his people in Barcelona and Santa Coloma, a suburb of Barcelona with a large Moroccan immigrant community. Ibra Rai carries forward this theme of immigration and relates it to a metaphorical love relationship with Andalucía. In a plaintive rai verse enhanced by the use of autotune, Ibra Rai sings the following lines in Moroccan Arabic:

> I'm headed to Tangier to send my greetings to Seville
> Oh, listen up and alleviate my affliction for you, o Andalucía
> I would get a visa just for you, for you.

Like Elena Vargas, Ibra Rai performs lyrics that underline the ease with which you can "greet" Seville from Tangier. His first line conjures up the physical proximity between Tangier and Spain's southern coast, which is visible from Tangier on a clear day. Indeed, in the video for the song, Ibra Rai points from his rooftop perch in Tangier to the coast of Spain when delivering the first line. He then apostrophizes Andalucía, addressing it in the second person. This move transforms Andalucía into a departed lover, separated from the speaker by the Strait of Gibraltar. In the last line, Ibra Rai expresses his desire to get a visa to visit his lover, Andalucía. Thus, the singer's allusions to Moroccan immigration to Spain are couched in a larger metaphor about the love that he and other Moroccans profess to Andalucía, presumably because of their cultural links to it.

The diverse range of meanings that al-Andalus has come to elicit in contemporary hip hop is perhaps best expressed in the work of Khaled (Jalid Rodríguez, b. 1990), a Spanish rapper of Moroccan descent.[117] The son of a Spanish father and a Moroccan mother, Khaled was born and raised in Granada's Albayzín neighborhood, which faces the Alhambra and has long served as a symbol of Granada's past life as the last Muslim kingdom on the Iberian Peninsula. (More recently, the Albayzín has become the home for many North African immigrants living in Granada.[118]) When Khaled was a teenager in Granada, he performed with the rap collective Kefta Boyz, named after a Moroccan dish made of spiced ground meat. In 2013, Khaled moved to Barcelona, where he became a founding member of Pxxr Gvng (pronounced "poor gang"), one of the most popular and influential Spanish rap groups of the past decade. The group, later renamed Los Santos, quickly rose to prominence by releasing several singles and mixtapes through YouTube, SoundCloud, and other online platforms.

As a member of Pxxr Gvng and later as a solo artist, Khaled has built a reputation as one of Spain's most inventive rappers. His lyrics are virtuosic in their multilingualism, weaving nimbly between Spanish and Moroccan Arabic, with occasional flourishes in French and English. His musical tastes are similarly diverse. While Khaled is most closely associated with the sub-genre of hip hop known as trap, his music has also drawn heavily on flamenco, which he often cites as one of his main musical influences.[119] Indeed, in his conversations with Spanish journalists, Khaled has stressed the continuities between flamenco and trap, noting that they are two musical genres that have given a voice to marginalized communities from southern Spain.[120] Khaled even called himself "a frustrated flamenco artist" ("un flamenco frustrado") in an interview with the newspaper *El Español* in 2017.[121]

In his statements to the Spanish press, Khaled has also frequently drawn attention to his intermediary position between different languages and cultures, as well as between Spain, his country of birth, and Morocco, his mother's country of origin. Reflecting on his dual background, Khaled told the interviewer from *El Español,* "Two cultures that collide. I consider myself Muslim, in my way. I've got the best of here and the best of there: I'm a Spanish Muslim. I have no homeland [*patria*]."[122] In a similar spirit, Khaled often refers to himself as *mestizo* (meaning, racially and culturally mixed), as, for example, when he told Spanish newspaper *El País* in a 2018 interview, "I'm *mestizo,* and I coexist with the two cultures every day of my life."[123] Al-Andalus is one of the cultural frameworks that Khaled uses to give voice to his self-proclaimed *mestizo* identity. In Khaled's music, the cultural legacy of al-Andalus is *mestizo,* floating between Granada and Tangier, Spanish and Arabic, as well as flamenco and trap.

All of these forces are at play in "Los Foreign" (2015), the first breakout hit that Khaled had with Pxxr Gvng. The song was the top single from *Los Yumas,* a mixtape that Pxxr Gvng recorded with rap duo Los Zafiros, made up of Dominican-Spanish rapper Big Jay and Cuban-French rapper Vicious. The video for "Los Foreign," shot in Barcelona's Raval neighborhood, has over fourteen million views on YouTube, an indicator of the song's stunning success.[124] Khaled is the first to speak on "Los Foreign." In the video, he is dressed all in black and sports a cane and a steaming cup of tea. Facing the camera, he mimics the sound of a machine gun and then shouts, "Agressif, ṣāḥbī," juxtaposing the French word for "aggressive" with the Moroccan Arabic word for "my friend." Building on this multilingual opener, Khaled lets loose a verse that moves with agility between French, Spanish, and Moroccan Arabic. I will offer the original lyrics below, followed by a translation in which I render the Spanish words in English:

C'est la classe!
Moviendo placas.
Tengo yinunas, tengo qaḥbas.
Bodas gitanas cantando con patriarcas.
Lléname la copa, Samara,
Que mis penas no se van con la ganja.
Classique, como "La tarara,"
Gitanas con pañuelo y moras con la chilaba.
Mi padre es de Huelva, la mama de Ṭanja,
Al-Andalus es mi raza!
Wallah pa' la nukhayla!
Estoy con los Yuma y los ḥarrāga,
Criao con los ṭanjāwa,
C'est bonne qualité, [ḥaḍāra?].[125]
Hey, mon frère, sīr t'hawa.
Had shī mqawwad, arf arf,
'Andak y'aṭṭik.

[C'est la classe!
Moving bricks.
I've got yinunas, I've got qaḥbas.
Gypsy weddings, singing with patriarchs,
Fill up my cup, Samara,
Since my sorrows don't go away with ganja.
Classique, like "La tarara,"
Gypsy women with headscarves and Moorish women with djellaba.
My father's from Huelva, mama's from Ṭanja
Al-Andalus is my race!
Wallah pa' la nukhayla
I'm with the Yuma and the ḥarrāga,
Raised with the ṭanjāwa,
C'est bonne qualité, [ḥaḍāra?].

> *Hey, mon frère, sīr t'hawa.*
> *Had shī mqawwad, arf arf,*
> *'Andak y'aṭṭik.*]

This verse, like all of Khaled's lyrics, poses a serious problem of translation. The challenge, for me, has been to figure out how to make Khaled's lyrics legible to an English-speaking audience without neutralizing Khaled's agile movements across languages. After all, to translate Khaled's lyrics into a single target language would be to miss the point of his multilingual pyrotechnics. The solution that I have proposed is to translate Khaled's Spanish (the predominant language in his work) into English, while preserving his phrases in Moroccan Arabic and French. This solution, I think, preserves some of the effect that Khaled's multilingual lyrics would have on a Spanish listener who is not of Moroccan origin.

My analysis of Khaled's verse hinges on his provocative claim that "Al-Andalus is my race!" What, I wonder, does it mean for Khaled to claim al-Andalus as his "race"? At first glance, the answer seems simple enough. Khaled is, as he narrates in the verse, the son of a mixed marriage between a father from Huelva (a city in southwestern Andalucía) and a mother from *Ṭanja* (the Arabic name for Tangier). Khaled's claim on al-Andalus thus rests, at least in part, on a family story that encompasses people on both sides of the Strait of Gibraltar. But Khaled's family story is only part of the picture. The rapper's performance of an Andalusi "race" also brings into play other dimensions of identity, such as class, immigration status, and language. On the last of these points, language, Khaled's lyrics suggest that to be "Andalusi" means not only to float between Spain and Morocco, but also to move between languages. Khaled's playful movements across languages reflect his bicultural upbringing, but they also allow him to stake out a position that is in solidarity with many marginalized groups in Spain.

Khaled places particular emphasis on the solidarity and similarity between "Moors" and "Gypsies" (that is, North Africans and *Gitanos* / Roma).[126] This theme emerges early in the song, when Khaled speaks of "Gypsy weddings, singing with patriarchs." When Khaled delivers this line in the video for "Los Foreign," he mirrors it with his body language: he straightens his back and claps his hands with his fingers spread wide, gestures that evoke the dancing and rhythmic handclapping that are common elements of flamenco and

Gitano performance. Building on this allusion, Khaled calls himself *"classique* like 'La tarara,'" citing an Andalusian folk song that is closely associated with *Gitano* performers, such as Camarón de la Isla (who is, not by coincidence, one of Khaled's musical heroes).[127] "La tarara" is also, as we have seen in this chapter, a mainstay in recent efforts to fuse flamenco and Moroccan Andalusi music. Khaled enacts a similar sort of fusion when he rhymes the song's title, "La tarara," with the word *chilaba* (djellaba), the name of the loose-fitting hooded garments often worn by Moroccans. Rounding out these efforts to map an alliance across ethnic groups, Khaled speaks of "Gypsy women [*gitanas*] with headscarves and Moorish women [*moras*] with djellaba." Notably, the word that Khaled uses to describe the headscarf (*pañuelo*) worn by some Gypsy women is the same word that is used, in Spanish, to describe the hijab worn by some Muslim women. Thus, in this line, the figure of the *Gitana* merges with that of the *Mora*, just as in Khaled's verse, Moroccans and *Gitanos* converge and share common cause. All these images place Khaled in a long line of authors and artists who have posited a deep connection between Spanish Muslims and Spanish *Gitanos*.

The rhyme on "La tarara" and *chilaba* is part of a chain of rhymes that bring into relief connections across different marginalized groups in Spain, including but not limited to the *Gitano* community. The assonance (or vowel rhyme) in *a-a* draws out the implicit associations between *Gitano* patriarchs (*patriarcas*), an Andalusian folk song ("La tarara"), a Moroccan garment (*chilaba*), the city where Khaled's mother comes from (*Ṭanja*), and the "race" (*raza*) of al-Andalus. The same rhyme scheme extends into the following lines, drawing out associations with new actors and cultural forces. After proclaiming "Al-Andalus es mi raza," Khaled gives a bilingual shout-out to the *nukhayla* (in Arabic, "the little palm"). This word, an extension of the vowel rhyme in *a-a,* could be a reference to Morocco (a land of palm trees) or perhaps a reference to Nujaila, a popular pastry shop in Granada's Albayzín neighborhood (and, if Instagram is any indication, one of Khaled's haunts in Granada).[128] In the next line, Khaled asserts, "I'm with the *Yuma* and the *ḥarrāga.*" The first italicized word, *Yuma,* is a Cuban slang term meaning "foreigner." The second, *ḥarrāga,* is a Moroccan colloquial term meaning "burners"; it refers to the immigrants who burn their documents before leaving the shore of North Africa so that European authorities will not return them to their countries of origin.[129] Khaled thus aligns himself with foreigners and undocumented immigrants and describes these groups with a multi-lingual web of synonyms that come from far-ranging contexts, from Cuba to Morocco. (To this web of synonyms, we could add the English term *foreign,* from the song's title.)

After the shout-outs to "the *Yuma* and the *ḥarrāga,*" Khaled adds a final detail to his autobiographical sketch, noting that he was "Raised with the *ṭanjāwa*" ("Criao con los *ṭanjāwa*"). This line combines the Spanish participle *criao* (in standard Castilian, *criado*), a syncopated form associated with working-class speakers, with the Arabic proper adjective for people from Tangier (*ṭanjāwa,* "Tangerines"). Through the repeated assonance in *a-a,* Khaled establishes an implicit association with the preceding rhyming words: *ḥarrāga, raza,* "La tarara," and so on. Khaled thus uses rhyme and juxtaposition to insert himself in intersecting categories of place, language, and class. He is, at once, a foreigner (*Yuma*), an immigrant (*ḥarrāga*), a working-class Spanish speaker (*criao*), a speaker of Moroccan Arabic, and a Tangerine (*ṭanjāwa*). As often happens with intersectional claims, none of these categories can be treated in isolation; they all reinforce and structure each other.[130]

Returning to Khaled's provocative claim that "Al-Andalus is my race," I think that we can understand this claim in light of the intersectional politics and verbal creativity that I have described above. Al-Andalus is, in part, Khaled's way of describing his identity as the son of Spanish and Moroccan parents. It cannot be reduced, though, to any kind of biological essentialism. Instead, al-Andalus functions here as a critical stance toward intersecting structures of power. Al-Andalus is the conceptual glue that binds together diverse groups who find common cause in their struggle against social and economic marginalization: "Moors" and "Gypsies," *Yumas* and *ḥarrāga,* men who sing "La tarara" and women who wear the djellaba, speakers of Moroccan Arabic and speakers of working-class Spanish. Khaled's lyrics seek to give voice to these diverse but allied groups and, in so doing, to give voice to a cultural legacy that the rapper calls the "race" of al-Andalus.

Khaled has returned to these themes in several of his songs, placing particular emphasis on the interrelations between the Moroccan immigrant community in Spain, the *Gitano* community in Spain, and the legacy of al-Andalus. The convergence of these intersecting strands is particularly prominent in the video for Khaled's song "Volando recto" (Flying straight, 2016).[131] The video was shot in Granada's Sacromonte neighborhood, a historic center of *Gitano* culture and the birthplace of many flamenco legends. The video depicts a celebration that is popularly known as "El Cristo de los Gitanos," a procession of a crucifix which takes place annually during Holy Week. The video's opening sequence establishes, in a few quick shots, the main themes that are in play. First, there are images of Khaled and his crew strutting through the streets of the Sacromonte during the nocturnal festivities for the "Cristo de los Gitanos." Then, there is an image of the Alhambra, illuminated against the night sky and seen from the perspective of the Sacromonte. Finally, as the camera shifts back to Khaled and his crew, there is a voice-over of a brief phone conversation between Khaled and a friend, speaking in Moroccan Arabic. In quick succession, then, the opening sequence juxtaposes images of one of Granada's most emblematic manifestations of *Gitano* culture (the "Cristo de los Gitanos"), an image of Granada's most famous Andalusi monument (the Alhambra), and a fragmentary recording that attests to the large Moroccan immigrant community that has made Granada its home. Khaled is, in the video, the common denominator uniting these diverse elements.

"Volando recto" continues Khaled's efforts to make flamenco and hip hop the main expressions of a long-standing cultural tradition rooted in southern Spain and tied to the region's *Gitano* and Moroccan communities. The song's video features lively images of the spontaneous flamenco performances that break out in the Sacromonte's streets and *cuevas* during the annual celebration of the "Cristo de los Gitanos." For instance, there are images of a flamenco guitarist playing in the street and of a female dancer striking a flamboyant pose in a bar. Throughout the video, Khaled and his companions are shown participating in the festivities, clapping along to the flamenco performances.

Khaled delivers most of his lines with the illuminated Alhambra in the background, serving as a frame for his performance (Figure 5.2). This staging establishes an implicit association between the memory of al-Andalus, Khaled's performance, and the images of the festivities in the Sacromonte. The video seems to suggest that the Alhambra and the cultural legacy that it represents are the historical scaffolding that supports the scene that unfolds in the video, making it possible for Khaled, a Spanish Muslim rapper of Moroccan descent, to pay homage to *Gitano* culture and to participate fully in an event that is closely associated with popular Catholic religiosity. I am reminded again here of Khaled's claim that "Al-Andalus is my race!" As I have

Figure 5.2. Khaled with the Alhambra in the background, in "Volando recto."
"Volando recto," produced by Shean Beats, directed by Alex Caballero, 2016.

argued, this claim does not only refer to Khaled's Spanish and Moroccan parentage but also to his ability to straddle seemingly irreconcilable divides of language, geography, class, ethnicity, and religion.

"Volando recto" is also a love letter to Khaled's hometown of Granada. Midway through the song, Khaled asserts, "I've never forgotten where I come from" (*Yo nunca me he olvidado de dónde vengo*). It is a line that he has also used in other songs, such as "Camarón" (2016). Although the repeated line might signal Khaled's love for his hometown, the phrase "where I come from" is ambiguous and allows for multiple interpretations. It can, of course, refer to a place of origin, but it can also refer to other forms of origin, such as family of origin, culture of origin, or socioeconomic class of origin. In "Volando recto," Khaled plays with these interlocking senses of what it means to come from somewhere. He suggests that "where he comes from" is a place with many layers.

Khaled drives this point home in a part of the video where he, while standing in front of the Alhambra, rhymes a line in Spanish and English, "Esto es gangsta rap, papi" (This is gangsta rap, *papi*), with a line that blends Spanish and Moroccan Arabic, "¡Viva wuld blādī!" (Long live *wuld blādī!*). In the second line, Khaled uses a common Moroccan Arabic phrase, *wuld blādī*, whose literal meaning is "son of my country." This phrase is frequently used in Morocco, and especially in Moroccan rap, to express pride in Moroccan identity. In other words, the "country" in question would seem to be Morocco. Yet, when Khaled transposes this common Moroccan Arabic phrase to a celebration in the Sacromonte, facing the Alhambra, the phrase takes on new meanings. Khaled's music outlines a lyrical "country" that embraces the Alhambra and the Sacromonte, Spanish and Moroccan Arabic, rap and flamenco. It is a "country" that straddles Granada's past as a major center in Muslim Iberia and Granada's present as a home to a diverse population of people from several ethnic and cultural backgrounds. This "country" is less a real place than it is an idea, an idea that is conjured into being through Khaled's music. Is it too much for me to call this idea "al-Andalus"? Certainly, the memory of al-Andalus looms in the background of much of Khaled's music, just as the Alhambra looms in the background of the video for "Volando recto."

Khaled is a recent iteration of a long-standing cultural tradition, whose genealogy I have sought to trace throughout this chapter. Like many of his precedessors, Khaled has used music to explore the deep cultural connections between the Iberian Peninsula and North Africa. Unlike many of his precedessors, Khaled has not pursued this project through a musical tradition that claims direct descent from al-Andalus. Instead, Khaled has adopted hip hop as the idiom for building musical bridges across the Strait of Gibraltar, while also establishing alliances among Spain's marginalized communities. Many of Khaled's precedessors have used the musical heritage of al-Andalus to explore interfaith, interethnic, transnational, or transregional relations. Khaled builds on this work but also brings into play new identity markers, such as class and language use. Indeed, language use might be the arena where Khaled has made his most innovative interventions. Khaled's playfully multilingual lyrics, which often feature translingual rhymes (like "La tarara" and *chilaba*), speak a tongue that cannot be reduced to a single national, ethnic, or religious category. Indeed, Khaled's music cannot even be reduced to a single musical genre—given the artist's propensity to include flamenco samples and aesthetics in his songs. It seems that Khaled's music, with its diverse range of languages and cultural references, is aimed at an audience that does not exist but might be on the horizon; or rather, it is aimed at many different audiences, none of whom will have a total command of the languages and cultural references that are in play. This problem of communication, which could be seen as a liability, is, in fact, the place where Khaled's greatest potential resides. After all, one way to *get* Khaled's lyrics is to notice that you missed something, or to realize that someone else might get them differently.[132]

Returning to one of the central premises of this chapter, I have argued that music—and, more broadly, sound—is a vehicle for engaging with and thinking about the legacy of al-Andalus in the present. Within this argument, Khaled's music teaches us something about how to listen for the sounds of al-Andalus. Khaled's music points to similarities that cut across cultural lines, but it does not attempt to resolve these similarities into a facile union that overlooks uneven distributions of power and ongoing challenges to linguistic and cultural legibility. If the lesson of al-Andalus is not one of overcoming difference but rather learning to live with it (indeed, even to derive pleasure from it), then Khaled's music could serve as a soundtrack, a very new beat that illuminates something about a very old time and place.

Epilogue

Cordoba / Illinois

The Central Illinois Mosque and Islamic Center stands a few blocks away from my house in Urbana, Illinois. The building's façade features three arches with red and white candy cane stripes (Figure E.1). The design is a nod to a famous feature of Europe's oldest Islamic heritage site, the Mosque of Cordoba, where visitors are dazzled by the sight of rows upon rows of red and white arches, stretching like a wondrous forest through the prayer halls (Figure E.2). The Central Illinois Mosque's façade, with its red and white arches, is a modest, though unmistakable, tribute to Muslim Cordoba. One of the mosque's founding members told me that he and the others who spearheaded the drive to build the mosque in the 1980s wanted it to evoke "the Qurṭuba [Cordoba] environment" and to recall "what Muslims did when they went to Europe."[1]

I mention the Central Illinois Mosque not because it is exceptional but precisely because it isn't. The mosque, like so many other examples discussed in this book, demonstrates that the traces of al-Andalus are widespread and pervasive, extending far beyond the lands where the civilization of al-Andalus took root and flourished. Put differently, al-Andalus does its work in many places, some of them quite unexpected. Artist Molly Crabapple has illustrated this point in her recent explorations of the traces of al-Andalus in New York City.[2] Even in my small hometown in central Illinois, thousands of miles from Cordoba, the local mosque, which I pass on a daily basis, offers me a reminder of the hold that al-Andalus has on the present. The mosque is an example of what I might call a vernacular al-Andalus, an Andalus that is woven into the fabric of everyday life, forming patterns that are all around us but that can easily go unnoticed. I doubt very much, for example, that many of my neighbors in Urbana have noticed the mosque's allusion to Muslim Cordoba or stopped to wonder how the mosque entwines our community with the legacy of al-Andalus.

Figure E.1. Central Illinois Mosque and Islamic Center in Urbana, Illinois. August 2021. Photograph by Eric Calderwood.

Figure E.2. Interior of Mosque-Cathedral of Cordoba. Universal Images Group / Getty Images.

While the memory of Muslim Cordoba continues to inspire diverse communities in the United States, from central Illinois to New York City, it has come under increasing pressure in Cordoba itself. In recent years Cordoba has witnessed tense, sometimes bitter debates about its Muslim heritage and the imprint of that heritage on the city in the present. These debates have coalesced around the city's most famous monument, commonly known as the Mosque of Cordoba or the Mosque-Cathedral of Cordoba.[3] The oldest section of the mosque was built in the late eighth century under 'Abd al-Rahman I, the first Umayyad emir of Cordoba. The mosque underwent several expansions in the ninth and tenth centuries, eventually growing to accommodate 40,000 worshippers. It was not only Cordoba's most important place of worship; it was also the city's main center of learning, where generations of scholars came to study and teach. Its life as a functioning mosque came to an end in 1236, the year of the Christian conquest of Cordoba. The city's new Christian rulers consecrated the building as a cathedral but decided to leave the mosque's basic structure and design intact. As art historian Jerrilynn Dodds has noted, the Christians who conquered Cordoba understood that there was more power in appropriating the extraordinary mosque than in destroying it.[4] As a result, much of the mosque's form and decoration survived for the next 300 years. The building did not suffer a major transformation until the sixteenth century, when Bishop Alonso Manrique, working against the opposition of the Cordoban community, ordered the construction of a large transept in the middle of the former mosque. The new addition, with its Gothic vaults and Mannerist touches, marked a sharp stylistic contrast with the Umayyad-era mosque that frames it. This stark juxtaposition of styles has remained in place since the sixteenth century. Today, the monument is a marvel and an oddity that elicits mind-bending descriptions: it is a cathedral framed by a mosque; a medieval Islamic heritage site with a sixteenth-century church at its center; the seat of Cordoba's bishop and the primary symbol of the city's Muslim heritage.

For the past several years the monument has been embroiled in a controversy that has exposed some big questions about its meaning, management, and cultural identity. The controversy has drawn in diverse constituencies and political forces, but, at its core, it has pitted two groups against each other: on the one hand, a loosely organized coalition of left-wing citizen activists and, on the other, the city's Catholic leadership—and especially its Cathedral Chapter (*Cabildo*), the ecclesiastical body that manages the Mosque-Cathedral complex. The confrontation between these two groups has spawned a host of thorny questions about al-Andalus's legacies, both tangible and intangible. Some of these questions revolve around issues of cultural identity, such as: Is the Mosque-Cathedral of Cordoba a Christian building, a Muslim building, or, rather, a building that confounds or transcends these religious categories? Is it an Andalusi building, a Spanish building, or a building that embodies a multilayered cultural palimpsest that predates, but informs, contemporary Spanish society? Other questions that have emerged in the heat of the controversy revolve around issues of ownership, such as: To whom do heritage sites, like the Mosque-Cathedral of Cordoba, belong?[5] This question of ownership has both a symbolic dimension and a literal one. In 2006 the Catholic Church registered the Mosque-Cathedral complex as its private property through an obscure legal procedure called "immatriculation."[6] The Church's surreptitious maneuver did not come to light for a few years, but when it did, it sparked an outcry from large segments of Cordoba's citizenry (and from Spanish citizens beyond Cordoba), who asserted that the monument was a public good, not the Church's private dominion. The disputes over the ownership of the Mosque-Cathedral, and of other monuments claimed by the Church through the same legal maneuver, are still in the courts and signal ongoing disagreements in Spanish society about the management of historical sites that, in many cases, are major sources of revenue from tourism.

But the question that I've posed about ownership is not, of course, limited to the issue of property rights. That is, it's not just about land deeds and revenues, but also about stories and the right to tell them. Indeed, the problems that interest me here are less juridical than symbolic. The questions surrounding Cordoba's most famous Andalusi heritage site are in many ways a microcosm for the larger questions that I've pursued throughout this book. Those questions include: What are the demands and claims that al-Andalus has placed on the present? Who has inherited the legacies of al-Andalus, and what have they done with them? How has the legacy of al-Andalus shaped (or served as a foil to) the construction of collective identities, in Spain and beyond? Who gets to tell the story—or rather, the *stories*—of al-Andalus, particularly when those stories enlist diverse actors, communities, periods, and political imaginaries? Cordoba's iconic Mosque-Cathedral is a Rorschach test in which viewers see diverse (and divergent) patterns of history. Thinking about the building, much like thinking about al-Andalus itself, demands thinking in multiple time scales and with multiple publics in mind. Building from that premise, I take the story of the Mosque-Cathedral as a concluding parable about the contested and elastic legacies of al-Andalus in the present.

The Building of Cordoba

Since the turn of the twenty-first century, the Cathedral Chapter of Cordoba has been engaged in a wide-ranging effort to stress the monument's Christian identity while downplaying, or even erasing, its Islamic identity. This effort has taken many forms and has unfolded in diverse media—in print and online, in exhibits and archaeological excavations, in signage at the site and in statements to the press. One way to track these efforts is to look at the various tourist brochures that the Cathedral Chapter has distributed at the site over the past four decades.[7] From 1981 to 1998, the brochures called the building the "Mosque Cathedral of Cordoba" (Figure E.3) and began with the following description:

> The Mosque-Cathedral of Cordoba is, according to F. Chueca, the foremost monument of all of the Islamic West and one of the most wondrous ones of the world. It sums up in its archaeological history the complete evolution of Umayyad art in Spain—that is, of the Hispano-Muslim style in the era of its greatest splendor.[8]

Citing the authority of Fernando Chueca (1911–2004), one of the most important Spanish architects of the twentieth century and the author of an earlier guide titled *La Mezquita de Córdoba* (The Mosque of Cordoba, 1968), the brochure's opening paragraph stressed the monument's Islamic identity, its influence throughout the Islamic world, and its close association with the Umayyad dynasty in al-Andalus. Continuing in this vein, the brochure went on to explain, "The fundamental parts of the building are the old minaret or tower, the courtyard, and the prayer room."[9] In other words, the brochure pointed visitors to the parts of the monument that made it legible as a mosque. This understanding of the building's primary characteristics gained additional legitimacy in 1984, when UNESCO declared the "Great Mosque of

Figure E.3. Tourist brochure for the Mosque-Cathedral of Cordoba, ca. 1981. From the collection of Miguel Santiago Losada.

Cordoba" a World Heritage Site. The UNESCO citation described the building as "an irreplaceable testimony of the Caliphate of Cordoba and it is the most emblematic monument of Islamic religious architecture."[10] Thus, for both the UNESCO authorities and the authors of the Cathedral Chapter's tourist brochures in the 1980s and 1990s, the building's claim to fame was its historic status as a mosque from Umayyad al-Andalus. Furthermore, the brochures from this period suggested a capacious vision of Spanish history that included al-Andalus and Islamic cultures as foundational elements. Such a vision allowed the brochure's authors to refer to "the Hispano-Muslim style" and "the complete evolution of Umayyad art in Spain."

In the late 1990s and with increasing vigor in the early twenty-first century, the Cathedral Chapter modified its tourist literature about the Mosque-Cathedral to reflect a different understanding of the building's history and identity. This evolution began in 1998, when the Cathedral Chapter published a new brochure titled *Brief Guide to the Holy Cathedral Church (Former Mosque of Cordoba)*. The change to the monument's official name, highlighting the building's current status as a cathedral while noting its former status as a mosque, was a subtle sign of things to come. Around the year 2000, the Cathedral Chapter issued a new brochure with a much more assertive vision of the monument's Christian identity and history. The new brochure was titled *The Cathedral of Cordoba: Living Testament of Our History* (*La Catedral de Córdoba: Testigo vivo de nuestra Historia*) (Figure E.4). Its opening section, titled "Mother Church of the Diocese," offered a stark illustration of the change in tone and vision. It began:

> The Cathedral Chapter welcomes you to this Holy Cathedral Church of Cordoba. The whole compound in this singular building that you are going to visit was consecrated as the mother Church of the diocese in the year 1236. In this beautiful and grandiose temple, since then and without missing a single day, the Chapter celebrates solemn worship and the Christian community gathers to listen to the Word of God and to participate in the Sacraments . . .

> In welcoming you to this Cathedral, the Cathedral Chapter asks that your visit to the building be respectful of the identity of this Christian temple, the Cathedral of Cordoba.[11]

Figure E.4. Cover of *La Catedral de Córdoba: Testigo vivo de nuestra Historia* (2015). Author's collection.

If you compare this opening statement to the one that appeared in the brochures from the 1980s and 1990s, some important differences immediately
become apparent. While the earlier brochures described the building as "the
foremost monument of all of the Islamic West," the introduction to the new
brochure did not make a single allusion to the building's previous life as a
mosque. The text's anonymous authors also went to great lengths to stress
the building's Christian identity ("the identity of this Christian temple") as
well as its continuous and uninterrupted function as a place of Christian worship, from 1236 to the present. Even more striking was their decision to relegate all five centuries of the building's history as a mosque to a sidebar titled
"The Islamic Intervention." For many local observers, especially critics of
the Cathedral Chapter's actions, the phrase "The Islamic Intervention" carried the implication that the five centuries of Muslim rule in Cordoba were
merely a parenthesis that did not fundamentally alter the longer and uninterrupted story of Iberian Christianity.[12]

One of the Cathedral Chapter's main strategies for upholding this view has
been to insist that the monument was, in fact, a church before it was a mosque.
In particular, the Chapter has claimed that the Umayyads built their mosque
on top of a Visigothic church called the Basilica of Saint Vincent. While there
is some scholarly debate on this issue, many archaeologists and historians
who have looked into this question over the past decade have concluded that
there is not much evidence to suggest the presence of a Visigothic basilica on
the current site of the Mosque-Cathedral of Cordoba.[13] Even a team of experts
hired by the Cathedral Chapter to find the remains of the Basilica of Saint
Vincent concluded, in a statement to the press in January 2020, "We have not
been able to identify a Christian basilica underneath the Mosque of Cordoba."[14] Although the prior existence of a Visigothic basilica at the site of the
Umayyad mosque is, at best, debatable, the church authorities have treated it
as an incontrovertible fact and have made it a centerpiece of their narrative
about the building's history.

This process gained steam in January 2005, when the Cathedral Chapter
opened a new Museum of Saint Vincent inside the Mosque-Cathedral.[15] The
new exhibit featured display cases with a selection of Visigothic and Roman
materials found on the site over the last century of excavations. The Cathedral Chapter's curators also made an important intervention in the oldest section of the existing structure, the mosque built under 'Abd al-Rahman I in

the eighth century. There, where tourists enter the building, the curators opened a patch of floor and replaced it with a glass viewing window that reveals pebble mosaic below. A nearby plaque (still there today) identifies the mosaic as part of the Basilica of Saint Vincent. The purpose of these interventions was clear: they implied that the Christian consecration of the building in 1236 and the subsequent insertion of a large transept and choir were not impositions on a Muslim structure but rather restorations of the building's original and long-standing Christian character, one that preceded and literally underlay the eighth-century mosque. This message was not lost on the Cordoban public. When a local journalist covered the inauguration of the Museum of Saint Vincent for the newspaper *Córdoba,* he wrote, "From now on, the Arab Mosque will no longer be able to be explained without first mentioning its historical origin: Christian. That of Saint Vincent."[16]

The new emphasis on the Christian Visigothic origins of the Mosque-Cathedral complex was also reflected in the official tourist brochures distributed at the site from the early 2000s until 2016. Under the heading "Origins," the text stated:

> Under all cathedrals, there is always a bed of hidden cathedrals . . . It is a historic fact that the Basilica of Saint Vincent was expropriated and destroyed in order to build on it the later Mosque, throwing into doubt the cliché [*tópico*] of the tolerance that was supposedly cultivated in Cordoba at that time. It was the city's principal church, a martyr's basilica from the sixth century which continued to be remembered and venerated by Christians for centuries after its destruction.[17]

This text, like the Museum of Saint Vincent, peeled back the layers of history to reveal "a bed of hidden cathedrals" underneath the mosque built by the Umayyads in the eighth century. Not only did the text assert the prior existence of a Christian church on the site, but it also took aim at the common perception that Muslim Cordoba was a place where Christians and Muslims lived together in relative harmony. In contrast with this popular vision of interfaith coexistence (or *convivencia*), the brochure suggested that Cordoba's Umayyad Muslim rulers violently usurped a venerable center of Christian worship. The story that thus emerged from this brochure, as well as from the exhibits about the Basilica of Saint Vincent, is that the present-day Cathedral of Cordoba, and the Cathedral Chapter that manages it, are the living heirs and representatives of a Christian community whose history and identity predate the advent of Muslim rule in the Iberian Peninsula, survived the "Islamic intervention" (to quote the brochure's words), and reemerged intact after the Christian conquest of the city in the thirteenth century.

In the face of the church's efforts to lay claim to Cordoba's most iconic monument and to stress its Christian identity, a group of citizen activists joined forces in 2013 to advocate for a different vision of the building's past, present, and future. They called themselves the "Platform for the Mosque-Cathedral of Cordoba: Heritage for All" (*Plataforma Mezquita-Catedral de Córdoba: Patrimonio de Todxs;* hereafter, "the Platform").[18] Their first high-profile action came in early 2014, when they launched an online petition demanding that the word "Mosque" be restored to the monument's official name, including in the tourist literature and on the monument's website. They also called for the Mosque-Cathedral to be administered by a public entity, rather than by the Catholic Church. The petition went viral and attracted nearly 400,000 signees, including such cultural luminaries as British architect Norman Foster and Spanish writer Juan Goytisolo. It also caught the attention of several major media outlets, including *Al Jazeera,* the *New York Times,* and *El País* (Spain's leading daily newspaper). This attention launched the Platform into the limelight—and into a confrontation with the Cathedral Chapter, one that continues to the present day.

What rankles the Platform's members and their allies is the impression that church authorities are engaged in a wholesale rewriting of local (and national) history. In an article published in 2020, leaders from the Platform asserted that the case of the Mosque-Cathedral of Cordoba illustrates "the damage that is inflicted on a monument when its history is falsified, its identity manipulated, its immaterial values mutilated, its narrative interpretation adulterated, its authenticity disfigured, and a substantial part of its character hidden."[19] In the same article, the authors accuse the church of "identity theft" and "symbolic destruction."[20] Similar views have surfaced in my conversations and interviews with the Platform's members over the past several years (since 2015). In my first conversations with Miguel Santiago, a spokesperson for the Platform, he accused the Catholic Church of "denying the true history of the monument" and of "nullifying history" (*ningunear la historia*).[21] In a similar vein, Antonio Manuel Rodríguez, another prominent figure in the Platform, told me that the Cathedral Chapter was "colonizing the Mosque" and "falsifying memory."[22]

For many of the Platform's members, what is at stake in this dispute is far more than a tourist site; it is a whole network of ideals and aspirations that they associate with Cordoba and al-Andalus. The Platform's members often refer to the Mosque-Cathedral, and even Cordoba itself, as a "paradigm."[23] For instance, Antonio Manuel Rodríguez called the building "a universal paradigm of respect for difference" in an op-ed piece published in *El País* in September 2013.[24] Rodríguez elaborated on this point in an interview with me in January 2015, when he told me:

> I belong to a culture whose core identifying feature [*germen identitario*] is inclusion and not exclusion . . . The Andalusi paradigm, far from being a myth, is a tool of extraordinary social utility in this day and age. And I believe that it is necessary for us to look for cultural paradigms that allow us citizens to be equal in rights, from a perspective of respect for difference. And that paradigm is architecturally in the Mosque of Cordoba.[25]

As this comment indicates, Rodríguez sees the Mosque-Cathedral of Cordoba as the architectural embodiment of a local tradition of *convivencia*. It is a view he shares with many of his colleagues in the Platform. Indeed, in an article published in 2020, representatives from the Platform hailed the Mosque-Cathedral as "a singular paradigm of artistic mixing and *convivencia* between cultures."[26] The Platform's dispute with church authorities carries such urgency because its stakes are not limited to adjudicating the past. The dispute, at its core, is not only about what Cordoba has been but also about what it will be. For the Platform's members, the Mosque-Cathedral has "social utility" (to use Rodríguez's phrase) because it encourages Cordoba's citizens—and people outside of Cordoba—to think about living with, and appreciating, cultural difference. Miguel Santiago summed up this vision when he told me, "We have a monument that makes the world realize that coexistence [*convivencia*] is possible, that mixing [*mestizaje*] is possible, that it is possible for us to live together, just as the different architectural styles live together, just as the different faiths have lived together."[27]

The Platform won an important victory in 2016, when the cultural department (*Consejería de Cultura*) of Andalucía's regional government ordered the Cathedral Chapter to restore the word "Mosque" to the monument's official name and publications.[28] The brochures for the site now refer to it as the "Mosque-Cathedral of Cordoba Monumental Complex" (Figure E.5). But the name change has not resolved the underlying disagreements about the building's meaning and management. If anything, the Cathedral Chapter has doubled down in its efforts to assert the building's Christian identity. As of this writing, tourist visits to the building still begin with a stop at the display window overlooking the supposed remains of the Basilica of Saint Vincent (even though several experts have cast serious doubt on the basilica's existence). Inside the building, there are periodic announcements over the loudspeakers reminding visitors, "You are on a cultural visit to a Catholic temple." This message is reinforced by the abundant Catholic iconography that the Cathedral Chapter has distributed throughout the most emblematic spaces of the former mosque. This practice is intensified during the Christmas and Easter seasons, when the building overflows with representations of Jesus and the Virgin Mary. Among the many incidents that have spawned an outcry from the Platform was the Cathedral Chapter's decision to place a large statue of Saint John of Avila next to the prayer niche (mihrab) built under the Umayyad caliph al-Hakam II in the tenth century. Another flare-up came in September 2019, when the Cathedral Chapter mounted an exhibit of 43 *Nazarenos,* depictions of Jesus carrying the cross, inside the iconic arches that stretch through the former mosque's prayer halls (Figure E.6). Representatives of the Platform have decried such acts as a "symbolic occupation" whose aim is to underline the building's status as a cathedral and to efface its Islamic heritage.[29]

Although Cordoba's Islamic heritage is central to the Platform's discourse, the city's Muslim community has been noticeably absent from the Platform's activities. In other words, the debates surrounding Cordoba's most famous Islamic heritage site have primarily involved non-Muslim actors who have looked to Cordoba's Muslim past as an important point of reference for understanding individual and collective identities in the present. At the same time, Cordoba's growing Muslim community (which numbers roughly 4,000) has, for the most part, remained on the sidelines of the ongoing dispute between the Platform and the church authorities. There are several reasons for this state of affairs. One of them has to do with the fresh memory of a conflict between a local Muslim leader and Cordoba's Catholic leadership in the early twenty-first century. In 2004 Mansur Escudero, the president of the Junta

Figure E.5. Cover of *Conjunto Monumental Mezquita-Catedral de Córdoba* (2020). Author's collection.

Figure E.6. Exhibit of *Nazarenos* in Mosque-Cathedral of Cordoba. Courtesy of Plataforma Mezquita Catedral.

Islámica, one of the leading Muslim organizations in Cordoba, petitioned the Vatican to convert the Mosque-Cathedral of Cordoba into an ecumenical space that would be shared by Christian and Muslim worshippers.[30] Although the Vatican rejected Escudero's petition, the Muslim leader continued to press his case over the following years, most notably by staging a prayer outside the Mosque-Cathedral in December 2006. Escudero's bid to make the Mosque-Cathedral an ecumenical space was ultimately unsuccessful, but it sparked a controversy in Cordoba and drew the attention of national and international media. After Escudero's death in 2010, the leadership of the Junta Islámica suspended his campaign to allow Muslims to pray in the Mosque-Cathedral. The organization's current president, Isabel Romero, has worked to improve relations with the city's Catholic leadership and has avoided wading into the dispute between the Platform and the Cathedral Chapter. She told me, in a recent interview, that she wanted to avoid the appearance of "a confrontation at the religious level," stressing that her organization wants to maintain good relations "with all faiths."[31]

While the Junta Islámica is mostly composed of white Spanish converts to Islam, the other major Muslim organization in the city, the Association of

Muslims in Cordoba, is primarily composed of immigrants from Muslim-majority countries in Africa, the Middle East, and South Asia. The association's president, Kamel Mekhelef, was critical of Escudero's campaign to turn the Mosque-Cathedral into an ecumenical space because he worried that the campaign would generate conflict between Muslims and Catholics in Cordoba.[32] Mekhelef and his association have also maintained a discreet profile in the ongoing dispute between the Platform and the Cathedral Chapter. In my conversations with him, he has stressed that he and the other members of his community are not interested in praying at the Mosque-Cathedral. He has, however, raised concerns about the fact that Muslim visitors to the Mosque-Cathedral often report being followed and even openly harassed by the security staff at the site. Mekhelef himself has experienced that harassment.[33]

An even greater concern for Mekhelef is what the recent controversies have revealed about how non-Muslim Spaniards imagine their relationship to Spain's Muslim heritage. On this point, he told me:

> There's an attempt to falsify history and to make people—that is, the Spanish themselves—believe that all that, that civilization was something alien to them. And that's not how it is because it is something that came from here. Because I've always said: it is Cordoban. Ibn Hazm was Cordoban. Abulcasis was Cordoban. They weren't from Arabia or Algeria or Morocco; they were Cordoban. And people—I'm talking about non-Muslims—should be proud of their history.[34]

The concern Mekhelef voices here is that the Cathedral Chapter's actions are symptomatic of a broader effort to excise Muslims from Cordoban and Spanish history. Mekhelef worries that cultural luminaries from Muslim Cordoba, such as the philosopher Ibn Hazm and the physician known as Abulcasis (Abu al-Qasim al-Zahrawi), have not been incorporated into narratives of collective identity at a local or national level. This problem, he suggests, has implications for how non-Muslim Spaniards imagine their relationship to Andalusi heritage sites, like the Mosque of Cordoba. It also has implications for how Muslim immigrants in Spain, such as Mekhelef himself, understand their place in the fabric of Spanish society. The big question that looms in the background of these reflections is: Are Muslims, both past and present, integral parts of Spanish culture, or are they somehow alien to it? While Mekhelef has not participated in the Platform's activities, he shares the Platform's sense that the Mosque-Cathedral of Cordoba is a flashpoint for the unresolved debates about what it means to be Cordoban and Spanish.

At the same time that the Mosque-Cathedral's Islamic heritage is under threat, business and cultural leaders in Cordoba are working to position the city as a major destination for Muslim tourism and as the leading European producer of halal food and services. The Junta Islámica and its sister organization the Halal Institute have been at the forefront of these efforts and have partnered with Cordoba's government to create the "Cordoba Halal Cluster," a group of businesses specializing in halal products and other services for Muslim consumers.[35] Isabel Romero, who is both president of the Junta Islámica and CEO of the Halal Institute, has acknowledged that the Andalusi legacy plays a pivotal role in promoting Cordoba to Muslim tourists, consumers, and investors. In an interview in August 2021, she told me:

> The name "Cordoba" is clearly identifiable in any part of the world—I would say any part of the world, but especially in the Islamic world. And it is associated with a series of values: science, research, development, civilization. That is to say, there is a whole compendium of values that are connected to the al-Andalus brand—and, of course, to the Cordoba brand . . . You don't have to build the brand because the brand is already easily recognizable.[36]

As Romero's comment illustrates, Cordoba is both a place and an idea: it is a place on the map and a place in discourse (or in many discourses). For Romero, the name "Cordoba" evokes such values as science and development, and she and her colleagues at the Halal Institute have leveraged those associations to promote Cordoba as a hub for Muslim tourism and Muslim-friendly business.

For the members of the Platform, the name "Cordoba" is also saturated with meaning, though the meaning that it elicits for them is slightly different. The Platform's Cordoba is the Cordoba of coexistence and respect for difference. The Halal Institute and the Platform have different investments (literally and figuratively) in "the Cordoba brand," but their projects are both premised on the belief that Cordoba *means* something—not only to the city's present-day residents but also to people who live far away from it. To substantiate their claim, I need only point to Cordoba House in New York or to the red and white stripes on the façade of the mosque near my house in Urbana, Illinois.

What are we to do, then, with the multiple meanings of Cordoba and al-Andalus? Although I have tried to avoid being overly prescriptive in this book, I do want to offer some final reflections on this question. First, I propose that to study the vast and multifarious afterlives of al-Andalus what we need is not an ontology of al-Andalus but rather a phenomenology of it. In other words, the primary question is not what al-Andalus *is* (or was) but rather how al-Andalus has *manifested* in diverse times and places to address different needs.[37] Second, I want to underline that representing al-Andalus is not a zero-sum game. Borrowing terms from Michael Rothberg, I would say that we need to move from a competitive understanding of al-Andalus to a "multidirectional" understanding of al-Andalus: that is, an understanding in which different articulations of the past confront each other in the public sphere without one eliminating the others.[38] Building from this premise, I propose that the aim of thinking about al-Andalus should be to increase complexity, rather than dispel it.[39] One way to honor this goal is to move beyond thinking of al-Andalus as a finite object of study and instead to think of it as a method. Al-Andalus as method means thinking across or beyond the boundaries that have defined academic disciplines in the United States and narratives of collective belonging throughout the world. I'm referring here to the continental boundaries between Europe, Africa, and Asia; the linguistic boundaries between Arabic, Spanish, Amazigh, Hebrew, French, and several other languages; the confessional boundaries between Christianity, Islam, and Judaism; as well as the political and ethical boundaries between self and other.[40] I'm not suggesting that al-Andalus, as method, is a magic wand that whisks away these boundaries; I'm simply saying that it never takes them for granted. Al-Andalus is a useful tool for mapping how these boundaries came into being and how they have structured different forms of collective identity. It is also a healthy reminder that all of these boundaries are permeable, subject to the flow of ideas and stories that move across space and time, like the arches of medieval Cordoba echoing far away in my neighborhood in Illinois.

Notes

Introduction

1. Rosemary R. Corbett offers a detailed account of this controversy in *Making Moderate Islam: Sufism, Service, and the "Ground Zero Mosque" Controversy* (Stanford, CA: Stanford University Press, 2017). See also Abigail Krasner Balbale, "Echoes of Cordoba," *Islamic Monthly,* June 17, 2012, https://www.theislamicmonthly .com/echoes-of-cordoba/; Feisal Abdul Rauf, *Moving the Mountain: A New Vision of Islam in America* (New York: Free Press), 154–160.

2. Feisal Abdul Rauf, "Building on Faith," *New York Times,* September 7, 2010, https://www.nytimes.com/2010/09/08/opinion/08mosque.html?smid=url-share.

3. I have drawn this information about Cordoba House's recent history from an interview I conducted with the organization's executive director, Naz Georgas, in August 2021.

4. All dates given in this book are CE (Common Era), unless otherwise noted.

5. Feisal Abdul Rauf, *What's Right with Islam: A New Vision for Muslims and the West* (New York: HarperCollins, 2004), 9.

6. Abdul Rauf, *Moving the Mountain,* 155.

7. The scholarship on this issue, and on the related term *convivencia,* is vast. For helpful introductions, see Eduardo Manzano Moreno, "Qurtuba: Algunas reflexiones críticas sobre el califato de Córdoba y el mito de la convivencia," *Awraq* 7 (2013): 225–246; Ryan Szpiech, "The Convivencia Wars: Decoding Historiography's Polemic with Philology," in *A Sea of Languages: Rethinking the Arabic Role in Medieval Literary History,* ed. Suzanne Conklin Akbari and Karla Mallette (University of Toronto Press, 2013), 135–161, https://www.jstor.org/stable/10.3138 /j.ctt4cgjd7.13; Maribel Fierro, "Al-Andalus, convivencia e Islam: Mucho ruido y pocas nueces," *Revista de Libros,* October 17, 2018, https://www.revistadelibros.com /discusion/al-andalus-convivencia-e-islam-mucho-ruido-y-pocas-nueces; Hussein Fancy, "The New *Convivencia,*" *Journal of Medieval Iberian Studies* 11, no. 3 (2019): 295–305, https://doi.org/10.1080/17546559.2019.1605242; Ross Brann, *Iberian Moorings: Al-Andalus, Sepharad, and the Tropes of Exceptionalism* (Philadelphia: University of Pennsylvania Press, 2021), 172–193; Hussein Fancy, "What Was

Convivencia? Spanish Medievalism at the Mid-Century" (unpublished manuscript, May 12, 2021), PDF file.

8. For example, Brian Catlos has argued that it was "the principle of convenience" (*conveniencia*), not *convivencia,* that guided Muslim–Christian interactions in medieval Iberia. *Muslims of Medieval Latin Christendom, c. 1050–1614* (Cambridge: Cambridge University Press, 2014), 522–525. See also the previously cited scholarship on *convivencia.*

9. In fact, Abdul Rauf was far from the only public figure in the United States to turn to the idea of *convivencia* in the early twenty-first century. In 2002, María Rosa Menocal published her best seller *The Ornament of the World: How Muslims, Jews, and Christians Created a Culture of Tolerance in Medieval Spain* (New York: Back Bay Books). In it, Menocal asserted that al-Andalus "was the chapter of Europe's culture when Jews, Christians, and Muslims lived side by side and, despite their intractable differences and enduring hostilities, nourished a complex culture of tolerance." Menocal, *Ornament of the World,* 11.

10. AbdoolKarim Vakil adopts a similar approach to *convivencia* when he observes that *convivencia* "retains the usefulness of a term under erasure." See Vakil, "Al-Andalus in Motion: Paths and Perspectives," in *Al-Andalus in Motion: Travelling Concepts and Cross-Cultural Contexts,* ed. Rachel Scott, AbdoolKarim Vakil, and Julian Weiss (London: King's College London, Centre for Late Antique and Medieval Studies, 2021), 28, ProQuest Ebook Central.

11. Many of the uses of al-Andalus mentioned here will be discussed at greater length in this book. For now, I point to the following sources: Al-Andalus Ensemble, *Andalusian Love Songs,* 2012, compact disc; Nawal El Messiri, "A Changing Perception of Public Gardens," in *Cairo: Revitalising a Historic Metropolis,* ed. Stefano Bianca and Philip Jodidio ([Turin]: Umberto Allemandi, 2004), 221–233; Yael Lerer, "The Andalus Test: Reflections on the Attempt to Publish Arabic Literature in Hebrew," *Jadaliyya,* May 16, 2012, https://www.jadaliyya.com/Details/25954; Eric Calderwood, *Colonial al-Andalus: Spain and the Making of Modern Moroccan Culture* (Cambridge: Belknap Press of Harvard University Press, 2018); Eric Calderwood, "The Invention of al-Andalus: Discovering the Past and Creating the Present in Granada's Islamic Tourism Sites," *Journal of North African Studies* 19, no. 1 (2014): 27–55; Hishaam D. Aidi, "The Interference of al-Andalus: Spain, Islam, and the West," *Social Text* 24, no. 2 (2006): 67–88; Balbale, "Echoes of Cordoba"; "Palestinian Wedding Hall Preserves Treasures of Its Cinematic Past," *Reuters,* March 5, 2019, https://www.reuters.com/article/uk-palestinians-cinema-idUKKC N1QM1A1; "El ISIS amenaza con más ataques a España en su primer video en castellano," *El País,* August 26, 2017, https://elpais.com/politica/2017/08/23/actualidad /1503514699_423271.html.

12. I'm referring here to the tendency to limit conversations about al-Andalus to a narrow circle of scholars based in Europe and the United States. There are, however, some important exceptions to this tendency. Among the scholars who

have preceded me in analyzing representations of al-Andalus in contemporary culture from the Middle East and North Africa, I highlight (in chronological order): Pedro Martínez Montávez, *Al-Andalus, España, en la literatura árabe contemporánea* (Málaga: Arguval, 1992); Reuven Snir, "'Al-Andalus Arising from Damascus': Al-Andalus in Modern Arabic Poetry," in *Charting Memory: Recalling Medieval Spain,* ed. Stacy N. Beckwith (New York: Garland, 2000), 263–293; Muhammad 'Abd Allah al-Ju'aydi, *A'indakum naba': Istid'a' al-Andalus fi al-adab al-filastini al-hadith* (Beirut: Dar al-Hadi li-l-Tiba'a wa-l-Nashr, 2002); William Granara, "*Extensio Animae:* The Artful Ways of Remembering 'Al-Andalus,'" *Journal of Social Affairs* 19, no. 75 (2002): 45–72; William Granara, "Nostalgia, Arab Nationalism, and the Andalusian *Chronotope* in the Evolution of the Modern Arabic Novel," *Journal of Arabic Literature* 36, no. 1 (2005): 57–73; Nieves Paradela, *El otro laberinto español: Viajeros árabes a España entre el siglo XVII y 1936* (Madrid: Siglo XXI, 2005); Ahmad al-'Adwani, *Zaman al-wasl: Al-Andalus fi al-qasida al-'arabiyya al-mu'asira* (Beirut: al-Intishar al-'Arabi, 2014); Jonathan Holt Shannon, *Performing al-Andalus: Music and Nostalgia across the Mediterranean* (Bloomington: Indiana University Press, 2015); Christina Civantos, *The Afterlife of al-Andalus: Muslim Iberia in Contemporary Arab and Hispanic Narratives* (Albany: SUNY Press, 2017). I address my indebtedness to these works later in the introduction.

13. I echo, here, Michael Rothberg's work on "multidirectional memory" and, in particular, his critique of approaches that understand collective memory as "*competitive* memory—as a zero-sum struggle over scarce resources." Michael Rothberg, *Multidirectional Memory: Remembering the Holocaust in the Age of Decolonization* (Stanford, CA: Stanford University Press, 2009), 3.

14. For this overview, I have drawn on several reference works and narrative histories, including E. Lévi-Provençal et al., "Al-Andalus," in *Encyclopedia of Islam,* 2nd ed., ed. P. Bearman et al., accessed September 11, 2021, https://doi.org/10.1163 /1573-3912_islam_COM_0054; Eduardo Manzano Moreno, *Conquistadores, emires y califas: Los omeyas y la formación de al-Andalus* (Barcelona: Crítica, 2006); Amira K. Bennison, *The Almoravid and Almohad Empires* (Edinburgh: Edinburgh University Press, 2016); L. P. Harvey, *Islamic Spain: 1250 to 1500* (Chicago: University of Chicago Press, 1990); L.P. Harvey, *Muslims in Spain: 1500 to 1614* (Chicago: University of Chicago Press, 2005); Mercedes García-Arenal and Gerard Wiegers, eds., *Los moriscos: Expulsión y diáspora—Una perspectiva internacional* (Valencia: Universitat de València, 2013).

15. For an introduction to these terminological debates, see Muhammad Rida Budshar, "al-Huwiyya al-thaqafiyya li-l-andalusiyyin al-muta'akhkhirin ba'da suqut Gharnata," *Qadaya fikriyya,* June 4, 2020, YouTube video, https://youtu.be /mWjWbomm6EA.

16. I discuss the terms "Berber" and "Amazigh" in Chapter 2. For introductions to the debates surrounding these terms, see Bruce Maddy-Weitzman, *The Berber*

Identity Movement and the Challenge to North African States (Austin: University of Texas Press, 2011), 1–4; Ramzi Rouighi, *Inventing the Berbers: History and Ideology in the Maghrib* (Philadelphia: University of Pennsylvania Press, 2019).

17. Vakil, "Al-Andalus," 41–42.

18. Stuart Hall, "Cultural Identity and Diaspora," in *Identity: Community, Culture, Difference,* ed. Jonathan Rutherford (London: Lawrence and Wishart, 1990), 226.

19. I draw here on Hall's insight that "identities are the names we give to the different ways we are positioned by, and position ourselves within, the narratives of the past." Hall, "Cultural Identity," 225.

20. Rachel Scott outlines a similar approach in her introduction to the recently published collective volume *Al-Andalus in Motion.* Scott explains that the volume seeks "to understand what al-Andalus *does* as a concept as it moves across different times and spaces, acquiring ideological freight and performing cultural work." Scott, "Introduction: Concepts, Origins, Aims," in Scott et al., *Al-Andalus in Motion,* 4.

21. Civantos, *Afterlife of al-Andalus,* 9. Translation is also the central framework for studying al-Andalus in Anna Gil Bardají, *Traducir al-Andalus: El discurso del otro en el arabismo español—De Conde a García Gómez* (Lewiston, NY: Mellen Press, 2009); Yuval Evri, *Translating the Arab-Jewish Tradition: From al-Andalus to Palestine / Land of Israel* (Berlin: Forum Transregionale Studien, 2016).

22. Scott, introduction to *Al-Andalus in Motion,* 4; AbdoolKarim Vakil, "Travelling with and through Al-Andalus," in Scott et al., *Al-Andalus in Motion,* 333.

23. Shannon, *Performing al-Andalus,* 7–11.

24. Shannon, *Performing al-Andalus,* 24, 30, 178–179; José Antonio González Alcantud, *El mito de al Ándalus: Orígenes y actualidad de un ideal cultural* (Cordoba: Almuzara, 2014), 13–19.

25. The origins of this nickname are discussed in Calderwood, *Colonial al-Andalus,* 266–285; Paradela, *Otro laberinto,* 135–145; Justin Stearns, "Representing and Remembering al-Andalus: Some Historical Considerations regarding the End of Time and the Making of Nostalgia," *Medieval Encounters* 15 (2009): 355–374, https://doi.org/10.1163/157006709X458891; Jonathan Glasser, *The Lost Paradise: Andalusi Music in Urban North Africa* (Chicago: University of Chicago Press, 2016), 3–16.

26. I thank Molly Crabapple for suggesting this phrase to me in a phone conversation on June 11, 2019.

27. Granara, *"Extensio animae,"* 62. Granara elaborates on this idea in "Nostalgia." Along similar lines, Shannon writes, "I suggest that performing Andalusian music in Syria, Morocco, and Spain can be interpreted as a means of performing and shaping rhetorical stances toward the past that influence projects oriented toward the present and the future." *Performing al-Andalus,* 16–17. See also Civantos, *Afterlife of al-Andalus,* 53, 292; Gil Anidjar, "Futures of al-Andalus," *Journal of Spanish Cultural Studies* 7, no. 3 (2006): 225–239, https://doi.org/10.1080/14636200601084014; Vakil, "Al-Andalus," 24.

28. I've taken some inspiration here from Carolyn Dinshaw's work on the temporal heterogeneity of medieval studies. See, in particular, Carolyn Dinshaw, "All Kinds of Time," *Studies in the Age of Chaucer* 35 (2013): 3–25, https://doi.org/10.1353/sac.2013.0025.

29. See, for example, Martínez Montávez, *Al-Andalus;* al-Juʿaydi, *Aʿindakum nabaʾ;* Civantos, *Afterlife of al-Andalus;* Shannon, *Performing al-Andalus.*

30. One of the scholars whose approach is closest to mine is Shannon, whose book "investigates the rhetorical uses of al-Andalus in contemporary Syria, Morocco, and Spain." *Performing al-Andalus,* 8. The most significant differences between Shannon's approach and mine are that I do not limit my focus to musical performance, and I also do not organize my study by national context. Instead, I try to show how many different cultural forms operate across national and cultural lines.

31. I play here with a famous phrase from Michel Foucault's *Discipline and Punish: The Birth of the Prison,* trans. Alan Sheridan, 2nd ed. (New York: Vintage Books, 1995), 31.

32. Quoted in Patrice Barrat, "Mahmoud Darwich poète de la blessure palestinienne," *Le Monde,* January 10, 1983. Here and throughout this book, the English translations are mine unless otherwise noted. I discuss Darwish's work at length in Chapter 4.

33. Charles Hirschkind, *The Feeling of History: Islam, Romanticism, and Andalusia* (Chicago: University of Chicago Press, 2021), 33.

34. See Martínez Montávez, *Al-Andalus,* 69–92; Civantos, *Afterlife of al-Andalus,* 129–130, 191–195; Waïl S. Hassan, "Al-Andalus in Brazil," paper presented at the annual meeting of the Middle East Studies Association, Washington, DC, November 19, 2017.

35. Bernard Lewis, "The Cult of Spain and the Turkish Romantics," in *Islam in History: Ideas, People, and Events in the Middle East* (Chicago: Open Court, 1993), 129–133; Muneeza Shamsie, introduction to "The Enduring Legacy of al-Andalus," special issue, *Journal of Postcolonial Writing* 52, no. 2 (2016): 127–135, https://doi.org/10.1080/17449855.2016.1164969; Amina Yaqin, "*La convivencia, la mezquita* and al-Andalus: An Iqbalian Vision," *Journal of Postcolonial Writing* 52, no. 2 (2016): 136–152, https://doi.org/10.1080/17449855.2016.1164972; Vakil, "Travelling," 317–319, 329–330.

1. The Arab al-Andalus

1. There are many videos of this performance on YouTube. My description is based on the following video: https://youtu.be/4I4d5bR46so, last accessed September 15, 2021. I would also like to thank Sama Dashti, Hanan Al-Alawi, Farah Al-Nakib, and Mahmoud Zibawi for their help tracking down information about Fayruz's performance at Cinema al-Andalus.

2. Ibn al-Khatib's poem appears in Ahmad b. Muhammad al-Maqqari, *Nafh al-tib min ghusn al-Andalus al-ratib,* ed. Ihsan 'Abbas (Beirut: Dar Sadir, 2004), 7:11–13. I have added some case endings to my transliteration of the original Arabic in order to reflect the poem's rhyme and cadence. My English translation is a modified version of the one that appears in James T. Monroe, *Hispano-Arabic Poetry: A Student Anthology* (Berkeley: University of California Press, 1974), 338.

3. For helpful discussions of this album, see Kenneth Sasin Habib, "The Superstar Singer Fairouz and the Ingenious Rahbani Composers: Lebanon Sounding" (PhD diss., University of California, Santa Barbara, 2005), 203, 392–408; Jonathan Holt Shannon, *Performing al-Andalus: Music and Nostalgia across the Mediterranean* (Bloomington: Indiana University Press, 2015), 139, 198.

4. Peter Wien has also analyzed the role that al-Andalus played in the formation of the Arab nationalist imaginary. See his *Arab Nationalism: The Politics of History and Culture in the Modern Middle East* (London: Routledge, 2017), 48–79. The difference between Wien's approach and mine is that I, unlike Wien, have chosen to emphasize *both* how the "Arab al-Andalus" enables certain forms of pan-Arab identity *and* how it excludes and marginalizes some non-Arab groups, especially North Africans.

5. Alexander E. Elinson, *Looking Back at al-Andalus: The Poetics of Loss and Nostalgia in Medieval Arabic and Hebrew Literature* (Leiden: Brill, 2015), 4.

6. For more on the opposition between al-Andalus and the Maghrib, see Elinson, *Looking Back;* Emilio García Gómez, *Andalucía contra Berbería: Reedición de traducciones de Ben Ḥayyān, Šaqundī y Ben al-Jaṭīb* (Barcelona: Publicaciones del Departamento de Lengua y Literatura Árabes, 1976); Camilo Gómez-Rivas, "Exile, Encounter, and the Articulation of Andalusi Identity in the Maghrib," *Medieval Encounters* 20 (2014): 340–351, https://doi.org/10.1163/15700674-12342178.

7. García Gómez, *Andalucía contra Berbería;* Elinson, *Looking Back;* Ramzi Rouighi, *Inventing the Berbers: History and Ideology in the Maghrib* (Philadelphia: University of Pennsylvania Press, 2019), 28–29, 37–42, 49–51; Jessica A. Coope, *The Most Noble of People: Religious, Ethnic, and Gender Identity in Muslim Spain* (Ann Arbor: University of Michigan Press, 2017), 1–38. Ethnic tensions in al-Andalus were not limited to relations between Arabs and Berbers. There were also tensions between Arabs and other non-Arab groups in al-Andalus, including Andalusi Muslims who traced their genealogy back to Iberian converts to Islam. For a prominent example from eleventh-century al-Andalus, see Göran Larsson, *Ibn García's Shu'ūbiyya Letter: Ethnic and Theological Tensions in Medieval Iberia* (Leiden: Brill, 2003).

8. A helpful illustration of this point may be found in the elegy that Ibn Shuhayd (d. 1035) wrote for Cordoba after its sacking. See Elinson's analysis of the elegy in *Looking Back,* 38–49.

9. García Gómez, *Andalucía contra Berbería;* Elinson, *Looking Back,* 117–150.

10. Al-Shaqundi's treatise was transmitted by al-Maqqari in *Nafh al-tib,* 3:187–222.

11. Al-Maqqari, *Nafh al-tib,* 3:191–192. The passage is also discussed in Elinson, *Looking Back,* 136–137. For a recent assessment of Yusuf b. Tashfin's knowledge of Arabic, see Mohamed Meouak, *La langue berbère au Maghreb médiéval: Textes, contextes, analyses* (Leiden: Brill, 2016), 152–155, https://doi.org/10.1163/9789004302358_003.

12. Elinson, *Looking Back,* 39–44, 136–142; Coope, *Most Noble,* 38–60.

13. There is an extensive body of scholarship on the Nahda. For helpful introductions, see M. M. Badawi and Pierre Cachia, introduction to *Modern Arabic Literature,* ed. M. M. Badawi (Cambridge: Cambridge University Press, 1992), 1–35; Tarek El-Ariss, introduction to *The Arab Renaissance: A Bilingual Anthology of the Nahda,* ed. Tarek El-Ariss (New York: Modern Language Association, 2018), xv–xxvii.

14. The relationship between the Nahda and European imperialism is complicated. In a sensitive reading of this problem, El-Ariss calls on scholars to understand the Nahda as a dynamic, multifaceted process that was "influenced by Arab exchanges and confrontations with Western Europe but never reduced to these exchanges and confrontations." El-Ariss, introduction to *The Arab Renaissance,* xx.

15. For examples of this phenomenon, see Eric Calderwood, *Colonial al-Andalus: Spain and the Making of Modern Moroccan Culture* (Cambridge: Belknap Press of Harvard University Press, 2018); Susan Martin-Márquez, *Disorientations: Spanish Colonialism in Africa and the Performance of Identity* (New Haven, CT: Yale University Press, 2008); Wien, *Arab Nationalism,* 48–57; Nieves Paradela, *El otro laberinto español: Viajeros árabes a España entre el siglo XVII y 1936* (Madrid: Siglo XXI, 2005), 135–145.

16. Paradela, *Otro laberinto,* 79–125; William Granara, "*Extensio Animae:* The Artful Ways of Remembering 'Al-Andalus,'" *Journal of Social Affairs* 19, no. 75 (2002): 50–53; Pedro Martínez Montávez, *Al-Andalus, España, en la literatura árabe contemporánea* (Málaga: Arguval, 1992), 25–36; Calderwood, *Colonial al-Andalus,* 170–207, 251–267.

17. Safa' Khulusi, *Bint al-Sarraj: Rihla ila Isbaniya* (Baghdad: Matba'at al-Ma'arif, [1952]).

18. Martinez-Gros asserts that Dozy's work "remained without rival" until the publication, in the middle of the twentieth century, of Lévi-Provençal's three-volume *Histoire de l'Espagne musulmane* (1944, 1950–1953). G. Martinez-Gros, "'Andalou', 'Arabe', 'Espagnol' dans l'*Histoire des musulmans d'Espagne* de Reinhart Dozy," *Studia Islamica* 92 (2001): 116, https://www.jstor.org/stable/1596193.

19. For example, Lévi-Provençal's three-volume *Histoire de l'Espagne musulmane* also ends with the collapse of Umayyad rule in the eleventh century. More recently, María Rosa Menocal's popular book on al-Andalus, *The Ornament of the World: How Muslims, Jews, and Christians Created a Culture of Tolerance in Medieval Spain* (New York: Back Bay Books, 2002), reflects a similar approach to narrating Andalusi history. Menocal describes her book as "an account of and

tribute to the culture of tolerance brought to Europe by the Umayyads" (282). In contrast, she frequently disparages the Almoravids and the Almohads as religious "fanatics" and "fundamentalists" who were fundamentally at odds with the cultural spirit of al-Andalus (37, 43, 283). Notably, when Menocal's book was translated into Arabic, it was published under the title *Al-Andalus al-ʿarabiyya* (The Arab al-Andalus) (Casablanca: Dar Tubqal, 2006).

20. Examples of these descriptions may be found in R. Dozy, *Histoire des musulmans d'Espagne jusqu'à la conquête de l'Andalousie par les Almoravides (711–1110)* (Leiden: Brill, 1861), 3:94, 107–109, 177, 222, 260, 284.

21. Dozy, *Histoire*, 3:304–308.

22. Dozy, *Histoire*, 3:308–309.

23. Dozy, *Histoire*, 3:313.

24. Dozy, *Histoire*, 4:261–262.

25. See, for example, Dozy, *Histoire*, 3:290.

26. Abigail Krasner Balbale lands on a similar conclusion in her discussion of Dozy's treatment of the twelfth-century figure Ibn Mardanish. Balbale writes: "For Dozy, the complex events in al-Andalus and North Africa during the twelfth century could be explained through race, religion, and nation—the terms and concepts that defined the nineteenth century." Balbale, *The Wolf King: Ibn Mardanīsh and the Construction of Power in al-Andalus* (Ithaca, NY: Cornell University Press, 2022), 4. I thank Balbale for sharing her manuscript with me.

27. My biographical sketch of Zaydan is based on three sources: Thomas Philipp, *Jurji Zaidan and the Foundations of Arab Nationalism* (Syracuse, NY: Syracuse University Press, 2010); Walid Hamarneh, "Jurjī Zaydān," in *Essays in Arabic Literary Biography, 1850–1950*, ed. Roger Allen (Wiesbaden: Harrassowitz Verlag, 2010), 382–392; Anne-Laure Dupont, "What Is a *kātib ʿāmm?* The Status of Men of Letters and the Conception of Language according to Jurjī Zaydān," *Middle Eastern Literatures* 13, no. 2 (2010): 171–181, https://doi.org/10.1080/1475262X.2010.487313.

28. The impact of European Orientalism on Zaydan's work is discussed in Anne-Laure Dupont, "How Should the History of the Arabs Be Written? The Impact of European Orientalism on Jurji Zaidan's Work," in *Jurji Zaidan: Contributions to Modern Arab Thought and Literature,* ed. George C. Zaidan and Thomas Philipp (Bethesda, MD: Zaidan Foundation, 2013), 85–121; Philipp, *Jurji Zaidan,* 31–32.

29. Stephen Sheehi summarizes and analyzes this novel in *Foundations of Modern Arab Identity* (Gainesville: University Press of Florida, 2004), 169–188.

30. Philipp, *Jurji Zaidan,* 32; Hamarneh, "Jurjī Zaydān," 384.

31. The only historical novel that Zaydan did not publish in *al-Hilal* was his first one, *al-Mamluk al-sharid*. For a complete list of Zaydan's novels, with their publication dates, see Hamarneh, "Jurjī Zaydān," 384–385.

32. On this point Taha Husayn wrote: "It is not at all an exaggeration to say that the founder of *al-Hilal* brought into being in the Arabic language this modern

science that we call the history of literature." Taha Husayn, "Athar *al-Hilal* wa-munshi'hi," in *al-Hilal: al-Kitab al-dhahabi, 1892–1942* ([Cairo]: Dar al-Hilal, [1942]), 135. See also Hamarneh, "Jurjī Zaydān," 390–392.

33. Philipp, *Jurji Zaidan*, 86–89; Sheehi, *Foundations*, 159–169; Wien, *Arab Nationalism*, 69.

34. Roger Allen, "Tāhā Husayn," in *Essays in Arabic Literary Biography, 1850–1950*, ed. Roger Allen (Wiesbaden: Harrassowitz Verlag, 2010), 137–149.

35. Husayn, "Athar *al-Hilal*," 135.

36. Husayn, "Athar *al-Hilal*," 135.

37. For Zaydan's concept of *kātib 'āmm*, see Dupont, "What Is a *kātib 'āmm?*"; Philipp, *Jurji Zaidan*, 85–86.

38. Jurji Zaydan, *Tarikh adab al-lugha al-'arabiyya*, ed. Shawqi Dayf (Cairo: Dar al-Hilal, 1957), 2:5.

39. Dupont, "What Is a *kātib 'āmm?*," 175.

40. Jurji Zaydan, *Tarikh al-tamaddun al-islami* (Cairo: Matba'at al-Hilal, 1902), 1:3.

41. Jurji Zaydan, "The Writers and Readers of Arabic," trans. Hilary Kilpatrick, in Philipp, *Jurji Zaidan*, 219. In a similar vein, Hamarneh asserts that Zaydan's novels created "an entirely new community of readers." Hamarneh "Jurjī Zaydān," 387.

42. Benedict Anderson, *Imagined Communities: Reflections on the Origin and Spread of Nationalism*, rev. ed. (London: Verso, 1991), 18–36.

43. Philipp offers several indicators of *al-Hilal*'s success and broad circulation in *Jurji Zaidan*, 89–90.

44. I build here on Philipp's discussion in *Jurji Zaidan*, 101–109. Ziad Fahmy's *Ordinary Egyptians: Creating the Modern Nation Through Popular Culture* (Stanford, CA: Stanford University Press, 2011) reveals additional limitations for applying Anderson's model to the study of nationalism in Egypt. Noting the high rate of illiteracy in early twentieth-century Egypt, Fahmy advocates for expanding the analysis of Egyptian nationalism beyond the elite realm of print culture through the incorporation of sources in colloquial Egyptian Arabic, including audio, audiovisual, and performance media. Although I find Fahmy's critique of Anderson compelling, my focus here is not on the rise of Egyptian nationalism but instead on the role that Jurji Zaydan's print ventures played in the formation of a particular brand of pan-Arab nationalism.

45. Dupont, "What Is a *kātib 'āmm?*," 181; Philipp, *Jurji Zaidan*, 53–64; Hamarneh, "Jurjī Zaydān," 387–388.

46. Jurji Zaydan, "Literary and Colloquial Arabic," trans. Paul Starkey, in Philipp, *Jurji Zaidan*, 196.

47. Philipp, *Jurji Zaidan*, 58; Dupont, "What Is a *kātib 'āmm?*," 178; Jurji Zaydan, "al-Mujtama' al-lughawi al-'arabi," *al-Hilal*, March 1893, 309–315. My argument in this paragraph is particularly indebted to Philipp's analysis of Zaydan's views on language. As Philipp argues, Zaydan saw the Arabic language as "the basis for a pan-Arab national identity." Philipp, *Jurji Zaidan*, 109.

48. For more on this historical context, see Philipp, *Jurji Zaidan*, 109–112; William Granara, "Nostalgia, Arab Nationalism, and the Andalusian *Chronotope* in the Evolution of the Modern Arabic Novel," *Journal of Arabic Literature* 36, no. 1 (2005): 64–65.

49. Jurji Zaydan, *Fath al-Andalus* (Cairo: Matbaʿat al-Hilal, 1903); Jurji Zaidan, *The Conquest of Andalusia*, trans. Roger Allen (Bethesda, MD: Zaidan Foundation, 2010). When citing passages from the novel, I have generally relied on Allen's published translation, though I have occasionally modified the wording or offered my own translation to emphasize different aspects of the Arabic. The novel is also discussed in Wien, *Arab Nationalism*, 69–76; Christina Civantos, *The Afterlife of al-Andalus: Muslim Iberia in Contemporary Arab and Hispanic Narratives* (Albany: SUNY Press, 2017), 125–126, 227–229.

50. Jurji Zaydan, *Sharl wa-ʿAbd al-Rahman* (Cairo: Matbaʿat al-Hilal, 1904); Jurji Zaidan, *The Battle of Poitiers,* trans. William Granara (Bethesda, MD: Zaidan Foundation, 2011). When citing passages from the novel, I have generally relied on Granara's published translation, though I have occasionally offered my own translations to emphasize different aspects of the Arabic.

51. Jurji Zaydan, *ʿAbd al-Rahman al-Nasir,* vol. 24 of *al-Muʾallafat al-kamila* (Beirut: Nobilis, 2003–2004). This novel has not been translated into English.

52. Writing about the first two novels in Zaydan's Andalus trilogy, William Granara observes that these novels were "part of a long project of writing historical novels to educate the rising urban readership of the glories of Arab history, and to foster pan-Arab patriotism among the masses." Granara, "*Extensio Animae*," 60.

53. Dupont, "History of the Arabs"; Wien, *Arab Nationalism*, 70–72.

54. See, for example, Zaydan, *Fath al-Andalus*, 15, 90, 103, 122, 156, 209; Zaydan, *Sharl wa-ʿAbd al-Rahman*, 18.

55. Charles Romey, *Histoire d'Espagne: Depuis les premiers temps jusqu'a nos jours* (Paris, 1839), 3:96–107.

56. For the composition of Tariq's army, see Eduardo Manzano Moreno, *Conquistadores, emires y califas: Los omeyas y la formación de al-Andalus* (Barcelona: Crítica, 2006), 166.

57. Zaydan, *Fath al-Andalus*, 108–109; Zaidan, *Conquest of Andalusia,* 189.

58. Zaydan, *Fath al-Andalus*, 182; Zaidan, *Conquest of Andalusia,* 305.

59. Taken from the cover of Zaydan, *Sharl wa-ʿAbd al-Rahman.* My italics.

60. Zaydan, *Sharl wa-ʿAbd al-Rahman,* 24; Zaidan, *Battle of Poitiers,* 30.

61. Zaydan's character is based on a historical figure discussed in Manzano Moreno, *Conquistadores,* 47.

62. Zaydan, *Sharl wa-ʿAbd al-Rahman,* 17; Zaidan, *Battle of Poitiers,* 22.

63. Zaydan, *Sharl wa-ʿAbd al-Rahman,* 85–86. Granara offers a slightly different translation in Zaidan, *Battle of Poitiers,* 101.

64. Zaydan, *Sharl wa-ʿAbd al-Rahman,* 9. For an alternate translation of the same passage, see Zaidan, *Battle of Poitiers,* 12.

65. Nancy Stepan, *The Idea of Race in Science: Great Britain, 1800–1960* (Hamden: Archon Books, 1982), 45–46, 83–110.

66. Jurji Zaydan, *Kitab 'ilm al-firasa al-hadith* (Cairo: Matba'at al-Hilal, 1901).

67. Zaydan, *Fath al-Andalus,* 30; Zaidan, *Conquest of Andalusia,* 54.

68. Zaydan, *Sharl wa-'Abd al-Rahman,* 71. Granara renders the phrase idiomatically as "He began to speak to her in Arabic with a strong Berber accent," in Zaidan, *Battle of Poitiers,* 85.

69. Zaydan, *Sharl wa-'Abd al-Rahman,* 5; Zaidan, *Battle of Poitiers,* 7.

70. Zaydan, *Fath al-Andalus,* 14–15. For an alternate translation, see Zaidan, *Conquest of Andalusia,* 23.

71. The embassy is discussed in Maribel Fierro, "Qāsim b. Asbag y la licitud de recibir regalos," in *Homenaje al profesor José María Fórneas Besteiro* (Granada: Universidad de Granada, 1995), 980–981; Mayte Penelas, *Kitāb Hurūšiyūs (Traducción árabe de las* Historiae adversus paganos *de Orosio)* (Madrid: Consejo Superior de Investigaciones Científicas, 2001), 27–28.

72. Zaydan, *'Abd al-Rahman,* 46.

73. Zaydan, *'Abd al-Rahman,* 46.

74. Zaydan, *'Abd al-Rahman,* 46.

75. Ildefonso Garijo Galán, introduction to *Libro de la explicación de los nombres de los medicamentos simples tomados del libro de Dioscórides,* by Ibn Juljul (Cordoba: Universidad de Córdoba, 1992), 9–23; Marie Geneviève Balty-Guesdon, "Al-Andalus et l'héritage grec d'après les *Ṭabaqāt al-umam* de Ṣā'id al-Andalusī," in *Perspectives arabes et médiévales sur la tradition scientifique et philosophique grecque,* ed. Ahmad Hasnawi, Abdelali Elamrani-Jamal, and Maroun Aouad (Leuven: Peeters, 1997), 335–336; Penelas, *Kitāb Hurūšiyūs.* Penelas offers a detailed discussion of the date and authorship of the Arabic translation of Orosius in *Kitāb Hurūšiyūs,* 27–42.

76. For the translation and transmission of Greek and Latin texts in medieval Iberia, see Dimitri Gutas, "What Was There in Arabic for the Latins to Receive? Remarks on the Modalities of the Twelfth-Century Translation Movement in Spain," in *Wissen über Grenzen: Arabisches Wissen und lateinisches Mittelalter,* ed. Andreas Speer and Lydia Wegener (Berlin: Walter de Gruyter, 2006), 3–21; Penelas, *Kitāb Hurūšiyūs;* Balty-Guesdon, "Al-Andalus"; S. J. Pearce, *The Andalusi Literary and Intellectual Tradition: The Role of Arabic in Judah ibn Tibbon's Ethical Will* (Bloomington: Indiana University Press, 2017), 22–29, https://doi.org/10.2307/j.ctt2005scn.

77. Zaydan, *'Abd al-Rahman,* 186. It is worth noting that neither France nor Italy existed as such in the tenth century.

78. Zaydan, *'Abd al-Rahman,* 43.

79. Paradela, *Otro laberinto,* 126–230; Martínez Montávez, *Al-Andalus.*

80. For Qabbani's writings about Spain, see Martínez Montávez, *Al-Andalus,* 149–171; Granara, "*Extensio Animae,*" 54–56. I discuss al-Haffar al-Kuzbari's work at greater length in Chapter 3. See also Ana María Ramos Calvo, "Visión de

España en la literatura árabe contemporánea: Dos ejemplos sirios," in *La traducción y la crítica literaria: Actas de las Jornadas del Hispanismo Árabe,* ed. Fernando de Agreda (Madrid: Agencia Española de Cooperación Internacional, 1990), 256–260; Fernando de Ágreda Burillo, "Salma Al-Haffar Al-Kuzbari," *Anaquel de Estudios Árabes* 18 (2007): 254–257; Granara, *"Extensio Animae,"* 57–58; Shannon, *Performing al-Andalus,* 67–68.

81. Salma al-Haffar al-Kuzbari, *Fi zilal al-Andalus: Muhadarat* (Damascus: Matabiʿ Alif Baʾ, n.d.), 61–62.

82. I build here on Jonathan Shannon's rich work on the place of al-Andalus in the modern Syrian cultural imaginary. Shannon has noted that many modern Syrian writers and musicians have used al-Andalus as "a powerful vehicle for the expression of pan-Arab sentiment" and have placed Syria and Syrians "at the heart of the story of al-Andalus." *Performing al-Andalus,* 54–57.

83. Chahine's film won a jury prize at Cannes. For discussions of the film, see Eric Calderwood, "Proyectando al-Ándalus: Alegorías andalusíes en el cine árabe moderno," in *Andalusíes: Antropología e historia cultural de una elite magrebí,* ed. José Antonio González Alcantud and Sandra Rojo Flores (Madrid: Abada, 2015), 213–219; Civantos, *The Afterlife of al-Andalus,* 91–97.

84. I have based this definition of the *musalsal* on the one offered in Christa Salamandra, "Past Continuous: The Chronopolitics of Representation in Syrian Television Drama," *Middle East Critique* 28, no. 2 (2019): 123, https://doi.org/10.1080/19436149.2019.1600880.

85. See Marwan M. Kraidy and Joe F. Khalil, *Arab Television Industries* (London: Palgrave Macmillan, 2009), 99–122.

86. I summarize here the industry history offered in Kraidy and Khalil, *Arab Television Industries,* 99–106; Salamandra, "Past Continuous," 123–124.

87. Rebecca Joubin, *The Politics of Love: Sexuality, Gender, and Marriage in Syrian Television Drama* (Lanham: Lexington Books, 2013), 32–38; Christa Salamandra, "Arab Television Drama Production and the Islamic Public Sphere," in *Visual Culture in the Modern Middle East,* ed. Christiane Gruber and Sune Haugbolle (Bloomington: Indiana University Press, 2013), 262–264.

88. Joubin, *Politics of Love,* 3–4; Salamandra, "Past Continuous," 123–124.

89. These historical dramas include *Saqr Quraysh* (2002), *Zaman al-wasl* (2002), *Rabiʿ Qurtuba* (2003), *Tariq* (2004), *al-Murabitun wa-l-Andalus* (2005), and *Muluk al-tawaʾif* (2005). This list is meant, not to be exhaustive, but instead to demonstrate the widespread popularity of al-Andalus in contemporary Arabic-language television drama. My discussion of this phenomenon builds on my work in Eric Calderwood, "El mito de al-Ándalus en el mundo mediterráneo moderno," in *Paradigma Alhambra: Variación del mito de Al Ándalus,* ed. José A. González Alcantud (Granada: Universidad de Granada, 2018), 121–160; and Calderwood, "Proyectando al-Ándalus," 232–240. See also John Shoup, "As It Was, and As It Should Be Now: Al Andalus in Contemporary Arab Television Dramas," *Trans-*

national Broadcasting Studies 1, no. 2 (2005): 191–198; Marlin Dick, "The State of the Musalsal: Arab Television Drama and Comedy and the Politics of the Satellite Era," *Transnational Broadcasting Studies* 1, no. 2 (2005): 182–184.

90. The trilogy is available on YouTube. Its awards are listed on Hatim 'Ali's Wikipedia page (in Arabic).

91. For SAPI's ties to the Asad regime, see Joubin, *Politics of Love,* 40.

92. *Saqr Quraysh,* episode 3, directed by Hatim 'Ali, 2002, https://youtu.be/I -xo79JWoFU.

93. *Saqr Quraysh,* episode 4, directed by Hatim 'Ali, 2002, https://youtu.be /e7VWWfFcJ9Q.

94. *Saqr Quraysh,* episode 23, directed by Hatim 'Ali, 2002, https://youtu.be /IDWZnBV66Sk. For 'Abd al-Rahman's poem, I quote from the translation in D. Fairchild Ruggles, *Gardens, Landscape, and Vision in the Palaces of Islamic Spain* (University Park: Pennsylvania State University Press, 2000), 42. The original Arabic poem appears in Ibn 'Idhari, *Kitab al-bayan al-mughrib fi akhbar al-Andalus wa-l-Maghrib,* ed. G. S. Colin and E. Lévi-Provençal (Beirut: Dar al-Thaqafa, [1967]), 2:60.

95. Elinson, *Looking Back,* 3–4.

96. For this figure, see Nicola Clarke, "'They Were the Most Treacherous of People': Religious Difference in Arabic Accounts of Three Early Medieval Berber Revolts," *eHumanista* 24 (2013): 518–520; Manzano Moreno, *Conquistadores,* 173–174.

97. *Saqr Quraysh,* episode 27, directed by Hatim 'Ali, 2002, https://youtu.be /BXuvYEysNgE.

98. Zaidan, *Battle of Poitiers,* 78, 84; Zaydan, *Sharl wa-'Abd al-Rahman,* 65, 71.

99. According to Clarke's review of the sources, Shaqya "was killed by what seem to have been some of his followers, perhaps indicating a power struggle." Clarke, "Most Treacherous," 519.

100. *Rabi' Qurtuba,* episode 1, directed by Hatim 'Ali, 2003, https://youtu.be /L4dLtzEyo7g.

101. Quoted in Christa Salamandra, "Creative Compromise: Syrian Television Makers between Secularism and Islamism," *Contemporary Islam* 2 (2008): 185, https://doi.org/10.1007/s11562-008-0060-0.

102. Samuel P. Huntington, *The Clash of Civilizations and the Remaking of World Order* (New York: Touchstone, 1997).

103. The "United Nations Year of Dialogue among Civilizations" is described in UN Resolution 55 / 23, available at www.un.org.

104. Press Release GA / 9497, November 4, 1998, www.un.org; my italics.

105. For this figure, see Ch. Pellat, "Rabi' b. Zayd," in *Encyclopedia of Islam,* 2nd ed., ed. P. Bearman et al., accessed September 5, 2021, https://doi.org/10.1163 /1573-3912_islam_SIM_6159.

106. *Rabi' Qurtuba,* episode 6, directed by Hatim 'Ali, 2003, https://youtu.be /B2uS68vqXYQ.

107. *Rabi' Qurtuba,* episode 6.

108. For a brief biography of Subh, see Manuela Marín, "Ṣubḥ," in *Encyclopedia of Islam,* 2nd ed., ed. P. Bearman et al., accessed September 5, 2021, https://doi.org /10.1163/1573-3912_islam_SIM_7111.

109. *Rabiʿ Qurtuba,* episode 5, directed by Hatim ʿAli, 2003, https://youtu.be /XEuyuVP_CW0.

110. *Rabiʿ Qurtuba,* episode 5.

111. Adam Gaiser, "Slaves and Silver across the Strait of Gibraltar: Politics and Trade between Umayyad Iberia and Khārijite North Africa," *Medieval Encounters* 19 (2013): 63–64; Rouighi, *Inventing the Berbers,* 212n36; P.B. Golden et al., "al-Ṣaḳāliba," in *Encyclopedia of Islam,* 2nd ed., ed. P. Bearman et al., accessed August 14, 2022, https://doi.org/10.1163/1573-3912_islam_COM_0978.

112. *Muluk al-tawaʾif,* episode 1, directed by Hatim ʿAli, 2005, https://youtu.be /s5hy5rOsyuw.

113. For example, in episode 9, ʿAbbad and his astrologer refer to the Almoravids as a *qawm ṭariʾūn.* In episode 11, ʿAbbad uses a related verb to express his fear that the Almoravids will "descend suddenly upon" (*yaṭruʾūn ʿalā*) the Iberian Peninsula to seize power in al-Andalus.

114. *Muluk al-tawaʾif,* episode 1.

115. Bruna Soravia, "ʿAbbadids," in *Encyclopedia of Islam,* 3rd ed., ed. Kate Fleet et al., accessed September 5, 2021, https://doi.org/10.1163/1573-3912_ei3_COM_24141.

116. *Muluk al-tawaʾif,* episode 1.

117. *Muluk al-tawaʾif,* episode 1.

118. Salamandra, "Past Continuous," 138.

119. *Muluk al-tawaʾif,* episode 30, directed by Hatim ʿAli, 2005, https://youtu .be/GcIrCrO2Aa0. The poem appears in *Diwan al-Muʿtamid b. ʿAbbad, malik Ishbiliya,* ed. Ahmad Ahmad Badawi and Hamid ʿAbd al-Majid (Cairo: al-Matbaʿa al-Amiriyya, 1951), 96. The translation is mine, though I would like to acknowledge Alexander Elinson's helpful input.

120. See Calderwood, *Colonial al-Andalus.*

121. Most of the Cordoba scenes in *Rabiʿ Qurtuba* were shot in Chaouen, but some of them were shot in other Moroccan cities. For example, a scene in episode 4 appears to have been shot in Funduq al-Najjarin in Fez. In the credits to *Rabiʿ Qurtuba,* the producers thank the regional governments of Rabat, Meknes, Fez, and Chefchaouen— which are all presumably locations used during the filming of the series.

2. The Berber al-Andalus

1. The event was covered by several sources in the Spanish media, including the newspaper *El País* and the press arm of the Spanish royal house. See, for example, Javier Arroyo, "Una muestra revive la construcción de Granada por los bereberes," *El País,* December 6, 2019, https://elpais.com/cultura/2019/12/05/actualidad/1575 569886_846459.html. My description of the exhibit is based on two visits I made to it in January 2020.

2. "La herencia bereber en Granada," *Canal Sur,* December 5, 2019, http://www
.canalsur.es/noticias/andaluc%C3%ADa/granada/la-herencia-bereber-en
-granada/1513607.html; "La Alhambra será la sede permanente de un gran museo
beréber," *Granada Hoy,* June 18, 2019, https://www.granadahoy.com/ocio/Alhambra
-sede-permanente-museo-bereber_0_1365164000.html.

3. Quoted in "Herencia bereber."

4. This is my translation of a passage from the official exhibit brochure, *La
Granada zirí y el universo beréber.*

5. Antonio Malpica Cuello, "La Granada zirí y el universo beréber. Un punto de
partida," in *La Granada zirí y el universo beréber* (Granada: Patronato de la Alhambra y Generalife, 2019), 13.

6. On this point, it is worth noting that one of the exhibit's assistant curators
was Bilal Sarr, a leading specialist on Zirid Granada, whose scholarship has un-
derlined the Zirids' "*berbérité*"—that is, in Sarr's words, the "authentically Berber
elements" of the Zirid kingdom in Granada. See Bilal Sarr, "'Quand on parlait le
berbère à la cour de Grenade': Quelques réflexions sur la berbérité de la taifa ziride
(al-Andalus, XIe siècle)," *Arabica* 63 (2016): 235, https://doi.org/10.1163/15700585
-12341000.

7. Malpica Cuello, "Granada zirí," 13.

8. For an introduction to the Marinid dynasty, see Maya Shatzmiller, *The
Berbers and the Islamic State: The Marīnid Experience in Pre-Protectorate Morocco* (Princeton, NJ: Marcus Wiener, 2000).

9. Perhaps the most prominent medieval antecedent for the phenomenon I discuss in this chapter is a genre known as *mafākhir al-barbar* or *mafāḍil al-barbar*
(the boasts / glories of the Berbers), which emerged in the eleventh century and became prominent in the fourteenth century. See Shatzmiller, *Berbers,* 31–38; Mehdi
Ghouirgate, "Un cas de nationalisme maghrébin médiéval: La littérature des
mérites des Berbères," in *Nation et nations au Moyen Âge: XLIVe Congrès de la
SHMESP* (Paris: Publications de la Sorbonne, 2014), 79–91. Rouighi notes a similar spirit of "Berberism," or Berber solidarity, among the Zirids and other *taifa*
rulers of North African origin in eleventh-century al-Andalus. Ramzi Rouighi, *Inventing the Berbers: History and Ideology in the Maghrib* (Philadelphia: University
of Pennsylvania Press, 2019), 59–61.

10. I give some examples of this phenomenon in Chapter 1. See also Amira K.
Bennison, *The Almoravid and Almohad Empires* (Edinburgh: Edinburgh University Press, 2016), 3; Abigail Krasner Balbale, *The Wolf King: Ibn Mardanīsh and
the Construction of Power in al-Andalus* (Ithaca, NY: Cornell University Press,
2022), 4–5, 25.

11. The bibliography on this topic is extensive. For introductions, see Jonathan
Wyrtzen, *Making Morocco: Colonial Intervention and the Politics of Identity*
(Ithaca, NY: Cornell University Press, 2015), 136–178; Eric Calderwood, *Colonial
al-Andalus: Spain and the Making of Modern Moroccan Culture* (Cambridge:
Belknap Press of Harvard University Press, 2018), 167–207.

12. For helpful introductions to debates surrounding the term *Berber*, see Bruce Maddy-Weitzman, *The Berber Identity Movement and the Challenge to North African States* (Austin: University of Texas Press, 2011), 2; Bennison, *Almoravid and Almohad Empires*, 9; Rouighi, *Inventing the Berbers;* Muhammad Shafiq, *Lamha ʻan thalatha wa-thalathin qarnan min tarikh al-Amazighiyyin* (Rabat: Dar al-Kalam, 1989), 9–17. Rouighi argues that before the Muslim Arab conquests of North Africa, no one thought that the inhabitants of northwest Africa belonged to a single ethnic group with a shared past.

13. Maddy-Weitzman, *Berber Identity*, 2; Rouighi, *Inventing the Berbers*, 18; Bennison, *Almoravid and Almohad Empires*, 9.

14. See, for example, Maddy-Weitzman, *Berber Identity*—in particular, the discussion of terminology on pages ix, 2–4.

15. For an introduction to the rich body of scholarship on this episode, see Calderwood, *Colonial al-Andalus*, 173–266; Wyrtzen, *Making Morocco*, 136–178; Susan Gilson Miller, *A History of Modern Morocco* (Cambridge: Cambridge University Press, 2013), 125–136.

16. These ideas can be traced back to nineteenth-century French writings about Algeria. See Edmund Burke III, *The Ethnographic State: France and the Invention of Moroccan Islam* (Oakland: University of California Press, 2014), 33–35; Maddy-Weitzman, *Berber Identity*, 40–41.

17. Wyrtzen, *Making Morocco*, 147.

18. For more on these figures, see Miller, *History of Modern Morocco*, 122–133; Calderwood, *Colonial al-Andalus*, 252–262; Wyrtzen, *Making Morocco*, 148–149, 159, 171–172, 283, 286.

19. In the early twentieth century, the Tharaud brothers published several influential works on Morocco, including *Rabat, ou, Les heures marocaines* (1918) and *Marrakesh, ou, Les seigneurs de l'Atlas* (1920). The Tharaud brothers also gave public lectures about Morocco and published actively in the French press. Unfortunately, I have not been able to locate the lectures that were the source for Balafrij and al-Fasi's translation. The Moroccan translators do not give the titles or publication information, but they do reproduce a letter (translated into Arabic) from the Tharaud brothers, approving the translation project.

20. According to the title page, the work was published in the year 1349 of the Islamic calendar, which corresponds to 1930/1931. At the beginning of the book, Balafrij and al-Fasi reproduce a letter from Shakib Arslan signed on 30 Ṣafar 1349 (July 27, 1930).

21. Ahmad Balafrij and Muhammad al-Fasi, foreword to *Azhar al-basatin fi akhbar al-Andalus wa-l-Maghrib ʻala ʻahd al-murabitin wa-l-muwahhidin* (Rabat: al-Matbaʻa al-Wataniyya, 1930/1931), 2–3.

22. I draw here on Benedict Anderson's classic work on nationalism, *Imagined Communities: Reflections on the Origin and Spread of Nationalism*, rev. ed. (London: Verso, 1991).

23. Balafrij and al-Fasi, foreword to *Azhar al-basatin,* 4.

24. Patrick J. Geary elaborates on this point, and provides several examples, in *The Myth of Nations: The Medieval Origins of Europe* (Princeton, NJ: Princeton University Press, 2002), 6–37. For more examples, from a range of nationalist projects, see Nadia Abu El-Haj, *Facts on the Ground: Archaeological Practice and Territorial Self-Fashioning in Israeli Society* (Chicago: University of Chicago Press, 2001); Anderson, *Imagined Communities,* 11–12; Alejandro García-Sanjuan, "Writing the History of al-Andalus: Spain and the West," in *The Routledge Handbook of Muslim Iberia,* ed. Maribel Fierro (London: Routledge, 2020), 620–637, https://doi.org/10.4324/9781315625959.

25. Balafrij and al-Fasi, foreword to *Azhar al-basatin,* 2.

26. Miller, *History of Modern Morocco,* 132–133; Wyrtzen, *Making Morocco,* 153–154.

27. Ahmad Balafrij ("A.B."), "Et maintenant?," *Maghreb,* May / June 1933, 50.

28. Balafrij, "Et maintenant?," 51.

29. For the history of *al-Salam,* see Hasna' Muhammad Dawud, *'Ala ra's al-thamanin* (Tetouan: Jam'iyyat Titwan-Asmir, 2011), 165–169.

30. Balafrij notes, for example, that 'Abd al-Mu'min was born to parents "from the Gumiya tribe," an important group from the central Maghrib. Likewise, Balafrij notes that Ibn Tumart came from the Berber-speaking Sous region and that he would "instruct the Berbers in their dialect." See Ahmad Balafrij, "'Abd al-Mu'min wa-ta'sis al-dawla al-muwahhidiyya (1)," *al-Salam* 2 (1933): 22, 24; Ahmad Balafrij, "'Abd al-Mu'min wa-ta'sis al-dawla al-muwahhidiyya (2)," *al-Salam* 3 (1933): 13.

31. Balafrij, "'Abd al-Mu'min (2)," 15.

32. Balafrij, "'Abd al-Mu'min (2)," 15.

33. Balafrij, "'Abd al-Mu'min (2)," 15.

34. Balafrij, "'Abd al-Mu'min (2)," 16.

35. I build here on ideas from Gonzalo Fernández Parrilla and Eric Calderwood, "What Is Moroccan Literature? History of an Object in Motion," *Journal of Arabic Literature* 52, no. 1–2 (2021): 97–123, https://doi.org/10.1163/1570064x -12341421. For Gannun's place in Moroccan literary history, see also Gonzalo Fernández Parrilla, *La literatura marroquí contemporánea: La novela y la crítica literaria* (Cuenca: Ediciones de la Universidad Castilla-La Mancha, 2006), 91–104.

36. For the earliest sources of Tariq's speech, see 'Abbas al-Jarari, *al-Adab al-maghribi min khilal zawahirihi wa-qadayahu* (Rabat: Maktabat al-Ma'arif, 1979), 59–65.

37. Gannun discusses Tariq's speech in his chapter on Moroccan literature from the period of the Islamic conquests of North Africa. Gannun also reproduces Tariq's speech in the second volume of *al-Nubugh,* in the section on the oratory genre (*al-khuṭab*). See 'Abd Allah Gannun, *al-Nubugh al-maghribi fi al-adab al-'arabi* (Tetouan: al-Matba'a al-Mahdiyya, [1937]), 1:9, 2:9–10. All of my references to Gannun's work are to the first edition (1937), unless noted otherwise.

38. Mohammed El Fasi, "La littérature marocaine," in *L'Encyclopédie Coloniale et Maritime,* fasc. 22 (Paris, 1940), 410.

39. This comment appears in a footnote that Gannun added to Shakib Arslan's 1942 review of *al-Nubugh al-maghribi.* Gannun's comment and Arslan's review are both reproduced in 'Abd Allah Gannun, *al-Nubugh al-maghribi fi al-adab al-'arabi,* 3rd ed. (Beirut: Maktabat al-Madrasa wa-Dar al-Kitab al-Lubnani li-l-Tiba'a wa-l-Nashr, 1975), 1:29n1. Gannun also defended the authenticity of Tariq's speech in his article "Hawla khutbat Tariq," *Da'wat al-haqq* 7 / 8 (1968): 111. For an overview of several opposing views regarding the authenticity of Tariq's speech, see al-Jarari, *al-Adab al-maghribi,* 53–67.

40. Gannun, *al-Nubugh al-maghribi,* 1:29, n. 1.

41. Gannun, *al-Nubugh,* 1:62, 70–75, 157–158; El Fasi, "La littérature marocaine," 412–414.

42. In addition to the examples analyzed in Chapter 1, see also Bennison's helpful discussion of this problem in *Almoravid and Almohad Empires,* esp. pp. 3–4.

43. Gannun, *al-Nubugh,* 1:27.

44. Gannun, *al-Nubugh,* 1:25.

45. Gannun, *al-Nubugh,* 1:25–26, my italics.

46. Gannun, *al-Nubugh,* 1:28.

47. Gannun, *al-Nubugh,* 1:30, 44, 54.

48. Gannun, *al-Nubugh,* 1:54.

49. Gannun, *al-Nubugh,* 1:54.

50. Gannun, *al-Nubugh,* 1:67.

51. For the promotion and expanded uses of Berber under the Almohads, see Mohamed Meouak, *La langue berbère au Maghreb médiéval: Textes, contextes, analyses* (Leiden: Brill, 2016), 156–168, https://doi.org/10.1163/9789004302358 _003; Bennison, *Almoravid and Almohad Empires,* 130–131; Mehdi Ghouirgate, "Le berbère au Moyen Âge: Une culture linguistique en cours de reconstitution," *Annales HSS,* July–September 2015, 577–605.

52. Gannun, *al-Nubugh,* 1:46.

53. Gannun, *al-Nubugh,* 1:47.

54. Gannun, *al-Nubugh,* 1:50.

55. For more on Mulin, see *al-Munadil al-ustadh Muhammad al-Rashid Mulin: Asalat fikr mutajaddid,* ed. Mustafa al-Jawahiri (Rabat: Matba'at Folio, 2002).

56. Muhammad al-Rashid Mulin, *'Asr al-Mansur al-Muwahhidi, aw, al-haya al-siyasiyya wa-l-fikriyya wa-l-diniyya fi al-Maghrib min sanat 580 ila sanat 595* ([Rabat?]: Matba'at al-Shamal al-Afriqi, [1961?]), 171–172. My citations refer to the second edition, which lacks a publication date but was probably published in the 1960s. In a prologue to the edition, 'Abd Allah Gannun refers to Morocco's independence (1956) and to Muhammad V's death (1961).

57. Mulin, *'Asr al-Mansur,* 164, 184, 194, 203, 212, 215, 220–221.

58. Mulin, *'Asr al-Mansur,* 264.

59. For Rabat's development under the Almohads, see Bennison, *Almoravid and Almohad Empires,* 309–325.

60. I build here on my earlier discussion of the mausoleum in *Colonial al-Andalus,* 289–298. See also Jennifer Roberson, "The Changing Face of Morocco under King Hassan II," *Mediterranean Studies* 22, no. 1 (2014): 57–83, muse.jhu.edu /article/547158.

61. Abdelwahab Benmansour, introduction to *Le Mausolée Mohammed V,* by Vo Toan (Casablanca: Sochepress, 1976), 18; Vo, *Mausolée Mohammed V,* 34.

62. Vo, *Mausolée Mohammed V,* 30, 38, 106–108.

63. Dolores Villalba Sola, *La senda de los Almohades: Arquitectura y patrimonio* (Granada: Universidad de Granada, 2015), 159, 238–239.

64. I discuss some of these allusions in *Colonial al-Andalus,* 295–296.

65. Vo, *Mausolée Mohammed V,* 38.

66. I discuss an example from the realm of tourism in Eric Calderwood, "The Invention of al-Andalus: Discovering the Past and Creating the Present in Granada's Islamic Tourism Sites," *Journal of North African Studies* 19, no. 1 (2014): 42–44.

67. According to the statistics published by the Centre Cinématographique Marocain, al-Nasiri's film sold more tickets in Morocco than any other film in the year 2006. The present analysis of al-Nasiri's film builds on an earlier discussion of the film in Eric Calderwood, "Proyectando al-Ándalus: Alegorías andalusíes en el cine árabe moderno," in *Andalusíes: Antropología e historia cultural de una elite magrebí,* ed. José Antonio González Alcantud and Sandra Rojo Flores (Madrid: Abada, 2015), 219–232. All my descriptions and quotations from the film refer to *'Abdu 'inda al-muwahhidin,* directed by Sa'id al-Nasiri (Casablanca: Hi-Com, [2006]), DVD.

68. Although most contemporary Arabic historical dramas set in al-Andalus are in Standard Arabic, the language situation in al-Andalus was considerably more fluid. Al-Andalus was a multilingual society where language use varied across historical periods as well as among different ethnic, religious, and social groups. On this point, see Consuelo López-Morillas, "Language," in *The Literature of Al-Andalus,* ed. María Rosa Menocal, Raymond P. Scheindlin, and Michael Sells (Cambridge: Cambridge University Press, 2000), 33–59.

69. I trace the origins of this phenomenon in Chapter 1. See also Marlin Dick, "The State of the Musalsal: Arab Television Drama and Comedy and the Politics of the Satellite Era," *Transnational Broadcasting Studies* 1, no. 2 (2005): 177–190; Christa Salamandra, "Past Continuous: The Chronopolitics of Representation in Syrian Television Drama," *Middle East Critique* 28, no. 2 (2019): 121–141, https://doi .org/10.1080/19436149.2019.1600880.

70. Atiqa Hachimi, "The Maghreb-Mashriq Language Ideology and the Politics of Identity in a Globalized Arab World," *Journal of Sociolinguistics* 17, no. 3 (2013): 269–296; Calderwood, *Colonial al-Andalus,* 204–205.

71. For recent scholarly accounts of this controversial episode in Ibn Rushd's career, see Maribel Fierro, "Ibn Rushd's (Averroes) 'Disgrace' and His Relation with the Almohads," in *Islamic Philosophy from the 12th to the 14th Century,* ed. Abdelkader Al Ghouz (Götttingen: Bonn University Press, 2018), 73–116; Bennison, *Almoravid and Almohad Empires,* 108–109, 261–262.

72. Sa'id al-Nasiri, in discussion with the author, January 20, 2020.

73. "Sa'id al-Nasiri: Sana'na kumaydiya tarikhiyya tadhak wa-tabki," *al-Quds al-'Arabi,* March 31, 2006, https://www.alquds.co.uk/?p=27461.

74. Al-Nasiri, in discussion with the author, January 20, 2020.

75. The most comprehensive study of this phenomenon is Maddy-Weitzman's *Berber Identity Movement.* See also Mohammed Errihani, "The Amazigh Renaissance: Tamazight in the Time of Mohammed VI," in *Contemporary Morocco: State, Politics and Society under Mohammed VI,* ed. Bruce Maddy-Weitzman and Daniel Zisenwine (London: Routledge, 2013), 57–69; Hassan Rachik, ed., *Usages de l'identité Amazighe au Maroc* (Casablanca: Imprimerie Najah El Jadida, 2006).

76. Maddy-Weitzman, *Berber Identity,* 7–8.

77. The novel is preceded, in the trilogy, by *Une enquête au pays* (1981, translated into English as *Flutes of Death*) and *La mère du printemps (l'Oum-er-Bia)* (1982, translated into English as *Mother Spring*). An introduction to the trilogy may be found in Stéphanie Delayre, *Driss Chraïbi, une écriture de traverse* (Pessac: Presses universitaires de Bourdeaux, 2006), 59–61, 307–311. More recently, Christina Civantos has analyzed *Naissance à l'aube* in *The Afterlife of al-Andalus: Muslim Iberia in Contemporary Arab and Hispanic Narratives* (Albany: SUNY Press, 2017), 130–137. Civantos situates Chraïbi's novel within a long tradition of literary representations of Tariq b. Ziyad and notes Chraïbi's creation of a powerful Amazigh identity for Tariq. In a similar vein, Edwige Tamalet Talbayev asserts that Chraïbi's novel rewrites "Andalusian Islam as the product of Amazigh probity" and mounts "an indirect indictment of Arabness." Talbayev, *The Transcontinental Maghreb: Francophone Literature across the Mediterranean* (New York: Fordham University Press, 2012), 91, https://www.jstor.org/stable/j.ctt1xhr5d6.

78. Driss Chraïbi, *Naissance à l'aube* (Paris: Seuil, 1986), 122–123; Chraibi, *Birth at Dawn,* trans. Ann Woollcombe (Washington, DC: Three Continents Press, 1990), 83. For each quote from the novel, I will give the pagination for the French original and Woollcombe's English translation. I should note, however, that my English translations sometimes depart from Woollcombe's published translation—either because I disagree with a translation choice that Woollcombe made or because I want to highlight a different aspect of the French.

79. Chraïbi, *Naissance à l'aube,* 184; *Birth at Dawn,* 129. Similar examples abound in the novel, including in the novel's first sentence, where Raho Ait Yafelman is

described as "a Berber, very tall and very thin." Chraïbi, *Naissance à l'aube*, 11; *Birth at Dawn*, 1.

80. Azwaw is also the protagonist of the previous installment in Chrabi's trilogy, *La mère du printemps (l'Oum-er-Bia)*. His tongue is cut out at the end of that novel.

81. Chraïbi, *Naissance à l'aube*, 55–56; *Birth at Dawn*, 31. Civantos discusses part of the same passage in *Afterlife of al-Andalus*, 133.

82. See, for example, Chraïbi, *Naissance à l'aube*, 88, 103; *Birth at Dawn*, 56, 67.

83. Chraïbi, *Naissance à l'aube*, 90–91; *Birth at Dawn*, 58.

84. Chraïbi, *Naissance à l'aube*, 88–89; *Birth at Dawn*, 57.

85. Burke traces the origins of these ideas in *The Ethnographic State*, 33, 140–141. See also Maddy-Weitzman, *Berber Identity*, 40–41.

86. Maddy-Weitzman, *Berber Identity*, 85–91, 123–127.

87. Chraïbi, *Naissance à l'aube*, 108–109; *Birth at Dawn*, 71.

88. Chraïbi, *Naissance à l'aube*, 137–138; *Birth at Dawn*, 94.

89. Chraïbi, *Naissance à l'aube*, 138; *Birth at Dawn*, 94.

90. Chraïbi, *Naissance à l'aube*, 175; *Birth at Dawn*, 121.

91. Chraïbi, *Naissance à l'aube*, 177; *Birth at Dawn*, 123. Ibn Yasin studied in Cordoba as a young man, but it is unlikely that he was there in 1054, when the Almoravid movement was already on the rise. See Bennison, *Almoravid and Almohad*, 27–28.

92. Chraïbi, *Naissance à l'aube*, 177; *Birth at Dawn*, 124.

93. Chraïbi, *Naissance à l'aube*, 185; *Birth at Dawn*, 129.

94. Chraïbi, *Naissance à l'aube*, 186; *Birth at Dawn*, 130.

95. The first verses revealed to Muhammad appear at the beginning of Sura 96, *al-'Alaq*.

96. Chraïbi, *Naissance à l'aube*, 186; *Birth at Dawn*, 130.

97. Chraïbi, *Naissance à l'aube*, 186; *Birth at Dawn*, 130.

98. Shafiq's moniker appears in Errihani, "Amazigh Renaissance," 58; Maddy-Weitzman, *Berber Identity*, 95. Maddy-Weitzman calls Shafiq "the preeminent intellectual of the contemporary Moroccan Amazigh movement." *Berber Identity*, 35.

99. Maddy-Weitzman, *Berber Identity*, 57–59; "Brief Biography of the Author," in *A Brief Survey of Thirty-Three Centuries of Amazigh History*, by Mohammed Chafik (Rabat: Institut Royal de la Culture Amazighe, 2004), 103.

100. Maddy-Weitzman, *Berber Identity*, 59.

101. Maddy-Weitzman, *Berber Identity*, 97–98; "Brief Biography."

102. See, for instance, Muhammad Shafiq's article "Ma hiya 'alaqat al-amazighiyya bi-l-'arabiyya fi judhurihuma al-kubra?," *Al-Bahth al-'ilmi* 25 (1976): 231–241.

103. Maddy-Weitzman, *Berber Identity*, 96–97.

104. Maddy-Weitzman, *Berber Identity*, 98.

105. Fadma Aït Mous, "Le réseau associative amazigh: Émergence et diffusion," in *Usages de l'identité Amazighe au Maroc,* ed. Hassan Rachik (Casablanca: Imprimerie Najah El Jadida, 2006), 150.

106. Aït Mous, "Le réseau," 150; Maddy-Weitzman, *Berber Identity,* 97.

107. For the role of IRCAM in the contemporary Amazigh movement, see Maddy-Weitzman, *Berber Identity,* 164–182; Errihani, "Amazigh Renaissance"; Dris Soulaimani, "Writing and Rewriting Amazigh / Berber Identity: Orthographies and Language Ideologies," *Writing Systems Research* 8, no. 1 (2016): 1–16, https://doi .org/10.1080/17586801.2015.1023176.

108. Mohammed Chafik, "Traduction du discours prononcé par Monsieur Mohammed Chafik à l'occasion de son entrée à l'académie du Royaume du Maroc," *Amazigh* 5 (March 1981): 12–18. I thank Bruce Maddy-Weitzman for providing me with a copy of this source.

109. Chafik, "Traduction," 17.

110. Chafik, "Traduction," 17, my italics.

111. Chafik, "Traduction," 18.

112. Shafiq addresses the origins and meanings of these terms in *Lamha,* 9–17; translated into English by Ali Azeriah as *A Brief Survey of Thirty-Three Centuries of Amazigh History* (Rabat: Institut Royal de la Culture Amazighe, 2004), 11–16. My quotations from this source are based on the text published in Arabic in 1989. In my notes, I will also point to the corresponding passages in Azeriah's translation, although my translations occasionally diverge from Azeriah's translations.

113. Shafiq, *Lamha,* 6; *Brief Survey,* 8. Shafiq refers here to a sound that is particular to the Amazigh language.

114. Shafiq, *Lamha,* 87; *Brief Survey,* 75–76.

115. Shafiq, *Lamha,* 88; *Brief Survey,* 77.

116. Shafiq, *Lamha,* 88; *Brief Survey,* 77.

117. For the languages spoken by Almoravid and Almohad rulers, I point again to Meouak's discussion in *Langue berbère,* 152–168.

118. Shafiq, *Lamha,* 48–49; *Brief Survey,* 41–42.

119. Shafiq, *Lamha,* 83; *Brief Survey,* 73.

120. Maddy-Weitzman, *Berber Identity,* 117–119, 131–139.

121. Maddy-Weitzman, *Berber Identity,* 159.

122. "Le manifeste berbère," accessed September 6, 2021, http://www.mondeberbere .com/chafik_manifeste-berbere.html.

123. "Manifeste berbère."

124. "Manifeste berbère."

125. "Manifeste berbère."

126. "Manifeste berbère."

127. "Manifeste berbère."

128. "Présentation," accessed September 6, 2021, https://www.ircam.ma/?q=fr /node/620.

129. For the controversy that surrounded the choice of an official script for Amazigh, see Soulaimani, "Writing"; Maddy-Weitzman, *Berber Identity,* 167–172.

130. Secrétariat Général du Gouvernement, *La Constitution,* July 29, 2011, http://www.sgg.gov.ma/Portals/0/constitution/constitution_2011_Fr.pdf.

131. My description of the conference is based on the published proceedings, edited by Moha Ennaji under the title *Amazighité et Andalousie / al-Amazighiyya wa-l-Andalus* (Fez: Centre Sud Nord, 2015).

132. For an overview of Leila Mezian's activities through her foundation, see Aziz Sijilmassi Idrissi, "Visión sobre la Fundación Doctora Leila Mezian," in *La Granada zirí y el universo beréber* (Granada: Patronato de la Alhambra y Generalife, 2019), 237–239.

133. Moha Ennaji, introduction to *Amazighité et Andalousie: Droit d'Appartenance et Hospitalité* (Fez: Centre Sud Nord, 2015), 1. Ennaji's introduction appears in French and Arabic in the published proceedings. My quotations are my translations of the French text, though the two texts are very similar.

134. For an introduction to Meddeb's work, see Hoda El Shakry, "Abdelwahab Meddeb and the Po / Ethics of Sufism," *Expressions maghrébines* 16, no. 2 (2017): 95–119, https://doi.org/10.1353/exp.2017.0021; Yasser Elhariry, *Pacifist Invasions: Arabic, Translation, and the Postfrancophone Lyric* (Liverpool: Liverpool University Press, 2017), 8–11, 134–151.

135. Abdelwahab Meddeb, "Berbérité d'al-Andalus," in Ennaji, *Amazighité et Andalousie,* 16.

136. Meddeb, "Berbérité," 16.

137. Meddeb, "Berbérité," 18.

138. Meddeb, "Berbérité," 18–19.

139. Meddeb, "Berbérité," 20.

140. Meddeb, "Berbérité," 20.

141. Meddeb, "Berbérité," 20.

142. See María Rosa Menocal, *The Ornament of the World: How Muslims, Jews, and Christians Created a Culture of Tolerance in Medieval Spain* (New York: Back Bay Books).

143. Meddeb, "Berbérité," 20.

144. Meddeb, "Berbérité," 20.

145. For instance, Ennaji, in his introduction to the conference proceedings, highlights the role Amazigh culture has played in "the strengthening of cultural exchanges and of coexistence." Ennaji, "Introduction," 1.

146. Meddeb, "Berbérité," 21–22.

147. Meddeb, "Berbérité," 22.

148. I have taken this quote from the brochure that was available at the entrance to the exhibit.

3. The Feminist al-Andalus

1. This quote and my description of the site come from a visit I made to the school on September 14, 2019. During my visit, I interviewed two teachers who have worked at the school for several decades. I would also like to thank Mohammed Gallab, who sent me additional information about the school, based on his conversations with a former employee.

2. Guadalupe Saiz Muñoz, "La escritora Janāṭa Bennūna (Apunte biográfico y aproximación a su obra narrativa)," *Miscelánea de estudios árabes y hebraicos* 37, no. 1 (1988): 241–257; Guadalupe Saiz Muñoz, "Šurūq, primera revista femenina en Marruecos," in *Homenaje al Profesor Jacinto Bosch Vilá* (Granada: [Universidad de Granada?], 1991), 2:811–822; Ana González Navarro and Gonzalo Fernández Parrilla, "From Khanata Bennouna to Leila Slimani: Moroccan Women Writers from the Margins to World Literature," in *Dialogic Configurations in Post-Colonial Morocco*, ed. Najib Mokhtari (Rabat: Université Internationale de Rabat, 2019), 291–308.

3. My description of the mural project is based primarily on Ms. Saffaa's Instagram account, where the artist documented each stage of the making of the mural and its launch in December 2016. I have also incorporated information from my emails and phone conversations with Ms. Saffaa and Molly Crabapple. I'm grateful to both artists for their assistance.

4. For the guardianship laws, see Human Rights Watch, "Boxed In: Women and Saudi Arabia's Male Guardianship System," July 16, 2020, https://www.hrw .org/report/2016/07/16/boxed/women-and-saudi-arabias-male-guardianship -system#.

5. This poem is preserved in Ahmad b. Muhammad al-Maqqari, *Nafh al-tib min ghusn al-Andalus al-ratib*, ed. Ihsan 'Abbas (Beirut: Dar Sadir, 2004), 4:205. The English translation is mine, though there are similar translations of the poem in María J. Viguera, "Aṣluhu li'l-maʿālī: On the Social Status of Andalusī Women," in *The Legacy of Muslim Spain*, ed. Salma Khadra Jayyusi (Leiden: Brill, 1992), 709; Asma Afsaruddin, "Poetry and Love: The Feminine Contribution in Muslim Spain," *Islamic Studies* 30, no. 1–2 (1991): 160.

6. Al-Maqqari, *Nafh al-tib*, 4:205.

7. See, for instance, Afsaruddin, "Poetry and Love," 159–160; Viguera, "Aṣluhu," 709; Nada Mourtada-Sabbah and Adrian Gully, "'I Am, by God, Fit for High Positions': On the Political Role of Women in al-Andalus," *British Journal of Middle Eastern Studies* 30, no. 2 (2003): 183–184, https://doi.org/10.1080/1353019032000126527.

8. Since the 2016 launch of "I Am My Own Guardian," the portrait of the young woman with the quotation by Wallada has become a mainstay in Ms. Saffaa's visual vocabulary and has figured prominently in many of the artist's works.

9. Lila Abu-Lughod, "Introduction: Feminist Longings and Postcolonial Conditions," in *Remaking Women: Feminism and Modernity in the Middle East*, ed.

Lila Abu-Lughod (Princeton, NJ: Princeton University Press), 22–23. I am also guided here by Marilyn Booth's illuminating studies of feminism in Egypt at the turn of the twentieth century. See Marilyn Booth, *May Her Likes Be Multiplied: Biography and Gender Politics in Egypt* (Berkeley: University of California Press, 2001), esp. pp. xx–xxxviii; Marilyn Booth, *Classes of Ladies of Cloistered Spaces: Writing Feminist History through Biography in Fin-de-Siècle Egypt* (Edinburgh: Edinburgh University Press, 2015).

10. Lila Abu-Lughod has insightfully analyzed how debates about feminism in the Middle East have become enmeshed with debates about cultural authenticity. See Abu-Lughod, "The Marriage of Feminism and Islamism in Egypt: Selective Repudiation as a Dynamic of Postcolonial Cultural Politics," in Abu-Lughod, *Remaking Women,* 243–269; Abu-Lughod, "Introduction," 14–15.

11. Lila Abu-Lughod, *Do Muslim Women Need Saving?* (Cambridge, MA: Harvard University Press, 2013).

12. Leila Ahmed, *Women and Gender in Islam: Historical Roots of a Modern Debate* (New Haven, CT: Yale University Press, 1992), 167, https://www.jstor.org/stable/j.ctt32bg61.

13. See, for example, Elora Shehabuddin, "Gender and the Figure of the 'Moderate Muslim': Feminism in the Twenty-First Century," in *The Question of Gender: Joan W. Scott's Critical Feminism,* ed. Judith Butler and Elizabeth Weed (Bloomington: Indiana University Press, 2011), 102–142; Abu-Lughod, "Introduction"; Abu-Lughod, *Muslim Women;* Booth, *Classes of Ladies,* 4–30.

14. Some of the scholars who have taken up this question in recent decades include Manuela Marín, *Mujeres en al-Ándalus* (Madrid: Consejo Superior de Investigaciones Científicas, 2000); Viguera, "*Aṣluḥu*"; Mª Luisa Ávila, "Las mujeres 'sabias' en al-Andalus," in *La mujer en al-Andalus: Reflejos históricos de su actividad y categorías sociales,* ed. María J. Viguera (Madrid: Ediciones de la Universidad Autónoma, 1989), 139–184; Kamila Shamsie, "Librarians, Rebels, Property Owners, Slaves: Women in al-Andalus," *Journal of Postcolonial Writing* 52, no. 2 (2016): 178–188, https://doi.org/10.1080/17449855.2016.1164968; Mourtada-Sabbah and Gully, "I Am"; Civantos, *Afterlife of al-Andalus,* 236–239.

15. Marín, *Mujeres en al-Ándalus,* 11–18; Viguera, "*Aṣluḥu,*" 711–713; Mourtada-Sabbah and Gully, "I Am," 183–186.

16. Henri Pérès, *La poésie andalouse en arabe classique au XIe siècle: Ses aspects généraux et sa valeur documentaire* (Paris: Adrien-Maisonneuve, 1937), 398.

17. See Ahmed, *Women and Gender,* 150–168; Shehabuddin, "Gender"; Abu-Lughod, *Muslim Women.*

18. Marín, *Mujeres en al-Ándalus,* 221–222.

19. Marín, *Mujeres en al-Ándalus,* 28–30; Viguera, "*Aṣluḥu,*" 715; Ávila, "Mujeres," 147; Mourtada-Sabbah and Gully, "I Am," 184.

20. Shamsie, "Librarians," 178. Civantos makes a similar point in *Afterlife of al-Andalus,* 239.

21. I echo, here, Foucault's famous description of his methodology in *Discipline and Punish*, 31.

22. I draw here on Saidiya Hartman's work on "critical fabulation" in Hartman, "Venus in Two Acts," *Small Axe* 12, no. 2 (2008): 1–14, https://muse.jhu.edu /article/241115. Hartman develops "critical fabulation" as a method for telling stories that were silenced by the violence of slavery. Although the forms of violence (and of silence) that I study here are not the products of slavery, I want to take up Hartman's invitation to use "critical fabulation" as a productive way of engaging with the problem of narrating experiences that are lost or silenced.

23. See, in particular, Booth, *Classes of Ladies*; Marilyn Booth, "Before Qasim Amin: Writing Women's History in 1890s Egypt," in *The Long 1890s in Egypt: Colonial Quiescence, Subterranean Resistance*, ed. Marilyn Booth and Anthony Gorman (Edinburgh: Edinburgh University Press, 2014), 356–398.

24. Booth, *Classes of Ladies*, 3.

25. A complete list of Fawwaz's subjects is in Booth, *Classes of Ladies*, 346–366.

26. Booth, *Classes of Ladies*, 90; Booth, *May Her Likes*, 14.

27. Zaynab Fawwaz, *al-Durr al-manthur fi tabaqat rabbat al-khudur*, ed. Muhammad Amin Dinnawi (Beirut: Dar al-Kutub al-ʿIlmiyya, 1999), 1:172–173, 290–295; 2:64, 417–421.

28. Booth, *Classes of Ladies*, 139.

29. I build here on Booth's insights about Fawwaz's productive reframing of material from earlier sources. See Booth, *Classes of Ladies*, 3.

30. Fawwaz, *al-Durr*, 2:417. Fawwaz takes this description from al-Maqqari, *Nafh al-tib*, 4:205, 207. Al-Maqqari attributes the second sentence to Ibn Bashkwal's *Kitab al-sila* (ca. 1139).

31. For the diverse meanings of *adab*, especially in the context of the nineteenth century, see Catherine Mayeur-Jaouen, introduction to *Adab and Modernity: A 'Civilising Process'? (Sixteenth-Twenty-First Century)*, ed. Catherine Mayeur-Jaouen (Leiden: Brill, 2020), 1–45, https://doi.org/10.1163/9789004415997; Michael Allan, *In the Shadow of World Literature: Sites of Reading in Colonial Egypt* (Princeton, NJ: Princeton University Press, 2016), 6, 76–77, 81–85, http://www.jstor.org/stable/j .cttlqlxshm; Booth, *Classes of Ladies*, 91–92.

32. See, for instance, Fawwaz's entry on ʿAʾisha bint Ahmad, in *al-Durr*, 2:64.

33. Fawwaz, *al-Durr*, 2:417. Fawwaz draws from al-Maqqari, *Nafh al-tib*, 4:208.

34. On the irony or tension embedded in Fawwaz's title, see Booth, *Classes of Ladies*, 92–95; Booth, *May Her Likes*, 34.

35. Fawwaz, *al-Durr*, 2:371. I thank Suzanne Pinckney Stetkevych for her advice about how to translate the term *al-maʿānī*.

36. Fawwaz, *al-Durr*, 2:418.

37. Fawwaz, *al-Durr*, 2:417; Booth, *Classes of Ladies*, 116. Fawwaz takes the comparison between Wallada and ʿUlayya from al-Maqqari, *Nafh al-tib*, 4:208. Al-Maqqari, in turn, takes it from Ibn Saʿid (d. 1286).

38. Fawwaz, *al-Durr*, 1:297. Fawwaz takes this description from al-Maqqari, *Nafh al-tib*, 4:287.

39. I quote here from Booth's lovely translation of the passage in *Classes of Ladies*, 115. The original passage is in Fawwaz, *al-Durr*, 2:82.

40. Booth, *May Her Likes*.

41. Booth, *May Her Likes*, 1–4.

42. Booth, *May Her Likes*, 28–31.

43. Warda al-Yaziji, "Shahirat al-nisa'," *Fatat al-sharq*, March 1916, 201. Al-Yaziji's essay is also discussed in Booth, *May Her Likes*, 96–98.

44. Al-Yaziji, "Shahirat al-nisa'," 201–202. To date Hassana al-Tamimiyya and Umm al-Saʿd bint ʿIsam al-Humayri, I have relied on Teresa Garulo, *Diwan de las poetisas de al-Andalus* (Madrid: Hiperión, 1986), 90–94, 135–137; al-Maqqari, *Nafh al-tib*, 4:166–170.

45. Al-Yaziji refers to her source as "the author of *Nafh al-tib*." Al-Yaziji, "Shahirat al-nisa'," 201.

46. Al-Yaziji, "Shahirat al-nisa'," 203. Al-Yaziji attributes this description to "Ibn Hassan," a typo for the Andalusi historian Ibn Hayyan (d. 1076). The same description appears, almost verbatim, in Fawwaz, *al-Durr*, 2:64. Al-Yaziji and Fawwaz take this description from al-Maqqari, *Nafh al-tib*, 4:290. Al-Maqqari, in turn, takes it from Ibn Hayyan.

47. Al-Yaziji, "Shahirat al-nisa'," 203–204. Parts of this passage are translated in Booth, *May Her Likes*, 96–97.

48. "Shahirat al-nisa': Sabiha, malikat al-Andalus," *Fatat al-sharq*, May 1916, 281–285. This article is discussed briefly in Booth, *May Her Likes*, 212–213.

49. For the spellings of Subh's name, see Fatima Mernissi, *Sultanes oubliées: Femmes chefs d'État en Islam* (Paris: Albin Michel, 1990), 65.

50. "Shahirat al-nisa'," 281.

51. "Shahirat al-nisa'," 284.

52. "Shahirat al-nisa'," 281.

53. Manuela Marín, "Ṣubḥ," in *Encyclopedia of Islam*, 2nd ed., ed. P. Bearman et al., accessed September 5, 2021, https://doi.org/10.1163/1573-3912_islam_SIM _7111. I also discuss the issue of Subh's Arabness in Chapter 1.

54. "Shahirat al-nisa'," 281.

55. "Shahirat al-nisa'," 282.

56. Booth, *May Her Likes*, 28.

57. For another example of this trend, see Booth's discussion of an article published in the journal *al-Hisan* in 1926. Booth, *May Her Likes*, 213.

58. I build here on my brief discussion of al-Haffar al-Kuzbari in Chapter 1. For her biography, see Fernando de Ágreda Burillo, "Salma Al-Haffar Al-Kuzbari," *Anaquel de Estudios Árabes* 18 (2007): 254–257; Pedro Martínez Montávez, *Al-Andalus, España, en la literatura árabe contemporánea* (Málaga: Arguval, 1992), 227–229; Clara María Thomas, "Cuatro narradoras sirias destacadas," in *Actas de las I*

Jornadas de Literatura Árabe Moderna y Contemporánea (Madrid: Universidad Autónoma de Madrid, 1991), 350–352.

59. From this period also date al-Haffar al-Kuzbari's novel *'Aynan min Ishbiliya* (ca. 1965) and her poem "Flamenco" (1962), in *Vent d'Hier* (Paris: Les Paragraphes Littéraires de Paris, 1966), 13–15.

60. Eric Calderwood, *Colonial al-Andalus: Spain and the Making of Modern Moroccan Culture* (Cambridge: Belknap Press of Harvard University Press, 2018), 167–207.

61. *Crónica de la Fiesta Mundial de la Poesía Árabe y IX Centenario de Aben Hazam* (Córdoba: Ayuntamiento de Córdoba, 1963); Martínez Montávez, *Al-Andalus,* 149–171; William Granara, "*Extensio Animae:* The Artful Ways of Remembering 'Al-Andalus,'" *Journal of Social Affairs* 19, no. 75 (2002): 54–58.

62. Salma Haffar de Kuzbari, *Influencia de la mujer árabe en nuestra historia y en nuestra literatura* (Madrid: Ateneo, 1963); al-Haffar al-Kuzbari, *Fi zilal al-Andalus,* 99–130.

63. Haffar de Kuzbari, *Influencia,* 3.

64. Haffar de Kuzbari, *Influencia,* 6–20.

65. Haffar de Kuzbari, *Influencia,* 15.

66. Haffar de Kuzbari, *Influencia,* 16–17.

67. Haffar de Kuzbari, *Influencia,* 17.

68. Haffar de Kuzbari, *Influencia,* 18.

69. Haffar de Kuzbari, *Influencia,* 18.

70. Haffar de Kuzbari, *Influencia,* 17.

71. Ágreda Burillo, "Salma Al-Haffar Al-Kuzbari"; Salma al-Haffar al-Kuzbari, *Basamat 'arabiyya wa-dimashqiyya fi al-Andalus* (Damascus: Manshurat Wizarat al-Thaqafa, 1993).

72. Al-Haffar al-Kuzbari, *Fi zilal al-Andalus,* 76.

73. Al-Haffar al-Kuzbari, *Fi zilal al-Andalus,* 76–77.

74. For more on this idea, see Booth, *Classes of Ladies,* 4–5; Ahmed, *Women and Gender,* 150–152.

75. I discuss the origins and political resonance of the adjective "Hispano-Arab" in Calderwood, *Colonial al-Andalus,* 167–207.

76. A notable example is that of Syrian author Qamar Kilani (1932–2011), whose *Awraq musafira* is a lyrical account of the author's journey to Spain. Kilani suffuses the narrative with allusions to the Arab influences on Spanish culture. She also includes a chapter titled "The Literary Women [*adībāt*] of al-Andalus." Kilani, *Awraq musafira* (Damascus: Dar al-Jalil, 1987), 117–119.

77. Mernissi, *Sultanes oubliées;* Fatima Mernissi, *The Forgotten Queens of Islam,* trans. Mary Jo Lakeland (Minneapolis: University of Minnesota Press, 1993). My quotations from this work come from Lakeland's English translation, unless otherwise noted. For all quotations, I also provide the pagination for the original French text.

78. Mernissi, *Forgotten Queens*, 1; Mernissi, *Sultanes oubliées*, 7.

79. Mernissi, *Forgotten Queens*, 2; Mernissi, *Sultanes oubliées*, 9.

80. Mernissi, *Forgotten Queens*, 9–16; Mernissi, *Sultanes oubliées*, 17–27.

81. Mernissi, *Sultanes oubliées*, 24. I have offered my own translation here because Lakeland's translation makes some important changes to the passage. Ibn Abi Zarʿ, who is quoted here, was an influential Maghribi chronicler who died after 1326.

82. A recent example of this trend is Farida Bourquia's 2014 biopic *Zaynab, zahrat Aghmat* (Zaynab, the rose of Aghmat), which I discuss in Eric Calderwood, "El mito de al-Ándalus en el mundo mediterráneo moderno," in *Paradigma Alhambra: Variación del mito de Al Ándalus*, ed. José A. González Alcantud (Granada: Universidad de Granada, 2018), 156–158. For debates about the social status of women during the Almoravid period, see Amira K. Bennison, *The Almoravid and Almohad Empires* (Edinburgh: Edinburgh University Press, 2016), 154–164.

83. Mernissi, *Forgotten Queens*, 14–16; Mernissi, *Sultanes oubliées*, 24–27. Marín offers a helpful discussion of the term *ḥurra* (pl. *harāʾir*) in Marín, *Mujeres en al-Ándalus*, 41–45.

84. Mernissi, *Forgotten Queens*, 16–17; Mernissi, *Sultanes oubliées*, 27–29.

85. Mernissi, *Forgotten Queens*, 16; Mernissi, *Sultanes oubliées*, 27.

86. Mernissi, *Forgotten Queens*, 17; Mernissi, *Sultanes oubliées*, 28.

87. Mernissi, *Sultanes oubliées*, 29. I have offered my own translation of this passage because Lakeland's translation makes significant alterations to the original.

88. For an introduction to this figure, see Guillermo Gozalbes Busto, *Al-Mandari, el granadino fundador de Tetuán*, 2nd ed. (Granada: T.G. Arte, 1993), 174–182.

89. For more examples of this phenomenon, see Calderwood, *Colonial al-Andalus*; José Antonio González Alcantud, "Los andalusíes hoy: Una elite viva frente al pasado futuro de al-Ándalus," in *Andalusíes: Antropología e historia cultural de una elite magrebí*, ed. José Antonio González Alcantud and Sandra Rojo Flores (Madrid: Abada, 2015), 15–57.

90. This blog was described as one of the "main information gateways for the Tunisian blogosphere" in Philip N. Howard and Muzammil M. Hussain, *Democracy's Fourth Wave? Digital Media and the Arab Spring* (Oxford: Oxford University Press, 2013), 129.

91. I am indebted here to Saddik Gohar's scholarship, which introduced me to Ghabish's work. Although Gohar and I focus on different elements of Ghabish's work, we converge in our assessment that Ghabish uses the heritage of al-Andalus to address contemporary political issues. On this point, Gohar writes that Ghabish's collection "reconstructs Andalusian mythology as a metaphor for contemporary reality in the Arab world calling for revolution and reform." Saddik Gohar, "Engaging Ancient Islamic Traditions in the Poetry of Saleha Ghabesh,"

Journal of International Women's Studies 12, no. 3 (2011): 139, http://vc.bridgew.edu /jiws/vol12/iss3/9. See also Saddik M. Gohar, "Toward a Revolutionary Emirati Poetics: Ghabesh's *Beman Ya Buthayn Taluthin?*," *Nebula* 5, no. 1–2 (2008): 74–87.

92. Saliha ʿUbayd Ghabish, *Bi-man ya Buthayn taludhin?* (Sharjah: Isdarat Daʾirat al-Thaqafa wa-l-ʿIlam, 2002), 5. I thank Wijdan Alsayegh and Issam Eido for their valuable feedback on my English translations of Ghabish's work.

93. Al-Maqqari, *Nafh al-tib*, 4:284–285.

94. Ghabish, *Bi-man*, 7.

95. Ghabish, *Bi-man*, 8–9. The poem is also in al-Maqqari, *Nafh al-tib*, 4:284.

96. Gohar strikes a similar note when he highlights Ghabish's "technique of adaptation . . . which includes recollection, rephrasing, and re-writing of ancient heritage and Andalusian legacies to fulfill contemporary purposes." Gohar, "Engaging Ancient Islamic Traditions," 135.

97. Al-Maqqari, *Nafh al-tib*, 4:284.

98. Ghabish, *Bi-man*, 19–20.

99. Ghabish, *Bi-man*, 56, 59.

100. Alexander E. Elinson, *Looking Back at al-Andalus: The Poetics of Loss and Nostalgia in Medieval Arabic and Hebrew Literature* (Leiden: Brill, 2015), 1; Rachel Arié, "Boabdil, sultan nasride de Grenade: Le personnage historique et la figure littéraire," in *Aspects de l'Espagne musulmane: Histoire et culture* (Paris: De Boccard, 1997), 94.

101. The line is reproduced in many sources, including Arié, "Boabdil," 94; María Rosa Menocal, *The Ornament of the World: How Muslims, Jews, and Christians Created a Culture of Tolerance in Medieval Spain* (New York: Back Bay Books), 245–246.

102. Arié, "Boabdil"; Civantos, *Afterlife of al-Andalus*, 165–205.

103. Ghabish, *Bi-man*, 49.

104. Ghabish, *Bi-man*, 51.

105. Quoted in al-Maqqari, *Nafh al-tib*, 7:11. I discuss various modern performances of Ibn al-Khatib's poem in Chapters 1 and 5.

106. Ghabish, *Bi-man*, 51.

107. Ghabish, *Bi-man*, 29, my italics.

108. Ghabish, *Bi-man*, 41–42.

109. For an introduction to this story and its Arabic sources, see Richard Serrano, "Jamīl Buthayna (7th c.) in the *Book of Songs* (10th c.): Man Out of Poetry," in *Reexamining World Literature: Challenging Current Assumptions and Envisioning Possibilities*, e-book (Taylor and Francis, 2020).

110. Ghabish, *Bi-man*, 40.

111. Quoted in "Saʿadat Saliha Ghabish," *Manarat*, https://www.youtube.com /watch?app=desktop&v=iBRHkFIVD6M.

112. The allusions to Buthayna Khidr Makki in Ghabish's collection are quite subtle, in large part because the identity of the title character, "Buthayna," remains

fluid and ambiguous throughout the collection. I would like to thank my colleague Wijdan Alsayegh for reaching out to Ghabish to ask about this aspect of her collection. Alsayegh learned from Ghabish that the first line of the poem "Fa-'asaka ya abati" is an allusion to Khidr Makki.

113. For example, Molly Crabapple's cover art for the zine *Al Andalus in New York* (New York: Hagop Kevorkian Center for Near Eastern Studies, 2019) features a poem by Wallada.

114. Civantos, *Afterlife of al-Andalus,* 236–265; Abderrahmane Bouali, ed., *Poemas marroquíes y al-Andalus* (Granada: Universidad de Granada, 2009), 60–67; Zeina Hashem Beck, *Louder than Hearts* (Peterborough: Bauhan, 2017), 62.

115. Quoted in JP Quiñonero, "Maram al-Masri," *ABC,* December 19, 2010, https://www.abc.es/internacional/maram-masri-primera-revuelta-201012190000 _noticia.html.

116. Maram al-Masri, *al-'Awda / El retorno,* trans. Rafael Ortega (Granada: Universidad de Granada, 2007), 7. My translations of al-Masri's work are from the Arabic text published in the 2007 edition.

117. Al-Masri, *al-'Awda,* 13.

118. Al-Masri, *al-'Awda,* 9. There appear to be typos in the last two lines of the Arabic text. In order to verify my translation of the text, I have also consulted the French edition of this poem, on which al-Masri collaborated. See Maram al-Masri, *Le retour de Wallada,* trans. Alain Gorius ([Neuilly?]: Al Manar, 2010), 22.

119. I discuss this novel in Chapter 1.

120. This comic is discussed in Allen Douglas and Fedwa Malti-Douglas, *Arab Comic Strips: Politics of an Emerging Mass Culture* (Bloomington: Indiana University Press, 1994), 143–149. I thank Luke Scalone for sending me scans of the comic from the Tunisian National Library.

121. For 'Ashur's biography, I have relied on Radwa Ashour, "Eyewitness, Scribe and Story Teller: My Experience as a Novelist," *Massachusetts Review* 41, no. 1 (2000): 85–92, https://www.jstor.org/stable/25091630; the author's biography in Radwa Ashour, *Granada,* trans. William Granara (Syracuse, NY: Syracuse University Press, 2003); and the obituaries published in 2014 in *The Guardian, Ahram Online,* and *El País.*

122. The first part of the trilogy was translated into English by William Granara as *Granada* (2003). The entire trilogy was translated into Spanish by María Luz Comendador and published as *Granada (Trilogía)* (Guadarrama: Ediciones del Oriente y del Mediterráneo, 2008). My English translations will come primarily from Granara's masterful translation, but I will, at times, make adjustments to his translations in order to highlight certain features of the Arabic text. For all quotations in English, I will give the page number in the original Arabic text, followed by the page number in Granara's translation.

123. My argument builds on the work of William Granara, "*A Room of One's Own:* The Modern Arabic Heroine between Career and Domesticity," in *Desire, Pleasure and the Taboo: New Voices and Freedom of Expression in Contemporary Arabic Literature,* ed. Sobhi Boustani et al. (Pisa: Fabrizio Serra, 2014), 3–11; Civantos, *Afterlife of al-Andalus,* 271–282; Caroline Seymour-Jorn, *Cultural Criticism in Egyptian Women's Writing* (Syracuse, NY: Syracuse University Press, 2011), 121–127, https://www.jstor.org/stable/j.ctt1j1w0bk. All of these scholars examine the role of 'Ashur's female protagonists in the struggle to preserve the cultural identity of Granada's Muslim community.

124. Radwa 'Ashur, *Thulathiyyat Gharnata,* 14th ed. (Cairo: Dar al-Shuruq, 2014), 9; Ashour, *Granada,* 2.

125. Ashour, "Eyewitness," 91.

126. 'Ashur, *Thulathiyyat Gharnata,* 31. I have made some small challenges to Granara's translation in Ashour, *Granada,* 25–26.

127. I am not the first scholar to note that 'Ashur's character Salima defies gender conventions through her pursuit of knowledge. For further reflections on this point, see Granara, "*Room of One's Own,*" 6; Civantos, *Afterlife of al-Andalus,* 272.

128. 'Ashur, *Thulathiyyat Gharnata,* 42. For a similar translation, see Ashour, *Granada,* 35.

129. Fawwaz, *al-Durr,* 2:64.

130. L. P. Harvey, *Islamic Spain: 1250 to 1500* (Chicago: University of Chicago Press, 1990), 333.

131. 'Ashur, *Thulathiyyat Gharnata,* 55; Ashour, *Granada,* 47–48.

132. 'Ashur, *Thulathiyyat Gharnata,* 151; Ashour, *Granada,* 141.

133. 'Ashur, *Thulathiyyat Gharnata,* 151; Ashour, *Granada,* 140.

134. 'Ashur, *Thulathiyyat Gharnata,* 123–124; Ashour, *Granada,* 115–116.

135. 'Ashur, *Thulathiyyat Gharnata,* 212; Ashour, *Granada,* 199.

136. 'Ashur, *Thulathiyyat Gharnata,* 311.

137. 'Ashur, *Thulathiyyat Gharnata,* 232; Ashour, *Granada,* 216.

138. 'Ashur, *Thulathiyyat Gharnata,* 232; Ashour, *Granada,* 216.

139. I build here on Granara's analysis of the same scene. Granara writes that, in the Inquisition scene, "The binaries of faith and reason, science and mythology, as traditionally drawn along gender lines, i.e. men are rational and women are emotional, are inverted, as the shrill and hysterical male seeks revenge on the rational, educated woman." Granara, "*Room of One's Own,*" 9.

140. 'Ashur, *Thulathiyyat Gharnata,* 241; Ashour, *Granada,* 224.

141. Civantos, *Afterlife of al-Andalus,* 274.

142. 'Ashur, *Thulathiyyat Gharnata,* 501–502.

143. Ashour, "Eyewitness," 90.

144. Ashour, "Eyewitness," 91.

145. Ashour, "Eyewitness," 91.

146. Ashour, "Eyewitness," 87–88.

4. The Palestinian al-Andalus

1. Yusuf al-'Isa, "Ya ukht Andalus, 'alayki salam," *Filastin,* November 5, 1932, 5, https://jrayed.org/en/newspapers/falastin/1932/11/05/01/article/10. The article's title is a quote from the first line of Ahmad Shawqi's poem "Al-Andalus al-jadida" (ca. 1913). I have accessed the article through Jrayed, the National Library of Israel's online archive of Arabic periodicals from Ottoman and Mandate Palestine.

2. For the 'Isa cousins and their newspaper *Filastin,* see Ami Ayalon, *Reading Palestine: Printing and Literacy, 1900–1948* (Austin: University of Texas Press, 2004), 58–64.

3. Al-'Isa, "Ya ukht Andalus," 5.

4. The earliest example I have found is an article titled "Al-Andalus wa-Filastin," published on November 16, 1921.

5. "Al-Andalus al-thaniyya" (The second al-Andalus) is the title of an article published in *Mir'at al-sharq* on February, 12, 1930, and of an article published in *al-Difa'* on December 5, 1934. "Al-Andalus al-jadida" (The new al-Andalus) was the title of a poem that 'Abd al-Razzaq al-Nasiri published in *al-Difa'* on June 19, 1936. There are several more examples of this theme in the newspapers in the Jrayed archive.

6. 'Abd al-Ghani al-Karmi,. "Nurid al-yawm adaban qawmiyyan 'anifan: Man yandab al-Andalus al-thaniyya 'amma qarib?," *Filastin,* December, 30, 1934, 5, https://jrayed.org/en/newspapers/falastin/1934/12/30/01/article/5. The italicized text is al-Karmi's quotation of al-Rundi's elegy for Seville (ca. 1248). My translation of the lines from al-Rundi's poem is a revised version of the translation that appears in James T. Monroe, *Hispano-Arabic Poetry: A Student Anthology* (Berkeley: University of California Press, 1974), 332.

7. Al-Rundi's elegy appears in Ahmad b. Muhammad al-Maqqari, *Nafh al-tib min ghusn al-Andalus al-ratib,* ed. Ihsan 'Abbas (Beirut: Dar Sadir, 2004), 4:486–488. It is a famous example of the city elegy genre, studied in Alexander E. Elinson, *Looking Back at al-Andalus: The Poetics of Loss and Nostalgia in Medieval Arabic and Hebrew Literature* (Leiden: Brill, 2015).

8. The two poems are "Filastin al-damiyya" (Bleeding Palestine, 1929) and "Filastin wa-l-Andalus" (1948), published in Muhammad Mahdi al-Jawahiri, *Diwan al-Jawahiri,* ed. Ibrahim al-Samarra'i et al. (Baghdad: Matba'at al-Adib, 1973–1977), 1:473; 3:315.

9. Al-'Abbushi later published the poem in *Jabal al-nar* (Baghdad: al-Sharika al-Islamiyya li-l-Tiba'a wa-l-Nashr, 1956), 16–19. In a footnote, he explained that he recited the poem at the event in Haifa in 1945.

10. For the symbolism of the *ghurāb* (crow or raven) in Arabic poetry, see James T. Monroe, "*Zajal* and *Muwashshaha:* Hispano-Arabic Poetry and the Romance Tradition," in *The Legacy of Muslim Spain,* ed. Salma Khadra Jayyusi (Leiden: Brill, 1992), 403.

11. Muhammad ʿAbd Allah al-Juʿaydi, *Aʿindakum nabaʾ: Istidʿaʾ al-Andalus fi al-adab al-filastini al-hadith* (Beirut: Dar al-Hadi li-l-Tibaʿa wa-l-Nashr, 2002), 163.

12. Al-Juʿaydi's book is the most detailed study of the invocations of al-Andalus in Palestinian literature, but the topic has also been addressed in other works, including Pedro Martínez Montávez, *Al-Andalus, España, en la literatura árabe contemporánea* (Málaga: Arguval, 1992), 134–137, 254–259; Reuven Snir, "'Al-Andalus Arising from Damascus': Al-Andalus in Modern Arabic Poetry," in *Charting Memory: Recalling Medieval Spain,* ed. Stacy N. Beckwith (New York: Garland, 2000), 277–286; Abdul-Rahim al-Shaikh, "The Political Darwīsh: '. . . In Defense of Little Differences,'" *Journal of Arabic Literature* 48 (2017): 105–111, https://doi.org/10.1163/1570064x-12341339.

13. Quoted in Patrice Barrat, "Mahmoud Darwich poète de la blessure palestinienne," *Le Monde,* January 10, 1983.

14. I draw inspiration here from Elinson's work on the poetics of nostalgia in *Looking Back.*

15. Burhan al-Din al-ʿAbbushi, *Shabah al-Andalus* (Damascus: Dar Muʾassasa Filastin li-l-Thaqafa, 2006), 26.

16. Al-ʿAbbushi, *Shabah al-Andalus,* 29–30.

17. The play that al-ʿAbbushi mentions here might be *Khuruj al-ʿarab min al-Andalus* (1936), which is cited in Mubarak al-Khatir, *al-Masrah al-tarikihi fi al-Bahrayn: Muqaddima wa-namudhaj, 1925–1953* (Bahrain: Wizarat al-Iʿlam, 1985), 177. But it could also be one of the many historical plays about al-Andalus that were staged in Palestine during the Mandate period. Among those plays were *ʿAbd al-Rahman al-Dakhil* (1924) and *Malik al-ʿarab fi al-Andalus* (1925), both written by Muhammad ʿIzzat Darwaza for the student theater troupe at the Najah School in Nablus, where al-ʿAbbushi was a student. See Nasri al-Jawzi, *Tarikh al-masrah al-filastini, 1918–1948* (Nicosia: Sharq Press, 1990), 14–15, 102.

18. For more on the politics of al-Jayyusi's first collection, see the poet's interview with Razmig Bedirian, "The Fascinating Life of Poet Salma Khadra Jayyusi," *The National,* April 16, 2020, https://www.thenationalnews.com/arts-culture/books/the-fascinating-life-of-palestinian-poet-salma-khadra-jayyusi-my-poems-are-about-being-human-1.1006785.

19. The poet mentions the circumstances in which she wrote the poem in an epigraph. Salma al-Khadraʾ al-Jayyusi, *al-ʿAwda min al-nabʿ al-halim* (Beirut: Dar al-Adab, 1960), 16.

20. Al-Jayyusi, *al-ʿAwda,* 16–17. I thank Jaafar Ben El Haj Soulami, Luke Leafgren, and Wijdan Alsayegh for their input on my translation of this poem.

21. Al-Jayyusi, *al-ʿAwda,* 20.

22. Similar themes can be found in the poems that Ahmad Shawqi and Muhammad Iqbal wrote about the Mosque of Cordoba in the early twentieth century. For discussions of these poems, see Martínez Montávez, *Al-Andalus,* 47–48;

Snir, "Al-Andalus," 266–269; Amina Yaqin, "*La convivencia, la mezquita* and al-Andalus: An Iqbalian Vision," *Journal of Postcolonial Writing* 52, no. 2 (2016): 136–152, https://doi.org/10.1080/17449855.2016.1164972.

23. Al-Jayyusi, *al-'Awda*, 23–24.

24. See, for instance, the use of the same word in the poem that al-Jayyusi dedicates "to the Arab *fidā'ī*," in *al-'Awda*, 56.

25. Al-Jayyusi, *al-'Awda*, 25–27.

26. Salma Khadra Jayyusi, ed., *Anthology of Modern Palestinian Literature* (New York: Columbia University Press, 1992), 265.

27. Jayyusi, *Anthology*, 265.

28. Tahera Qutbuddin translates and analyzes Tariq's speech in *Arabic Oration: Art and Function* (Leiden: Brill, 2019), 327–332. I discuss the debates surrounding the authenticity of Tariq's speech in Chapter 2.

29. Quoted in Qutbuddin, *Arabic Oration*, 328.

30. Harun Hashim Rashid, *Safinat al-ghadab* (Kuwait: Maktabat al-Amal, 1968), 108–109. All ellipses are in the original Arabic.

31. Rashid, *Safinat al-ghadab*, 110–111.

32. Rashid, *Safinat al-ghadab*, 113–116.

33. For an example, see Elinson, *Looking Back*, 45–47.

34. For several allusions to al-Andalus in the work of the writers listed here, see al-Ju'aydi, *A'indakum naba'*, 87, 91, 163–164, 167–169, 209–215, 227–228, 247–254, 288–296, 312, 316; Martínez Montávez, *Al-Andalus*, 254–259; Snir, "Al-Andalus," 271–272, 277–286; al-Shaikh, "Political Darwīsh," 105–111; Najat Rahman, "Threatened Longing and Perpetual Search: The Writing of Home in the Poetry of Mahmoud Darwish," in *Mahmoud Darwish: Exile's Poet*, ed. Hala Khamis Nassar and Najat Rahman (Northampton, MA: Olive Branch Press, 2008), 48–53; Jeffery Sacks, *Iterations of Loss: Mutilation and Aesthetic Form, al-Shidyaq to Darwish* (Fordham University Press, 2015), 31–43, 68, https://doi.org/10.2307/j.ctt130h9gq.

35. Salma Khadra Jayyusi, "Foreword: Mahmoud Darwish's Mission and Place in Arab Literary History," in Nassar and Rahman, *Mahmoud Darwish*, viii, xi.

36. For Darwish's biography, I have relied primarily on Khaled Mattawa, *Mahmoud Darwish: The Poet's Art and His Nation* (Syracuse, NY: Syracuse University Press, 2014); Nassar and Rahman, introduction to *Mahmoud Darwish*, 1–10.

37. Darwish recounts this part of his childhood in his first memoir, *Yawmiyyat al-huzn al-'adi*, 2nd ed. (Beirut: Dar al-'Awda, 1978), 36–39; *Journal of an Ordinary Grief*, trans. Ibrahim Muhawi (Brooklyn: Archipelago Books, 2010), 11–14.

38. Darwish, *Yawmiyyat*, 38; Mattawa, *Mahmoud Darwish*, 14; Ilan Pappe, *A History of Modern Palestine*, 2nd ed. (Cambridge: Cambridge University Press, 2006), 157.

39. For an overview of Darwish's work from the 1960s, see Mattawa, *Mahmoud Darwish*, 3–61.

40. Mattawa, *Mahmoud Darwish,* 15, 24, 65; Ilan Pappé, *The Forgotten Palestinians: A History of the Palestinians in Israel* (New Haven, CT: Yale University Press, 2011), 125, http://www.jstor.org/stable/j.ctt1nphsk.

41. Mattawa, *Mahmoud Darwish,* 15, 71–93; Pappé, *Forgotten Palestinians,* 125.

42. Mahmud Darwish, *Uhibbuki . . . aw la uhibbuki* (Beirut: Dar al-Adab, 1972), 56–57. The English translation is mine, though I have drawn heavily on the published translations in Snir, "Al-Andalus," 281–282; Mahmoud Darwish, *The Music of Human Flesh,* trans. Denys Johnson-Davies (London: Heinemann, 1980), 50.

43. For al-Andalus as "the lost paradise," see Eric Calderwood, *Colonial al-Andalus: Spain and the Making of Modern Moroccan Culture* (Cambridge: Belknap Press of Harvard University Press, 2018), 266–285; Justin Stearns, "Representing and Remembering al-Andalus: Some Historical Considerations regarding the End of Time and the Making of Nostalgia," *Medieval Encounters* 15 (2009): 355–374, https://doi.org/10.1163/157006709X458891; Jonathan Glasser, *The Lost Paradise: Andalusi Music in Urban North Africa* (Chicago: University of Chicago Press, 2016), 3–16; Nieves Paradela, *El otro laberinto español: Viajeros árabes a España entre el siglo XVII y 1936* (Madrid: Siglo XXI, 2005), 135–145.

44. Darwish, *Yawmiyyat,* 33–34. The English translation is my revision of Muhawi's translation in Darwish, *Journal,* 8–9. There are brief discussions of the same passage in al-Shaikh, "Political Darwish," 108–109; Sacks, *Iterations of Loss,* 31.

45. Najat Rahman advances similar ideas in her analysis of Darwish's poem, "Aqbiya, Andalusiyya, Sahra'" (1986). In that poem, as Rahman notes, al-Andalus "is invoked not as 'the lost paradise,' but rather as the future promise and a point of intersection." Rahman, "Threatened Longing," 49.

46. In addition to the examples I consider here, see also the allusions to al-Andalus in Mahmud Darwish, *Madih al-zill al-'ali,* 2nd ed. (Beirut: Dar al-'Awda, 1984), 53–54, 94; Mahmud Darwish, *Hisar li-mada'ih al-bahr* (Amman: al-Dar al-'Arabiyya li-l-Nashr wa-l-Tawzi', 1986), 89, 93–94, 112–114.

47. Quoted in Barrat, "Mahmoud Darwich."

48. Aristotle, *Poetics,* trans. Richard Janko, in *The Norton Anthology of Theory and Criticism,* ed. Vincent B. Leitch et al., 2nd ed. (New York: Norton, 2010), 95. I build here on ideas that I first piloted in *Colonial al-Andalus,* 74–75.

49. Mahmud Darwish, *Ward aqall* (Casablanca: Dar Tuqbal li-l-Nashr, 1986), 9. My English translation draws inspiration from the existing translations in Mahmoud Darwish, *Unfortunately, It Was Paradise,* trans. and ed. Munir Akash and Carolyn Forché (Berkeley: University of California Press, 2013), 5; Mahmud Darwish, *Menos rosas,* trans. María Luisa Prieto, 4th ed. (Madrid: Hiperión, 2010), 21.

50. *The Qur'an,* trans. M.A.S. Abdel Haleem (Oxford: Oxford University Press, 2004), 145.

51. Darwish, *Ward aqall,* 77. I thank Ahmad Diab for bringing this poem to my attention. The poem is also discussed in al-Shaikh, "Political Darwish," 110–111.

52. Mahmud Darwish, *Ahad 'ashar kawkaban* (Beirut: Dar al-Jadid, 1992), 9–10. The ellipses are in the original Arabic. Clarissa Burt published an English transla-

tion of the entire suite of "Eleven Stars" in Mahmoud Darwish, *The Adam of Two Edens,* ed. Munir Akash and Daniel Moore (Syracuse, NY: Syracuse University Press, 2000), 149–170. I have decided to offer my own translations of the work because I disagree with some of the choices Burt made in her translation. I have erred on the side of literal translation because I feel that Burt's looser translation obscures some of the poem's allusions to al-Andalus. I would like to thank Alexander Elinson and Luke Leafgren for their input on my translation.

53. Mahmoud Darwich, *La Palestine comme métaphore: Entretiens,* trans. Elias Sanbar and Simone Bitton (N.p.: Actes Sud, 1997), 118.

54. Darwish, *Ahad 'ashar kawkaban,* 29–31.

55. See, for instance, Darwish's allusion to "the song of the Gypsies going to al-Andalus" in *Hisar,* 23.

56. Darwish, *Ahad 'ashar kawkaban*, 33-51. See also al-Shaikh, "Political Darwish," 105–108.

57. Darwish, *Ahad 'ashar kawkaban,* 23–24. The ellipses are in the original Arabic.

58. Elinson, *Looking Back,* 15–49.

59. Darwish, *Ahad 'ashar kawkaban,* 12.

60. Darwish, *Ahad 'ashar kawkaban,* 24.

61. Darwish, *Ahad 'ashar kawkaban,* 9.

62. For this practice, see Jonathan Holt Shannon, *Performing al-Andalus: Music and Nostalgia across the Mediterranean* (Bloomington: Indiana University Press, 2015), 92–93.

63. The entanglements between Lorca, the Andalusi heritage, and modern Arabic poetry are explored in Martínez Montávez, *Al-Andalus,* 195–219; Lubna Safi, "To Africanize Spain: Twentieth-Century Spanish Poetry and the Persistent Forms of al-Andalus," *Comparative Literature* 73, no. 4 (2021): 421–441, https://doi.org/10.1215/00104124-9313105.

64. Darwish, *Ahad 'ashar kawkaban,* 13–14. The final ellipses are in the original Arabic.

65. Darwish, *Palestine comme métaphore,* 118.

66. Darwish, *Ahad 'ashar kawkaban,* 29.

67. See, for example, the audience's reaction to the line in a YouTube recording of Darwish reading the poem: https://youtu.be/_iP3jyWp_gE, accessed on May 25, 2022.

68. Pappe's *History of Modern Palestine* offers a helpful overview of the period between the Oslo process (1993) and the rise of the second intifada (2000). In particular Pappe notes, "From 1994 onwards, Israel began a construction effort, including building new settlements and expanding old ones, and erecting border fences that delineated the partition of the West Bank prior to negotiations" (243).

69. A good example of this trend is Salim al-Za'nun's poem "Al-Andalus . . . wa-Filastin: Ya ukht Andalus" (Al-Andalus . . . and Palestine: O sister of Andalus), published in *Ya ummat al-Quds* ('Amman: al-Mu'assasa al-'Arabiyya li-l-Nashr, 1995), 391–392. The poem revives the trope of Palestine as the "sister of al-Andalus" and

invokes the figure of Tariq b. Ziyad. The poem's speaker also addresses the Andalusi poet Ibn Zaydun, saying, "O Ibn Zaydun, we stand in need / not of good poetry but of a sword in our hands."

70. In addition to the poem analyzed here, see also the Andalus-themed poems in Musa Hawamida, *Shajari a'la,* (Beirut: al-Mu'assasa al-'Arabiyya li-l-Dirasat wa-l-Nashr, 1999), 27–29, 33–35; Musa Hawamida, *Jasad li-l-bahr . . . rida' li-l-qasida* ('Amman: Dar Nun, 2015), 95–98.

71. Musa Hawamida, *Min jihat al-bahr* (Beirut: al-Mu'assasa al-'Arabiyya li-l-Dirasat wa-l-Nashr, 2004), 64–65.

72. Hawamida, *Min jihat al-bahr,* 65.

73. 'Adwan Nimr 'Adwan, *'Awdat al-muriski min tanahhudatihi* (Ramallah: Markaz Ugharit al-Thaqafi, 2010), 5.

74. 'Adwan, *'Awdat al-muriski,* 68.

75. 'Adwan, *'Awdat al-muriski,* 60.

76. 'Adwan, *'Awdat al-muriski,* 45.

77. 'Adwan, *'Awdat al-muriski,* 50.

78. 'Adwan, *'Awdat al-muriski,* 50.

79. 'Adwan, *'Awdat al-muriski,* 51.

80. 'Adwan, *'Awdat al-muriski,* 52–53.

81. 'Adwan, *'Awdat al-muriski,* 56.

82. 'Adwan, *'Awdat al-muriski,* 56.

83. 'Adwan, *'Awdat al-muriski,* 96.

84. 'Adwan, *'Awdat al-muriski,* 101.

85. 'Adwan, *'Awdat al-muriski,* 119.

86. 'Adwan, *'Awdat al-muriski,* 120.

87. Hoda El Shakry, "Palestine and the Aesthetics of the Future Impossible," *Interventions: International Journal of Postcolonial Studies* 23, no. 5 (2021): 688, https://doi.org/10.1080/1369801X.2021.1885471.

88. Quoted in El Shakry, "Palestine," 670.

89. El Shakry, "Palestine."

90. In addition to the cases I consider here, I would like to point to the one discussed in S. J. Pearce, "The Medieval Fantasy That Fuels Israel's Far Right," *Washington Post,* March 1, 2019, https://www.washingtonpost.com/outlook/2019/03/01/medieval-fantasy-that-fuels-israels-far-right/. Pearce examines how a right-wing Israeli group has claimed a famous figure from eleventh-century al-Andalus.

91. I build here on a few works that have proposed translation as a model for understanding the modern legacy of al-Andalus: Anna Gil Bardají, *Traducir al-Andalus: El discurso del otro en el arabismo español—De Conde a García Gómez* (Lewiston, NY: Mellen Press, 2009); Christina Civantos, *The Afterlife of al-Andalus: Muslim Iberia in Contemporary Arab and Hispanic Narratives* (Albany: SUNY Press, 2017); Yuval Evri, *Translating the Arab-Jewish Tradition: From al-Andalus to Palestine / Land of Israel* (Berlin: Forum Transregionale Studien, 2016).

92. I thank Yael Lerer for sharing materials related to her project. For my discussion, I have relied primarily on the information in Yael Lerer, "The Andalus Test: Reflections on the Attempt to Publish Arabic Literature in Hebrew," *Jadaliyya,* May 16, 2012, https://www.jadaliyya.com/Details/25954; Yael Lerer, "Translating Arabic into Hebrew in an Apartheid Country," *The Funambulist,* podcast audio, June 23, 2015, https://thefunambulist.net/podcast/the-funambulist-podcast/yael-lerer-translating-arabic-into-hebrew-in-an-apartheid-country.

93. Quoted in Lerer, "The Andalus Test."

94. Lerer, "Translating Arabic."

95. This quote comes from "About Andalus Publishing," on the publisher's website: http://www.andalus.co.il/?page_id=220.

96. Lerer, "The Andalus Test."

97. See Evri, *Translating;* Yuval Evri, "Return to al-Andalus beyond German-Jewish Orientalism: Abraham Shalom Yahuda's Critique of Modern Jewish Discourse," in *Modern Jewish Scholarship on Islam in Context: Rationality, European Borders, and the Search for Belonging,* ed. Ottfried Fraisse (De Gruyter, 2019), 337–354, https://doi.org/10.1515/9783110446890-019; Almog Behar and Yuval Evri, "From Saadia to Yahuda: Reviving Arab Jewish Intellectual Models in a Time of Partitions," *Jewish Quarterly Review* 109, no. 3 (2019): 458–463, https://doi.org/10.1353/jqr.2019.0015. Michal Rose Friedman has drawn a more mixed picture of Yahuda's ideological legacy in "Orientalism between Empires: Abraham Shalom Yahuda at the Intersection of Sepharad, Zionism, and Imperialism." *Jewish Quarterly Review* 109, no. 3 (2019): 435–451, https://doi.org/10.1353/jqr.2019.0016. Friedman notes, for example, that Yahuda's professed commitment to Jewish-Arab reconciliation stood in tension with his embrace of the Revisionist Zionist Movement.

98. Quoted in Evri, *Translating,* 5.

99. I take these phrases from the title and subtitle of Salim Sha'shu', *al-'Asr al-dhahabi: Safahat min al-ta'awun al-yahudi al-'arabi fi al-Andalus* (Tel Aviv, 1979).

100. There is an extensive body of work on this term. For helpful introductions, see Ella Shohat, "The Invention of the Mizrahim," *Journal of Palestine Studies* 29, no. 1 (1999): 5–20, https://www.jstor.org/stable/2676427; Lital Levy, "Historicizing the Concept of Arab Jews in the *Mashriq,*" *Jewish Quarterly Review* 98, no. 4 (2008): 454–455, https://doi.org/10.1353/jqr.0.0024; Meirav Aharon, "Riding the Culture Train: An Ethnography of a Plan for Social Mobility through Music," *Cultural Sociology* 7, no. 4 (2012): 151, https://doi.org/10.1177/1749975512457137; Ruth Margalit, "Miri Regev's Culture War," *New York Times,* October 20, 2016, https://www.nytimes.com/2016/10/23/magazine/miri-regevs-culture-war.html.

101. Pappe, *History,* 174–179, 210–211; Shohat, "Invention"; Meirav Aharon, "Just Like Democracy: Ethnography of Realpolitik in a City of Immigrants," *Journal of Levantine Studies* 2, no. 1 (2012): 71–91.

102. Lerer, "The Andalus Test." In a similar vein, Pappe notes that the Zionist community in early twentieth-century Palestine "aspired to be an integral part of Western culture and looked for ways of eliminating any Middle Eastern or Arab characteristics in their society." *History*, 88.

103. "Ruh jadida," https://arabjews.wordpress.com/2011/04/11/%d7%a8%d7%95 %d7%97-%d7%92%d7%93%d7%99%d7%93%d7%99%d7%94-%d7%a8%d7%95 %d7%97-%d7%97%d7%93%d7%a9%d7%94-2011/#more-4.

104. "Ruh jadida."

105. "Ruh jadida."

106. For the history of the Israeli Andalusian Orchestra, I draw on Aharon, "Riding the Culture Train"; and Noy and Aharon's documentary *Fine Tuning* (2010), which Aharon generously shared with me.

107. Aharon, "Riding the Culture Train," 460.

108. For an introduction to the various names and historical narratives ascribed to "Andalusi music," see my discussion in Calderwood, *Colonial al-Andalus*, 230–250; as well as Glasser, *Lost Paradise;* Carl Davila, *The Andalusian Music of Morocco: Al-Āla* (Wiesbaden: Reichert, 2013).

109. Aharon, "Riding the Culture Train," 456.

110. My description is based on the notes I took on the night of the performance and also on the recording I made of the performance. I would like to thank Maria Goldshtein for helping me to translate some fragments from my recording.

111. I translate from the concert program, titled *L'Orchestre Andalou d'Israël Ashdod: Saison de concerts 2019.*

112. For an analysis of Macias's complex positioning between North Africa, France, and Israel / Palestine, see Aomar Boum, "Unmuted Sounds: Jewish Musical Echoes in Twenty-First Century Moroccan and Israeli Soundscapes," in *Jewish-Muslim Interactions: Performing Cultures between North Africa and France*, ed. Samuel Sami Everett and Rebekah Vince (Liverpool: Liverpool University Press, 2020), 181–185, https://doi.org/10.2307/j.ctv19prrm2.15.

113. Jalal Chekara, personal communication with author, August 30, 2020.

114. Quoted in "Orquesta Andalusí de Ashdod," *Shalom,* June 24, 2018, https://www .rtve.es/play/videos/shalom/shalom-orquesta-andalusi-ashdod/4643799/.

5. The Harmonious al-Andalus

1. My description is based on the performance I attended on April 26, 2019. I would like to thank Ronnie Malley for allowing me to record the performance and for responding to my questions about his work.

2. These works include Malley's one-man show *Ziryab, The Songbird of Andalusia,* which premiered at Chicago's Silk Road Rising Theater in 2016.

3. For the various tellings and uses of the Ziryab story, see Dwight F. Reynolds, *The Musical Heritage of al-Andalus* (London: Routledge, 2021), 62–82,

https://doi.org/10.4324/9780429281655; Carl Davila, *The Andalusian Music of Morocco: Al-Āla* (Wiesbaden: Reichert, 2013), 46–54, 73–121; Jonathan Holt Shannon, *Performing al-Andalus: Music and Nostalgia across the Mediterranean* (Bloomington: Indiana University Press, 2015), 37–40. Reynolds wisely cautions that much of what we know about Ziryab comes from sources written centuries after his death. As a result, Ziryab's contributions to the musical heritage of al-Andalus are a matter of debate. On this point, see Reynolds, *Musical Heritage,* 81–82. Despite this ambiguity, many modern-day musicians have posited a direct link between their performance practice and Ziryab's legacy, a phenomenon documented in Shannon, *Performing,* 38–40, 103, 138–144.

4. Habib analyzes this song in Kenneth Sasin Habib, "The Superstar Singer Fairouz and the Ingenious Rahbani Composers: Lebanon Sounding" (PhD diss., University of California, Santa Barbara, 2005), 392–408. For introductions to the *muwashshah* form, see Reynolds, *Musical Heritage,* 156–174; James T. Monroe, "*Zajal* and *Muwashshaha:* Hispano-Arabic Poetry and the Romance Tradition," in *The Legacy of Muslim Spain,* ed. Salma Khadra Jayyusi (Leiden: Brill, 1992), 398–419; Shannon, *Performing,* 43–44.

5. I discuss a performance from the album in Chapter 1.

6. Ronnie Malley, in discussion with author, April 26, 2019.

7. I build here on the work of Shannon and Hirschkind, who treat music and performance both as important legacies from al-Andalus and as tools for thinking about how those legacies operate in the present. See Shannon, *Performing al-Andalus,* 7–9; Charles Hirschkind, *The Feeling of History: Islam, Romanticism, and Andalusia* (Chicago: University of Chicago Press, 2021), 102–103.

8. Patricia Álvarez, in discussion with author, January 28, 2020.

9. In recent years there have been several excellent studies of North African Andalusi music, including Jonathan Glasser, *The Lost Paradise: Andalusi Music in Urban North Africa* (Chicago: University of Chicago Press, 2016); Davila, *Andalusian Music;* Amin Chaachoo, *La música andalusí, al-ála: Historia, conceptos y teoría musical* (Cordoba: Almuzara, 2011). For examples of recent attempts to combine flamenco and North African Andalusi music, see Matthew Machin-Autenrieth, "Spanish Musical Responses to Moroccan Immigration and the Cultural Memory of al-Andalus," *Twentieth-Century Music* 16, no. 2 (2019): 259–287, https://doi .org/10.1017/S1478572218000324; Brian Scott Oberlander, "Deep Encounters: The Practice and Politics of Flamenco-Arab Fusion in Andalusia" (PhD diss., Northwestern University, 2017), https://www.proquest.com/dissertations-theses /deep-encounters-practice-politics-flamenco-arab/docview/1883375527/se-2; Ian Isaac Goldstein, "Experiencing Musical Connection: Sonic Interventions in Mediterranean Social Memory" (PhD diss., University of California, Berkeley, 2017), https://www.proquest.com/dissertations-theses/experiencing-musical -connection-sonic/docview/1925028679/se-2; Shannon, *Performing al-Andalus,* 152–154.

10. I retain the problematic term *Gitano* (Gypsy) because it is the term that many performers, including Heredia Maya, have used to describe themselves. In using this term, I also follow the lead of recent scholarship on *Gitano* culture in Spain, including Matthew Machin-Autenrieth, *Flamenco, Regionalism and Musical Heritage in Southern Spain* (London: Routledge, 2017); Samuel Llano, "Flamenco as Palimpsest: Reading through Hybridity," in *Transnational Spanish Studies,* ed. Catherine Davies and Rory O'Bryen (Liverpool: Liverpool University Press, 2020), 161–175.

11. See, for example, the comments about Moroccan music in Pedro A. de Alarcón, *Diario de un testigo de la guerra de África,* ed. María del Pilar Palomo (Seville: Fundación José Manuel Lara, 2005), 429, 472.

12. I build here on an earlier discussion of *andalucismo* and Spanish colonialism in Eric Calderwood, *Colonial al-Andalus: Spain and the Making of Modern Moroccan Culture* (Cambridge: Belknap Press of Harvard University Press, 2018), 116–141.

13. Calderwood, *Colonial al-Andalus,* 116–141.

14. For helpful introductions to these debates, see Machin-Autenrieth, *Flamenco,* 19–34; Llano, "Flamenco as Palimpsest."

15. Manuel de Falla, *El "cante jondo" (canto primitivo andaluz): Sus orígenes, sus valores musicales, su influencia en el arte musical europeo* (Granada: Editorial Urania, 1922); Federico García Lorca, "Importancia histórica y artística del primitivo canto andaluz llamado 'cante jondo,'" in *Poema del cante jondo,* ed. Mario Hernández (Madrid: Alianza, 1982), 146–168; Machin-Autenrieth, *Flamenco,* 25; Oberlander, "Deep Encounters," 99–100, 128–129.

16. Falla's essay appeared in a brochure that was published on the occasion of the contest. The essay was first published anonymously but was later attributed to Falla and published under his name.

17. Falla, *El "cante jondo,"* 6.

18. Falla, *El "cante jondo,"* 7–8.

19. Falla, *El "cante jondo,"* 8.

20. For an introduction to Infante's work and its influence on *andalucismo,* see Calderwood, *Colonial al-Andalus,* 116–141.

21. This argument appears in Blas Infante, *La verdad sobre el complot de Tablada y el Estado libre de Andalucía,* 2nd ed. (Granada: Aljibe, 1979), 76–77; Blas Infante, *Orígenes de lo flamenco y secreto del cante jondo (1929–1933)* (Seville: Junta de Andalucía, 1980), 165–166.

22. Infante first published this etymology in 1931, in *Verdad,* 76. He repeated it in *Orígenes,* 166.

23. Infante's etymology appears to refer to the Arabic phrase *fallāḥ mankūb* (ill-fated peasant). This etymology has been reproduced in many works that have followed in Infante's footsteps, including Antonio Manuel, *Flamenco: Arqueología de lo jondo,* 3rd ed. (Cordoba: Almuzara, 2020), 36–40, 155.

24. Infante, *Verdad,* 77.

25. Francisco José García Gallardo and Herminia Arredondo Pérez, "La música de la casa: La colección de discos de Blas Infante," in *La Casa de Blas Infante en Coria del Río* (Seville: Centro de Estudios Andaluces, 2004), 132–133; Calderwood, *Colonial al-Andalus,* 130–133.

26. Infante's unpublished notes about the performance are collected in Enrique Iniesta Coullaut-Valera, *Blas Infante: Toda su verdad. Volumen II, 1919–1933* (Granada: Atrio, 2003), 227–232. The Moroccan Andalusi repertoire is composed of eleven suites called *nūbāt* (sing. *nūba*), as described in Davila, *Andalusian Music,* 7–12, 28–34; Chaachoo, *La música andalusí,* 115–119; Glasser, *The Lost Paradise,* 14–16. The term is sometimes spelled *nawba.*

27. Quoted in Iniesta Coullaut-Valera, *Blas Infante,* 232.

28. Rodolfo Gil Benumeya, "La música andaluza en la zona francesa," *África,* March 1932, 57. I discuss Gil Benumeya's work in Calderwood, *Colonial al-Andalus,* 133–140.

29. Calderwood, *Colonial al-Andalus,* 232–248.

30. Rubén Gutiérrez Mate, "El aflamencamiento de Tetuán (1912–1936)," *Música oral del Sur* 8 (2009): 141–155; Rubén Gutiérrez Mate, "La prensa como testigo fiel de los años dorados del flamenco en Tetuán durante el Protectorado español de Marruecos," *La Madrugá: Revista de Investigación sobre Flamenco* 7 (2012): 109–133. As Gutiérrez Mate documents, flamenco also reached audiences in colonial Tetouan through radio and cinema.

31. Gutiérrez Mate, "Aflamencamiento"; Gutiérrez Mate, "Prensa."

32. For al-Qasri's biography, see Ahmed Ouiriarhli Ameur, *La Colombe blanche et Touhami Kasri: Un destin commun* (Tetouan: Imprimerie Khalij Al-Arabi, [2002]); Rubén Gutiérrez Mate, "Tetuán comarca cantaora," *La nueva Alboréa* 22 (2012): 64–65.

33. The story appears in Ouiriarhli Ameur, *La Colombe blanche,* 71–73. For definitions of the *mawwāl,* see Amina Alaoui, "El canto andalusí: Aproximación histórica y geográfica a la herencia andalusí," *Papeles del Festival de música española de Cádiz* 2 (2006): 309; Chaachoo, *La música andalusí,* 124.

34. Gutiérrez Mate, "Aflamencamiento," 152–153; Chaachoo, *La música andalusí,* 103.

35. For information about Sabarezi's work at the conservatory, see Fernando Valderrama Martínez, *Historia de la acción cultural de España en Marruecos (1912–1956)* (Tetouan: Editora Marroquí, 1956), 423, 428.

36. Mohamed El Yamlahi Ouazzani recollects the performance in "Abdessadak Chakara: Une vie, une melodie," in *'Abd al-Sadiq Shaqara: Haya wa-naghma* (Tetouan: Jam'iyyat Titwan-Asmir, 1996), 43. El Yamlahi Ouazzani refers to Sabarezi by her first name, "Clara," by which she is affectionately remembered in Tetouan today.

37. 'Ali al-Zakari, "al-Fannan 'Abd al-Sadiq Shaqara," in *'Abd al-Sadiq Shaqara: Haya wa-naghma* (Tetouan: Jam'iyyat Titwan-Asmir, 1996), 11.

38. Al-Zakari, "al-Fannan," 14; El Yamlahi Ouazzani, "Abdessadak Chakara," 45.

39. Al-Zakari, "al-Fannan," 14; El Yamlahi Ouazzani, "Abdessadak Chakara," 45.

40. See, for example, al-Zakari, "al-Fannan," 13–15; El Yamlahi Ouazzani, "Abdessadak Chakara," 43–44.

41. *Medieval Courtly Monody: Arabian-Andalusian Music,* Atrium Musicae and Moroccan Orchestra of Tetuán, Musical Heritage Society, 1973.

42. Dwight Reynolds, "The Re-creation of Medieval Arabo-Andalusian Music in Modern Performance," *Al-Masaq: Journal of the Medieval Mediterranean* 21, no. 2 (2009): 185, https://doi.org/10.1080/09503110902875442.

43. Shaqara performed, for example, at the World of Islam Festival in London in 1976. El Yamlahi Ouazzani, "Abdessadak Chakara," 44.

44. Eduardo Castro, "Primer encuentro de música andalusí en Granada," *El País,* June 23, 1980, https://elpais.com/diario/1980/06/24/cultura/330645606_850215 .html; Oberlander, "Deep Encounters," 147–149.

45. Quoted in Castro, "Primer encuentro."

46. Quoted in Castro, "Primer encuentro."

47. Miguel Acal, "Con José Heredia Maya," *ABC,* April 14, 1983, 23. Heredia Maya's translation of the term *maqāma* is loose. As Michael Cooperson notes, the term *maqāma* derives from the verb "to stand" and usually refers to an Arabic literary genre that consists of short narrative texts that showcase feats of linguistic virtuosity. See Cooperson's introduction to *Impostures,* by al-Hariri (New York: NYU Press, 2020), xix–xxvii.

48. The work's title is also glossed in Machin-Autenrieth, "Spanish Musical Responses," 269; Oberlander, "Deep Encounters," 18–19; Goldstein, "Experiencing Musical Connection," 56.

49. Quoted in Acal, "Con José Heredia Maya."

50. Quoted in Rosana Torres, "El encuentro de músicas y pueblos, escenificado en *Macama jonda,*" *El País,* April 17, 1983, https://elpais.com/diario/1983/04/18 /cultura/419464816_850215.html. The quote is attributed to an unnamed member of the orchestra from Tetouan.

51. Machin-Autenrieth, "Spanish Musical Responses," 268–269; Acal, "Con José Heredia Maya"; Torres, "Encuentro."

52. I would like to thank Ana María Tenorio Notario at the Central Andaluz de Documentación del Flamenco for sharing a copy of this recording with me.

53. Quoted in Acal, "Con José Heredia Maya," 23.

54. This quote and the following descriptions of the show refer to the production that was staged in Seville and broadcast on Spanish Television in 1983.

55. Machin-Autenrieth, "Spanish Musical Responses"; Eric Calderwood, "The Invention of al-Andalus: Discovering the Past and Creating the Present in Granada's Islamic Tourism Sites," *Journal of North African Studies* 19, no. 1 (2014): 27–55.

56. Josep Lluís Mateo Dieste, *La "hermandad" hispano-marroquí: Política y religión bajo el Protectorado español en Marruecos* (Barcelona: Bellaterra, 2003);

Susan Martin-Márquez, *Disorientations: Spanish Colonialism in Africa and the Performance of Identity* (New Haven, CT: Yale University Press, 2008); Calderwood, *Colonial al-Andalus.*

57. I draw inspiration, here, from D. Fairchild Ruggles's essay on the Mosque of Cordoba: "The Stratigraphy of Forgetting: The Great Mosque of Cordoba and Its Contested Legacy," in *Contested Cultural Heritage,* ed. H. Silverman (Springer, 2011), 51–67, https://doi.org/10.1007/978-1-4419-7305-4_2.

58. For several examples, see Machin-Autenrieth, "Spanish Musical Responses"; Oberlander, "Deep Encounters"; Shannon, *Performing al-Andalus,* 152–154.

59. See, for instance, the artists interviewed in *Tan cerca, tan lejos: La Orquesta Chekara y el flamenco,* directed by Pepe Zapata (Música es Amor, 2010), DVD; and in Elena Muñoz and Nadia Messaoudi, eds., *Flamenco de Orilla a Orilla* (Seville: Junta de Andalucía, 2013), https://www.juntadeandalucia.es/servicios /publicaciones/detalle/77085.html.

60. Goldstein offers a more detailed analysis of this mode of musical fusion in "Experiencing Musical Connection," 56–76.

61. For a helpful introduction to Moroccan immigration to Spain at the turn of the twenty-first century, see Bernabé López García and Mohamed Berriane, *Atlas de la inmigración marroquí en España* (Madrid: Taller de Estudios Internacionales Mediterráneos, 2004). Silvia Bermúdez has studied how these migratory trends have been reflected and negotiated in Spanish popular music in *Rocking the Boat: Migration and Race in Contemporary Spanish Music* (Toronto: University of Toronto Press, 2018).

62. This dynamic has been analyzed in Machin-Autenrieth, "Spanish Musical Responses"; Shannon, *Performing al-Andalus,* 119–162.

63. I will refer to Jalal Chekara by the Spanish spelling of his name because it is the spelling under which Chekara has published his two studio albums: *La Chekara y el flamenco* (Música es amor, 2008) and *Tan cerca, tan lejos* (Música es amor, 2014). I have pieced together Chekara's biography from several sources, including a telephone interview I did with the artist on August 31, 2020. I have also drawn information from the liner notes of Chekara's albums; Zapata's documentary *Tan cerca, tan lejos* (2010); Goldstein, "Experiencing Musical Connection," 51–76; Muñoz and Messaoudi, *Flamenco,* 28, 50–51.

64. *Tan cerca,* directed by Zapata; Goldstein, "Experiencing Musical Connection," 63–64.

65. Arantza Coullaut, "Morente presenta hoy su espectáculo 'Sonidos de Al Andalus' en Málaga," *El País,* August 31, 2000, https://elpais.com/diario/2000/09 /01/cultura/967759213_850215.html; Ángel Álvarez Caballero, "Persiguiendo la esquiva fusión," *El País,* September 4, 2000, https://elpais.com/diario/2000/09/05 /cultura/968104801_850215.html.

66. Goldstein, "Experiencing Musical Connection," 62–63; Jalal Chekara, interview with author, August 31, 2020.

67. Most recently, the two joined forces for a show called "Tesela" (2020), reviewed in Fernando Torres, "Estrella Morente, la voz flamenco de Al-Ándalus," *Sur,* February 29, 2020, https://www.diariosur.es/culturas/musica/estrella-morente -flamenca-20200228232320-nt.html.

68. Jesús Arias, "El árabe por bulerías," *El País,* May 1, 2001, https://elpais.com /diario/2001/05/02/andalucia/988755742_850215.html.

69. Quoted in Arias, "El árabe por bulerías."

70. Jalal Chekara, telephone conversation with author, August 31, 2020.

71. This label appears on the cover of the album *Tan cerca, tan lejos,* as well as in the promotional materials for many of Chekara's performances. Machin-Autenrieth also discusses it in "Spanish Musical Responses," 260.

72. The track is titled "Yarahtini," an allusion to the Shaqara song that inspired it.

73. *Multaka* was performed in the gardens of Seville's Alcázar, one of the city's most emblematic Andalusi heritage sites. "Multaka," accessed September 6, 2021, https://www.actidea.es/archivo/nochesalcazar2008/?page_id=46.

74. Goldstein, "Experiencing Musical Connection," 45–46, 71–72.

75. Amina Alaoui, telephone conversation with author, October 7, 2020. Several of Fez's elite families claim descent from al-Andalus, as discussed in José Antonio González Alcantud, "Los andalusíes hoy: Una elite viva frente al pasado futuro de al-Ándalus," in *Andalusíes: Antropología e historia cultural de una elite magrebí,* ed. José Antonio González Alcantud and Sandra Rojo Flores (Madrid: Abada, 2015), 15–57.

76. Amina Alaoui, "Alcantara," *Alcantara,* Auvidis, 1998, compact disc, liner notes, 3.

77. Amina Alaoui, telephone conversation with author, October 7, 2020.

78. Alaoui, telephone conversation with author.

79. Alaoui, telephone conversation with author.

80. "Andalusi music" is an umbrella term that covers several interrelated music performance traditions found throughout North Africa. These musical traditions are known by several different names, each of which is linked to a particular region in North Africa. For *gharnāṭī,* see Glasser, *The Lost Paradise,* 25–26, 32–33; Alaoui, "Canto," 307–308. Although the *gharnāṭī* repertoire is today often associated with eastern Morocco and western Algeria, Alaoui told me that it was frequently performed in Fez during her childhood. Telephone conversation with author, October 7, 2020.

81. Amina Alaoui and Ahmed Piro, *Musique Arabo-Andalouse du Maroc: Gharnati,* Auvidis, 1995, compact disc.

82. Alaoui, "Alcantara," 3.

83. Lorca popularized the term *duende,* especially in his lecture "Juego y teoría del duende" (1933). Amina Alaoui cites Lorca's lecture in "Canto,"

289–290; "Prose pour un arc-en-ciel," *Arco Iris,* ECM, 2011, compact disc, liner notes, 7.

84. Davila, *Andalusian Music,* 323; Shannon, *Performing al-Andalus,* 104–106; Alaoui, "Canto," 289; Reynolds, *Musical Heritage,* 30, 55.

85. Alaoui, "Canto," 289.

86. Alaoui, "Canto," 289. Alaoui repeats this argument in "Prose," 7; Alaoui, "Réminiscences de la culture arabe dans le fado," *Sigila* 11 (2003): 78.

87. The phrase comes from Lila Ellen Gray, *Fado Resounding: Affective Politics and Urban Life* (Durham, NC: Duke University Press, 2013), 22. As Gray's book illuminates, debates about the origins of fado often intersect with debates about Portuguese national identity. This issue is also addressed in Goldstein, "Experiencing Musical Connection," 10–26.

88. Gray, *Fado Resounding,* 1–13.

89. Gray, *Fado Resounding,* 81.

90. Alaoui, "Réminiscences," 55.

91. Alaoui, "Réminiscences," 55. See also Alaoui, *Arco Iris,* liner notes, 24.

92. Alaoui, "Réminiscences," 70.

93. Alaoui, "Réminiscences," 59–62.

94. Alaoui, "Réminiscences," 62–67. For an introduction to the *zajal,* see Reynolds, *Musical Heritage,* 156–163; Monroe, "*Zajal.*"

95. Alaoui, "Réminiscences," 76–79.

96. Alaoui, "Réminiscences," 56–57.

97. Goldstein, "Experiencing Musical Connection," 17. Goldstein offers a detailed analysis of a track on the album, "Fado Al-Muʿtamid," at pp. 10–26.

98. Alaoui, "Prose," 6. My translations vary slightly from George Miller's published translation of Alaoui's essay.

99. Alaoui, "Prose," 7.

100. Glasser, *The Lost Paradise,* 26.

101. Ibn Khafaja, *Diwan Ibn Khafaja* (Beirut: Dar Sadir, 1961), 117. My translation is based on the one that appears in Glasser, *The Lost Paradise,* 23–24.

102. Glasser, *The Lost Paradise,* 27–28.

103. Glasser, *The Lost Paradise,* 25.

104. For my account of the poem's transmission history, I draw on María Jesús Rubiera Mata, "De nuevo sobre las tres morillas," *Al-Andalus* 37 (1972): 133–143; María Jesús Viguera Molins, "'Tres morillas', entre al-Andalus y Jaén," in *Estudios de Frontera, 9: Economía, derecho y sociedad en la frontera,* ed. Francisco Toro Ceballos and José Rodríguez Molina (Jaén: Instituto de Estudios Giennenses, 2014), 833–843; Julián Rozas Ortiz, *Música y poesía en Jaén: El cantar de las Tres morillas ante el panorama de la lírica tradicional* (Jaén: Diputación Provincial de Jaén, 2002).

105. Rozas Ortiz, *Música y poesía,* 56–57.

106. Shannon, *Performing al-Andalus,* 129–131; Lubna Safi, "To Africanize Spain: Twentieth-Century Spanish Poetry and the Persistent Forms of al-Andalus," *Comparative Literature* 73, no. 4 (2021): 421–441, https://doi.org/10.1215/00104124 -9313105.

107. Alaoui, "Réminiscences," 66.

108. Several examples are discussed in Hisham D. Aidi, *Rebel Music: Race, Empire, and the New Muslim Youth Culture* (New York: Vintage Books, 2014), xxiv–xxv; Eric Calderwood, "Spanish in a Global Key," *Journal of Spanish Cultural Studies* 20, no. 1–2 (2019): 53–65; Paula Pérez-Rodríguez, "Hibridismo y estetización hispanoárabes: Pliegues espaciotemporales y mestizaje en el hip hop," in *El cine como reflejo de la historia, de la literatura y del arte en la filmografía hispano-brasileña,* ed. María Marcos Ramos ([Salamanca?]: Centro de Estudios Brasileños, 2019), 563–581. Additional examples include the allusions to al-Andalus in Sa-Roc, "The Moors of Alhambra," January 18, 2013, YouTube video, https://youtu.be/l_7Sj0 na5z4; Abd Al Malik, "Le jeune Noir à l'épée," *Le jeune Noir à l'épée,* vol. 1, Gibraltar Label, 2018, compact disc.

109. I'm playing here on the trope of "street flow," which is in common use in hip-hop circles, including in Morocco. In fact, one of the pioneers of the Moroccan rap scene was the Tangier-based group Zanka Flow, whose name combines the English word "flow" with the Moroccan Arabic word for "street." Their work is analyzed in Jairo Guerrero, "Zanka Flow: Rap en árabe marroquí," *Romano-Arabica* 12 (2012): 125–157.

110. Calderwood, "Spanish," 56–63; Pérez-Rodríguez, "Hibridismo."

111. My discussion of this collaboration is deeply indebted to one of its producers, Yolanda Agudo López, who shared information and materials about the song. I also thank Cristina Moreno Almeida for her input. Moreno Almeida offers an insightful discussion of H-Kayne in *Rap Beyond Resistance: Staging Power in Contemporary Morocco* ([Cham]: Palgrave Macmillan, 2017), 34–41, 75–77, 87–89.

112. Toteking, H-Kayne, and Oum, "Hip Hop Exchange," *La diversidad de las músicas de Marruecos,* Fabricantes de Ideas / FNAC, 2009, compact disc.

113. Haze illustrates the style in his 2010 hit "Rap flamenco."

114. Sayflhak, featuring Haze, "Sma O Bhar (Aire y Mar)," October 11, 2013, YouTube video, https://youtu.be/aLdgPskAYoM.

115. The so-called Invincible Armada did not depart from Seville, but Haze's allusion to it likely refers to the fact that Seville was Spain's richest and most populous city at the height of the country's imperial power in the sixteenth century.

116. For introductions to current debates about race in Spain and Morocco, see Bermúdez, *Rocking the Boat;* Martin-Márquez, *Disorientations;* Chouki El Hamel, *Black Morocco: A History of Slavery, Race, and Islam* (Cambridge: Cambridge University Press, 2013); Cynthia J. Becker, *Blackness in Morocco: Gnawa Identity*

through Music and Visual Culture (Minneapolis: University of Minnesota Press, 2020).

117. I build here on my earlier discussion of Khaled in Calderwood, "Spanish," 56–63.

118. Francisco Javier Rosón Lorente, *¿El retorno de Tariq? Comunidades etnorreligiosas en el Albayzín granadino* (Granada: Editorial de la Universidad de Granada, 2008); Calderwood, "Invention."

119. Peio H. Riaño, "Khaled: 'Soy musulmán español. No tengo patria,'" *El Español,* May 26, 2017, https://www.elespanol.com/cultura/musica/20170526 /218978443_0.html; "Improvistas #29—Khaled," interview by Raquel Ruiz, May 15, 2018, YouTube video, https://youtu.be/Zf83VwlaBTM.

120. Riaño, "Khaled"; "Improvistas #29."

121. Quoted in Riaño, "Khaled."

122. Quoted in Riaño, "Khaled."

123. Quoted in HJ Darger, "Khaled: 'Tutankamon no tenía Nike y era un chulo igual,'" *El País,* March 28, 2018, https://elpais.com/elpais/2018/03/26/tentaciones /1522059439_540412.html.

124. Los Santos, "Los Foreign," February 8, 2015, YouTube video, https:// youtu.be/wjNRk63XFdk.

125. I am unsure of my transcription of the last word in this line. I believe that Khalid says *ḥaḍāra* (civilization, or culture).

126. Both *Gitano* (Gypsy) and *Moro* (Moor) are vexed terms that have often been used pejoratively. I will, nonetheless, retain both terms here, in large part because Khaled himself uses them. Both terms have recently been the object of a process of "taking back," in which some Spaniards of Roma or North African descent have appropriated them and used them to their own ends. Such is the case, I believe, with Khaled's use of these terms.

127. Khaled devotes the track "Camarón" (2016) to Camarón de la Isla. The rapper speaks of his admiration for Camarón in "Improvistas #29."

128. I thank Paula Pérez-Rodríguez for drawing my attention to Khaled's shout-outs to Nujaila on Instagram.

129. Hakim Abderrezak, *Ex-Centric Migrants: Europe and the Maghreb in Mediterranean Cinema, Literature, and Music* (Bloomington: Indiana University Press, 2016), 67–88, https://www.jstor.org/stable/j.ctt1c3gwsd.

130. I draw here on Kimberlé Crenshaw's influential work on intersectionality. See, for instance, Crenshaw, "Mapping the Margins: Intersectionality, Identity Politics, and Violence against Women of Color," *Stanford Law Review* 43, no. 6 (1991): 1241–1299, https://www.jstor.org/stable/1229039.

131. Khaled, "Volando recto," April 2, 2016, YouTube video, https://youtu.be /mXb15vEJ9tY.

132. I'm riffing here on Doris Sommer's observations in *Bilingual Aesthetics: A New Sentimental Education* (Durham, NC: Duke University Press, 2004), 64.

Epilogue

1. Waleed Jassim, personal communication, July 14, 2021. As of this writing (September 2022), the mosque is under renovation, and it is unclear whether the façade will retain the Cordoba-inspired design that has been there since the 1980s. My description of the mosque is based on observations I made between 2014 and 2022.

2. See Molly Crabapple et al., *Al Andalus in New York* (New York: Hagop Kevorkian Center for Near Eastern Studies, 2019).

3. I build here on ideas I piloted in Calderwood, "The Reconquista of the Mosque of Córdoba," *Foreign Policy,* April 10, 2015, https://foreignpolicy.com/2015/04/10/the-reconquista-of-the-mosque-of-cordoba-spain-catholic-church-islam/. The debates surrounding the Mosque-Cathedral of Cordoba have received significant attention from scholars and journalists around the world. From the rich body of work on this topic, I would like to highlight D. Fairchild Ruggles, "The Stratigraphy of Forgetting: The Great Mosque of Cordoba and Its Contested Legacy," in *Contested Cultural Heritage,* ed. H. Silverman (Springer, 2011), 51–67, https://doi.org/10.1007/978-1-4419-7305-4_2; Michele Lamprakos, "Arquitectura, memoria y futuro: La Mezquita-Catedral de Córdoba," *Quintana* 17 (2018): 43–74, https://doi.org/10.15304/qui.17.5604; Avi Astor, Marian Burchardt, and Mar Griera, "Polarization and the Limits of Policitization: Cordoba's Mosque-Cathedral and the Politics of Cultural Heritage," *Qualitative Sociology* 42 (2019): 337–360, https://doi.org/10.1007/s11133-019-09419-x; Brian Rosa and Jaime Jover-Báez, "Contested Urban Heritage: Discourses of Meaning and Ownership of the Mosque-Cathedral of Córdoba, Spain," *Journal of Urban Cultural Studies* 4, no. 1–2 (2017): 127–153; Plataforma Mezquita-Catedral de Córdoba. Patrimonio de Todxs, "La Mezquita de Córdoba: Un caso de destrucción simbólica del patrimonio," *erph* 27 (December 2020): 185–207, https://doi.org/10.30827/e-rph.v0i27.17906. For my overview of the monument's history, I've relied on the sources cited here, as well as Jerrilynn D. Dodds, "The Great Mosque of Córdoba," in *Al-Andalus: The Art of Islamic Spain,* ed. Jerrilynn D. Dodds (New York: Metropolitan Museum of Art, 1992), 11–25.

4. Dodds, "Great Mosque," 24.

5. In posing this question, I build on the insights of Rosa and Jover-Baez, "Contested"; Astor, Burchardt, Griera, "Polarization"; Alejandro García Sanjuán, "¿De quién es la Mezquita de Córdoba?," *Diario de Sevilla,* September 20, 2018, https://www.diariodesevilla.es/opinion/tribuna/Mezquita-Cordoba_0_1283871634.html; Susan Slyomovics, "Is *Patrimoine* 'Good to Think With'?," *Journal of North African Studies* 25, no. 5 (2020): 689–696, https://doi.org/10.1080/13629387.2019.1644887.

6. My discussion will not focus on the debates over property and "immatriculations," but these issues have been analyzed in depth in Astor, Burchardt, Griera, "Polarization"; Rosa and Jover-Baez, "Contested," 144–149.

7. I would like to thank Marta Jiménez and Miguel Santiago for sharing many documents from their personal archives, including copies of the brochures going back to the 1980s. The brochures are also discussed in Ruggles, "Stratigraphy"; Astor, Burchardt, Griera, "Polarization"; Plataforma Mezquita-Catedral de Córdoba, "Mezquita de Córdoba"; Rosa and Jover-Baez, "Contested."

8. *Guía breve de la Mezquita Catedral de Córdoba* (Cordoba: Monte de Piedad y Caja de Ahorros de Córdoba, n.d.). I have taken this quote from the 1981 edition of the brochure, but the same text appears in the 1993 edition.

9. *Guía breve.*

10. UNESCO, "Historic Centre of Cordoba," accessed September 10, 2021, https://whc.unesco.org/en/list/313/. In 1994, UNESCO expanded its World Heritage designation to include all of Cordoba's historic center.

11. I have taken this quote from the brochure that I picked up when I visited the site in March 2015. I have a scan of a brochure from the early 2000s, and it includes the same statement.

12. Calderwood, "Reconquista"; Plataforma Mezquita-Catedral de Córdoba, "Mezquita de Córdoba."

13. Fernando Arce Sainz, "¿Hubo un precedente cristiano en el origen de la mezquita de Córdoba?," *Al-Andalus y la Historia,* December 20, 2019, http://www.alandalusylahistoria.com/?p=1647; Susana Calvo Capilla, "Analogies entre les grandes mosquées de Damas et Cordoue: Mythe et réalité," in *Umayyad Legacies: Medieval Memories from Syria to Spain,* ed. Antoine Borrut and Paul M. Cobb (Leiden: Brill, 2010), 289–290. In 2017 Cordoba's mayor assembled a team of experts to study the disputes surrounding the Mosque-Cathedral. Their report, released in 2018, concluded that there is no reliable evidence showing that there was a Christian church on the land where the Umayyad mosque was built. See Juan B. Carpio Dueñas, Alejandro García Sanjuán, and Federico Mayor Zaragoza, "Informe: Comisión de expertos sobre la Mezquita Catedral de Córdoba," September 15, 2018, 1–3, https://www.cordoba.es/doc_pdf_etc /AYUNTAMIENTO/Informe_Comision_Expertos_Mezquita-Catedral_15-09 -18.pdf.

14. Quoted in A. Moreno, "Los arqueólogos de la Iglesia no localizan la basílica cristiana bajo la Mezquita de Córdoba," *Público,* January 18, 2020, https://www .publico.es/sociedad/arqueologos-iglesia-no-localizan-basilica-cristiana-mezquita -cordoba.html.

15. Ruggles, "Stratigraphy," 57–58.

16. "San Vicente," *Córdoba,* January 20, 2005, https://www.diariocordoba .com/cultura/2005/01/20/san-vicente-mezquita-catedral-38810391.html.

17. I take this quote from the brochure that was available at the site around 2006. I thank Marta Jiménez and D. Fairchild Ruggles for providing me with photographs of this edition of the brochure. In later editions (such as the one from 2015), the Cathedral Chapter kept the quoted text but removed the phrase, "throwing

into doubt the stereotype of the tolerance that was supposedly cultivated in Cordoba at that time."

18. I build here on my work in Calderwood, "Reconquista." See also Plataforma Mezquita-Catedral de Córdoba, "Mezquita de Córdoba"; Astor, Burchardt, Griera, "Polarization."

19. Plataforma Mezquita-Catedral de Córdoba, "Mezquita de Córdoba," 192.

20. Plataforma Mezquita-Catedral de Córdoba, "Mezquita de Córdoba," 192, 205.

21. Miguel Santiago, interviews with author, January 8 and 30, 2015.

22. Antonio Manuel Rodríguez, interview with author, January 9, 2015. Rodríguez's work is analyzed in Hirschkind, *Feeling of History,* 54–68.

23. The idea of the "Cordoba paradigm," as Elena Arigita has shown, was formulated by Iranian-Canadian philosopher Ramin Jahanbegloo, who developed it in several essays published in the years following the 9 / 11 attacks. See Elena Arigita, "The 'Cordoba Paradigm': Memory and Silence around Europe's Islamic Past," in *Islam and the Politics of Culture in Europe: Memory, Aesthetics, Art,* ed. Frank Peter, Sarah Dornhof, and Elena Arigita (Bielefeld: Transcript, 2013), 21–40. In my interviews with members of the Platform, several of them noted Jahanbegloo's influence on their work.

24. Antonio M. Rodríguez Ramos, "Un paradigma en peligro," *El País,* September 4, 2013, https://elpais.com/cultura/2013/09/04/actualidad/1378322235_891541 .html.

25. Antonio Manuel Rodríguez, interview with author, January 9, 2015.

26. Plataforma Mezquita-Catedral de Córdoba, "Mezquita de Córdoba," 190.

27. Miguel Santiago, interview with author, January 30, 2015.

28. Plataforma Mezquita-Catedral de Córdoba, "Mezquita de Córdoba," 194.

29. Plataforma Mezquita-Catedral de Córdoba, "Mezquita de Córdoba," 198–199.

30. Juan G. Bedoya, "Los musulmanes piden en Roma poder rezar en la mezquita de Córdoba," *El País,* March 11, 2004, https://elpais.com/diario/2004/03/12/sociedad /1079046003_850215.html. Mansur's initiative is discussed in Arigita, "Cordoba Paradigm," 33–36; Ruggles, "Stratigraphy," 56–57.

31. Isabel Romero, interview with author, August 4, 2021.

32. Arigita, "Cordoba Paradigm," 35.

33. Kamel Mekhelef, interview with author, January 30, 2015. For more accounts of harassment at the Mosque-Cathedral, see Calderwood, "Reconquista"; Jihad Abaza, "Police Followed Me Around Cordoba's Mosque—All I Did Was Wear a Hijab," *Middle East Eye,* November 2, 2016, https://www.middleeasteye.net/opinion /police-followed-me-around-cordobas-mosque-all-i-did-was-wear-hijab.

34. Kamel Mekhelef, interview with author, January 30, 2015.

35. This project is described on the Halal Institute's website, accessed September 10, 2021, https://www.institutohalal.com/the-halal-institute-participates-in -the-creation-of-the-cordoba-halal-cluster/.

36. Isabel Romero, interview with author, August 4, 2021.

37. This reframing takes inspiration from David Damrosch, *What Is World Literature?* (Princeton, NJ: Princeton University Press, 2003), 6.

38. Michael Rothberg, *Multidirectional Memory: Remembering the Holocaust in the Age of Decolonization* (Stanford, CA: Stanford University Press, 2009), 1–12.

39. I'm riffing here on Hayden White's gloss of Maimonides in *The Practical Past* (Evanston, IL: Northwestern University Press, 2014), x.

40. In a similar spirit, scholars in the burgeoning field of Mediterranean studies have proposed the Mediterranean as another frame of inquiry that disrupts existing paradigms. See, for example, Brian A. Catlos, "Why the Mediterranean?," in *Can We Talk Mediterranean? Conversations on an Emerging Field in Medieval and Early Modern Studies,* ed. Brian A. Catlos and Sharon Kinoshita (Cham: Palgrave Macmillan, 2017), 1–17.

Acknowledgments

The journey that led me to this book began long ago, in the fall of 1998, when, after graduating from high school, I moved to Spain to study flamenco at a dance academy in Seville. My high school education had given me a decent command of Spanish and some rudimentary notions about the history of al-Andalus, but it had not prepared me for the astonishing beauty I would find in Andalusi heritage sites, like the Alcázar of Seville or the Mosque of Cordoba; nor had it prepared me to think about the very complicated ways in which the legacies and memories of al-Andalus operate in the present, animating diverse cultural expressions, collective identities, and political projects. This book is my attempt to take stock of those complex operations and to work through some of the questions that I first formulated—or, at least, intuited—as a wide-eyed teenager. In the time that has elapsed since that first stint in Spain, I have acquired scholarly tools that have helped me to think critically about the history of al-Andalus and its cultural afterlife. But along the way, I have tried to preserve the excitement, curiosity, and even wonderment that first led me to this object of study.

Although the seeds of this project were planted long ago, the book did not begin to take shape until 2011, when I received a postdoctoral fellowship at the Michigan Society of Fellows to do research on representations of al-Andalus in contemporary culture. The fellowship at the University of Michigan not only gave me time to read widely and to test out new ideas, but it also landed me in a wonderful community of colleagues, who encouraged my work with their feedback and camaraderie. Among the many colleagues who supported my work on this project at Michigan, I would especially like to thank Lydia Barnett, Hussein Fancy, Elizabeth Hinton, Enrique García Santo-Tomás, Mayte Green-Mercado, Michele Hannoosh, Alexander Knysh, Donald Lopez, Karla Mallette, Cristina Moreiras-Menor, Yopie Prins, Anton Shammas, and Ryan Szpiech.

I wrote *On Earth or in Poems* while working at the University of Illinois at Urbana-Champaign, where I have been a faculty member in the Program in Comparative and World Literature since 2014. I am immensely grateful to my colleagues at the University of Illinois for supporting my work and inspiring me with theirs. I would especially like to thank my colleague Javier Irigoyen-García for reading parts of the manuscript and for responding to numerous inquiries over the years. I would also like to thank the following colleagues who have contributed to the project with their input and encouragement: John Barnard, Antoinette Burton, Ken Cuno, Carolyn Fornoff, Maria Gillombardo, Jim Hansen, Waïl Hassan, Rana Hogarth, Lilya Kaganovsky, Brett Kaplan, Susan Koshy, Craig Koslofsky, Jean-Philippe Mathy, Rini Bhattacharya Mehta, Justine Murison, Allyson Purpura, Dana Rabin, Manuel Rota, Bruce Rosenstock, Dede Ruggles, Rob Rushing, Nora Stoppino, Pollyanna Rhee, Carol Symes, Renée Trilling, Jonathan Tomkin, Angeliki Tzanetou, and Craig Williams. In addition, I want to thank two librarians, Paula Mae Carns and Laila Hussein Moustafa, for their tireless efforts to track down many of the sources I discuss in this book. I have also had the privilege of working with some very talented graduate research assistants, who have helped me to sift through a vast archive of material about al-Andalus. They are Mary Casey, Katherine Crosby, Mohammad Gallab, Elias Shakkour, and Dana Shalash. Finally, the work for this book would not have been possible without the generous financial support of several units at the University of Illinois. This support included a fellowship from the Center for Advanced Study, a fellowship from the Unit for Criticism and Interpretative Theory, an Arnold O. Beckman Award from the Campus Research Board, and a Conrad Humanities Scholar award from the College of Liberal Arts and Sciences. These awards allowed me to conduct research abroad and to take time away from teaching to finish writing the manuscript.

On Earth or in Poems illustrates how the legacies of al-Andalus have energized diverse communities and projects around the globe. As befits a book on this topic, my research has allowed me to connect with colleagues and to form friendships on multiple continents. These relationships have nourished my work on this project, teaching me much of what I know about al-Andalus, while bringing joy and companionship to the learning process. Although I have always treasured these relationships, I came to have an even deeper appreciation for them at the height of the COVID pandemic, when I was cut off from many of the professional and personal networks that had given life to this project. I cannot do justice here to all the help I received while working on this project, but I do want to acknowledge some of the colleagues and friends who have contributed to this project over the years. I would first like to thank Hussein Fancy, Carolyn Fornoff, Jonathan Glasser, and Daniel Pollack-Pelzner for reading early drafts and providing me with helpful feedback. Likewise, I thank the members of the Early Modern and Mediterranean Worlds Workshop at the University of Chicago for giving me feedback on a draft of Chapter 2, and the members of the "Musical Afterlives of al-Andalus" workshop for giving me feedback on an excerpt from Chapter 5. I would also like to thank the following colleagues for responding to questions, suggesting ideas, and helping me locate relevant materials: Malek Abisaab, Ruanne Abou-Rahme, Sabahat Adil, Yolanda Agudo López, Sumayya Ahmed, Hisham Aidi, Yolanda Aixelà Cabré,

Wijdan Alsayegh, Cristina Álvarez Millán, Elena Arigita, Anna Assogba, Avi Astor, Jamal Bahmad, Abigail Balbale, Mohamad Ballan, Dia Barghouti, Almog Behar, M'hammad Benaboud, Jaafar Ben Elhaj Soulami, Amira Bennison, Jacob Ben Simon, Ayelet Ben-Yishai, Noel Blanco Mourelle, Marilyn Booth, Mohamed Reda Boudchar, Aomar Boum, Olga Bush, Adolfo Campoy-Cubillo, Sanae Chairi, Fatme Charafeddine, Basma Chebani, Laryssa Chomiak, Peter Cole, Raph Cormack, Francis Cuberos, Hasna Daoud, Carl Davila, Ahmad Diab, Antonio de Diego, Simon Doubleday, Anne-Laure Dupont, Issam Eido, Emran El-Badawi, Alex Elinson, Hoda Elsadda, Hoda El Shakry, Brad Epps, Helena de Felipe, Gonzalo Fernández Parrilla, Daniela Flesler, Jocelyn Frelier, Allen Fromherz, Yoni Furas, Adam Gaiser, Alejandro García-Sanjuan, Tania Gentic, Naz Georgas, Luis Girón, Itzea Goikolea-Amiano, Ian Goldstein, Luz Gómez García, Camilo Gómez-Rivas, José Antonio González Alcantud, William Granara, Lila Ellen Gray, Mayte Green-Mercado, Faisal Hamadah, Olivia Harrison, Nizar Hermes, Daniel Hershenzon, Ahmed Idrissi Alami, Sarah Irving, Waleed Jassim, Marta Jiménez, Rebecca Joubin, Behnaz Karjoo, Jo Labanyi, Travis Landry, Luke Leafgren, Yael Lerer, Elad Levy, Samuel Llano, Matthew Machin-Autenrieth, Bruce Maddy-Weitzman, Susan Martin-Márquez, Miguel Martínez, Catherine Mayeur Jaouen, Kamel Mekhelef, Hosni Mlitat, Aurélien Montel, Luisa Mora Villarejo, María Teresa Morales Rodríguez, Cristina Moreno Almeida, Abdelbaar Mounadi Idrissi, Philip Murphy, Farah al-Nakib, Brian Oberlander, Caitlyn Olson, Valérie Orlando, Rafael Ortega, Karim Ouaras, Juan Palao, Vanessa Paloma Elbaz, Nieves Paradela, Bob Parks, S.J. Pearce, Pablo Pérez-Mallaína Bueno, Paula Pérez-Rodríguez, José Miguel Puerta Vílchez, Almudena Quintana Arranz, Zineb Rabouj, Jen Rasamimanana, Isabel Romero, Javier Rosón, Michael Rothberg, Bárbara Ruiz-Bejarano, Christa Salamandra, Benita Sampedro, Miguel Santiago, Bilal Sarr, Mohammed Sawaie, Luke Scalone, Rachel Schine, Samuel Scurry, Edwin Seroussi, Jonathan Shannon, Eyad Shehab, Reuven Snir, David Stenner, Suzanne Stetkevych, Jessie Stoolman, Edwige Tamalet Talbayev, Francisco Trujillo, José Luis Venegas, Christopher Witulski, Jonathan Wyrtzen, Khaled Youssef, Rachid Zegrane, and Mahmoud Zibawi. I also want to thank some of the artists who granted me interviews to discuss their work: Amina Alaoui, Patricia Álvarez, Jalal Chekara, Molly Crabapple, Ronnie Malley, Said Naciri, and Ms. Saffaa.

It has been a true honor and privilege to work with the entire staff at Harvard University Press. I want to express my deepest gratitude to my editor, Sharmila Sen, for taking a chance on me when I was an unpublished author and for supporting me through the writing of two books about the legacy of al-Andalus. I appreciate her advocacy for this project, her curiosity about its subject matter, and her helpful feedback on the manuscript. I also want to thank editorial assistant Olivia Woods for responding to numerous inquiries with intelligence, patience, and kindness. I thank the two anonymous reviewers for their insightful and constructive feedback on the manuscript. And thanks to Angela Piliouras for shepherding the book through the production process with precision and care. I would also like to thank

Stephanie Vyce, the Director of Intellectual Property at Harvard University Press, for helping me to secure permissions for the images in this book. Every effort has been made to identify copyright holders and obtain their permission for the use of copywritten material. Notification of any additions or corrections that should be incorporated in future reprints or editions of this book would be greatly appreciated.

I could not have written this book without the support of my family and friends, who have surrounded me with love and laughter and have shown patience and understanding during the periods when I went underground to work on this project. I thank my parents, Nancy and Stephen Calderwood, for nurturing my love of reading, languages, and travel—all of which have played a role in the making of this book. I also thank Susan Abraham, Audrey Calderwood, Michael Calderwood, Becky Curtiss, Skip Curtiss, Patricia Estevan, Catharine Fairbairn, Charlie Frazier, Karen Frazier, Connell Jones, Karen Jones, Peter Kitlas, Avital Livny, Prashant Mehta, John Meyers, Ben Miller, Jacob Okada, Greg Pollock, Rachel Pollock, Aaron Rackoff, Sandy Steiner, David Sucunza, Nick Valvo, Serena Van Buskirk, and Arnold Weinstein.

Finally, I thank my wife, Jamie Jones, who continually inspires me with her brilliance and sustains me with her love and kindness. She has seen this book at every stage of its journey and has discussed it with me over countless meals and walks, at home and abroad. She has read drafts of every chapter and provided crucial feedback. And whenever I've hit a roadblock, she has rallied my strength by reminding me of the spirit of adventure that has always animated this book and our life together.

Index